ACADEMIC FREEDOM AND APARTHEID

Academic Freedom and Apartheid

*The Story of the World
Archaeological Congress*

Peter Ucko

Duckworth

First published in 1987 by
Gerald Duckworth & Co. Ltd.
The Old Piano Factory
43 Gloucester Crescent, London NW1

ISBN 0 7156 21807 (cased)
ISBN 0 7156 2191 2 (paper)

British Library Cataloguing in Publication Data

Ucko, Peter
    Academic freedom and apartheid: the story of the World
    Archaeological Congress.
    1. World Archaeological Congress: (*Southampton*)
    I. Title
    930.1   CC51

    ISBN 0-7156-2180-7
          0-7156-2191-2 Pbk

Photoset in North Wales by
Derek Doyle & Associates, Mold, Clwyd
and printed and bound in Great Britain by
Redwood Burn Limited, Trowbridge

Contents

Everyone concerned with the battle for liberation in South Africa and the ending of apartheid should read this book. The issue of the cultural boycott as a major instrument in isolating South Africa is fundamental to the whole process of liberation. Here is the first major account of what it means. It should be required reading for all academics but equally it is essential for those who wish to understand the meaning and principles of solidarity in the struggle.

Bishop Trevor Huddleston

Foreword
by Neal Ascherson

This book is the story of a great battle. It is not a simple story, but battles on this scale are complex, obscure and tragic even when they end in victory. The tale of the 1986 World Archaeological Congress at Southampton, as Professor Ucko tells it, reminds me of Stendhal's vision of Waterloo: an immense engagement commenced without the participants knowing where it would lead to (let alone how desperate it would become), fought on shifting ground by disparate coalitions of forces arriving on the battlefield at different moments. As in many such affaiors, some troops changed sides and others were accidentally cut down by their own allies. But it ended in victory for those who supported Professor Ucko. The wounds and the anger will take long to heal. But the scale of the victory, and its importance, will – I think – become steadily more impressive as the years pass.

The outline of the events described here can be briefly described, as they appear from outside to one who is only a journalist and who took no part in them. Professor Peter Ucko started work on organising this World Archaeological Congress, a huge event which attracts several thousand participants, as long ago as 1982. His understanding was that the Congress would break new ground, by laying special emphasis on African and Asian archaeology and by redefining the science as an activity performed in – and on – a living world of sentient and suffering human beings, to whom archaeology owed a responsibility located not only in the past but equally in the present. In this sense, the Congress would have been historic in any case. It intended nothing less than the transfer of archaeology from a European orientation towards the past to a world-wide, world-conscious orientation towards the present and the future.

This gave Professor Ucko labours enough. But in 1985, the present came to meet the Congress with unexpected energy. South Africa was entering new convulsions. Southampton city council, the local students' union who had offered premises, the Association of University Teachers and the influential Anti-Apartheid Movement made it clear that they would not agree to the presence of South African scholars at the Congress. They demanded an academic boycott, at a moment when the issue of economic sanctions against South Africa was being fiercely debated both in Britain and the United States. They warned that they would withdraw financial support, and accommodation, and that they would organise demonstrations of protest if South Africans attended.

Peter Ucko's postion was a desperate one. It also became plain that if he persisted with invitations to South African scholars – themselves in no way personally tainted by support for apartheid and, on the contrary, in many cases displaying impressive intellectual battle honours in the struggle – archaeologists from Africa, much of Asia and eastern Europe would not attend, and the whole point of this Congress would be lost.

On the other hand, to 'disinvite' the South Africans would be a step into unknown territory. Peter Ucko long ago learned to hate racialism, both in its blatant form and when it comes disguised in the needs of 'value-free' scientific research. But he could foresee – even to an extent sympathise with – the disbelieving horror of decent, 'liberal' scholars in Europe and North America at a move which seemed to violate the precept that academic freedom is an absolute moral imperative. Much of the archaeological establishment would react with incomprehension, and anger. He ran the risk of making himself a pariah and – worse – of creating a devastating schism in the whole archaeological world.

This is the story of how a very brave man wrestled with his own doubts and fears, overcame them, and took the decision to go ahead with the Congress without the South Africans. As a narrative, it is not only constantly exciting, but it is the chronicle of a tremendous and fundamental argument about the responsibilities of science, carried through on both sides with a merciless intensity. Not all the arguments here are scrupulous or fair. None is negligible.

In the event, the Congress was overwhelmingly successful, even though many great names in the discipline stayed away to register their own protest. The price in damage – personal, financial, organisational – is still being paid, but total schism did not take place as a result. Instead, the new course on which the Congress intended to set out has been much more sharply and usefully illuminated by the struggle which this book records. As Professor Ucko says, 'archaeologists and anthropologists are immersed in the evidence of man's inhumanity to man over many time periods and in countless areas of the world ... It is precisely people such as the archaeologists and anthropologists who should not wish simply to stand aside and condone by inaction.'

London   N.A.
1 June, 1987

Preface

This book is concerned with a number of apparently unrelated topics – archaeology, conference organisation, the international academic community, the South African apartheid regime – and the way that they became inextricably bound together in the story of the World Archaeological Congress (WAC). It is a story not only fascinating in itself, but one with far-reaching implications, some still unfolding as this book goes to press – for the story is not yet over. I have written the story in some detail, so that readers may enter into the complexity of the events in sufficient depth to imagine what their own reactions might have been, if they themselves had been involved in them. To this extent it is not important whether or not the decisions that were taken are considered to have been right or wrong. My intention, in the following pages, is to inform by the accurate recording of events. I have not tried to persuade, but it is my account, and as such is written from my own perspective.

In speaking of accurate recording of events I do not suggest that there can ever be just one version of an incident, or just one view of what was said, and implied, in a decision or meeting. This is a very personal book, and the perceptions presented are indeed also personal, and are very much my own. Nevertheless, the order of events, and what was actually said by participants in them, are as accurate as I have been able to establish, both from written records and, as far as practicably possible in a short period of time, with the actual people to whom I refer in the book.

Since the book is a personal account of my own view of events it is bound to be, in part, autobiographical. I have therefore included some of my own history and much of my own thinking as it has become modified over the years. I have also, in places, and especially at the beginning of the book, given some rather frank personal assessments of friends and colleagues. These are included partly so that the readers can judge for themselves my own prejudices and preconceptions as I moved from one situation to another, and partly to show how events proved several of my preconceptions to be totally wrong, whereas many were only partially correct, and yet others appear to have been well founded. The book is in part a chronicle of the way in which friends and enemies can be lost and created. It describes how previously unsuspected facets of some people's personalities were revealed, facets which, in many cases, would never have been discovered in other contexts.

I am aware that what I have written may cause offence and even unhappiness to some of those who appear in the book, but I believe that it is essential to try to convey the extent to which personal relations and interactions are so crucial in the development of historic incidents, and particularly in committee affairs. My aim has not been to insult nor to suggest that my own views of other individuals – friends or opponents – are any more correct or insightful than any one else's views. Their importance is solely in the context of the ways that events developed and decisions were taken.

The importance of such human likes and dislikes, personal assessments of other people's qualities and failings, and preconceptions about one person's strength versus another's weakness is evident in many contexts, not only in committee meetings or confrontations. The story of the Congress shows that these factors are significant in the very structure of a conference, where it is the interplay of session organisers, the interactions of participants and those chairing sessions, and the relationship of academic with administrator which may make or break such an enterprise.

Even before the ban on South African/Namibian participation, the World Archaeological Congress promised to be a somewhat unusual meeting. From the beginning, the organisers were determined to have participation from all over the world, including the Third and Fourth Worlds (see glossary). It was also unusual in that some 25 books were planned to result from the Congress's four and a half days of carefully planned meetings, an enterprise which was based on our determination to hold an academically successful and significant Congress.

I have described the academic planning for the Congress in considerable detail, in the hope that others in the future, who take on the organisation of an international academic conference, will be able to use this book, to some extent, as a sort of manual. I hope, however, that this attention to detail (especially in Chapter 2) does not obscure the drama of the events that took place.

The essence of the drama, and the most important reason of all for writing this book, lies in the banning of South African/Namibian participation from the Congress and the chain of events that followed from this decision. The decision to impose the ban struck at the foundations of what had, until then, been unquestioningly accepted – that the principle of academic free speech transcended all other principles or, at the very least, was somehow immune to the political situation of any particular time. In the following pages I chart the anguish and anger that were created by this decision. That they were created in the forms that they were resulted from the fact that it was a group of British academics who decided on the ban, without reference to the policies of the present British government. There was in this case no hiding behind a government's refusal to grant visas to South Africans – as had happened with other conferences in other countries. Instead, there was an explicit decision to impose the ban. In this book I describe the various factors that led to the decision in all their complexity, and try to show how different people encouraged or supported the ban for different reasons. Some of these reasons were purely pragmatic ones either to avoid disruption by anti-apartheid groups and organisations, or to try to maximise the number of participants from those countries who would not attend if South Africans were present. Less pragmatic reasons included the wish to demonstrate solidarity with the black majority of South Africa who, through the African National Congress (ANC), called for such a boycott and, similarly, a desire to support African and Indian archaeologists who would not have been able to attend the Congress without such a ban.

It was not, I think, merely coincidence that this ban was imposed by a group of archaeologists. Of course, in 1985 and 1986 other conferences in Britain with high profiles must also have been affected by the international events involving South Africa at that period, given all the discussion about the imposition of sanctions, culminating in the State of Emergency and the subsequent cancellation of the right freely to report events in that country. However, those in the press who were surprised that archaeologists, of all people, decided to stand up and be counted on this issue misunderstood the nature and current state of the study of archaeology.

As Chapter 2 sets out to show, approaches to archaeology have changed fundamentally over the past twenty years, at least in some parts of the world. Yet archaeology remains a study of human societies of whatever date in whatever part of the world. Archaeologists and anthropologists (see glossary) are immersed in the evidence of man's inhumanity to man over many time periods and in countless areas of the world. It could be argued that the full realisation of the past should lead to an attitude of non-interference in other people's affairs, but equally it must be recognised that it is precisely people such as the archaeologists and anthropologists who should not wish simply to stand aside and condone by inaction. Their studies nowadays are largely concerned with social processes, including social mechanisms which allow the imposition of slavery or discrimination on grounds of colour or race, and are no longer focussed on excavation simply for the recovery of technology or artwork with which to fill museums.

The WAC was, from the beginning, an exceptional event because it put great emphasis on giving equal status and weight to those interested in the past who were not professional archaeologists or anthropologists. As well as academics from other disciplines, it included some from nations, tribes and cultural groups whose material culture has been, and indeed still is, excavated by archaeologists. The voices of these groups added a new dimension to the WAC proceedings, speaking, as they alone could, as objects of archaeological investigation (often carried out by archaeologists of alien cultures) – a dimension which was totally new to the vast majority of the archaeologists present at the Congress. In them, the present and the past were fused, not because they were not fully part of the modern world of 1986, but because they claimed for themselves a greater right to 'their' past than that of the archaeologist or anthropologist.

It was this unique dimension of the occasion, coupled with the almost equally rarely heard voice of Third World archaeologists, that has led me to adopt an unusual procedure for Chapter 8 of this book. Echoing what I have written above, I have allowed representatives of the WAC administration, of academia and of the Fourth World to speak for themselves. The aim of Chapter 8 is to capture the spirit of the occasion, not only to report the academic discoveries and discussions which were covered in the sessions, and which will be judged on their merits when published by Allen & Unwin as post-Congress books.

This book is addressed to several different kinds of readers and contains a variety of messages and stories. I have shown it in various draft stages to colleagues (some involved in the WAC and some not), friends (some in favour of the ban and some not) and acquaintances (whose views I do not know). The wide range of their reactions has surprised me – some want more personal details about the 'players' in the 'drama', others want a smaller cast altogether, some want more academic content, others feel other chapters are too detailed, some find the 'villains' sympathetic, whereas others find it almost impossible to read about them. All have said that they were fascinated by the story and have learned at least something from it.

In order to make the book easier to understand, and details of events and personalities simpler to follow, especially for non-archaeologists, I have included a chronological chart of events (page 243), a diagram of the structure of the international academic organisations concerned (page 276), a list of the members of the main committees (pages 278-79), a glossary of terms and organisations appearing in the book (page 252), and a list of abbreviations (page 243).

I have tried to remedy some of the deficiencies in the book on the basis of the comments from those who have read one or other of the drafts. There is one person, however, whose contribution is not sufficiently explicit in the book – that of Sue Stephenson – whose role is understated. Throughout the years of preparation, as well as during the Congress, she was indescribably supportive of the whole endeavour and of me personally. This is all the more surprising for Sue had written to me via Colin Renfrew (her then Head of Department) before she had even met me, to say that she would never work past 5 pm! She knows that I cannot thank her enough for that support, but I can at least thank her formally, here, for reading an early draft of the manuscript. In the following pages I acknowledge the role of some of my Departmental staff in the WAC. Two of these, Dr Tim Champion and Dr Steve Shennan, also read and made many constructive comments on an early version of the book. It has been quite impossible to do full justice to the role of the Departmental students throughout the Congress, most of them showing a willingness to work long hours unrewarded which should augur well for their futures! One who contributed a paper to the Congress (to be published in a post-Congress book) is Brian Molyneaux, a postgraduate research student from Canada, who has also spent night after night away from his thesis in order to get a clean manuscript of this volume to the publisher by the given deadline. Without him this book could not possibly have been published so soon. Peter Stone's role in the Congress is reported in the book, and I owe him renewed thanks for having criticised it in detail. Another major character in the book, Paul Crake, not only worked through the final manuscript, but was driven by it to write up his own perception of the WAC, a piece which I have included in Chapter 8.

I owe sincere thanks to two medical friends of mine – Dr Andrew Manasse commented on an early draft and Professor Robert Boyd criticised the penultimate version. Several people, including Professor David Bellos, Dr Robert Layton and Mr Alan Whitehead, have commented on parts of early drafts, and I am particularly grateful to Professor Michael Day, Professor David Harris, Mr Derek Hayes, Professor Colin Renfrew, Professor Thurstan Shaw, and Sir David Wilson for comments on the whole of the book. Two others, who were not involved in the academic running of the Congress, provided me with very helpful comments on the whole book, and I am most grateful to Julie Elford and Paul Lashmar.

One of these readers suggested to me that I will, inevitably, be attacked for writing this book as an 'ego trip'. So far it has certainly not been, for I do not feel anything beyond exhaustion at the effort to publish a record of events as quickly as possible. Should the book be a commercial success, profits will be used to facilitate the participation at archaeological meetings of those from countries who cannot themselves afford to attend such gatherings.

Almost all the readers have complained at the lack of substance that I have given to Jane Hubert in the following pages. In my perception, however, she is there on *every* page. Jane is also an anthropologist of long standing who has read every version of the book and altered it in both style and content. The closeness of our relationship which, according to some, is not apparent in this book, is perhaps best illustrated by the fact that, at a moment when everything seemed hopeless and I was on the verge of abandoning the Congress, she invoked the memory of an Australian Aboriginal friend of mine, Gloria Brennan. Gloria had fought for the rights of her people until her death and I had visited her in Australia as she was dying, just after the ban on South Africa was imposed. Only Jane could and would have known that that was exactly the right thing to have said to me at that moment of my self-pity. For me much of the WAC is Jane and vice versa.

Southampton   P.J.U
1 June, 1987

Introduction

Friends and colleagues have often asked me over the past year what it has felt like to be at the centre of an international controversy. Some have asked what, if anything, in my past has enabled me to stand up to the pressures. I was unable to give any reasonable response to these questions.

This book may serve as a belated sort of answer. It is also, by implication, somewhat of an exploration of my own weaknesses and strengths as they emerged, often much to my own surprise, during this traumatic period.

As an academic archaeologist it was both strange and unexpected that I should find myself at the centre of an emotional political controversy regarding South Africa. What is even more surprising is that it was the second time something of this sort had happened to me, though the only similarity between the two situations is that they both concerned the apparent injustices of the dominant group of whites towards the non-white, indigenous populations of their own and other countries. In yet a third situation I was in danger of being in conflict with both an African nationalist regime and its ex-colonial predecessor.

There was nothing specific in my upbringing (that I can remember or identify) which might have led me to become involved in the aspirations of indigenous populations. I was not sufficiently politically aware, as a young man, to try to discover why my father, as a German Professor of Medicine, chose to settle in England in the 1930s rather than in Ethiopia, Thailand, or South Africa, which were the alternative homelands offered to him at that time. I was born in Buckinghamshire and brought up there during and after the war with no exposure to any other culture (except to the Swiss through a family with whom we shared our house). My first experience of a wider world was not until 1955, at the North Western Polytechnic in London, where I struggled to take my GCE Advanced Levels, the only non-Cypriot in the Greek class, and one of very few whites taking French and English. I thrived in this very un-English environment and began, at last, to hear the other side of the stories I had heard, becoming quite well informed about the shocking exploitation of the island of Cyprus and learning much from my African and Indian fellow-students.

Never the less it was really by chance that I studied anthropology (which was the study, at that time at least, of other cultures) at University College London, because this was the only means by which I could, as an undergraduate, read Egyptology, that unwavering obsession I had had since I was 11. It was through these anthropology courses that I not only had the chance to read about the practices and beliefs of other peoples, but also to be taught by, and to meet, academics who had respect for the beliefs and activities, often far-removed from their own, of the people of other cultures.

Later, I became a postgraduate student of Egyptology and Prehistory at University College London and the Institute of Archaeology in London where John Evans, who features throughout many of the following pages, had recently been appointed Professor and was one of my supervisors. My doctoral thesis was on the interpretation of prehistoric figurines from Egypt, the Near East, and the Mediterranean. Subsequently I was, for some ten years, a Lecturer in Anthropology at my old college, continuing to be engrossed in prehistoric cultures, and publishing articles on a variety of subjects including disease in ancient Egypt, the application of scientific techniques to archaeological objects, and the ways that material culture, such as articles of clothing, was used by different cultures to express the age and status of the individuals concerned. I also edited a series of books on 'Art and Society' and initiated a research seminar series which resulted in the publication of two books for which I was the editor. Both books were based on revised precirculated papers which were discussed at small conferences and both – one on the domestication of plants and animals and the other on settlement and urbanisation – became textbooks.

However, it was probably my joint book with Dr Andrée Rosenfeld on *Palaeolithic Cave Art* which led me to accept a position in Australia where I hoped to be able to study artists who were still carrying out rock paintings.

In 1972 I became Principal of the Australian Institute of Aboriginal Studies in Canberra, a semi-governmental research Institute set up in the 1960s to record for posterity the languages and customs of the Aborigines, whose culture was assumed to be dying. I arrived there as a relatively cloistered academic, still sceptical about anything approaching 'action research' and with no hint of doubt about the sacred right of academic archaeologists and anthropologists to dig up, and into, whatever they pleased, regardless of whose lands, cultures or beliefs were being disrupted and overturned. I found that my Institute was a totally white institution – whites gave out money to whites, through white committees, to study the blacks. Very quickly this seemed to me to be an untenable situation and, as I met more and more Aborigines, whose interest and involvement in their own culture was at least as great as any academic's, I began to see, at first-hand, how a combination of European-derived committee structures, the English language, and so-called academic 'objectivity' could silence the voice of a whole population living in the same land but with a different cultural background.

By the time I left Australia in 1980 the situation had, at least in relation to the Institute, radically altered. Government had accepted the importance of research (as well as the need for secure archiving of materials) and the budget had been increased very substantially. Aborigines were now members of its controlling Council, were full members of its powerful academic Advisory Committees, and controlled their own research budget. My successor, as Principal of the Institute, was an Aborigine. These changes had not been made without some violent opposition, but they had been successful.

The main political involvement of the Institute during this time was with the documentation of Aboriginal Land Rights. With the Aboriginal Land Rights (NT) Act passed in 1976, Aborigines could lay claim to those parts of vacant Crown Lands in the Northern Territory that they considered to be theirs. To do this they had to work within the framework of a white judiciary, within laws and using procedures that were entirely unknown to them. It was self-evident to me that, at this point, the academics and scholars had no option but to leave the comfort of their cloistered walls, and enter the real world, to step away from their long-held academic priorities and to participate and help in the fight for the survival of the culture and heritage of the indigenous peoples whose lands, lives and belief systems had, until now, been merely the subjects of academic study.

In 1980, having returned to England to live, I was sent by the British Council to advise the new Robert Mugabe Government in Zimbabwe on the setting up of 'culture houses' throughout the country. I was shocked by the way the Ian Smith regime had managed to manipulate the archaeological evidence about the site of Great Zimbabwe, to ensure that it was not publicly acknowledged that it had been built by the indigenous black population, and appalled that the archaeologist who had been sacked for refusing to cover up the archaeological evidence was not supported by other archaeologists in any part of the world, including Britain. I was revolted to see how a white regime was able, over many years, to reduce proud and individual cultural groups to confusion, dependency and social malaise. I also learnt the undeniable fact that in much of what we call the Third World the presentation and examination of the past is in the hands of a white minority. My report, and subsequent publications, documented the way that the archaeological service in Rhodesia had not catered for the interests of the majority population, and also urged the new Zimbabwean Government to recognise the cultural wealth of its many constituent cultural groups.

In 1981, after having accepted the Chair of Archaeology at Southampton University, I was approached to become National Secretary of the British Congress of the International Union of Pre- and Protohistoric Sciences (IUPPS), to be held in 1986. I eventually agreed to organise the conference *on condition that it would take as its most serious commitment the full participation of the countries of the Third World*, to end the European domination of previous Congresses. As this book outlines, the academic programme of the World Archaeological Congress had this aim in mind, so that the subjects which were chosen for debate were those which would allow not only archaeologists but also others interested in the past, from anywhere in the world, to participate as equal members in the meeting.

The following chapters detail the events surrounding the Congress's ban on

South African and Namibian participation. In looking back at this period, I cannot help being aware of the parallel with my Australian experience, for, at that time, in 1985, I was not a formal member of Anti-Apartheid and I was still politically naive enough to be ignorant of the national policy of the Association of University Teachers regarding South Africa. For months I acted as a traditional academic would, arguing that academic freedom was more important than anything else, and I claimed to myself and others that one could be totally against apartheid while at the same time doing nothing about it in the sphere of academia. Shockingly, it took many months for my Australian experiences to make me realise what a patronising stance I was adopting.

This book records the emotions and pressures involved in this whole debate. It says quite a lot about the nature of archaeological enquiry and of the European and North American domination of the subject, but it also reveals the great quality of many people involved in archaeology and other studies of the past. It is a powerful force which made me stand up against many of my friends and colleagues in Britain, the USA and South Africa on this issue and which deprived me of the long-awaited chance to finish two neglected books. It is indeed a striking story that nine new Directors of the Congress were willing to join a beleaguered garrison besieged by their academic colleagues, and that an historic decision was made by my erstwhile Executive Committee colleagues who resigned so that the confrontation of principle between academic privilege and humanitarian involvement might continue. Apart from the South African apartheid issue, there was a wider set of considerations about the treatment of other peoples' cultures, past and present, that were of major importance and that focused on the nature of the IUPPS. The IUPPS is the only official international body that exists to foster the academic discipline of archaeology, to which I have devoted my life. It is a dinosaur which continues to seek to manipulate the world situation according to its archaic Western European preconceptions about what is relevant and important and what is not. It does so by devices such as the imposition of white rules and regulations which no one bothers to explain and by the manipulation of bureaucratic procedures. What became clear to me during 1985 and 1986 is that my priorities do not conform to those of some of my academic colleagues. I do not share the views of those who believe, for example, that a piece of archaeological research is so sacrosanct that it should allow us, in the name of academic free intercourse, to disregard the call from the African National Congress (ANC), the National Union of Students (NUS), the Association of University Teachers (AUT), the Commonwealth, the European Economic Community (EEC) and – for that matter – the United Nations (UN), to over-ride the Eurocentric, self-important, academic self-indulgence of those who claim to know better than anyone else what others should believe and practise.

I believe that apartheid, as practised by the current South African regime, is an abomination, whose historical roots are European, and is part of our guilt (like the killing of Tasmanian Aborigines). This particular abomination is legalised and institutionalised, and it is this which makes it wholly unlike any other example of discrimination and oppression in the world of 1987.

Archaeology is my interest and my life. I believe, and teach, that the study of the past is important for all, from primary school children to adults. I believe that to be able to identify with a past, and to be proud of it, helps people to have respect for themselves and for the group of people from whom they have derived. I have as much respect for the Aboriginal leader who explains past events to his people as for the Druid who genuinely believes that Stonehenge is a sacred place, or for my colleague down the corridor who believes that he can scientifically date his site to a particular year BP (see glossary). I am quite obviously out of step with those who believe that, by definition, it is the European rules and attitudes which should determine our actions.

For reasons such as these, many of us now face the accusation that we have irreparably divided the archaeological world over the issue of apartheid versus 'free speech'. In fact, to discuss the issue of academic free speech is almost an obscenity in the context of South Africa, where the majority of the population lack far more fundamental freedoms than that of discussion. I do not know why archaeologists, any more than any group of people who happen to study the same subject, should be expected to share all the same values, political or ethical. What has driven me, as an academic, into politics over the past few years has been best summed up in a letter from Dr I. Torbe to *The Times* which, along with letters from the Vice Chancellor of the University of Southampton, the President of the Southampton AUT and many others, was not published by that newspaper:

> When I read in a contribution to the debate on the exclusion of South Africans from the WAC the clause 'of course I am opposed to apartheid' I know that the next word will be 'but'. What that really means is that the onus of doing anything about it lies on everybody else. The dockers at Southampton, where at least one-sixth of the trade passing through the port is with South Africa, are expected to place their jobs in jeopardy; grocers, greengrocers and fruiterers to sacrifice a portion of their livelihood; sportsmen and women and entertainers to forgo lucrative tours; but academic freedom must remain sacrosanct.

I pray the WAC has now helped to establish a secure future for world archaeology which can make its contribution to the recognition of the unique variety of human cultures, past and present. To become a humane subject archaeology must itself show that it is not merely the plaything of a particular social class or of a particular stage in industralised development. I hope that the story of this book, which represents a virtual revolution in practice and self-awareness, is a record of the development of such a future role for the past.

1. How Not to Finance a Congress

I suppose I must have been vaguely aware that there existed a worldwide international archaeological organisation. Friends in Australia had come back from a meeting in Nice, France, in 1976 furious that no academic interest or arrangements had been made for regions such as the Pacific, and resplendent with stories of booze and French hospitality. In 1981 I certainly knew no details about this organisation, not even its name.

IUPPS is a Union linked through the International Council for Philosophy and Humanistic Studies (ICPHS) to UNESCO (see page 276), with the aim of promoting the study of prehistory and protohistory through the organisation of international congresses, through the patronage of international scientific publications and, in general, by the collaboration of scholars from all countries in enterprises that contribute to the advancement of prehistoric and protohistoric sciences. It is supposed to hold major Congresses every five years. In fact this story should begin with its meeting in October 1981 in Mexico City. I remember that the first I heard of the Mexico meeting was from a future colleague in Southampton, who had just come back from it, and who told me that virtually no one had turned up, despite lavish entertainment and finance from the Mexican Government. Apparently almost nobody had been told about the Congress in advance. Later I was told that it had been chaotic and that the greatest frustration had been the lack of any detailed programming. At that meeting in Mexico, apparently, there was, not for the first time, serious discussion about whether or not such Congresses were worth continuing (see page 220). Indeed, a review of the meeting reported that 'the fears for the future of the Congress have become greater and the need to change the format of the Congress more urgent'. As a result the three British members of the IUPPS Permanent Council who were present – Professor John Evans (Director of the London Institute of Archaeology), Dr David Wilson (Director of the British Museum), and Professor Colin Renfrew (newly appointed Disney Professor of Archaeology at Cambridge) – were asked by the IUPPS Secretary-General, Professor Jacques Nenquin of the University of Ghent in Belgium, whether Britain would offer to host the next IUPPS Congress scheduled to meet in 1986. Apparently he made this approach because he believed that Britain was capable of running a successful Congress, which would remove the bad taste of the Mexican experience, and also because no acceptable bid had been received from any country. The IUPPS is supposed to work through a Permanent Council composed of up to four members from each country in the world. It is this Permanent Council which is supposed to decide, by a secret ballot, between the various countries offering to hold the next Congress. According to the IUPPS Statutes, only the Permanent Council can take this decision.

In this case, however, because the Permanent Council had no offer to accept or reject, it apparently decided in principle that if Britain were to make a formal offer to host the XIth Congress, such an offer should be accepted (presumably by the International Executive Committee which meets annually, as the Permanent Council would not meet again for another three years). The three British members returned home apparently committed to hosting the XIth IUPPS Congress, despite the fact that they had no money to do so, no firsthand experience of running a very large international meeting, and no one to organise it. I suspect that their move was partly nationalistic, as the first of the IUPPS Congresses had taken place in England in 1932 and they did not want to see the glorious tradition die, and partly from a genuine desire to make the next IUPPS Congress into a truly world Congress. As John Evans said later to the National Committee, the British wished to maintain 'our international standing in these fields'. Apparently my name was mentioned as a possible National Secretary in discussions between the three British members of the IUPPS Permanent Council and my old friend Dr John Alexander of the University of Cambridge, who was also at the Mexico meeting and who had published reviews of previous IUPPS Congresses, in which he had discussed the desirable form of its future activities.

I had returned to my Buckinghamshire cottage from Australia in December 1980, and in May 1981 I was appointed to the Chair of Archaeology at the University of Southampton, a position I was to take up in January 1982, succeeding Professor Colin Renfrew. Meanwhile I was to teach back in my old academic home of University College London, and I planned to renovate the cottage, write up some of the work that I had done in Australia and act as a Consultant to the new Government of Zimbabwe (see Introduction). I was also nervously waiting to see whether Jane Hubert (then Forge) would also leave Australia permanently to join me in my new life back in England.

I cannot remember when exactly Professor Colin Renfrew rang, on the first of many occasions, to say that he had been asked by the British members of the IUPPS to get me to agree to become National Secretary for the 1986 Congress to be held in London. He explained that the country appointed to host each IUPPS Congress has to appoint its own National Secretary, who then also becomes a voting member of the International IUPPS Executive Committee. I replied that I was not interested, pointing out that I had organised enough conferences, in England and Australia, to last a lifetime, that I hated all I had heard about really big congresses, and that I was one of the few who for that reason, had not even thought of going to Nice in 1976.

Colin Renfrew kept up the pressure, to which were added telephone calls from John Evans and David Wilson. No one mentioned the fourth British member of the IUPPS Permanent Council, Leslie Alcock, Professor of Archaeology in the University of Glasgow, whom I had never met.

I was not at all swayed by this pressure, for none of the three were people with whom I had all that much in common. Colin was about my own age, and we had known each other throughout somewhat parallel careers before I went to Australia. Indeed he had taken on the running of the research seminar series after I left. I knew him as a very clever establishment character, with a Cambridge background, who had stood as a Conservative Parliamentary candidate in 1967 and made massive inroads into the then Labour majority. John Evans was a far different matter. I had known him well for many years, first as my professor when I was an undergraduate and subsequently as my supervisor during postgraduate studies. I had excavated at Knossos in Crete under his directorship and had travelled with him and his wife across Greece. It was a fairly close relationship – I remembered having driven him in my car to his driving test. We both particularly enjoyed foreign cultures and languages, and we had a considerable degree of mutual respect. But I knew enough of him to realise that he would not make a good President of any Congress, for leadership was not one of his qualities. David Wilson seemed to represent almost everything I detested in England; by repute he was only seen with those of seniority and influence. We had only a nodding acquaintance, and I suspected that he would indeed only nod if he thought he might gain some advantage by so doing.

The line eventually put to me was that there was no one else with my experience of organisation to take on the position of National Secretary, and also that the job should be done by a professor. I had to agree that it was difficult to think of anyone who would be able to do it except Colin Renfrew himself. It was also true that, so far, I had only limited commitments since returning to England, and 1986 seemed very far away. But I was really secretly attracted to the proposal for two quite different reasons. The first was entirely personal. I thought that Jane might not join me, and I would then be badly in need of full-time distraction. If she did come, it was an enterprise we could tackle together and also be able to travel overseas together. The second was that I would have the chance really to involve people from the Third and Fourth Worlds in such a meeting. I knew I would agree to the idea if various conditions were acceptable – that I would be able to organise the meeting in such a way that real work would be carried out during the Congress by groups of people who would not normally ever have the chance of getting together.

I met the four British members of the IUPPS Permanent Council in London on 16 November 1981 in John Evans' room at the Institute of Archaeology. Apparently, as Chairman of the host country's Executive Committee, John Evans also became President of the IUPPS until the next

Congress, five years later. Given the absence of any government funding, they had already been discussing possible alternative sources of finance, primarily through Mr Robert Kiln of Kiln and Co., Underwriting Agents at Lloyds and Mr Brian Palmer of Legal and General Insurance in the City of London, but also from learned societies and grant-giving bodies, and had chosen names of those who could be invited to join National and Honorific Committees. Their idea was that the Congress should be held in London with the British Museum playing a major supportive role. They offered me the position of National Secretary. I suggested immediately, as I did later, that it should be Colin in his new role as senior professor at Cambridge. I also asked for clarification whether, if I refused, I would in any case be co-opted on to the Executive Committee in my own right, and I asked for more time to consider the offer. I mentioned too, even at that early date, my feeling that London might not be the ideal location for the academic sessions, for in any meeting that I might organise I would be concentrating on the work and not on the social programme; a small campus location might be more appropriate, with the formal Plenary Session located in London.

I thought hard about what to do. I thought I realised the amount of work that such a Congress organisation would involve, and I debated with myself and with Jane, whether I wanted to continue to be seen as an organiser or whether I now needed time exclusively for research and writing. I tried again to get Colin to take on the position himself. This time it was Dr Jane Renfrew who tried to convince me that I should do it rather than he. I consulted some of my new colleagues in the Southampton Department of Archaeology, who also encouraged me to take it on. Finally I formulated the conditions under which I would be prepared to accept the position of National Secretary. Among these were: that I would not be responsible for any money-raising (in any case all was supposedly already arranged on that front); that the primary aim of the Congress would be real academic discussion (which therefore implied both precirculation of papers and post-Congress publications); that there would be meaningful world participation from the Third World and from Fourth World indigenous peoples; and that the Congress would cater for the interests of both young archaeologists and students. To my great surprise, and growing horror, all the conditions were immediately accepted without any modifications.

I was determined to have the academic working sessions outside London, for only in that way would I be able to ensure an intimate atmosphere despite the huge number of expected participants, and ensure that the aim would be work rather than theatres and nightclubs. I also needed exceptional conditions such as free accommodation to help the Third and Fourth Worlds. How could I persuade the Executive, of which I was still not a member, to forgo its commitment to hold the meeting in London?

Nor was it clear to me how I could get the University of Southampton interested. In December I began meetings with John Hiett, an apparently bluff and well-meaning Welshman who was the University's Conference Officer. To my horror he said straightaway that it was impossible even to contemplate such a large and unusual Congress in a place like Southampton. In order to sway him I stressed the importance of such a Congress, not only to the University but also to his own future conference activities, and I tried to infect him with my excitement over the overall concept and plan for the Congress. In the end I succeeded. He then put in an impressive amount of work in the battle to get the Congress to Southampton. Early in 1981, he introduced me to Fay Pannell, who had received an OBE for conference organisation. Since then she had retired to Hampshire. Together, and in close consultation with me, they drew up the first outline Congress budget, a formula which was so good that it lasted as the basic outline for activity throughout the next five years.

Armed with this detail I went back to the Executive and argued the case for concentrating the academic sessions within a limited university campus without the distractions of London. David Wilson was the main opponent, stressing the importance of luxury food and drink for the august foreigners, as well as the possible implications for raising London City financial support. Colin Renfrew was more supportive because, it turned out, he wanted to put in a Cambridge bid for the Congress. The principle that the Congress need not be necessarily held in London was agreed in February 1982. The flood gates were then open for vying bids. I now had to leave it to John Hiett to come up with a concrete, attractive offer. He worked hard at this, even investigating the possibility of using the QEII liner if 4,000 participants were really to attend.

The next move was forced upon us, I learnt, by the rules of the IUPPS, about which I still knew next to nothing. The British Executive had to set up a British National Committee, both under John Evans' Chairmanship, a back-to-front procedure about which I complained to the Executive Committee but which we could not alter. I had only a few months to get the Executive to add to the list, which it had been considering at its first meeting in November 1981, the names of some of the archaeologists and anthropologists whom I wanted to see play an active part in the Congress. What was worse was that I had to come up with some agreed principles of planning and organisation in time for the first National Committee meeting now scheduled for the end of April 1982. All this was made even more complicated by the fact that I was still not the National Secretary, and the Executive Committee had still not decided whether or not I was a member of it in my own right as Professor of Archaeology at Southampton University. Colin was the first to give way on the location of the Congress, partly because he had discovered that the facilities in Cambridge were not suitable and partly because he was now worried that Cambridge colleagues were not in favour of a large Congress. However, having earlier fought for Cambridge, he could no longer insist on London. John Evans was the next. He wrote to me confirming that the IUPPS had previously approved Britain as the location for its Congress without specifying a particular town. At a Saturday Executive Committee meeting only David held out. He was forced to agree that if raising financial support would not be affected by a dual location of the Congress, he also would go along with the Southampton venue. At that same Executive meeting I insisted that the financial support from the City of London which had been mentioned so often should now be produced. This was not to be.

As the day of the National Committee grew nearer I applied pressure. 'It strikes me that it would be courting disaster,' I wrote to John, 'if the decision as to where the conference is to be held had not been taken by the Executive prior to the National Committee meeting. Otherwise, I can envisage that several people on the National Committee will have a view and will wish for time to put in counter bids.' Using much of Hiett's information, I also submitted a detailed argument in favour of Southampton over Oxford or Cambridge, and of Southampton and London together over London by itself. A few days before the National Committee meeting, members of the Executive Committee met with one of Southampton University's Deputy Vice Chancellors, the Conference Officer, Fay Pannell and myself and looked over the campus. Over lunch the Deputy Vice Chancellor offered a university reception, a 20 per cent reduction on rooms in Halls of Residence, free use of meeting rooms, cheap printing facilities, and the free supply of audiovisual equipment and possibly also of technicians. I was not sure then, and am still not sure now, whether it was these special concessions, or the free flow of gin which I had instructed Sue Stephenson, our Departmental secretary, to supply before lunch, which clinched the deal.

Meanwhile I had also been concentrating on my weak position within the Executive Committee, if indeed I joined it, and I was becoming more and more suspicious of the financial backing for the Congress. I decided to turn to an old contact of mine, Derek Hayes, a solicitor at the London firm of Macfarlanes. I remembered him, with some awe, as the toughest man I had met in a long time when, years ago, he had managed to retrieve my book, *Anthropomorphic Figurines from Predynastic Egypt and Neolithic Crete*, from an inactive publisher so that it could be published within one of the publication series of the Royal Anthropological Institute. Since then he had handled some minor legal matters for me but I had not kept in close contact. I began to point out to John Evans that we were badly in need of legal advice, not least to form ourselves into a charitable company if we ever did receive the promised City financial support. I rang Derek Hayes a few days before the National Committee meeting. He sounded exactly as I remembered him, quick and alert and to the point, and he agreed to meet us in the morning before the National meeting.

By now there was even more obscurity about the nature of the City's financial backing and we did indeed badly need someone to explain the implications of the insurance policy that was apparently being suggested. I was desperate to get firm details of the offer and, in the end, saw Brian Palmer with John Evans the day before the National Committee meeting. Palmer was more than reassuring. An insurance slip would be easy to get. Would a quarter of a million risk coverage be sufficient? All that would be needed in return would be invitations to a special party at the British Museum and special invitations to the Plenary Session. We did indeed need Derek to sort out fact from fantasy ...

Derek's presence at the Executive meeting was reassuring to us all, and his experience and knowledge shone through to us amateurs. Even David, who pretends to be very expert in such matters, was visibly impressed. I convinced the Executive that we needed a formal association with Macfarlanes and Derek Hayes was asked to prepare the necessary papers for us to become a company limited by guarantee. I still felt that I needed Derek on the Executive, but meanwhile he accepted, on behalf of Macfarlanes, to be our legal adviser.

At the National Committee meeting, attended by 26 of the 46 invited members, John Evans summarised the way the IUPPS functioned. He stressed that in Mexico in 1981 'it had been decided that a major effort must be made to attract non-European and especially third world members'. The National Committee accepted my appointment as National Secretary as well as the likely dual locations of Southampton and London. More important, the Committee also supported my main recommendation which was to base the Congress on 'several major inclusive themes (which) would form the central core of the Congress's working sessions and that papers for discussion for these sessions would be circulated in advance, and that discussion would be the main aim of such sessions'.

Early in May 1982 John Evans flew to the IUPPS International Executive Committee meeting in Florence, a meeting which he informed me was not worth my bothering about although I had been invited to attend it, and reported that he could now formally invite the Union to hold its XIth Congress in London and Southampton in 1986 'despite many financial problems which still had to be sorted out'. At that meeting the IUPPS was officially told that the Congress would concentrate on the participation of people from outside Europe and would be organised around major themes. It was also at that moment that, in apparent breach of the rules, John Evans was 'formally elected' President of the IUPPS. According to a letter of 10 May from Jacques Nenquin, Secretary-General of IUPPS, I was also somehow 'elected', 'acting on the recommendation of the Permanent Council' (although my name could not have been put forward with any authority at the time of the Mexico Congress), by almost the same group of Western Europeans who were later to throw us out of IUPPS at the special meeting in Paris in 1986 (see Chapter 5). There were other prophetic hints at that meeting in Florence. Jacques Nenquin, who had failed to turn up to a meeting of the Pan African Association on Prehistory and Related Studies (previously the Pan African Congress) in Nairobi in 1977, where he had been due to preside as one of its Vice Presidents, was now beginning to refer uneasily to that body's new statutes and reorganisation (which were to reject any contacts with South Africa and South Africans). John Evans' mention of the money problems was also prophetic. Just before Christmas 1982 these led to my first and only resignation from the whole enterprise.

I had based my 1982 budget on what I had been told was a guaranteed minimum of £150,000 from the City of London. David Wilson had mentioned this sum at the National Committee meeting, as well as an annual grant of £5,000 which he expected we would get from the British Academy, and he had warned the Committee that each person's registration fee would be about $250, at 1986 prices (excluding dinners and accommodation). Assuming 2,000 participants I was working on an assumed budget of about £400,000 – a figure which I desperately tried to maintain, more or less, throughout the years, despite all the ups and downs, as well as the planned changes, which were to befall the Congress.

The main items apart from administration, printing and postage, meeting rooms, equipment, and secretariat (c £128,000), were interpreters (£28,000), precirculated papers (£30,000), travel, consultations and seminars leading to the development of the academic programme (£30,000), financing of Third World participants (£30,000), and transportation in Southampton and to London (£39,000). These divisions more or less accurately reflected my major concerns: of Third/Fourth World participation, precirculated papers for thematic sessions, a high academic standard, and an efficient secretariat. By the time I had to pay the first bills – for such things as fares, stationery, telephone calls, and secretarial assistance – it had become all too clear that, despite the reassuring promises of David Wilson and their tacit acceptance by John Evans and Colin Renfrew, there was in fact no money available or in sight, except for £5,000 from the British Academy (with the assumption that this amount would be repeated each year). All the words about the City of London's input of £150,000 appeared to be just a pipe dream. By now I had become so involved in the plans for the Congress that I was loth to give it all up. On the other hand, it had been one of my main conditions from the start that I would not become involved in money raising – indeed it was largely because of my dislike of this role that I had left the job I loved in Australia. Telephone calls between members of the Executive Committee became nightmarish as grant-giving bodies, banks, personal contacts and all other possible leads were pursued by several of us. Some leads were successful but most were not; funding a Congress was quite a different matter from funding an excavation, which held out the promise of striking new discoveries. I was spending all my time doing exactly what I had said I would on no account do. John Evans was trying to get action from Brian Palmer, but apparently to no avail. It was also impossible to get John to take any conclusive action – he simply agreed that everything looked terrible. The only development was that he suddenly wrote to agree that the Congress should be 'a joint London/Southampton affair' ... 'subject of course, to the monetary guarantees actually being forthcoming at this end on this joint basis'.

By October, John Hiett, the University's Conference Officer, was again taking fright and urging reconsideration of the whole Congress. Only a few months before he had even been suggesting that the University should underwrite the whole costs of the Congress, and take any profits deriving from it. There was suddenly a flicker of hope. Brian Palmer had apparently written to Robert Kiln who was now apologising on his and Brian Palmer's behalf for the lack of promised guarantee, and was suggesting a complex arrangement of insurance company guarantees together with his own personal guarantee. Again nothing happened. The Executive Committee meeting in November deferred almost all of its business, though it did appoint Derek Hayes as Honorary Treasurer and the Executive took the necessary steps to be recognised as a charity. Discussion was depressing. It focused more or less exclusively on whether to cancel altogether if there was no financial movement by the end of December, or whether to attempt to hold a much smaller and more limited conference. Everything appeared to be lost when Mr Kiln reported to me that no support appeared to be forthcoming from within the City. At the end of November an actual slip was said to have been agreed in principle by the insurers, but this had no effect on the banks I approached in order to try to raise actual cash.

Towards the end of December I decided that the issue had to be forced into the open, so I resigned. The effect was startling. Within the month the insurance policy was not only firmly promised (it was issued at the end of February 1983) by Legal and General and a few other insurance companies, but it guaranteed 'losses up to £150,000 for net loss of expenses, costs and/or commitments sustained or incurred in the event of the number of "booked delegates failing to exceed 3,000" and "losses up to £400,000 for net loss of expenses, costs and/or commitments sustained or incurred solely and directly in consequence of the cancellation, postponement or abandonment of said Congress due to any cause beyond the control of the Assured" '. Eventually, after being rebuffed by Midland Bank, we were given an overdraft facility of up to £150,000 by National Westminster Bank on the basis of our £7,000 unique insurance policy. It was assumed that I had withdrawn my resignation, and Derek was busy dealing with government tax regulations, finding auditors, drawing up covenant forms, and advancing the money from Macfarlanes in order to pay for the insurance cover. The Executive Committee members became the Directors of a Company limited by guarantee.

However I was still far from reassured. How were we ever going to be sure of the 3-4,000 participants, and how were we ever going to be able to finance the running costs of the Congress in 1984, 1985 and 1986 before the registration fees had been received and after the overdraft facility had been used up? We desperately needed to raise another £150,000 of support before the Congress could be regarded as really viable with 2,000 or 3,000 participants and able to do all we intended. The one immediate positive and exciting result of the overdraft facility was that I could go ahead and produce the Congress's First Announcement.

In March and June 1983 there were meetings of the Executive and National Committees. They were mainly concerned with the academic and other programmes. But they were also full of warnings, reported even in journals such as *Antiquity*, about the negative reactions that had been expressed both in Britain and overseas to our statement in the First Announcement that the registration fee would be about £200. Lengthy discussions on both occasions led to the agreement that future Congress announcements would stress that the £200 was at predicted 1986 prices, and included a proportion for government tax. Announcements would also make clear how the sum had been arrived at, and would stress that as there was no government financial support for the Congress, all income would derive from registration fees. In this context the National Committee also urged a specially reduced student registration fee.

At this same round of meetings, after I had returned from my first meeting of the international Executive Committee in Lund in Sweden (see page 35), I alerted members to my continuing disquiet about the IUPPS organisation, in particular the number of vacancies in many of the Third World countries' representation on the Permanent Council, and I urged as wide a circulation as possible of all Congress Announcements.

Much of the remainder of 1983 (and for that matter 1984) was devoted to the chase after money. The Executive, on the basis of Derek's and my separate and detailed recommendations, had by this time chosen Martlet, in the spring of 1983, as the Congress's Conference organiser at a fee of £25,000, plus £10 per registered participant. By the summer we had been given or promised about £52,000, but there was still little hope in sight and we were in overdraft. The Executive set up a Finance Committee but, by the end of 1983, it had accomplished nothing. Colin Renfrew and I met with the secretariat of the British Committee of UNESCO and did other canvassing. We had hopes of some financial support for the Third World from that source, but 1984 was obviously to be the crunch period when we would either have to find money or finally abort the whole enterprise.

Mentally, I had adjusted to thinking of a break-even on the basis of 2,000 rather than 3,000 participants. This feeling was borne out by my visit to my first big Congress, the meeting of the International Union of Anthropological and Ethnological Sciences (IUAES) in Quebec and Vancouver, held in August 1983. At this meeting of the sister organisation to IUPPS (also under the overall control of ICPHS), which also had specialist sections dealing with archaeology and, like IUPPS, leaves the organisation of its Congresses to the host country which takes full responsibility for it, I learnt a lot of hard lessons. I returned to England more than ever determined either to find the money needed to do what I wanted, or to cancel our Congress before it was too late and too much effort and money had been committed.

By the time I reached the Canadian Congress I was beginning to have doubts about Martlet's suitability to run the WAC and, by the end of the year, I was seriously considering changing to a different conference organiser. Each time that I was on the verge of taking the final plunge the problem was always recognised, with a promise to do better in the future. One lovely example caused some amusement. Participant No 1458 on the computer printout was named as UIB – the nearest Martlet could get to UCKO! Against all the failures there was the asset of Alex Ross, whose computer programme was so essential for the academic side of the Congress (see page 38). My Canadian experiences led me to compose a vivid report for both Martlet and the Executive Committee from which I quote part of the main section dealing with administration and finance:

IUAES 1983 has lost a lot of money and [the limited registered charitable company] will have to declare itself bankrupt unless retrospective efforts to raise face-saving finance succeed – and this despite an extremely able National Secretary who has been paid a half-time salary for two years and despite the hiring of a professional conference organisation company on a per capita rate (who, admittedly, seemed to be there only to handle registrations, to organise a (hopeless) salmon barbecue, and for the production of (illegible) name-tags). We have many lessons to learn from this – most of which I think we have already foreseen. The Canadian National President predicted 5,000 paying participants – a figure which was never challenged ... The Canadian National Secretary took his own sensible decision to base his budget on 3,000 but only 2,500 turned up – we must continue to base our budget on 2,000 and we have an adequate insurance guarantee ... The Canadians made some bad errors of judgement; they decided the University of British Columbia could not house 5,000 and therefore based their Vancouver Congress on down-town hotel prices and lost a mint when few turned up and they had to pay penalty clauses to the down-town hotels, bus companies, etc – we must stick to our concept of the University campus and accommodation being the centre with the City being there as an overflow facility. The Canadians lost control of their academic programme so that those who witnessed the Quebec disaster opted out and did not travel on to Vancouver ...

Aside from administration there was more fury vented on the lack of publication plans than on anything else – no abstracts were copied or printed and IUAES has no publication plans for proceedings – people said the Congress was an exercise in tourism, not a scientific/academic exercise. We must continue to avoid the production of copied abstracts and must find a solution to the publication (and precirculation of papers) problems. We must avoid the vast majority of Third World participants to receive financial assistance from the Congress being from the Indian continent. The Canadian Congress was appalling in this regard – I was reminded of Australia in the early 1970s; endless Whites discussed endless non-White problems ...

IUAES had 6,000 responses to their *c* 30,000 first mailing (admittedly, a mailing shot which did not mention costs/registration fee) and *c* 2,500 attended over the two located meeting places. However, by 1 January 1983 (their official deadline) only 400 had paid their registrations. IUAES had virtually no student attendance (despite an offered reduced fee); no one seems to know why. We should consider appointing someone as Student Liaison Officer.

One thing that was really lovely, was to see Welcome to IUAES (IUPPS) notices on road signs, at the airport, and on University Campus signs. I think we should do the same ...

We must state in all official correspondence/announcements that no refunds of 'Registration Fees' will be allowed unless there are medical certificates to justify such re-funding. We should stick to our previous Executive decision to allow no free registrations – and we should follow IUAES in giving 'grants' to Third/Fourth World participants to cover such Congress registration fees. Volunteers/students who work for the 1986 Congress, and receive no other payment, can also, following IUAES, be given 'free passes' – ie worth the £200 registration Fee.

With this experience behind me I realised that relying on Sue, the Departmental secretary, for part-time secretarial assistance was simply not good enough. The Congress had to have its own secretariat, and I took on a full time secretary. I also frantically urged Colin Renfrew to get results from his Finance Committee and even to use his personal contacts in high places to get the Government to take on the financial responsibility for the Congress – the incessant search for money having become potentially the death of our endeavours. I wrote to Colin in January 1984:

'We' (IUPPS, British members of the Permanent Council, British Archaeology, Britain, whichever level you wish to choose) actually face a disaster scene. It is only a few months ago that I saw/witnessed/participated in a charade of disreputable academic collapse in Canada. I saw a 'good' National Secretary in mental collapse, a UNESCO Congress in disrepute, Canada reviled as inadequate to the task (by White academics, Israelis, and several Black countries), and anthropology/archaeology suffer (probably) irreparably.

Colin's Finance Committee finally met without me or the President in February and, although agreeing in principle that 'this was the moment for a firm attempt to obtain more support from the government', in fact put its only effort into a special reception to be held in the presence of the Duke of Gloucester at the British Museum in November at £250 per double ticket. In March, the Department of the Environment finally responded to a Parliamentary Question about the Congress by hoping that it would be a resounding success but declining to provide any direct assistance. Meanwhile Colin and I were still applying to UNESCO, through the British secretariat, for financial assistance for Third World participants, and I was in contact with the Wenner-Gren Foundation for Anthropological Research in New York for financial support for all parts of the budget.

At this stage the revised budget we were working to had, as its major divisions, Congress Promotion (£27,000), Academic Programme (£38,000),

Assistance to the Third World (£90,000), Administration (£77,000), Precirculated Papers (£8,000), Supplies (£20,000), Lunches and teas (£80,000), and Transportation (£38,000).

During the summer there were more meetings of the Finance Committee and many more letters from me to Colin and from him to possible sponsors – but still no significant results and no real attempt to pressurise Government. We were all beginning to get seriously rattled. Colin and I in particular had one violent public disagreement over the 1983 commitment to pay 'expenses' to academic organisers amounting, where needed, to the equivalent of the £200 registration fee. It was the first serious dispute on a point of principle we had had, and both of us were upset by it. I could not give way, since facilitating the work of the academic programme was essential for the Congress's success.

I needed urgent action. I decided to tackle the University and the City of Southampton to gain more than verbal support. First a lunch for the City's Conservative Leader and executive members of the Council, organised by the University's Conference Officer. This led to agreement to provide a Civic Reception – but that was all. Then a change of local government, to Labour Leader Alan Whitehead, who first responded by announcing major archaeological excavations to coincide with the Congress, and then offered major financial and other support, amounting to some £40,000 – as well as a close working relationship and friendship which began in July 1984 and continues to this day. The Congress, now named the World Archeological Congress, could at last be officially launched through its Second Announcement (see page 47) at a special ceremony on 27 September 1984 at the British Museum attended by Allen & Unwin, its principal publisher (see page 45-6), Southampton City Council, and English Heritage (see pages 40-2). Caroline Jones became the new Congress secretary. A few days later I flew back from France where I had been explaining the Congress programme to a conference on Palaeolithic art, to attend the Finance Committee's British Museum Reception.

Armed with the support of the City of Southampton, I went on to the attack with the University via memos and meetings. This led first to an offer of only a reception and then, aided by a joint communication from the Conference Officer and the previous Deputy Vice Chancellor (who had first negotiated the switch of the Congress from London to Southampton), an offer to match the City's contribution.

The next miracle came in the guise of the quiet voice of Dr Tim Champion, of my Department, who was the Congress's Liaison Officer. He told me that he had a message from Dr Peter Addyman that I should ring him about a possible major Congress sponsor. At the end of November I went to London to meet Ian Skipper, Peter Addyman and Anthony Gaynor of Cultural Resource Management Ltd, the commercial company which manages the Jorvik Viking Centre for the York Archaeological Trust. I had previously heard a story about Ian Skipper: apparently one day he had been driven up to the York excavations wearing a suit, and in immaculately polished shoes, and had offered his services to a startled site supervisor who, on noting his dress, said there was nothing he could do there, and sent him away. Luckily for archaeology Mr Skipper left his credentials. Even more luckily, Peter Addyman went through the visitors list, noticed Mr Skipper's expertise in financial matters, and bothered to follow him up. This extraordinary man had then taken over Addyman's life. Single-handedly he moved York archaeology into a new league, attracting international admiration for its flair, and financial success, in the public display of archaeological remains.

I liked the man on sight, sensed his strength and power, and yet hated the views he expressed on private health schemes versus the National Health Service! To put it another way, my explanation of the Congress situation and the ensuing discussion went perfectly (with Peter and Anthony almost totally silent until asked by Ian if they agreed with his approach during our discussions), so that I really believed that I would now be able to forget the Congress' financial problems and needs. But the non-Congress discussions over the lunch which followed were almost as disastrous as the pre-lunch session had been good. I returned to Southampton by train and reported to Jane that I was sure that I was the only person that she knew who had gained and lost £150,000 in one day!

I suppose I must have known really, at some level or other, that Ian would have enjoyed a good argument. Peter confirmed by phone that the offer was still on and, at the end of November, Cultural Resource Management Ltd guaranteed to the World Archaeological Congress any shortfall up to a total of £150,000 out of its advertising budgets for 1985/1986 and 1986/1987. In return the Congress would include the Jorvik Viking Centre in its Congress itinerary of tours, would publicise the Centre during the Congress in stalls and exhibitions, and would identify a particular public lecture as deriving from its support. Most, or all, of these suggestions were ones that I had suggested to the York meeting, and I could see nothing but good in all of them. They went even further. If the Congress made a profit, a fund would be established to give subventions to special categories, such as Third Worlders, to attend future international conferences or for whatever other objective I might decide upon.

By the end of 1984, therefore, Ian Skipper's Cultural Resource Management Ltd appeared to be offering me the glorious vision of at last being able to forget financial problems altogether. It seemed as if Caroline Jones and I could now concentrate on the huge job of organising the academic side of the Congress, and that we could make sure that the right participants from each country could really get the grants they needed to be able to attend and make the meeting a resounding success.

The Executive Committee met on 17 December 1984. I had plenty of Christmas presents to offer in addition to the news revealed at the official launch of the WAC. But it was John Evans who reported the first good news, that HRH The Prince of Wales had agreed to become the WAC 1986 Patron. Further details of the academic programme (page 257) were all approved and responsibility for the programme was again vested in me. Even the non-academic programme was beginning to take some shape – receptions at the University of Southampton, in the Southampton Guildhall, in the British Museum and, following the Plenary Session, in the Royal Festival Hall. Then we reached financial matters. First, Derek announced that the British Museum Reception had produced a net profit of £13,500. Then there was emerging news of activity, and promised activity, by Colin Renfrew, David Wilson, John Evans and Leslie Alcock in approaching an even wider variety of possible sources of funding. Next I tabled the newspaper report of the £40,000 from the City of Southampton and slipped in the news of £1,000 for Third World participants from the Esperanza Trustees of the Royal Anthropological Institute. I was beginning really to enjoy myself as I tabled a confidential University of Southampton Minute specifying its support of £40,000, and I made the Executive read a letter from IBM (located just outside Southampton) offering sponsorship of £1,500. During the prolonged period of overall amazement I led the Executive formally to record in the Minutes that the strategy of locating the main business of the Congress outside London had paid off fully and handsomely.

I then tabled a revised budget. I led the Committee slowly through several minor adjustments to it and I forced them to concentrate on further possible actions by them to raise more sponsorship. Only Caroline knew that the next item on the agenda, simply listed as 'other news', would cause the real shock. The President read out the agenda title and moved on, assuming that it had become a non-item. I restrained him and without comment tabled the offer of sponsorship of '£150,000 for Third World delegates and specialists in ancillary fields' from the Cultural Resource Management Ltd (York). As the Committee read through the letter there were hisses of surprise, which I can still hear. Under the agenda item 'Date and venue of next meeting' it was simply minuted that 'it was felt that a meeting was probably not needed in the near future'. Back in Southampton, Caroline and I celebrated by ordering the computer system which was to save us when it came to the academic programme.

2. Academic Planning

I am one of those people who always seem to take on too much and feel terribly overcommitted. I have never bothered, therefore, to go to a conference or congress unless I had good reason to think that there will be relevant and interesting things to learn from it. From the very beginning I saw the Congress as a means to advance everyone's knowledge through the unique worldwide participation of people gathered together exceptionally in one place.

I am also very bad at taking in a complex argument, or a mass of data, by just hearing it. I need to be able to read and reflect. From my very first conference, in the 1960s, I developed a system for the precirculation of papers which, though costly, very reliant on excellent chairing of each session and demanding a high degree of commitment from the participants, is the only way to get the most out of conferences. By precirculated papers I do not mean abstracts of papers. These are nearly always quite useless – being written at great speed, at a level of generality that renders them completely unusable and divorced from the content of the full-length paper.

Precirculation of papers has other implications beyond finance, not least that papers must be ready, copied and dispatched in sufficient time for participants to be able to read them before attending a meeting. Such papers should therefore be well-thought out, in-depth contributions to knowledge, and their authors must be given a short time at the conference itself to update them, in the case of new interpretations or new discoveries, or to illustrate them if necessary. Such a system focuses attention on discussion.

I was aware from the beginning of the importance of hard work and efficient organisation, with the aim of producing papers revised, in the light of informed Congress discussion, for post-Congress publication. This was as far away as it possibly could be from the scheme of traditional large Congresses, which are based on very short addresses from a rostrum, in a context usually aimed primarily at social intercourse. I am told that large Congresses do not often result in post-Congress publications, and where they do it is usually due to the energy of a particular session organiser. What I was aiming at, despite the huge number of people who might come to the Congress, was informality, and free discussion within informal groups who must themselves operate under the overall Congress umbrella.

As I became more and more aware of the IUPPS, I realised that these aims were in direct contrast to those enshrined in the IUPPS Statutes.

Luckily no one in Britain was aware of the arcane nature of these directions, which order the host country to behave in certain specified ways while at the same time claiming that matters are left entirely in the hands of that country's organising committees.

Moreover there were a number of further challenges facing the organiser of an international meeting to be held in 1986, for archaeology was poised at a series of critical points in its development.

In Britain, since the 1960s, and the advent of the so-called 'New Archaeology', the archaeological fraternity had been involved in self-examination of its aims and methods. It was a period of discussion and introspection. What should the core course of a Single Honours Archaeology degree consist of? How many staff should a Department have? Is Archaeology really a *discipline*? What is the role of Scientific Archaeology – or is it Archaeological Science? What is the relationship of Archaeology to History – or is it just part of historical enquiry? What is its relationship to Anthropology – or is it just the Anthropology of past times? What is its environmental/ecological basis – and, therefore, its association with Geography? There were other questions too, such as the apparent divisions between the academic and the local 'practitioner', and between amateur and professional.

There was also the problem how to bring 'world archaeology' into this turbulent scene. To begin with, the term was rarely defined, despite the existence of a British-based journal of this title, and most of my British colleagues would have to be made to realise what we were talking about. It was a staggering fact that in the 33 British universities which taught some kind of archaeology, only four taught an obligatory component of World Prehistory and none had obligatory courses in either African or New World Archaeology. Apart from a few members of staff in London University and Oxbridge Colleges, British 'world archaeological' endeavour was almost exclusively focused on Europe and based on a few British Schools of Archaeology in places such as Athens, Rome and Ankara. Archaeology in Britain, in its university teaching and its interpretative base, was under serious risk of becoming merely parochial.

There was the further problem that most European archaeology, unlike British, Scandinavian, American and Australian, remained essentially based within the art- and culture-historical tradition (with interests somewhat removed from those being investigated via the 'New Archaeology' tradition). Much archaeological work in Europe, therefore, continued to focus on questions of chronology, typology, 'diffusion', technology, and movements of culture(s) and peoples, which were remote from anthropology and other social sciences. In fact the very existence of the IUPPS reflected an historical split away from the interests of the so-called ethnological sciences, the responsibility of the IUAES. What was equally important was the on-going debate as to whether 'science-based' archaeology was merely a set of techniques or a different approach and set of methodologies.

Early on it was decided that the academic programme would not attempt to evaluate the relative merits of these various national or international approaches. The programme must allow for all approaches, at the same time focusing on the most interesting approaches to archaeology, and themes to which all could contribute. Some specialist subjects also had, by definition, an international character, and would also have to be included. One example was the investigation of early hominids/hominoids (and early Pleistocene material) where physical material from sites as diverse as China, Africa and Europe may be anatomically compared and analysed according to various schemes of evolution. Indeed it is in the context of this very early material that the international aspect of archaeology is often stressed, with the oft-stated claim that archaeology can demonstrate the common basis of humanity.

There were other problems, too, specific to the IUPPS. This organisation aims to cover both prehistoric and protohistoric cultures, and the latter are difficult to define and categorise. To make matters worse, there was a tradition in the IUPPS of including at least part of the Medieval period and cultures within its brief – although how even to translate the term 'Haut Moyen-Age' into English is open to some debate.

It was clear, therefore, that whoever was to choose the topics for the academic programme would be stepping through a minefield of misunderstanding and potential disaster.

To add to the problems was my own determination to explore the political role of archaeology and its involvement in the everyday lives of Fourth World peoples who have their own attitudes, beliefs and studies to and of the past. There was potential trouble here too. The Third World archaeologists had learned methods and aims from an imperialist past. These issues needed public discussion, and also to be brought into relationship with the Fourth World situations where, so often, the people had simply borne the brunt of archaeological activity. All this would require a new self-awareness on the part of archaeologists from western countries who should be examining the role and position of archaeology and archaeologists within their own societies and education systems. Early on therefore, I determined to handle this whole theme myself, and I knew that I would need the best academic helpers I could identify, if the session were not to plunge into disorder.

From the beginning I had one principal asset. This was the total contempt in which the International IUPPS Executive (its Western European members) was held by Colin Renfrew and David Wilson, and it was their overall attitude that led to some pretty cavalier actions (see page 90) about which John Evans and I expressed some concern. Nevertheless, in the context of the academic programme, all our Executive (with the exception of Derek Hayes, who kept out of such discussions, and Leslie Alcock, who missed some of these particular meetings) were united in their dissatisfaction with the kind of archaeological approach that many members of the International Executive Committee stood for.

This urge to ignore the 'old-fashioned' European/continental approach to archaeology was tempered by the realisation, shared by Colin and myself, that many of our colleagues would be unhappy in Southampton if they could not huddle together in specialist cliques to view their own new discoveries. Indeed the same approach was true of several of our British colleagues. In Colin this led to a series of self-contradictory statements and advice as the years of programme development went on. However, some things would have to be kept very fluid until the last possible moment. If there were to be 3-4,000 participants, specialist meetings would be needed in order to stop them destroying the proposed precirculated paper thematic sessions, whereas if there were less than 2,000 participants few, if any, such specialist sessions would be needed.

More than anything – again from the very beginning – I was absolutely determined to keep control over the academic programme, particularly the thematic sessions. I decided to do so in the most correct way possible, by getting the Executive to vest the responsibility in me, but to keep them informed at every meeting about each of my moves regarding session organisers (however much such detail might bore them). I also took care to try to have sponsorship and contracts vested in me, so that, in any case of dispute, I had effective clout. I did not trust any of the members of the Executive sufficiently as judges of their colleagues to know which would be the most appropriate organisers of academic sessions specifically devoted to cross-cultural approaches to a subject matter. The academic organisers needed to be very exceptional people who would not only be loyal to the Congress, devoting much time to the enterprise, but exceptionally creative and far-sighted. Ideally they should also be good at dealing with their session participants, their future contributors to a book. With these qualities in mind there would have to be more than one organiser to each session, for only by having a combination of people could the width and quality needed be achieved. The Executive Committee also wanted to spread the interest and involvement in the Congress as widely as possible across Britain (and possibly, via co-organisers, across the world). I obviously had a huge job of consulting ahead of me, and I spent an immense amount of time travelling around.

As described in the previous chapter, 1982 was fraught with financial uncertainty, but the National Committee meeting in April gave me some marvellous support. It accepted the major suggestion that 'the Executive Committee reserved the right to refuse to accept papers for discussion within the core sessions' and, instead, to place unsuitable offerings within a separate category of heterogeneous 'Working Papers'. Up to now IUPPS had always accepted all offered papers from anyone, however mad or hopeless they might be. This was because their Congresses had never aimed to be occasions primarily for scholarly work, but for social meetings and the setting up of informal contacts. The Committee also accepted my view that the Congress must involve younger scholars, research students and, if possible, undergraduates. Lastly, with enormous implications for the future of the Congress, National Committee members agreed on people who would be 'Liaison Officers', whose job would be to get in touch with IUPPS Commissions – groups of specialists with named office holders who were supposed to meet between Congress meetings – and to report back to me, for I was made responsible to the Executive Committee for the whole of the Congress' academic programme.

The IUPPS Commissions worried us. They were almost all concerned with a particular archaeological period or area, with a huge emphasis on Western Europe. The Executive Committee was convinced that unless we could override them by my suggested core sessions, the Congress would be an academic failure with nothing to interest archaeologists from the rest of the world. Typical of the IUPPS, these Commissions were not even mentioned in its Statutes. They just threatened to sit there like a dead weight around our necks. Some of them made no sense at all, such as Commission 17, 'Iron Age Cultures: America', for there is no Iron Age in the Americas! The few other Commissions dealing with non-European areas also worried me. On the face of it, it was difficult to imagine why Indians should wish to discuss 'Iron Age Cultures: India' (the title of one of the few non-European IUPPS Commissions) in Nice, Mexico or Southampton rather than with their own experts at meetings of large numbers in their own country. Similarly it was not really clear why 'The Neolithic of the Old World: Africa' or 'Iron Age Cultures: Africa' (other IUPPS Commissions) should not be best discussed at the regular meetings in various countries in Africa of the Pan African Association on Prehistory and Related Studies. The plan was to get the Liaison Officers to persuade most of these Commissions to agree either not to meet at all or to come under the umbrella of the thematic core sessions – whatever these might turn out to be. The choice of some of these Liaison Officers was made very carefully. Some, like Professor David Harris of the Department of Human Environment, Institute of Archaeology, London, and Professor Michael Day of the Department of Anatomy, St Thomas' Hospital Medical School (who had to be especially invited to join the National Committee), had been known to me for many years and, in 1986, were to come to the rescue of the Congress at its worst time of adversity.

By the time of the First Announcement, right at the beginning of 1983, the Executive Committee had approved a whole set of suggestions. Since participation was to be really worldwide, it was essential to have at least several themes which would accommodate universal interests. Just as important was the decision to extend the traditional participation at IUPPS Congresses to include non-archaeologists such as guides, site and museum custodians, as well as indigenous experts about the past. All this meant that it was essential to have themes which would allow such non-archaeologists to be, and to be seen to be, equal contributors to, and in, those particular themes at least. The first thing to do, therefore, was to make sure that the world would indeed know about the Congress and would come to it. That of course meant money and very wide advertisement of the programme. Here we could not count on the IUPPS at all, for by now we had been made aware of how useless the IUPPS organisation had been in the past. Some members of the Permanent Council of the IUPPS claimed that they did not know that they were on the Council, and others said that they were unable to find out the way the organisation was supposed to function. More and more letters complained about lack of communication and it was clear that the situation regarding Commissions was chaotic. Professor Desmond Clark of the Department of Anthropology, University of California, Berkeley, had not been able even to discover who were the officers of the subcommission on 'The Earliest Industries of Africa'. We were continually finding ourselves trying to make excuses for the lack of organisation and telling people whether or not they were part of Commission membership. Perhaps the most representative example was the letter from Professor Fred Wendorf, of the Department of Anthropology, Southern Methodist University, Texas, one of the four American members of the IUPPS Permanent Council who was later to have nothing to do with the Congress because of its ban on South Africa. Having organised a meeting at the Mexico Congress, he had not been told that his own 'Commission for Near East Prehistory Terminology [had been] abolished at the meeting in Florence in 1982'. This whole matter turned out to be even more bizarre when a 1984 publication on the origins and development of food producing cultures claimed to be held under the auspices of the 'Commission on Terminology of the Prehistory of the Near East and North Africa' of the IUPPS. Professor Wendorf went on to complain to Professor Nenquin of lack of courtesy on the part of the IUPPS, and he reported that he had had 'considerable difficulty in maintaining communications with the Secretary-General of the IUPPS'. Meanwhile this member of the Permanent Council had not even realised that Professor Nenquin was the Secretary-General. He had been writing, to no avail, to the 1976 National Secretary, Professor Henry de Lumley, of the Laboratoire de Préhistoire, Musée National d'Histoire Naturelle, who was later to appear to take such glee in hosting the meeting in Paris which was to expel our Congress from the IUPPS! Certainly we could count neither on good will towards the IUPPS nor on an up to date mailing list. The confusion regarding Commission membership seemed to know no end (even for those so immersed in IUPPS affairs, such as Professor de Lumley, who had invented the Commissions in the first place). Sometimes it fell to me to have to inform, or possibly remind, Secretary-General Nenquin of the previous resignation, or even death, of a Commission Member, Chairman or President.

The Congress also needed a visible symbol. During 1982 and early 1983 we prepared our mailing lists. Over the years we mailed some 30,000 people, using names and addresses from journals, personal contacts, and the names suggested by respondents themselves. The symbol was a message about the aims of the Congress which was produced in 12 languages and read:

> This meeting of archaeologists and others who are interested in the past is to
> be a truly international one. Most of the main subjects to be discussed should
> be of interest to people all over the world. The working sessions will take place
> at the University of Southampton and a significant event during the Congress
> will be the opening of a major new exhibition at the British Museum in
> London.

This symbolic gesture was welcomed by many, only one person complaining
at the supposed inaccuracy of the Pidgin English and one staff member of
the Smithsonian Institution in Washington lamenting the absence of
Hebrew! We kept the symbol in our Second and Final Announcements,
running it together with our logo of Stonehenge and our new name, 'The
World Archaeological Congress'. Unfortunately, though I am not sure
whether anyone spotted it, there was an evident clash between this world
message and the fact that IUPPS restricts its languages for Congresses to
English, French, German, Italian, Russian and Spanish.

The IUPPS also insists on French as the only language acceptable for
official Congress matters, including Congress programmes. Professor David
Bellos, of the Department of French in the University of Southampton, was
persuaded by me and Jane, at our house-warming party, to translate into
French all of the First Announcement that we could fit onto the pages. This
whole question of the official use of French was to cause us problems later
on.

At this stage the programme could still not be finalised or announced
publicly, as we still awaited developments regarding negotiations about the
specialist Commissions. The Executive Committee supported the principle
of delaying any final decisions about the number and length of meetings
until we had received and analysed responses to the first two Congress
Announcements – that is to say, not for another two and a half years.

One of the major decisions had been whether or not to have one overall
major theme throughout the Congress. This was decided against simply
because any such all-embracing theme would be so vacuous as to be
meaningless. Instead the Executive Committee agreed on five major themes
which would run concurrently and thus force participants to make choices.

Before I describe these themes in some detail, I should stress that I was
well aware of some of the implications of parallel sessions. It would be
essential for participants to have a timetable efficient and accurate enough
for them to be able to choose realistically what they wanted to do each hour
of the day. Again, this plan was borne out by my Canadian trip (see pages
17-18):

> The whole academic side was, in fact, a shambles – ... papers had been
> accepted without any assessment of quality, the Programme Committee

members gave up early on and made individual members decide on their own rules (eg. some said that only one paper could be given by any one person while others allowed two or three by the same person within the same session), those who offered a paper received letters saying they were in charge of a symposium – and those who actually arrived suddenly found themselves saddled with unknown speakers/papers/chairmen. The computer was incorrectly programmed, whereby a symposium supposedly concerned with folk law was programmed to include one on diet, and so on. The printed programme announced speakers and papers which were non-existent, referred to rooms and sessions which were already occupied or which duplicated others, and so on. Of the c 150 announced symposia, there were perhaps 15 which actually took place with the correct chairman and number of speakers – and these only took place because of the initiative and dedication of individual co-ordinators of symposia – who had previously been in touch with their respective speakers. In most cases only up to two of eight or more advertised speakers (and/or chairmen) turned up. One heartening thing was that on the rare occasion that a high quality debate did take place, it appeared to fascinate ... This suggests that our format of informed discussion of precirculated papers should succeed.

Even with only 1,000 participants, let alone a possible 4,000, we had to have an efficient and imaginative computer programming system. Here we relied on Alex Ross of Martlet, and subsequently on our own Christmas 1984 Octopus computer system which Caroline and especially Paul Crake, who joined the secretariat later, were to master and grow to hate and love.

An attractive programme, which forces choices to be made by participants, should allow a marvellous opportunity to two groups: publishers and makers of cassettes. I had been determined from the moment I accepted the Secretaryship that the Congress should result in first-rate post-Congress books – otherwise conference-going is simply tourism with nothing left for posterity. What could be more exciting for a publisher than to know that a thousand or more people were aware of exciting events going on nearby, which they were unable to attend because of their participation in other sessions, all eager potential buyers of the volumes or, if they could not wait that long, potential purchasers of cassettes which would catch the whole intellectual excitement of debate. To my mind these two activities, book publishing and cassette recording, would not be in conflict. Books would consist of selected and revised Congress contributions (with the addition of some chapters commissioned later to fill any gaps), while cassettes would reveal the cut and thrust of debate from which, after a period of reflection, the printed book would develop. Whenever I could, I sought to carry out these dreams by writing, meeting and talking to publishers and recording companies. My Executive thought I was completely mad and that I had absolutely no chance of success. By the spring of 1983 I had approached 27 publishers and one particular recording firm.

After endless thought and discussions it was decided to make animals one of the main thematic subjects of the Congress. By the time of the First Announcement this theme was called 'Cultural Attitudes to Animals including Birds, Fish and Insects', with sub-divisions which would cover 'categorisation, usage, domestication, art depictions, etc'. I had focused on this topic for many reasons. At one extreme was the possibility of securing sponsorship for a topic linked to pets; at the other, was the chance of interesting art experts, scientific archaeologists, philosophers and indigenous groups – a mixture of people who had probably never been brought together before. By the time of the National Committee meeting in June 1983 I had successfully recruited a social anthropologist, Dr Tim Ingold of the University of Manchester, to take part-control of the whole theme, and he and I were busy creating sub-themes as well as seeking the best people to handle them. Among the things which Dr Ingold and I hoped to see come out of this meeting was a world perspective which would focus on the nature of the varying relationships that can develop between humans and animals. This realisation, in its turn, would lead to the question: what actually is an animal or a human? Such an approach should, when developed, force archaeologists to become aware of their own individual and cultural preconceptions and would draw attention to a set of attitudinal questions and problems. We in Britain, for example, normally consider the hyena to be wild, and untrainable, yet the ancient Egyptians appear to have 'domesticated' it and forcibly fed it! Our preconceptions about our relationships and interactions with animals come under scrutiny when we move beyond the normal level of trying to ascertain from any excavation simply what animals were eaten. Thus the recent discovery of the 'sacred animal necropolis' at Saqqara in Egypt, where thousands of ibis, hawk and baboon mummies were found, challenges European conceptions of the distinction between animal and human. It is all too easy to suggest simply that animals were themselves regarded and worshipped as manifestations of the gods, for the animals, mummified after death, were sacred to the god and appear not to have been sacred in themselves. In this theme, therefore, animal domestication anywhere in the world would be considered in the context of the appropriation, domestication and exploitation of animals at particular times and in particular areas.

Discussions about who would, in the end, be asked to help with the running of this theme highlighted another of my problems. As plans became known, many of my colleagues became keener and keener to be part of the whole endeavour. Some were even abusive when not chosen, others accepted more understandingly, and a few refused offers because they were already overcommitted. The 'appropriation, domination, and exploitation of animals' sub-theme was given to Dr Juliet Clutton-Brock, Principal Scientific Officer, Department of Zoology, in the British Museum (Natural History) and her husband Professor Peter Jewell, of the Physiological

Laboratory, University of Cambridge, in order to try to avoid a family row – which, in the event, it totally failed to do (see page 63)!

I had published several articles over the previous five years which examined the way that the past – known from archaeological discoveries - had been used by different groups, both in Australia and in Africa, to legitimate their political actions. It was not surprising, therefore, that by the time of the First Announcement the detailed programme was further advanced for this theme, called 'Archaeological "Objectivity" in Interpretation', than for others. The divisions of the main theme were into 'Multiculturalism and ethnicity in the archaeological record', to be run by, at least, Dr Steve Shennan (of my own Department), and 'Individual and group self-expression through material culture (objects for defence and warfare, for status and show, etc)', by Dr Ian Hodder of the Faculty of Archaeology and Anthropology, University of Cambridge, and possibly one other. In the latter case I was trying to add an ethnographer to the archaeologist and I had to arrange that the two should meet; but, in the end, the suggestion did not work out. The next division was called 'Archaeologists' views of the past'. Topics to be covered were listed as 'factors influencing choices of interpretations available to the professional archaeologist; interpretations of sites presented to tourists; interpretations presented in museums; etc'. By June I was still having immense difficulty finding the right organisers for these sensitive topics. I was beginning to consider my old friend Professor Carmel Schrire, of the Department of Human Ecology, Rutgers State University of New Jersey, and Associate Professor Mark Leone of the Department of Anthropology, University of Maryland as an interresting combination of views. Since both were in the United States, I was also trying to identify a sort of contrary-spirit, later to be Mr Peter Gathercole of Darwin College, Cambridge, to act as administration anchorman, and intellectual sparring partner, in England. The last sub-theme was 'Archaeological time scales and indigenous perceptions of the past' which I kept under Jane's and my control – at least for the moment.

In working out the details of this whole theme I wanted to show that a world archaeological approach to archaeology as a 'discipline' revealed how subjective archaeological interpretation has always been. It would also demonstrate the importance that all 'rulers', 'leaders' and politicians have placed on the legitimisation of their positions through the 'evidence' of the past. 'Archaeological Objectivity in Interpretation' is strikingly absent from most archaeological exercises in interpretation – a world perspective reveals how this subjectivity is at the very basis of the study of the past. The plan was that this Congress would, for the first time, draw public attention to these complex aspects of archaeology. Discussion would focus not only on the conscious manipulation of the past for national political ends (as did Smith's Rhodesian regime with Great Zimbabwe or the Nazis with their racist use of archaeology), but also on the way archaeologists themselves have been influenced in their interpretation by the received wisdom of their times (both in the sort of classificatory schemes which they considered appropriate to their subject, and in their dating of materials because of their assumptions about the capabilities of the humans concerned). It was also important to show that Britain was not immune to changes of interpretative fashion. Even Stonehenge had been subjected to the most bizarre collection of interpretations over the years, including all sorts of references to Myceneaens and Phoenicians. Although, at first sight, it is tempting to assume that this is different from attempts by politicians to claim that the extraordinary site of Great Zimbabwe was constructed by Phoenicians using black slaves, the difference is not really all that easy to sustain.

Realisation of the flexibility and variety of past human endeavour all over the world should direct attention back to the very basis of much archaeological interpretation: the question of how to equate static material culture objects with dynamic human cultures, how to define and recognise the 'styles' of human activity, as well as their possible implications. Here I was thinking, for example, of how the recent work, extending back only over some twenty years, of exploration and recording of Laura rock art (in North Queensland, Australia) epitomised some of these points, for here the questions of art styles and iconography became central to Aboriginal claims to the land. If archaeologists could demonstrate that there is cultural continuity from the excavated rock peckings of more than 13,000 years ago to the more recent rock paintings and through them to the living Aboriginal myths and traditions, then such works of art are no longer just remnants of prehistoric activity, and the creation and possible income from suggested parks and guided tours cannot be assumed as of right to belong to the European, who only recently 'discovered' Australia.

All these factors in turn lead to a new consideration of how different societies choose to display their museum collections and conserve their sites. As the debates about who should be allowed to use Stonehenge, and how it should be displayed, make so clear, objects or places are considered important at one time and 'not worth bothering about' at others. Who makes these decisions and in what contexts? Who is responsible, and why, for what is taught in schools or in adult education about the past? Is such education based on a narrow local/regional/national framework of archaeology and history, or is it orientated towards multiculturalism and the variety of human cultural experiences in a worldwide context? What should the implications be for the future of archaeology?

The third main theme, 'Interactions between "Central" and "Peripheral" Cultures', would cover 'imperialism; colonialism; centralised and non-centralised societies; States; literacy; etc'. I quickly fixed on the two people I wished to take this on, for I thought that the intellectual sparks might fly between them and I could trust them to nominate reliable co-organisers for sub-themes. They were Michael Rowlands of the Department of Anthropology, University College London, and Tim Champion. Tim had now to be relieved of another of the jobs, organising post-Congress tours, which he had offered to do. World archaeology should focus attention on questions and definitions which the archaeologists of a particular area or nation all too often take for granted. Just as we often assume that it is obvious that one tool or piece of equipment is more efficient than another (without wondering what are the social or behavioural advantages of, for example, switching from horse to tractor), so we often assume that it is obvious that one society is more complex than another. We, in Europe, are prone simply to assume that writing must be a significant stage in the development of the complexity of human societies. A narrow parochial approach to the past allows us to ignore the complexity of non-literate civilisations and cultures such as those of the Inca of Peru or of Benin in Nigeria. In Peru excavations over the past few years have shown that this vast non-literate State organisation was capable of building and maintaining some 23,000 km of 'roads' and supporting between 6 and 12 million people through an efficient socio-political organisation with an integrated diversity of populations from the desert to the High Andes. Recent archaeological investigations at Huanuco Pampa have uncovered evidence which suggests that Inca socio-political control was effected through an efficient hierarchy of regional administrative centres located in the Empire's hinterland. The evidence of monumental architecture, the use of developed metallurgical technology and the apparent political stability in this vast Empire is an achievement which rivals the better-known civilisations of the Old World. In discussions I asked Michael and Tim to examine these problems in a way that would allow consideration of these essential questions in the context of human cultural development anywhere in the world. Such an approach would, we hoped, focus attention on what we actually mean when we call something 'socially complex'. The sub-themes would consider subjects such as Processes of State Formation, Domination, Subjugation, Literacy and Communication, Centre-Periphery Relations, and Imperialism, Colonialism and Incorporation.

The fourth theme, on the Social and Economic Contexts of Technological Change, was really chosen primarily to 'hide' as many specialist IUPPS Commissions as possible, and also to provide another forum within which people of various backgrounds could contribute equally. The whole topic does, of course, have its own intrinsic importance but it is a somewhat more 'traditional' approach to the human past, focusing on technological development and technological evolution. A world archaeological orientation would, again, stress the different reasons and contexts for the adoption of particular pieces of equipment, as well as the reasons why apparently more efficient items of technology may be ignored by one culture but adopted by another. It was particularly important for subjects such as innovation, procurement and exchange, and intensification to be treated as processes, but I had not suggested any thematic sub-divisions, while I tried unsuccessfully to convince Colin Renfrew that he should take on this whole theme and accommodate within it as many of the specialist IUPPS Commissions as possible. At that time Domestication of Plants had been placed within this theme and, largely because Dr Ian Glover of the Institute of Archaeology in London was not willing to take on its organisation, also the IUPPS Commission on Prehistory of the Pacific.

The last of the major themes was called 'Archaeology and the very remote past'. It had already been split into three sub-themes, 'Archaeology and the origins and dispersal of modern man' under Dr Paul Mellars of the Faculty of Archaeology and Anthropology at the University of Cambridge, 'Man at *c.* 18,000 years ago' under Dr Clive Gamble of my Department, and 'The Pleistocene/Holocene boundary' under their joint control. This was the only major theme which originated from suggestions put to me by others; and it was the one about which I had most qualms, because not only did it rely entirely on professionals only, but it had to accommodate some seven specialist IUPPS Commissions, with Commission Presidents and Secretaries scattered all over Europe, the USA and Australia. The first approach had come from Clive Gamble in May 1982, and a month later from Paul Mellars. Of all the people I was entrusting to run sessions Paul Mellars was the one about whom I knew least. When we met to discuss his proposals he appeared ponderous, cautious in his views and very slow-spoken. I was therefore particularly keen to force Clive Gamble on him as a co-organiser, although 'Man at *c.* 18,000 years ago' was less a theme in any meaningful sense than the choice of a particular (though very interesting) moment in time. In fact I need not have been worried at all about this aspect of Paul Mellars. From 1983 onwards he did much more than just the required letter-writing and he took the whole enterprise very seriously: he and I were to become close friends. Clive Gamble's subject matter suddenly became of international importance as the construction of a dam threatened the archaeology of southwestern Tasmania, and telegrams of protest were sent from the WAC (later ratified by the IUPPS International Executive Committee) to the then Australian Prime Minister (Malcolm Fraser, who was later one of the seven members of the Commonwealth Eminent Persons Group on Southern Africa) and other Ministers known well to me from my Australian days.

If all these themes really worked out there would only need to be separate meetings of a few specialist IUPPS Commissions: those which could not be fitted in elsewhere, such as 'History of Prehistoric and Protohistoric Archaeology', 'Physical Dating Methods in Prehistory', 'Data Management and Mathematical Methods in Archaeology', 'The Earliest Hominids', 'Copper and Bronze Age Cultures', and 'The Archaeology of the High Middle Ages', some of which were active groups of specialists, and others who had done nothing in between the five-yearly IUPPS Congresses. One further meeting had been offered by Dr Henry Cleere, on behalf of the

Council for British Archaeology, of which he is Director, on 'Public Archaeology and Cultural Resource Management', although it remained obscure whether it was Henry Cleere or John Alexander who was to organise it.

The programme was a vast one – and so it had to be if it was to have the impact we wanted, for indeed we had high hopes of what could result from such a Congress. For me, world archaeology should be a vibrant approach to the understanding of the past. It forces everyone to be humble, to be self-critical of their own interpretations, and to be aware of the constraints and pressures under which they make, interpret and publish their findings. My intention was that a critical self-awareness, combined with a sense of awe of past human endeavours, would be one of the main benefits with which archaeologists from almost all over the world would depart from the Congress.

In May 1983 I went to my first IUPPS International Executive Committee meeting with John Evans, an occasion of ostentation and money-wasting in the University of Lund, with a 'work agenda' which was worth no more than a letter or two. I could see why John considered all these meetings a sheer waste of time. It was clear that Professor Bertha Stjernquist, our hostess from the Department of Archaeology, and Dr Kurt Böhner – previously of the Römisch-Germanisches Zentralmuseum in Mainz, who appeared to be a cheery old man who was clearly feeling unwell and suffering from the effects of the journey to Lund – were unable to imagine anything that departed from a traditional presentation of recent discoveries. Yet they would, as things stood, be responsible for one of the specialist meetings on medieval archaeology at the Congress. The one thing that woke up this group of elderly western Europeans who purported to represent world archaeology, was our First Announcement. This was sufficiently worrying for them to comment on the high price of the registration fee and to quote the Statutes at us regarding the necessity for specialist Commission meetings and pre-Congress publications of the 'state of the art' papers by them. It was clear that this group had not, any more now than later, the remotest understanding of, or sympathy with, the views of the British Congress as conveyed in the message from me, as the National Secretary, in the circulated First Announcement and published in several journals, such as *Antiquity*:

> I hope that everyone who receives the first announcement about the XIth Congress of IUPPS 1986 will treat the multilanguage introductory statement with the importance that it deserves.
>
> The suggested format of this Congress is different from previous ones. The participation of professional academic archaeologists continues, of course, to be crucial to the success of the Congress but, in addition, the 1986 Major Themes are designed to widen the field of participants to include those from all continents, countries, nations and cultural groups who are in any way involved in studying the past, whether as guides, or as custodians of

monuments, or as trainees on excavations, or involved in some other way with archaeological projects.

Personally, I believe that the major aims of the Congress will have succeeded only if in 1986 new and continuing dialogues are established between people from diverse backgrounds with diverse preconceptions who share a common interest in comprehending the cultural processes which have contributed to past human cultures. It is my intention that out of this Congress there will develop an increased understanding and appreciation of our global heritage and the variety of attitudes that we bring to it.

Only Professor Jacques Nenquin, Secretary-General of IUPPS, appeared to understand the aims and intentions of the British programme. Jacques Nenquin appeared to be a most genial and cultured person, fluent in languages, and replete in extensive personal contacts with many of the archaeologists within IUPPS and in the writings of many of those who formed part of the 1986 Congress programme. It was enjoyable to be in his, and his wife's, company, and reassuring to feel that he, at least, was in fundamental agreement with the British plans for the vitalisation of the Union's academic activities.

In June 1983 the meeting of the National Committee received a report on the IUPPS reaction to the programme in Lund, and not only rejected its possible implications but unequivocally, and much to my delight, gave precedence in any potential dispute over offered papers to the thematic sessions.

The question of who should be entrusted to run the various sessions could not be deferred for ever. The plan was to announce them, or as many of them as possible, in the Second Announcement which was due out before the end of 1984.

Tim Champion's name was beginning to be mentioned more and more by me, both as a session organiser and as Congress Liaison Officer. As one of my staff, Tim was to be one of several people who surprised me, not only over the South Africa issue but also in his gutsy reaction to subsequent events and his vigorous defence of the ensuing position of the Congress. Another name deliberately brought up by me at this time was Dr David Lewis-Williams of the Department of Archaeology, University of Witwatersrand, whom I was considering as a possible co-organiser of the session on animals and art. I asked the Executive whether it had qualms about a South African. No one had, despite the fact that I alerted them to the possibility of future trouble. I remember saying to Jane and others that we might be about to take a dangerous decision in appointing a South African, but that he was clearly the most innovative person around in this field and we were, after all, operating within a UNESCO organisation which insisted that activities should be open to everyone. I was therefore encouraging Tim Ingold and his co-organiser, Mark Maltby, Research Fellow in the Faunal Remains Unit in my Department, to take on Dr Lewis-Williams to help Associate Professor Meg Conkey, of the Department of Anthropology, State University of New York at Binghamton, who was to be asked to organise the animals and art session. Above all, I thought that the two, who had apparently never met, should prove an unbeatable academic combination, although a successful theme would create problems about the more traditional IUPPS Commission on rock art. As Meg Conkey had not attended the meeting in Chicago where we were supposed to meet, I was totally dependent on Carmel Schrire for character assessments of both these potential organisers/editors. However, Tim Ingold had met Meg Conkey in June 1983 and was enthusiastic about inviting her to organise the art session. In October and November we took our decision. Meg Conkey and David Lewis-Williams were appointed joint organisers of the meeting on 'The representation of animals in parietal (see page 247) and prehistoric art', although I was still worried at the absence of a link person in Britain whom I knew personally and with whom administrative matters could be dealt with efficiently and quickly. Carmel Schrire spoke at length with David Lewis-Williams in January 1984. Another major decision for Jane and me was to give up the organisation of the vitally important session on indigenous concepts, and to entrust it to Dr Robert Layton, a colleague in Australia who had just taken up the post of Reader in the Department of Anthropology in Durham University, and to Professor David Bellos who was to contribute actively, together with others from the School of Modern Languages in the University of Southampton, in creating a sub-theme on the past as revealed through European literary sources.

Some of these chosen organisers had still to be 'educated' before they would really be able to cope with the job presented to them in the way that was wanted. A considerable amount had therefore been built into the budget for the development of the academic programme. I used part of this sum to visit Santander in Spain to attend a mini-conference on rock art, in order to spread the news of the Congress, to recruit participants and to stimulate ideas to be discussed – but primarily to explain to Professor Hans-Georg Bandi, of the Seminar für Urgeschichte of the University of Bern, who was also the Swiss representative on the IUPPS Executive Committee, what I thought he should organise within a rock art context at the Congress. In fact the whole of 1983 was a series of consultations and discussions about the academic programme, not only within Britain but overseas. Paul Mellars in particular had many of the IUPPS Commission Presidents and Secretaries to liaise with. He went to Siena in Italy for a meeting of one of the Palaeolithic Commissions where he hoped to be able to reach agreements with one at least of the Polish Kozlowskis who were Commission Officers, and he returned having done so, and marvelling at the Christian paintings which he had not seen previously.

Someone had to attend the December meeting of the Pan African Association on Prehistory and Related Studies in Jos, Nigeria. Because of the subject matter of his sub-theme, ' Multiculturalism and ethnicity in archaeological interpretations' it was Steve Shennan who got the chance to go. There he seconded an amendment which led to the motion:

> The IX Pan African Association on Prehistory and Related Studies: unequivocally condemns the practice of apartheid and any other forms of discrimination; rejects racist criteria used anywhere to restrict education research, and employment opportunities for 'non-white' South Africans and Namibians; within the range of interest of Pan African Association: calls for a cessation of all contacts with South African institutions; calls for the censure of colleagues and institutions maintaining links with South African institutions.

This motion was passed by that Association of archaeologists, an Association officially affiliated to the IUPPS (see page 276). It was at this meeting in Jos that Steve Shennan first met Dr Alex Okpoko of the Department of Archaeology in the University of Ibadan, who was to become Visiting Research Fellow in my Department in 1985/6, and who was to play such an important role in the whole drama of the period. Throughout the next two years overseas travel was supported wherever relevant and possible. One example was the attendance at an archaeology and education conference in Ravello, Italy, by Peter Stone, a postgraduate in my Department who was later appointed Congress Student Liaison Officer. A special effort was also made regarding the travel of colleagues who could spread the news and details of the Congress in eastern Europe.

The Executive considered the student question, and having learned from the Canada Congress what not to do, wanted to involve them as much as possible. It discussed a student registration fee of only £52. There was one breakthrough to report. The University of Sheffield took the lead in announcing that it would find funds for its archaeologists (and possibly students who were to give papers) to attend the Congress. Colin Renfrew undertook to try to get other universities to follow Sheffield's lead.

I was still engrossed in seeking publishers and had meetings lined up in the States where I was due to give a paper in November. David Wilson clearly thought I would be unable to cope with all the work, and moved that money should be kept aside in our budget for financial assistance to help me in the future (1985 and 1986) with substitute teachers. Indeed I was still running a department and undertaking my full teaching load. I was to come to bless him for this foresight.

Throughout this time responses to the First Announcement were coming in each day. Some 1,500 had arrived from 86 countries by the end of 1983. Further large direct mailings were undertaken in the USA to members of organisations such as the Society for American Archaeology, greatly assisted by Professor Schrire. All these responses were fed into Alex Ross's computer system, so that their names, addresses and main interests and the subjects of any papers they wished to present to the Congress were recorded. All session organisers received copies of relevant forms selected by me, and were supposed to be ready by the beginning of 1984 to provide me with the title of their sessions, the titles of sub-themes, and the names of contributors to their sessions with paper titles, as well as the number of days which they thought would be appropriate for their meeting. By the end of 1984 the theme organisers should have decided on the length of precirculated papers, contribution by contribution. They were expected to have written to contributors who had not yet completed a Congress registration form but whom they wanted to participate in their sessions.

This whole exercise was both vast and complex, and it was very competently handled by my then secretary, Ann Lewis. She not only had to work in very unsatisfactory conditions and be on top of the details of the arrangements, but also had to enter into a mountain of form-specific correspondence with Alex Ross. Computer printouts littered tables and floors.

It was planned to produce the Second Announcement as early as possible in 1984. In it I was determined to outline the scope of each topic to be discussed at the Congress, as well as giving a rough idea of the length of each session. Before then, however, the whole financial situation would have had to become viable and, I was determined, a publisher found. Only then would it be timely to have an official launch of the Congress.

Consultations throughout Britain continued with actual meetings between session and sub-theme co-ordinators, lengthy telephone calls about the intentions and development of some of the sessions, and endless letters to organisers with suggestions and ideas about other possible contributors and topics. The appointed Liaison Officers were putting in an enormous amount of work in corresponding with IUPPS Commission officials. No one now doubted that this was going to be a Congress primarily devoted to hard work and the 'advancement of knowledge'.

One of the main problems concerned the relationship between the IUPPS Commissions on the Pacific, the Indian Iron Age and the Peopling of the Americas, as well as the original intention of the Commission on Origins of Cities. In the end, after many discussions between several of the potential organisers, it was decided to subsume some under themes and to create a new specialist meeting on Iron-Age Societies in South Asia, under the control of Robert Knox of the Department of Oriental Antiquities in the British Museum. Another area which had to be discussed at length concerned the wider role of archaeology in education. After numerous sessions with Peter Stone and Robert MacKenzie, who were later both appointed co-editors of a post-Congress book, the Executive Committee agreed to make this an important part of the Congress. In some cases, as with David Bellos, my discussions covered possible political problems during the Congress, as between Arabs and Israelis, and led to the development of a relationship of trust and close friendship.

Another relationship which was growing more and more important was with Paul Mellars. We tried desperately to get answers from Commission office-holders such as Professor de Lumley and to work out the implications of thematic versus more traditional, verbal presentations of Pleistocene material. In June, we went to Paris to see Professor de Lumley and Professor

Yves Coppens of the Laboratoire d'Anthropologie at the Musée de l'Homme. It was difficult to imagine them doing any of the detailed work which this Congress demanded of all of its organisers. Paul and I discussed many things, personal and professional, and we were getting accustomed to each other's pace, but he could not hide his incredulity when he learnt that an unknown number of my third-year undergraduates were arriving that evening on the boat train from Southampton, to take me up on my offer of a post-Finals dinner wherever I turned out to be on the last night of their exams. Paul was clearly tempted to stay but, in the end, domesticity demanded his return to Cambridge. Not long after he wrote to me, wryly, about his horizons having broadened!

Much of the trouble with the Pleistocene sessions involved clear definitions of the questions to be discussed, whether physical anthropologists should be co-organisers with archaeologists for the session on the origins/dispersal of Modern Man (a suggestion to co-opt Dr Chris Stringer of the British Museum (Natural History) being refused by Paul Mellars), whether the origins of agriculture should be incorporated into the meeting on the Pleistocene/Holocene boundary, and how far dating methods and techniques, as well as the results of such scientific dating, should feature within these themes. On all of these decisions there were a great many letters to be written by both Paul Mellars and Clive Gamble. Clive had the additional problem of what to do with the Americas, for he had strong doubts about some of the very early dates attributed to some of the excavated material. Liaison and Commission Officers all received lengthy letters from Paul and me and decisions had to be taken about who should work with whom. In the end various compromises and formal associations between theme meetings and Commissions were agreed.

Towards the end of March 1984 my activities had again been diverted. Following Colin Renfrew's efforts to involve the Historic Buildings and Monuments Commission for England (later to be colloquially called 'English Heritage') in the WAC, Lord Montagu of Beaulieu (its new Chairman) asked to see me in London. With Colin, who was one of the English Heritage Commissioners, present he announced to me that English Heritage wished to undertake a major excavation in the vicinity of Southampton in connection with the Congress. He requested me to draw up a list of suitable sites so that the Commission could choose one as quickly as possible. In answer to my questions he made it clear that by suitable he meant both visually attractive and with quick access from Southampton (up to 20 minutes drive), as well as academically worthwhile and with potential as a continuing tourist attraction and Information Centre long after the WAC had finished. It was my strong impression that the Chairman intended a site with impressive walls. I was unhappy about the situation I had been placed in whereby I was expected to choose a site suitable for excavation, and worried that a massive excavation of a walled city (Medieval Southampton?) would divert the Congress away from its primarily 'prehistoric' brief. On the other hand, of course, an important excavation could only be attractive to Congress participants.

As we left the room, Colin Renfrew looked surprised and delighted. He said that the whole idea had been Lord Montagu's own and had not been discussed, as far as he knew, with any of the Commissioners, or with members of his Ancient Monuments Advisory Panel.

By the middle of April I had consulted with endless people about possible sites, most particularly with Dr Geoffrey Wainwright (Principal Inspector of Ancient Monuments, English Heritage). I wrote to Lord Montagu that we had narrowed the choice down to some three sites, and hoped to put in a joint recommendation by June. If he wanted the excavation to feature in our Second Announcement a decision would have to be taken by July so that it could be included as a Special Announcement.

In the end I wrote the letter alone (27.5.84), but with the full knowledge of Dr Wainwright, and suggested various possible excavations which could be undertaken separately or in different combinations. I started by recapping what I understood to be his major concerns 'that the Commission be seen publicly to be associating itself positively with the decision that Britain should host the 1986 Congress of the IUPPS; and that, in the context of archaeology at least, the Commission wishes to be seen to be significantly more than an agency which *only* responds to rescue demands, or an agency which is *solely* concerned with the commercial development of sites'. Then I listed in some detail a number of possible sites of varying dates and interest, commenting on some of the advantages and disadvantages of each of them. I also stressed that any such excavation should be undertaken only if there was also substantial extra funding for Medieval Southampton, to coincide with the Congress. I finished with five points:

1. Many of my colleagues would only accept the need for new excavations of the 'attractive' sites of the kind mentioned [by me] from the Iron Age, if the Commission was seen to be funding such excavations from additional, *non-Rescue* monies, if such activity was seen to be linked to the elucidation of specific archaeological problems or questions, and then only as a special response to the circumstance of the WAC 1986.

2. What will, and should, live on as a testimonial to the Commission's support for the WAC is not so much the structures and material revealed by excavation but ... permanent Information Centres and guide books. Many believe that major effort should be devoted to creative interpretation and presentation of our heritage and that this should be at least as important as excavation at this time. Having said this, there is no doubt that limited excavation of the kind suggested [by me] at, for example, Old Sarum, would be both academically worthwhile and visually impressive to visitors/tourists.

3. The Iron Age 'package' suggested [by me] is not an 'all or nothing' situation. One or more of the suggested sites could be omitted without forfeiting the overall idea ...

4. All [my] suggestions afford the Commission a unique opportunity not only to make a major and visible contribution to the WAC but also to make

public their commitment to local archaeological organisations ... Furthermore, if the whole suggested activity would be seen to result in local
Education Officers becoming attached to, and responsible for, one or more
Information Centres at various important sites, much potential opposition to
the overall scheme would be dissipated.

5. Your idea to carry out excavation(s) in connection with the 1986 WAC is
an exciting one with great potential ... from the Congress' side we would do
everything possible to try and arrange the 1986 Congress programme of
meetings to facilitate as frequent visits as possible to excavations arranged by
you in connection with its meeting ...

On 3 August I was telephoned by Colin Renfrew from the actual meeting
which was to decide the location of the excavation. He asked if the WAC
would object to the site being Maiden Castle in Dorset – not one of the sites
ever mentioned by me. I said that it would obviously be highly attractive to
Congress participants but was much too far away for regular visits, but I
presumed I was not being asked for a professional view. On Saturday 4
August Geoffrey Wainwright telephoned to explain the choice of site in
detail. There was just time to include this news in the Second
Announcement and then to deny any WAC responsibility for this highly
contentious decision, which was the subject of several letters to *The Times*.

By now there was considerable interest in the Congress from local
Southampton media, and I was interviewed by BBC Radio Solent and the
press. However, there was no point pushing my session organisers much
further until I could prove that the wider world really appreciated their
efforts. The best way to do that was for me to prove the Executive
Committee wrong by finding a publisher. In any case, I would never be able
to precirculate the thematic papers if I could not get this major item funded
by a publisher. The organisers knew roughly how many post-Congress books
were expected to derive from their sessions, and that the plan was to
precirculate papers by April 1986 in groupings which the session organisers
would by then have determined to be discussed under Chairs chosen by
them. Following the Congress, they would have to select the good
contributions. The authors of these would then be given until Christmas to
revise their papers for publication. By January 1987, the publisher should
be receiving the finished texts based on precirculated papers, and by
April/May 1987 the texts deriving from the more traditional Congress
sessions.

My enquiries with publishers had shown, not surprisingly, that most of
them wanted to know more about the programme when it had been
developed, nearer the time of the Congress. That did not help me. All the
publishers I met were charming, and many of them said they would be
interested in publishing a few selected volumes, but my problem here was
that some wanted the same volumes and I also had a horror of having to
deal with a multiplicity of publishers with different formats, contractual
terms, and styles. I knew that I needed help and that I should be trying

something out of the ordinary. I approached my old friend Colin Haycraft, of Duckworth, who had published many of my previous endeavours, particularly the very successful series of books based on precirculated conference papers which had begun with the pioneering work on the Neolithic Revolution, *The Domestication and Exploitation of Plants and Animals*. Duckworth had already offered to publish one or two of the Congress books and I knew that Colin, an independent publisher, could not afford to take any more volumes at the £2,000 per book advance that I was demanding. I discussed the assets of the Congress books as I saw them – a unique chance to break into the archaeology market in a big way, a wide range of potential buyers in different disciplines, an international audience, and a more or less guaranteed set of delivery dates. We also discussed the huge size of the project and the fact that few British publishers would be able either to handle the quantity of books that I was insisting on (up to 40) or the total financial advance (£80,000). I was, of course, guessing and bluffing over these numbers as I did not know how many participants there would be.

Colin, who had apparently previously been approached by Robin Denniston of Oxford University Press (OUP) about the possibility of joint ventures, now suggested to him that they should take on the Congress project under their joint imprint. Negotiations proceeded during May and June with some of the OUP Delegates, to convince them that the Congress books would not be ordinary collections of second-rate papers and that this was indeed an effective way to break into the archaeological market. Mr Denniston appeared to be enthusiastic and keen to beat his rivals, Cambridge University Press (CUP) and Academic Press, to an important venture. I did not disabuse him of his belief that CUP was about to move in with an offer, although Robin Derricourt of CUP had shown no real interest in the whole project. Eventually the idea of cooperation with Duckworth came to nothing, to my regret, but Colin Haycraft encouraged me to write a long document to OUP and, at the beginning of July, Robin Denniston recommended to his Delegates that they publish up to 40 books from the Congress, which was expected to have 4,000 participants. I was to be General Editor and they would pay £40,000 in advance. 'The Press,' Robin wrote, 'will enter an important academic area in which they had previously not maintained a strong presence.' I departed for fieldwork in Crete in a sort of dream. There I heard that the Delegates had rejected Robin Denniston's recommendation and when I returned to Southampton I found that he was almost as upset and disappointed as I was. The best he could offer was to return to his Delegates to get them to publish 20 books for which there would be no £2,000 advance per book. That was of no help to me at that time.

After that it was somewhat difficult to get going again. However Colin Ridler of Thames and Hudson had had the initiative already in January to approach me even before I had written to them. We met for lunch, with the

Chairman, Thomas Neurath. Again I waited with baited breath. Eventually Mr Ridler wrote:

> I hope you enjoyed our talk last week as much as I did. It was stimulating to hear about your ambitious plans for the 1986 Congress, and we came away and thought seriously about the idea that we might boldly take on the full 40 titles that you were expecting to create. Sadly the harsh realities of what all those would entail were borne in on us when we got back to the office and began to consider just how much of the firm's time and effort this mammoth undertaking would consume. Even though, as you suggested, one should be able to make sensible preparations in advance, taking on extra freelance staff etc, the sheer logistical problem I think would be too great for us, and – more importantly – would possibly prevent us from doing some of the other things that we might want to achieve that year.

The next encounter was with Longmans. Andrew MacLennan wrote after our meeting in September:

> I was glad to see you ... and have a chance of discussing in more detail your superbly ambitious plans for the 1986 IUPPS Congress. I cannot honestly believe that you will be able to achieve the full range of targets you have set yourselves, but even if it only comes halfway up to your most optimistic expectations it should still be incomparably prolific, productive and valuable. I wish you every possible success with it.
>
> As far as a publishing connection is concerned, I have been giving very careful thought to the great quantity of notes I made during our conversation; I have also done some very rough-and-ready figure-work, and discussed the whole colossal project with the Director of the University and Further Education Division here. It seemed to me on the face of it highly unlikely that we would be able to underwrite the scheme in the manner you proposed, but clearly it promises to be an occasion of such exceptional importance that it would have been wrong to dismiss it out of hand as impossible for us without having gone through the possibilities and implications very carefully.
>
> I must report, however, that even the most sympathetic consideration retires baffled before the scale of the whole operation! Just taking the figures you gave me at the time, and looking only at the top half of the Conference Programme (ie the Major Themes), your plans would generate 22 (perhaps more) full-scale volumes, each of considerable complexity ... probably one is thinking in terms of at least a quarter of a million pounds in straight money, not counting all the effort, time, enthusiasm, confidence and forestalled opportunities elsewhere that the operation would involve ...
>
> I am sorry to write at such length, but you were so interesting and persuasive an advocate for your very splendid vision of what the Congress hoped to do that I thought I should explain in some detail why we would have to fall back: we certainly didn't just dismiss the idea through an inability to think large when the opportunity offers.

I knew of only one further possibility of finding a single publisher to take on all the books, and with a sufficient advance to cover the costs of precirculation – Academic Press (whose UK branch had shown little interest). Colin Renfrew and Carmel Schrire both approached Bill

Woodcock, and he and I met in Chicago in November where I was giving a paper on Australian Aborigines and anthropology. All the publishers with whom I had negotiated till now were the sort of people I knew well through my previous experiences of publishing – they were well and widely educated, charming, and enthusiastic. Bill Woodcock was somewhat different. We met in the foyer of a preposterous hotel in Chicago with a cascading multi-coloured waterfall and his first remark was 'I am a hard businessman and I therefore have no interest in your project'. By the time we parted, much later, his eyes were as near to sparkling as I am sure they ever are. He was very serious, and I knew it, and he did not want to be beaten by any publisher in Britain. I could hardly believe that I had managed to reach my dream situation again, but Bill Woodcock assured me that he had never yet been turned down by his company. I still did not dare breathe a word to anyone but Jane. Thank goodness I did not, because at the beginning of January Bill Woodcock finally managed to get himself to tell me that he had indeed been overruled, solely because the owners of Academic Press had decided to diversify into real estate and television. I do not know which of us was the more upset, though Bill stressed the possibility of his trying the company again in September and, later on, offering to publish four or five books.

Twice so near, and twice overruled by those even higher up. I gave up for several months. Eventually I had no choice but to confront the ghastly issue of trying to achieve contracts for groups of books or even individual volumes; at least Duckworth would be able to publish a follow-up of our previous, very successful, domestication volume. I saw numerous publishers and started drawing up the list of publishers and books for presentation to the Executive Committee, which had not heard anything official from me about publication arrangements for a long, long time.

Things did not start in an auspicious way with George Allen & Unwin, for Roger Jones had been 'so sorry to have cancelled our meeting [in July] at the last minute'. Nor did he get back in touch with me, as he had suggested, in September. At least Roger had to make the journey down to see me in Southampton (in early March 1984)! I was only trying to interest this very correctly dressed, apparently cold, and somewhat terrifying person in a few volumes. I no longer remember whether it was he who cleverly led me on or whether I chose to tell him about OUP, Academic Press, Longmans and the rest, but by the end of our meeting I had gone right through the Congress plans with him and had promised him several documents and details. I now wrote a new updated presentation of the suggested publication venture, knowing that Allen & Unwin would be approaching outside readers (several of whom I contacted) for the Board to make a decision in early May. It was clear that Roger Jones was vitally interested in the whole project. He sent me the outside reports on the venture, which were basically very positive, but rang a few days later to say that Allen & Unwin would not proceed with the venture, as it now stood, since it was altogether too formidable a proposition. He did suggest, however, that I get in touch a few days later and that we might be able to talk about fewer titles and a smaller advance.

I went to see him in his London office on 18 May and together we hammered out the details of a contract based on up to 25 books with an immediate advance of £5,000 and a further advance of £25,000 whenever needed for precirculation of papers. While I sat unable to breathe, he went upstairs to see Merlin Unwin. Eventually he returned and asked me to join them. I was welcomed as Series Editor of a huge undertaking and was quite unable to be articulate.

On receipt of the final draft of the proposed Agreement a few days later I wrote to Derek Hayes:

> I am going to try for Executive approval by telephone or writing (as opposed to calling a special Executive Committee meeting). Somehow or other I must stop Allen & Unwin from going cold on the whole thing or even thinking about it realistically!

By 31 May the Executive had indeed agreed, and the contract was finally signed on 18 June 1984. From then on Roger Jones stood by the Congress and his Series Editor in a way that almost defies description.

The plans for the official launch of the Congress at the end of September could now really go ahead, and the Second Announcement could be finalised. I had started to make more and more use of Paul Crake, a graduate from my Department who had somehow stuck around the Department since graduating, doing drawings and cartography for various members of staff and who had become indispensable in our chaotic life. He and Ann Lewis finalised the details of the Second Announcement, and it was seen through the press by Ann with the help of Colin Renfrew.

It was at this point that Dr Paul Mellars came up with a brilliant idea regarding precirculated papers. He suggested that a way to minimise the invidious position that post-Congress book editors would find themselves in, when having to tell their participants that contribution would not be included in a post-Congress book, could be to bind the precirculated papers into volumes which could count as official publications. Such publications of precirculated papers would help participants with grant-giving bodies, and would enable bibliographical reference to the papers without the need to include data-packed but otherwise unacceptable chapters in post-Congress volumes. This was a typically constructive suggestion from Paul Mellars, whose interest in the details of the Congress had been unflagging ever since our first detailed discussions together. It was immediately accepted both by the Executive Committee and by Allen & Unwin.

In September Jane and I flew to join John Evans in Bucharest for the meetings of the IUPPS Permanent Council and International Executive Committee, and we were able to table proof copies of the Second Announcement. As usual there appeared to be no important business for either group and, as usual, there appeared to be procedural irregularities.

Members not yet elected to the Permanent Council were present at its meeting and others, like Professor Stjernquist of Lund, who should have been retired/promoted to the Comité d'Honneur (see page 283) resolutely claimed the right to stay on the Executive Committee and Permanent Council. At the first meeting there were questions and comments about the high registration fee, and dark mutterings about the Second Announcement. There was also an apparent threat by the Germans, particularly by Dr Konrad Weidemann, Director of the Römisch-Germanisches Zentralmuseum in Mainz, to ask difficult questions about the Announcement when it was to be discussed in detail later in the week. During the next days of the usual excursions and official meals, I made a point of talking to as many of the International Executive Committee as possible about the details of the Congress. I talked at some length to Dr Weidemann and established some understanding with him, which was to prove important in the future when Jane, Caroline and I went to see him in Mainz (page 51). In his opinion the best thing which could happen in Southampton was that the IUPPS would simply become an organisation dealing with the prehistory and protohistory of Europe, leaving a smaller group to have their own Congress dealing with world archaeology. When the Second Announcement came up again on the agenda, the only question raised by the Germans was about the meaning of the term 'Fourth World'. By and large the reaction could be taken to have been positive, and it was a relief to John and me that, this time round, we had been able to head off any formal comment about the almost total absence of French translation in the Second Announcement. If there had been such a formal objection, we could not have afforded to do anything about it.

Never the less the meetings, as usual, left an unpleasant taste in my mouth. Once again there were the same old faces from Western Europe with pretences to run a world organisation. But this time it had been even more unpleasant because the IUPPS system of self-appointment of new members to the Permanent Council had been revealed and publicly questioned by me, and Dr Pal Patay of the National Museum, Budapest, had publicly attacked Secretary-General Nenquin for administrative inactivity. I was beginning to realise why the British members of the IUPPS had always been so dismissive of its International Executive Committee and the whole organisation. The Bucharest meeting, however, was useful in two way. I was able to talk to Dr Patay at length and to come to a detailed arrangement with him about major Hungarian participation in the Congress, by which we would offer grants to all those Hungarians who could reach England by their own means, and I was able to work through the rock art responses and draft programme with Dr Bandi.

The Second Announcement was made public on 27 September following meetings of the Executive and National Committees. It included Special Announcements about the contract with George Allen & Unwin, special exhibitions in the British Museum and Southampton's John Hansard and

City Art Galleries, Southampton City's decision to undertake a major excavation to coincide with the Congress, and the offer to Congress participants of a unique chance to see a major excavation by English Heritage at the important Iron Age site of Maiden Castle. At this 'Official Public Launch' at the British Museum, John Evans was in the Chair. Guest speakers were Lord Montagu of Beaulieu (Chairman of the HBMC), Mr Rayner Unwin (Chairman of the Holding Company of Allen & Unwin), and Councillor Alan Whitehead (Leader of the Southampton City Council). There had been news and press releases from the City and the University of Southampton, as well as from the British Museum and English Heritage, and there was significant press coverage of the event, all of it very positive except for some criticism of the proposed excavation at Maiden Castle.

The Congress's Second Announcement was now an impressive document which we hoped would significantly increase the numbers registering. It was reprinted in the Spring of 1985 in order to announce that HRH the Prince of Wales had become our Patron and that our major sponsor was Heritage Projects Ltd (York) (a change of Company from that mentioned on page 20 but still under Ian Skipper's control). This academic programme is reproduced in full in Appendix IV (page 258). It shows how successful we had been in subsuming IUPPS Commissions and in converting session organisers to the idea of precirculation of papers.

The main change made in the 1985 36-page Final Announcement was not only that all the organisers of sessions were updated and that some new sub-themes had been introduced, but that the names of *all* 1,750 participants who had offered papers were individually listed under each academic session and sub-session, together with the countries from which they had submitted their registration forms – *all*, that is, *except* those from South Africa and Namibia whose names were 'whited'-out at the very last moment.

3. The Banning of South African and Namibian Participation

On the face of it, the first half of 1985 was continuing according to plan, albeit hectically. Most of my work on the Congress took place after 5 pm when Departmental matters were supposed to ease off. The evening sessions tended to go on far into the night, and through weekends, and every available moment was crammed full, of dictation or planning for the next stage, or deciding a particular tricky problem which had been referred to me from session organisers, Martlet, Paul, or Caroline. It really was a case of there not being enough hours in each day and I had to master all the details of all the subjects. Normally Caroline had to take dictation in the train up to London, even, on one occasion, coming with me on the train just for this reason, and travelling straight back to Southampton. On many occasions she and I attended meetings of session organisers, and Paul and I were busy at several meetings of the Local Communities Committee, which had been set up to involve the minority groups in the City with the Congress. I also continued to try to raise more funds, but now some of these were for items which for the first years I had never dreamt might be possible. In particular I tried, more or less unsuccessfully, to interest the Southampton Chamber of Commerce in sponsoring a 30-strong television message system, Viewpress, for the WAC. Other attempts were made to obtain additional funding to allow for more Third World participation, through bodies such as the British Council. My new initiatives were also aimed at seeing as large a contingent as possible from East European countries and the USSR, preferably along the same sort of lines as agreed with Dr Patay for the Hungarians – that if they got themselves to England we would give grants to cover registration, food and accommodation. I therefore travelled to Yugoslavia, both to spread the news about the Congress and also to attend a meeting of the IUAES Executive Committee whose agenda, in marked contrast to those of IUPPS Executive meetings, was packed with important policy matters (including relations with IUPPS). I side-tracked Steve Shennan to Moscow on his way back from fieldwork in Cameroon, so that he could bring us details of the fantastic news that the USSR was intending to send an especially big and diverse group of participants, including both archaeologists and ethnographers. While there he was also privileged to meet Professor Anatoly Khazanov and was, we hope, a contributory factor to the plans which proved successful in getting the USSR authorities to allow Professor Khazanov to emigrate with his family to Israel. It was a strange feeling that while I was talking to Professor Yuri Bromley of the Institute of Ethnography (Moscow) in Belgrade about Khazanov, there was Steve in Moscow actually carrying messages to the man himself – a meeting which I know made a profound impression on Steve. The Third World had, of course, not been forgotten. I sent Robert MacKenzie, then Visiting Fellow in the Department of Adult Education in the University of Southampton and organiser of the session on 'The past in education', to various East African countries, and Robert Knox, organiser of the 'Chalcolithic, Bronze and Iron Age Cultures in South Asia' session, to meet various archaeologists in India. I started making extensive use of, and trusting, Olivia Harris, Lecturer in the Department of Social Anthropology, Goldsmith's College, London and who was to chair the session 'Conflicting priorities' in the sub-theme 'Indigenous perceptions of the past', because of her exceptional knowledge of South America. In the end we commissioned her to find out about, and make arrangements for, South American Indian participation in the Congress.

Whatever the activity, and whichever the country concerned, I tried to interest the archaeologists not only in the Congress but also in the IUPPS organisation as a whole. The latter was hard work, as those who had heard of it, such as Professor Senake Bandaranayake of Sri Lanka with whom I had a long meeting at Heathrow airport, considered the organisation an irrelevancy. The more archaeologists I talked to, the more annoyed I became that this unique world organisation amounted to so little, and that so many countries were not even fully represented on it. Much of this frustration and annoyance surfaced at the April IUPPS Executive meeting in Madrid (and in subsequent correspondence), at which there was really no working justification for us to be there at all, but John and I still enjoyed being together overseas. My anger at the renewed attack by Professor Ripoll-Perello, then Director of the National Archaeological Museum in Madrid, and Jacques Nenquin on the lack of French in the WAC programmes was diverted by my relief that the International Executive agreed that it would not meet again before the Southampton September Congress. As I said at the time, this seemed to rule out IUPPS Executive Committee action even if the South African issue were to explode – little did I know!

My relationship with Secretary-General Nenquin was becoming strained, as is revealed by the correspondence which followed this meeting. In answer to an attempted reprimand that I had misled Zimbabwean archaeologists as to how they should nominate representatives to the IUPPS Permanent Council, and to his remark that it had been so nice to meet me again, I answered petulantly:

> I was somewhat amazed at your letter of 29 April 1985. I found nothing 'nice' about the International IUPPS Executive meeting ... Re Zimbabwe, I am glad to see some movement at last! I received a telex and I telexed an answer. I told them to contact you, and that a provisional look at suggested names might

take place at the Executive meeting in Madrid but that a final decision would be taken by the Conseil Permanent in September 1986. Are you suggesting that this information was incorrect? Incidentally they deny having *ever* heard from you regarding their situation 'En cours de reorganisation'.

Re Sri Lanka, I was surprised to see the way that you presented the Executive nothing of this submission (in *stark* contrast to the way that you had put 'Propositions pour la tenue du XIIe Congrès de l'IUPPS en 1991' on the agenda).

Re Madagascar, you will I hope be receiving nominations for the vacant two positions in the near future. One of the members of the Conseil Permanent denies having ever received any letter from you about the vacant two positions.

Re USSR, I understand that one of their members of the Conseil Permanent claims that two further names were proposed by them several years ago, but they have never even received an acknowledgement letter, let alone seen any result.

I hope that your Minutes will accurately reflect the lack of action taken so far by the Secretariat regarding the recruitment of full country memberships for non-Western European countries. I personally intend to do everything in my power to inform all such countries: (a) about their rights, and (b) the correct procedures to be followed in order for them to be considered at the first meeting of the Conseil Permanent in September 1986.

When Caroline can find the time she will send you, as offered, the names of enrolled persons from those countries where you have been apparently unable to find anyone with whom to communicate! Meanwhile, wherever appropriate, we will continue to stress the international value of IUPPS. I was unhappy that you did not report on the IUAES initiatives as recounted to you by Vice Chancellor Sunderland, particularly about how he has managed to organise *meaningful* international participation in that organisation.

May I take it for granted that, as Secretary-General, you will not seek retrospective sanction for arguing that *this* Congress communication should have been written to you in French?

PS I look forward to receiving your Minutes in the near future.

I could have added that I was still incensed by his claim at the Madrid meeting, in the context of the enforced use of French by the IUPPS, that the IUPPS had a tradition of never voting on issues (for what use, then, were instructions about voting in its Statutes?).

Professor Nenquin's undated reply was simple 'Don't be silly!'

In May, Jane, Caroline and I spent two days in Mainz with Dr Konrad Weidemann and Dr Horst Böhme in order to get the details of the Medieval sessions sorted out in time for the Final Announcement. Again it was clear that at least these Germans were simply not interested in a world perspective, and would be happy if the IUPPS officially became merely a European organisation. They also refused to countenance the organisation of their sessions around precirculated papers. Later in May the Executive Committee meeting in London was absolutely normal. Discussion focused on such things as the provision of cassette recordings of the Congress, and the details of the Final Announcement. These included approval of the addition of Professor David Lowenthal of the Department of Geography, University College London, as an organiser of a new sub-theme on 'Heritage and the Law: indigenous claims against the modern state' and the appointments of Drs B. Bender and J. Gledhill of the Department of Anthropology, University College London, C. Tilley of Trinity Hall, Cambridge, and M. Larsen of the Department of Archaeology, University of Copenhagen, to co-organise sub-themes of the thematic session on 'Comparative Studies in the Development of Complex Societies'.

My June and July were similarly crammed with such activities, including many theme and Commission meetings, consultation with Greek archaeologists in Athens and discussions about Japan and China. Paul Mellars and Caroline went to Paris to consult Professor Henry de Lumley and, more particularly, Jean Combier, Directeur des Antiquités Préhistoriques de la Région Rhone-Alpes, about several of the Pleistocene sessions. A meeting in Amsterdam with Professor 'Carlos' van Regteren Altena was entrusted to Paul Crake, to finalise arrangements about the 'Settlement, Cultural and Religious Relationships Between People and States in the Middle Ages: High and Later Middle Ages (900-1200 AD)' session.

This surface normality was, however, far from the reality of the situation, for in just over one month the whole of the Congress was to be shaken to its core.

It is difficult for me to answer the question often put to me as to when I realised that the South African issue was to hit the Congress. In several senses, I had been first aware that it might from the moment I took on the position of National Secretary, with the special brief to involve the Third World as fully as possible. In that sense I suppose my answer must be that I had always assumed that South Africa would cause problems at some stage. After all, already in the late 60s, I had warned a friend who was trying to decide whether or not to take up an academic post in South Africa that if he did so we would probably never be able to work together again. Equally I hoped, until August 1985, that the Congress would somehow be able to avoid total confrontation with this, and other political issues. These were not thoughts which I merely kept to myself. At the very first meeting of the Executive Committee I pointed them out and, on my advice, we removed the term 'delegate' from our (and later, Martlet's) vocabulary and from then on we always insisted that people attending the Congress were individual participants. Until now I had hoped that this insistence on the individual nature of participants would allow worldwide attendance in the 1986 Congress.

My actions reveal that I continued to assume that problems would occur, if not necessarily or exclusively about South Africa. By early 1983 I was already worried enough about some of the future political problems that would almost certainly arise during the lead up to the Congress, and probably during the meeting itself, to mention them to the Executive Committee. I was not convinced that the Executive members had taken my warnings about such problems – Israelis and Arabs, South Africa, Russian and East European defections – seriously; certainly they were not willing to discuss them before anything concrete actually occurred. I, on the other hand, felt that I might need protection, and I saw Professor John Roberts, then Vice Chancellor of Southampton University, and requested a high-powered committee, under his chairmanship, to oversee the University's interest. After much pressure the Committee was approved by Senate and Council by the end of the year; ironically, although several of my fears were, in the event proved to be correct, the Committee was never convened. In 1986, it was quietly disbanded so that the South African issue would never have to be formally debated within the University.

My concern with the role of archaeology in the modern world and collaboration with South Africa in particular, surfaced in July 1983 on the occasion of a meeting between students, including Peter Stone, and Professor Lewis Binford, of the Department of Archaeology at the University of New Mexico, Albuquerque. We all met together, over drinks, after he had been awarded an Honorary Degree at the University of Southampton. On that occasion I questioned why he had never spoken out on behalf of the Australian Aborigines during his period of fieldwork there, and criticised his current choice of fieldwork area, namely South Africa, if he was not to speak out there either. The latter point was also the cause of heated disagreement when I met Professor Carmel Schrire in Chicago in November 1983, for she was full of excitement about her recent fieldwork in South Africa and her plans for extending work there.

The truth about my feelings on these potential crises was that they were likely to shatter the Executive Committee, and it was probably for this reason that I had been so worried about the individuals on the Committee when I first took up my position on it. Certainly, whenever I did mention the South African issue and how it could be compatable with our emphasis on the Third World, and in particular on African participation, it received scant attention and no apparent sympathy, especially from David Wilson who argued that there was no reason to discuss the issue before we had to. These Executive Committee discussions, most usually brought up in the context of considering whether to approach companies with close connections with South Africa for sponsorship, were never minuted. David and I usually preferred to back away from such subjects, by agreeing not to approach such companies, for the sake of Executive Committee unity.

Even my report to the Executive Committee in January 1984 of Steve Shennan's news that the Pan African Association on Prehistory and Related Studies had passed a motion censuring all contact with colleagues and institutions in South Africa was passed over as quickly as possible, with a simple instruction to me to keep the Committee posted as to subsequent developments, although it was minuted that the Pan African Association's decision was 'likely to have implications for the 1986 Congress and [would] presumably be discussed by the International Executive Committee of the IUPPS'. To Steve himself, when he told me that he himself had seconded the amendment to the motion, I remarked 'God knows what you have done to our Congress'. I then worried more and more about it and repeatedly asked for copies of the Minutes of the Jos meeting both from Steve and from Jacques Nenquin. Meanwhile I could only assume that the African archaeologists would be taking their resolution most seriously. I tried in vain to get into contact with some of my Nigerian archaeological friends to find out about any subsequent actions or events.

As the State of Emergency of 1985 was announced in South Africa (July 20), and some of the events were shown on television (more than 1,200 people detained without trial and at least 15 killed in clashes with the police and army during the first week and at least 129 killed by the middle of August), Jane kept asking how this was going to affect the Congress. The first real indication of trouble came from the Anti-Racism Committee of Southampton University's Students' Union, in early March and, slightly later, the South African issue was raised officially at one of our Local Community Committee meetings. As the evidence grew of local preoccupation with the issue of South Africa, and as the international news, including the USA's and Britain's veto of the UN's call for mandatory sanctions, grew more and more disgraceful, so I was becoming clearer and clearer that it was indeed the most vital of all the political issues that confronted us, for the demands were for the imposition of an academic ban on South Africa/Namibia. The UN adopted a resolution calling for voluntary sanctions (with Britain and the USA abstaining), and the Commonwealth Group of Eminent Persons issued its damning report on South Africa.

I must have been aware that there could be no single winner in this situation. In the end it would be a matter of personal conscience and personal commitment. I was deeply worried about our British Executive Committee members if a ban was demanded and became the only way for the Congress to proceed, for there was little from previous Executive, or private, discussion to indicate that they did not put 'academic freedom of speech' above all else. Perhaps more important, they were unlikely to share my own feeling of admiration that the Anti-Apartheid Movement had acquired sufficient power in Britain to put on such pressure. I guessed that John Evans would be likely to have most understanding of the effects that apartheid had on human beings, but it would be a theoretical concern only. Colin Renfrew was also an interesting case to try to understand, for he had a violent hatred of the South African apartheid regime which, funnily enough, would make him more inclined to send financial help to the ANC, or fight for them, than to support an academic ban. I thought he might need convincing that a ban could actually do some good. My mental summing-up of David Wilson and Derek Hayes was that, although the former would no doubt stress his abhorrence of the apartheid regime, both would spend most of their time saying that they refused to bow before 'blackmail'. I still did not know Leslie Alcock well enough to make any predictions but, by phone, he seemed calmly prepared to support a ban on

South African participation. As for myself, I was too busy at that moment talking to trusted friends about what one should or could do, and consulting others with recent experience of international meetings, to work out an explicit philosophy for myself. I learnt, for example, that already in 1981, the Tanzanians had forced the withdrawal of South African participants from a meeting of the Association of Applied Linguistics in Lund. I was sure that we could not ignore the call for the cultural isolation of South Africa by the ANC, which represents the vast majority of non-whites in South Africa. Also, as a Congress devoted to Third World involvement, we could not be seen to be part of the British Government's stand against the wishes of the Commonwealth and the EEC to impose sanctions on South Africa. Jane seemed to have no doubts what should happen, nor any doubts about the line that I personally would take.

Local pressures from the City of Southampton, the Southampton Branch of the Association of University Teachers, the Southampton Community Relations Office, and Southampton University students, as well as the National pressures of Anti-Apartheid and others had now become acute. Letters were being exchanged between some of these groups and rumours were rife. I began to receive warnings about possible student action later described retrospectively in a letter from the President of the Students' Union as:

> … inevitable uproar among students [which would lead] to disruption of the Congress by withdrawing the Union's provision of rooms and services, and non-violent direct action of anti-apartheid protestors (of which the majority of students are in sympathy or actively support) hindering the smooth running of the Congress.

As the Community Relations Officer put it, on behalf of the Southampton Council for Racial Equality, a great number of ethnic minority groups would not participate in the Congress and, at the very least, South African participation would cause 'a great deal of hostility and ill feeling' and, at worst, total disruption. I confronted the local pressure groups, arguing, very strongly, that academic matters – and academic freedom – were 'above' politics, and that, in any case, the participants from South Africa in the Congress included blacks as well as whites. I well remember one of these meetings in early June, where it was brought home to me, very forcibly indeed, by the Chair of the Southampton Anti-Apartheid Group, David Hoadley, that UNESCO, to which IUPPS is affiliated, had banned all cultural interaction with South Africa. Although in one sense I felt that I 'won' each point of the arguments with David Hoadley, I could tell that at no stage did I really move him from his position, and I was well aware that several members of the Local Communities Committee, who witnessed the debate, were totally unmoved by my eloquence. I had no doubt that David would be returning, again and again, to the fray. Belatedly, I started to do my homework. Equally, I well remember searching the IUPPS Statutes for John Evans' assurance that IUPPS was concerned with the participation of individuals, irrespective of their colour, creed, politics, or philosophical convictions. To my horror, I discovered nothing of the sort and therefore rang Secretary-General Jacques Nenquin in Belgium. There is in fact no such statement in the Statutes of the IUPPS, despite all their impressive-sounding claims. The only mention of such a concern is a bland statement about collaboration with scholars from all countries.

The pressures were building on me and though, in my role as National Secretary for an IUPPS Congress, I still resolutely defended the pre-eminence of academic freedom of speech, I did so with growing disquiet and unease. Much of this was due to the quality and conviction of the counter-arguments being put to me by Anna Ridehalgh of the Southampton Anti-Apartheid Group, and Roger Ingham of the local AUT. Secretary-General Nenquin told me that I was indeed right about the Statutes but that he had written a letter in 1982 to the President stating that the IUPPS condition for its Congresses was that 'all bona fide scientists are to be admitted to its venue, irrespective of nationality, philosophical conviction or religious faith' (and see page 235). John Evans could not find the letter, and it took Professor Nenquin a long time to find a copy of it. Throughout this time I was on the phone to Jacques Nenquin almost daily, and it was at about this time that I learnt that he was 'personally active in the anti-apartheid movement' in Belgium.

By August I was convinced that our device of removing the word 'delegate' from all our literature would not be sufficient, given the State of Emergency in South Africa, and the official ANC and the AUT national policy that no individual from South Africa should be allowed to participate in overseas cultural activities unless the ANC had made such a person an exception.

Councillor Alan Whitehead, Leader of the City Council, then spoke to me on several occasions regarding the withdrawal of financial and other support by the City if South African participation in the Congress was to take place. As he put it, rather more gently than he had in person:

> I am writing to place on record that I would be most unhappy about the presence of a number of South African participants at the forthcoming WAC. As you know, the Majority Group on the City Council, and Southampton Labour Party both have a clear policy in support of the ending of Apartheid in South Africa, and against the participation of citizens of South Africa while the present regime exists …

Quite separately from the local pressures, and much more significant to me personally, was the growing evidence that some countries, particularly in Africa, would not let their nationals participate if South Africa was represented at our Congress. I received information, via Dr Okpoko, that at least Nigerians would not be able to attend if South Africans were allowed to, a view later confirmed in writing by the Nigerian High Commission. As the Honourable Minister of External Affairs for the Federal Republic of Nigeria wrote:

> ... if South Africans were admitted to the Congress, so long as the apartheid regime persists, Nigerians would not be able to attend. I think that this would probably apply to nationals of other OAU [Organisation of African Unity] countries, since the OAU has prohibited cultural intercourse with South Africa.

There were also phone calls from SWAPO [Southwest Africa Peoples' Organisation] and the ANC, as well as from the office of the High Commissioner of the Republic of Zambia, and messages via the Anti-Apartheid Movement from the Zimbabwe High Commission and the Botswana High Commission. I learnt that the Anti-Apartheid Movement was about to write formally to the Ambassadors/High Commissioners of thirty countries. I was under no delusion about the seriousness of such a threat of withdrawal by African countries. I was very much aware of the problems at that very moment being faced by the International Stoke Mandeville Games Federation (for paraplegics).

I determined to see John Evans urgently and privately for it was obvious that our Final Announcement, whose layout was currently being entrusted to, and finalised by, Caroline and Paul, could not be issued with the names of individual South African participants and organisers of sessions, before the Executive had determined its South Africa policy once and for all. Jane and I went to John's country house on Sunday 3 August, where I explained that all the indications were that we would shortly be receiving written and specific demands from the pressure groups and sources of our funding. I made it plain that I was finding it more and more intolerable to have to defend our own stance over the South African matter. John listened to all this with sympathy but growing horror. I am the first to admit that this whole issue is both emotional and complex, but John's performance that long evening was remarkably worrying. It was as if he had totally failed to take in any of the signs and warnings of the previous years. His initial reaction was reasonably straightforward. He said quite simply that he would not continue with the WAC if the South Africans, or anyone else, were to be banned. Yet, at the same time, he had absolutely no answer to the series of pragmatic issues that might confront us if we did not ban the South Africans. It was Jane who moved the argument away from just the simple pragmatics, and the more she argued the quieter John became. He was obviously in distress. It was decided that the Executive should consult, if necessary by phone, at as late a date as possible before the Final Announcement had to be printed. Meanwhile I would brief everyone as far as possible before going to Crete for three weeks fieldwork.

I continued my confrontation with the anti-apartheid group, the AUT, the Students' Union and so on to try to find out, as much as possible, what their pressure really amounted to. I was getting nowhere with my arguments that South Africans were both black and white and that our grants were being given out to the black South Africans, for the point at issue was whether *any* South African should be allowed to participate and the policy being presented was that there should be no collaboration with South Africa in any shape or form (and see Appendix X, page 286, for the most recent statement on this issue from Anti-Apartheid). I was aware that the net was drawing in, for not only were people on the University campus, including some of my own staff, now talking openly about what the Executive would do, but members of the Executive Committee were about to leave the country on fieldwork expeditions. I myself was scheduled to go to Australia and Papua New Guinea on 9 September. I noticed with grim fascination that the annual Council meeting of the International Stoke Mandeville Games Federation adopted a resolution which read in part:

> It is in the interests of the ISMGF and the future of international paraplegic sport that teams from South Africa no longer be accepted to take part in the Games ... It is with great regret that this action is seen as vital for the continued survival of the ... Games.

The situation moved one step further with the confirmation in writing from Councillor Whitehead of his previous verbal commitment to refuse all City support to a Congress which allowed any South African participation.

Jane and I debated whether to cancel our Crete work for the year, but decided against it because nothing would actually happen while we were away and obviously this would be our last fieldwork for two years. Before and after our work in Crete I again phoned or met all the Executive members I could get hold of. Derek Hayes was taking a purely pragmatic view of the whole affair, and considered the ban therefore inevitable, though commenting that he was personally inclined against the banning of, and sanctions on, South Africa, and hated to be blackmailed by anyone. I also confronted the President of the Students' Union again and urged her to correct some of the errors in her previous document circulated to her members, and I tried to convince her that things were much more complex than she realised. Courteously she pointed out that whatever the details of the case, the overall principle remained the same.

The evidence that Third World participants would withdraw if South Africans were present was becoming firmer and firmer, and there were now phone calls making it clear that Indian participation would also be at risk, especially those employed by the Indian Archaeological Service.

A new element was the suggestion that without a ban on South African participation some, at least, of the Scandinavian archaeologists would not attend the Congress. This was later confirmed in a letter to me about a discussion with a senior Swedish archaeologist who stressed that:

> if the South Africans were to attend, Swedish archaeologists would be obliged to withdraw, because of the policy of the Swedish Government that there

should be no contacts, commercial, cultural, or whatever, with the Republic of
South Africa.

There was only one moment when I thought I might be going mad, for when
I talked to Steve Shennan about the forthcoming ghastly decision which
would have to be taken by the Executive, he simply remarked that it was
obvious that we would have to ban South Africa and that he was amazed
that we had got away for so long without having to do so. Given South
Africa's State President Botha's long-awaited address of August 15 to his
National Party and the world, which had promised so much but instead had
offered nothing – 'we have never given in to outside demands and we are not
going to do so' – it was difficult not to agree with Steve.

The Executive phone conference between all of us except Leslie Alcock
(who was travelling out of reach of any phone) took place at 11.30 am on
Saturday 7 September. I confined my remarks to factual statements. I
started by pointing out that there were currently 27 South Africans or
participants who had filled in their forms with South African addresses. I
stressed that one reason for the urgency for an immediate decision was that
the Final Announcement, unless altered, would be sent out the next week
stating all the names of participants presenting papers as well as their
countries. I pointed out that in the case of the 'Past in Education' session
this happened to place A.D. Mazel (South Africa) up against T. Mudariki
(Zimbabwe) and that Robert MacKenzie, the session organiser, would
resign if this happened. Obviously it would also be, at the very least, acutely
embarrassing to Taka Mudariki, who would presumably be unable, or
would refuse, to participate. I then outlined the details of the national and
local AUT position, the statements made by the Students' Union, the
University and local City branches of Anti-Apartheid, and I informed the
Executive of Councillor Whitehead's insistence that Southampton City
support would only continue to be given if 'South African citizens' were
banned. I also told them that the evidence suggested that the same
circumstances would arise in other Cities such as Edinburgh if we tried to
move the Congress elsewhere in Britain. John Evans started the ball rolling
– I could not believe my ears. He said that the situation was a conflict of
repugnancies, but that over the last few weeks he had been carefully
watching the newspapers and he now felt that there would be no WAC if we
accepted South Africans. He also wanted to dissociate himself from
apartheid. The next was David Wilson who picked up John's description of
a 'repugnant decision' and said that the matter ought really to be an
international decision and not simply one for the Executive Committee. A
basic belief of his, he said, was that there *should* be communication, and
therefore he might resign from the WAC if the Executive decided to ban the
South Africans, though at the moment he was in two minds. It was a case of
blackmail, which he detested but, in practice... Colin Renfrew followed,
saying that he felt similarly to David. Conferences should be free speech,

but principles could not prevail in this case and whatever was decided would create an unfortunate situation. He felt that non-discrimination was as important a principle as anti-apartheid. If only, he continued, we could get a UNESCO ruling and then pragmatically go along with it. Then we would be able to say that it was not *our* decision but we could refer to that ruling. Derek Hayes spoke only in his role as Treasurer and said that we simply could not afford to accept South Africans as participants and thereby lose the Third World or the sponsorship, and that we should therefore bow to the pressures. John Evans then spoke again, saying that perhaps the ban would do good, but it was David Wilson who formally proposed that South African participation should be withdrawn, and the Committee unanimously agreed. The fact that the Congress, which had no Government financial support, would be bankrupt if it was cancelled now, had weighed heavily with several members of the Executive. Time was then spent working out the overall lines of the Executive's statement which would be issued to the Press. David spoke of 'force majeur' and Colin of the importance that the act should be seen not to have been of our own making. Finally the main wording was agreed and the decision reiterated that South African names would now be omitted from the Final Announcement, and John Evans said that he would let Secretary-General Nenquin know immediately.

The local AUT and Anti-Apartheid representatives were clearly delighted at the decision. From this time onwards they and their colleagues were as helpful and supportive as they had previously been critical.

By the time I left for Australia on 9 September I had rung as many as possible of the organisers whose sessions included South African participants. One of the oddest phonecalls, in the light of her subsequent actions, was my first ever conversation (on 9 September) with Meg Conkey, co-organiser of the 'Cultural attitudes towards animals in art' session with David Lewis-Williams from South Africa. She said that she totally approved of the ban and although sad about Lewis-Williams, she had no real regrets about it. She also made joking reference to Carmel Schrire's position and said she would make a point of dealing with her herself. The opposite reaction came from David Phillipson in Cambridge, organiser of the session on 'Iron-using peoples in sub-Saharan Africa', for he immediately resigned in protest at the ban and wrote courteously to his participants explaining his reasons; however he chose to remain on the National Committee and was one of the very few who agreed to debate the issue (on radio with Thurstan Shaw). I also signed a letter to all the WAC co-organisers, which was to be sent out with a copy of a confirmatory letter from John Evans to Secretary-General Nenquin as well as the final version of the press release which the Executive had drafted on the telephone. I also wrote formally to each of the South Africans concerned, stressing that the Executive's decision was *not* aimed at them as individuals or as scholars. I also wrote personal letters to David Lewis-Williams and others that I knew personally in South Africa. These letters were to reach the recipients before the press release of 19 September was issued.

Poor Caroline had the job of co-ordinating the Executive's modifications to the draft press release which we had circulated. She had to ring me in Australia on numerous occasions. Nevertheless I must stress, in view of many subsequent attacks made on me, that the final version was decided by the President, John Evans, as I was not even in the country. Despite all subsequent press coverage and comment by such as Martin Biddle, of Christ Church Oxford, the Executive's statement was not merely concerned with pragmatics, for the press release stated, quite clearly, that '... South Africa and its apartheid regime placed it outside all normal principles and regulations...'. Also, contrary to accusations against me personally by Professor Nenquin, it was in fact the President, John Evans, who was supposed to telephone him and was thus responsible for the fact that the Secretary-General apparently had to learn of the decision from others.

While I was in Australia and Papua New Guinea I had meetings with the Executive Committee of my former Institute and with old friends and colleagues. In both countries I received promises that they would investigate the possibilities of financial support for their archaeologists and others to enable them to participate in the Congress. While I was so far away, trying to enthuse, to explain the aims of the Congress and to commission contributions to it, I little knew, despite all the phone calls between us, that Caroline, Sue and Jane were keeping quiet about the reactions to the ban. In Australia I sensed from old friends, such as Professor Jack Golson and Dr Rhys Jones of the Department of Prehistory at the Research School of the Australian National University, and others, that the initial reaction of disbelief about my news might easily turn to condemnation. This was not the occasion, however, to explore these matters further, for Australia was keen to see if it should make a bid for the 1991 Congress or, more likely, become the host of a smaller inter-congress, and I had to attend meetings to explain the complexities of such an undertaking. In Papua New Guinea, however, I sensed no doubts about the ban, either from the white or the native archaeologists whom I met, such as Les Groube and Joe Mangi, of the Archaeology Section of the Department of Anthropology and Sociology, University of Papua New Guinea.

I returned to my desk in Southampton at the end of September to learn the shocking news of the premature death of Professor Glynn Isaac of the Peabody Museum at Harvard, who was a co-organiser of one of our Pleistocene sessions. I had written to Glynn in June asking him to help us with the postage of Final Announcements in the States, but he was in China at the time. I had also just written to him from Australia saying that I expected Professor Desmond Clark, of the Department of Anthropology, University of California, to resign because of the ban and urging Glynn to stick with us. My prediction had been correct. Professor Desmond Clark not only resigned but subsequently canvassed others to join his boycott. What shocked me, however, was his claim that he was sure that Glynn would have responded negatively to our Executive decision, particularly as, so I am reliably informed, Glynn never had the chance to make any comment on my letter (despite the fact that it was carried by hand from Australia to the States by Professor David Harris). Professor Desmond Clark later lost many previous admirers when he chose the occasion of Glynn Isaac's memorial service in January 1986 in England to raise the subject with people.

So far the number of withdrawals from the Congress was quite small, but some of those that had been received were accompanied by such virulent, and often personal, abuse against me that all the members of the Executive Committee were upset by it. In one instance a letter was so disgusting that Sue Stephenson hid it and only remembered it in 1987 when we were discussing this book! In fact, it was less surprising that one of those who lived in South Africa should assume that my name was not English and should urge me to go back to where I had come from, than that another of those banned, with whom I had had extensive discussions about possible participants in the Congress, should accept the decision as appropriate. Despite many people's fears, Professor Carmel Schrire's letter of resignation was polite and clear and gave no warning of her subsequent public campaigning, together with people like Professor Desmond Clark, to make people withdraw from the Congress. Professor Lewis Binford also campaigned against the Congress and wrote, characteristically:

> I am outraged at your decision to exclude South African prehistorians from *your* upcoming meeting. To equate scientists who are generally liberal with the repressive policies of the Boer government is silly and out of place in the broader scientific community. To equate the participation in science with representatives of political positions is to obviate the role of science in the modern world.
>
> This action further confirms my opinion that you are trying to use archaeology for your own short-sighted political goals. This is an abuse of power not unlike other abuses that you say you are against!
>
> I withdraw my participation in your ill-advised *show* in protest. I insist that you delete my name from any advertisements or programs that you are distributing.

Although very upsetting, I should not really have been surprised. Carmel Schrire, in a letter to me, had reported him as saying:

> ... If the Third World can't face 'science' they should stay home in the mealie fields.

There were also others who went to ridiculous extremes; the Director of a local Archaeological Trust not only tried to block his staff from attending the Congress but actually sent a copy of the cheque which he had been on the point of sending to me, as if to say, 'Look what you have now lost'! (at a later meeting of his Executive Committee he was directed to remove his ban).

Totally out of character, as far as I was concerned, was my old friend Peter Jewell's intemperate personal attack on me which appeared to compare the Executive Committee to hyenas and jackals who were out to knock our South African colleagues in a petty way. In resigning as a co-organiser of the academic session which Juliet Clutton-Brock continued to organise, Professor Jewell appeared more upset about the genocides of small communities occuring in several parts of the world than about the situation of the blacks in South Africa who, he claimed, were numerous and strong, and whose numbers were increasing rapidly. He was the first of my friends to take the opposite view to my own, but by far the most violent and, when I had recovered from the shock of such an attack from someone I had known intimately for so many years, I replied to his letter by accepting his resignation, and added:

> If you wish to talk about 'indefensible and preposterously hypocritical stances' maybe you should reconsider your own position. As a member of the AUT you are pretending to support national policy which is that there should be 'a total academic boycott of South Africa'.

Those who knew the Jewell/Clutton-Brock household reported fierce arguments about the whole issue. A month later, after Professor Jewell had written to others (including another of my old friends, Professor David Harris) about his own point of view, I received another letter from him which now focussed its attack on the current AUT policy and assumed that the Executive had been intimidated, harassed and blackmailed into total compromise. He then went on to boast of his own insistence that South Africans should participate in meetings which he himself organised, and concluded with expressions of good will to our inalienable friendship. Thinking of the quiet-spoken Southampton AUT representative, the genuine and enthusiastic Anti-Apartheid campaigners, and the courageous and palpably honest Leader of the Southampton City Council, who had discussed the issues with us, and put pressure on us, I could not get myself to respond to Peter's letter, and I kept out of his way until after the Congress was over. Others, whom I had never met, also attacked me personally.

There was also increasing evidence that, had the ban not been imposed, Africans, probably Indians, and several East Europeans would not have been able to attend. Councillor Whitehead, Leader of the Southampton Council, having kept his word not to make public statements during the period of decision-making by the Executive Committee, now wrote to congratulate the Executive and to notify us of his Council's September resolution to enforce the UN's cultural boycott, and he remarked that 'your action was timely, in that I doubt whether I could have held off for too long after the passing of that item in full Council'. Another very welcome letter of support came from Dr Henry Cleere who spoke about the sadness of having to exclude colleagues from South Africa but found that 'the decision of the Executive Committee is wholly laudable'.

I was having long discussions by telephone with Colin Renfrew. He was in correspondence with a South African colleague and was obviously impressed by a long and reasoned letter from Professor Tobias of the University of Witwatersrand, whom many recognised as a fighter against apartheid, and Colin was getting cold feet. Neither he nor Leslie Alcock were able to attend the October 15 Executive Committee meeting but Colin had phoned in a suggestion for compromise, whereby participants would not mention that they were South Africans but register as international scholars, a suggestion immediately rejected by the Executive. I also had been impressed with Professor Tobias' letter and had prepared a detailed draft answer to him which, with the addition of a paragraph to be written by John Evans, was accepted after the Executive had reasserted its South African ban, this time considering only purely pragmatic grounds. I reproduce the texts of both letters:

Dear Professor Ucko, *Re: Rejection of South African participants in the World Archaeological Congress*

I have received your letter of 9 September 1985, informing me that 'the Executive Committee ... has decided that it cannot accept your participation in the above 1986 meeting' and that 'This decision reflects the policy of numerous organisations who call for "a total academic boycott of South Africa".

I understand that a similar letter has been received by most, if not all, of those who were proposing to participate in the Congress and who are resident in South Africa. These include Dr J.D. Lewis-Williams, co-organiser of one of the themes of the Academic Sessions of the Congress.

In my case, this letter was received although I have been a member, since September 14, 1976, of the Permanent Council which is 'le principale organe directeur de l'UIPPS' (paragraph 10 of the Constitution of the International Union of Prehistoric and Protohistoric Sciences); and, moreover, am Vice-President of Commission 6 (The Earliest Hominids) of IUPPS and have been for the last ten years or more.

I write now to reiterate my request, conveyed to you by telex, and to Professor Evans by telephone, that your Executive Committee urgently reconsider its decision. In support of this request, I should like to make several points:

(1) *Authority to take such a decision*

Both Professor Evans and Professor Nenquin have confirmed that the decision was taken by the Executive Committee of the British national organising committee, and not by the Comité Executif or the Permanent Council that are the governing bodies of IUPPS. I seriously question whether a national organising committee has the authority to take such a decision.

Nothing in the Statutes of IUPPS gives authority to national organising committees to make such a decision, as a study of Section VII of the Statutes makes clear. Indeed, it is implicit in the Statutes of the International Union that its congresses will be open to delegates of all countries. Thus, paragraph 3 refers to 'la collaboration de savants *de tous les pays*' (underlining mine).

All meetings of IUPPS have been organised on this basis since the first congress in London in 1932. Therefore, what your national organising committee is proposing to do constitutes a radical departure in the policy of an International Union and one whose policy has been in existence for over half a century. The proposal that such a far-reaching departure from the International Union's policy be made is not, I submit, in the province of a national organising committee to effect. Such a proposal should, at the very least, have been referred to the Comité Executif, but preferably to the Permanent Council, or even the General Assembly of IUPPS, *before* any decision in the matter was taken.

The conclusion is inescapable that this decision was *ultra vires* and should be reversed.

(2) *Stated reason for your Executive Committee's decision*

The reason for the Executive Committee's decision given in your letter is that 'This decision reflects the policy of numerous organisations who call for "a total academic boycott of South Africa".' I am unable to comprehend, let alone condone, that a national committee, charged with organising a Congress *on behalf of an International Union*, could allow itself to be influenced by any other than the policy of the International Union on whose behalf it is acting. IUPPS has *not* called for 'a total academic boycott of South Africa': the matter has *not* been put to its Permanent Council, General Assembly, or international Comité Executif, as Secretary-General Nenquin informed me on 19 September 1985. The policy of 'numerous organisations' should not have been allowed to override the IUPPS policy of the universality of science and scholarship and freedom of participation by all bona fide scientists.

When I enquired of Professor Evans whether Her Majesty's Government had indicated that South Africans (including British subjects resident in South Africa) were to be debarred from entering the United Kingdom to attend the Congress he replied that this was not the case.

In other words, neither the political arm of the country concerned, nor the International Union on whose behalf your committee is organising the Congress, has instructed, or advised, your committee to take the decision it has done.

I conclude that the reason given for your Executive Committee's decision is not acceptable.

(3) *Implications of your Executive Committee's decision*

I am sorry to say that this is the first occasion known to me when *one's fellow-scientists* have taken a decision to exercise political discrimination against a group of their fellows.

Of course there have been previous occasions when problems have arisen. But in all such cases, one's colleagues have sought and desired the presence of scholars irrespective of race, politics or national origin; whereas it has been the political arm, the national government, that has restricted (or sought to restrict) the entry of persons from certain countries. The present issue constitutes a clear departure from these precedents since for the first time (known to me) the organisers themselves have decided to deny the right of participation to a group of scholars. This is a deplorable development in the history of the infringements upon the free interchange of ideas. Moreover it is an ineluctable implication of your committee's decision that it constitutes a serious breach of the long-recognised, long-respected principle of the universality of science and scholarship.

That your Executive Committee is aware of this aspect one may infer from the statement in your letter that 'in so far as this decision may be seen to lessen its commitment to the free interchange of ideas between all "bona fide scientists" the Executive regrets its decision'. I do not believe that this expression of regret is sufficient to counteract the violence done to a basic principle of international scientific intercourse.

Another implication of the Committee's decision is that, by keeping out all South African participants, you are in effect identifying all those researchers with the policies of South Africa. To being so identified, a number of my colleagues and I take exception. Some of us, like myself, have spent decades opposing racism and apartheid; we work for institutions like the Universities of the Witwatersrand and Cape Town which are non-segregated, whose policies are predicated upon non-racial admissions of students, non-racial appointments of staff members and strong opposition to apartheid in educational matters. I personally have played an active part in the ongoing fight for academic freedom and against racism since 1948. These things are mentioned here not as a plea that exceptions should be made in such cases; I mention them to show how offensive it is to such people to be virtually held responsible and to be forced to suffer for a government's policies, with which they may be totally out of sympathy. At least one person who has received a letter of denial from you is a 'coloured' South African.

By accepting, *de facto*, that the policies of a country are relevant to the decision whether or not to accept fellow-scientists' participation in a Congress, your Committee opens up a dangerous precedent. Is your Committee refusing participation also to scholars from other countries whose policies are repugnant to you, for example those which deny freedom of movement to scientists?

I submit that all such factors are not relevant to the case. The overriding principle, with which I should have thought all members of your Committee must be in sympathy, is that of the universality of science and scholarship. I do not cavil with the fact that some organisations and individuals (though not the British Government at the EEC recently) feel that they can achieve political objectives by cultural boycotts of South Africa, but I do maintain that it is quite wrong that this should be allowed to influence the operations of an organisation dedicated to the promotion of prehistoric and protohistoric sciences.

Many people noted with pleasure that both your First and Second Announcements proudly proclaim, in twelve languages, that 'This meeting ... is to be a truly international one'. How very sad that, when your Third Circular is about to be printed, with names of countries and participants in it – as Professor Evans informed me – your Committee should have reneged on this fine principle.

(4) *Personal considerations*

I do not plead for exceptions to be made to your Committee's decision; that would be as reprehensible as the initial decision. Nevertheless, let me illustrate how hurtful and unjust your decision has been (and you are hurting individual colleagues, not the country or its policies – since none of us was attending as an official representative of our country or its government). May I mention again, briefly, that I personally have a long record of fighting against apartheid. I am as strongly opposed to political discrimination in science (which your Committee's decision amounts to) as I am to racial discrimination. I am a member of the Permanent Council and Vice-President of an IUPPS Commission. My invitations to be a congress participant and symposiast have carried me to nearly every corner of the globe; and I was an active participant, symposium organiser and chairman at the Nice Congress of the IUPPS in 1976 and at the Mexico City Congress in 1981. Furthermore, I happen to be a British subject, as well as a South African national. It is particularly painful, under these circumstances, that the first country in which *a group of fellow-scientists* have resolved to keep out myself and others from here is Great Britain.

Against this background, you will appreciate that I am unable to accept the validity or the moral defensibility of your decision; and that my conscience compels me to express my opposition to it by whatever proper channels are open to me.

Conclusion

In the light of the foregoing, I urge your national Executive Committee to reconsider this matter urgently and to reverse its decision.

As this matter affects the policy and the welfare of the International Union as a whole, I am sending a copy of this letter to the Secretary-General, Professor Jacques Nenquin. I am also sending a copy to the President of my Commission, Collège de France Professor Yves Coppens, whom I normally help run the Commission.

Your Committee's early response would be appreciated.

Yours sincerely,
(Professor) P.V. Tobias

Dear Professor Tobias

Further to my letter of 2 October I have to inform you that the Executive, at its meeting today, considered your letter in detail and decided not to reverse its decision.

In reaching this decision, and conveying it to you, the Executive wished to acknowledge the accuracy of various of the statements that you make in your letter of 23 September 1985 and to make various matters explicit. In so deciding the Executive acknowledges both the quality of your letter ... and your personal reputation regarding apartheid. The Executive wishes to be entirely frank with you, and it does not feel that it has anything to hide. I therefore deal with the various points in your letter in the order that you raise them.

1. You are no doubt correct that, technically, only the Permanent Council of UISPP can take an overall decision about the non-acceptance of participants. This fact was recognised by the National Executive when it took its original decision as is made clear in the enclosed press release (which you may not have seen previously). Nevertheless the Committee was convinced that in this instance the urgent need for a quick decision precluded reference to the Permanent Council, or even the International Executive Committee, and also

that no other decision was possible if the Congress were to take place as planned.

2. The Executive Committee believes that it acted responsibly in taking its decision because the organisations referred to in my letter of 9 September were in a position to disrupt the Congress entirely. Southampton City Council, which has been backing it very strongly, would have withdrawn both its cooperation and its financial support. The total financial loss would have amounted to at least £100,000, nearly a quarter of the total Congress budget, and other severe difficulties would have arisen as well as the Council's non-cooperation. The Southampton University Students' Union, which controls the main accommodation to be used by the Congress, made it clear that it would withdraw provision of rooms and services, and would in addition engage in 'non-violent direct action' against the Congress. The local branch of the Association of University Teachers, which has a *national* policy of total boycott of any form of cultural contact or exchange with South Africa, also indicated that it would take action against the Congress if South Africans participated. Lastly, the Anti-Apartheid Movement wrote to the Ambassadors and High Commissioners of thirty countries about the matter, and we are convinced that had South African participation not been publicly disallowed the number of withdrawls from the Congress would have been very high, with further serious consequences for its financial viability, and even more for its academic value.

3. We do indeed keenly regret the breach of the principle of free academic interchange implicit in our decision. Nevertheless we do not think that it is unreasonable to weigh against this the damage to the Congress and its wider goals likely to result from ignoring the increasing pressures from many quarters, official as well as unofficial, for a clear signal of disapproval of the South African Government's apartheid policy. Among the former, in addition to the various UN and UNESCO resolutions, there is the acceptance by the British Government itself (FCO Press Conference, 25 September 1985) of the restrictive measures proposed by the EEC, which include discouraging scientific and cultural agreements with South Africa. The Executive's decision was in no way *ad hominem*; most of the members of the Executive have friends and colleagues who are 'hurt', 'offended', or 'insulted' by its decision. All of the Executive sincerely regret that outstanding academic colleagues (including 'coloured' and 'black' South Africans), some of whose contributions had been previously solicited and grant-aids approved, are affected by its decision and perhaps even more so, that acknowledged fighters against racism and apartheid are similarly affected.

4. The Executive is truly committed to the WAC 1986 being truly international. If South African participation had been allowed *very few, if any*, of our colleagues would have participated from Africa (apart from South Africa), Eastern Europe, China, etc – let alone Australian Aborigines, Inuit, San [Bushmen] peoples, etc. Now that South African participation is not allowed, it is possible for it to be indeed an (almost) truly international meeting.

There remain a few heterogeneous points which have not been incorporated conveniently under the numerical order of attempting to answer your letter of 23 September, but they nevertheless deserve mention:

(a) Throughout the agonising period of decision-making regarding South African participation, the Secretary General has been kept fully informed by phone. Following a telephone call on the Monday after the Executive's Saturday decision, the enclosed confirmation letter (of 19 September 1985) was sent to Professor Nenquin.

I reiterate that the Executive does not treat this matter as anything other than one of major concern, and certainly has not (and does not) seek to hide anything.

(b) As stated above, the question of principle is now in the hands of the International IUPPS Executive/Conseil Permanent. Its Statutes are lamentably vague on the point at issue. Our Executive has fully reported the matter to the Secretary General at the earliest opportunity. It must be noted that IUPPS (and other bodies) affiliated to UNESCO (through ICPHS) *appear* to be in direct conflict with their 'parent' body in having South African membership of their governing councils.

(c) In voicing their regrets regarding their non-participation in WAC 1986, South Africans affected by the Executive's decision have written variously saying 'I sympathise with your underlying anti-apartheid sentiments and would be prepared to accept this discrimination if I felt that something would be achieved by it', 'I accept that it is impossible to separate one's personal policies and actions, whatever they may be, from one's institutional and national affiliations. Given this, I feel that an Academic boycott is appropriate at this time'. Others have, of course, written in a different vein.

(d) Several of our compatriots have resigned over the issue. *The Executive has not taken its decision lightly.*

I do not believe that the above will, necessarily, convince you of the correctness of the Executive's decision but I do sincerely hope that it will convince you both of its sincerity and of its anxiety in this matter. Few of us find it easy to judge between two points of principle which appear, at least on the face of it, incompatible. Let us all at least hope that we, as an Executive, have taken the right decision for 1986.

Yours sincerely
P.J. Ucko

As the Minutes of that Executive Committee meeting of October 15 state:

> The Treasurer reiterated his view, which the Executive Committee accepted, that had South African attendance not been prevented for the WAC 1986 then the financial viability of the whole Congress would have been likely to have collapsed. It was with this advice in mind that the Executive, mindful of its duties as Directors ... reiterated its view that, on purely pragmatic grounds, the Executive had no other option than to repeat its previous decision to ban South African participation from the Congress.

The Executive also added Namibia to its South African ban for the same reasons that the latter had originally been imposed. Leslie Alcock and Colin Renfrew were immediately telephoned with the news of these decisions, and both agreed with them.

The Executive Committee also had some other business and noted that the first instalment of £75,000 of the York sponsorship money had been safely received. This had been a hair-raising business, for the money had been due in on 1 September but, despite written reminders as well as innumerable telephone calls from Australia to England and then within

England, it was only received at the end of September. It was not only that we could not finalise the cover of the Final Announcement, nor decide about a pre-Congress excursion to York, before we received payment, but neither Peter Addyman nor I had any idea of how Ian Skipper would react to the ban on South Africa, for I had been unable to speak to Ian from Australia when he was in the West Indies. He had not yet responded to my letter of October in which I suggested a meeting to discuss 'several important points on an informal basis'. I simply had to assume that his co-Director Peter Addyman had kept him informed.

I was also able to report to the Executive Committee that the Council of the Australian Institute of Aboriginal Studies had now agreed to support Australian participation in the Congress and would be advertising grants in the press. We also tackled the first cases of replacement of session organisers due to withdrawals. In the light of subsequent events it is ironic for me to record that I had made alternative plans for Michael Day's session should he resign because of his known friendship with Professor Tobias!

Finally, the Committee decided that a National Committee meeting should be held as soon as possible.

It often felt to me at that time that I stood alone, except for Jane. We had endless discussions and she, like me, felt that the decision to ban was essentially an ethical one and that everything else was secondary to it, while the Executive appeared to be held together by pragmatic considerations. In any case, the letters which came in often appeared to be aimed at me personally. No doubt sensing this loneliness, Paul Crake wrote me an official letter in which he referred to some of the recent events in South Africa, and concluded:

> I do not think that I could, in all conscience, have continued working for the Congress (if the Executive had permitted South African participation). I could certainly not have mustered as much enthusiasm for the whole of this marvellous enterprise. The Executive Committee has taken a hugely courageous decision, and one for which I offer you my wholehearted support.

And that is exactly what he did, taking over the whole very sensitive and very time-consuming organisation of grant awards and grant payments.

Not long after, Steve Shennan also wrote to me, making it clear that his support for our ban was based on grounds of principle and not just on pragmatic considerations; he chose this time to write 'because of the weight of opposition which has been building up'. Another form of support was Caroline's unremitting devotion to her work, which also sustained me, even though I suspected that she herself might not be in agreement with the ban.

It was almost as if those academics who reacted with outrage could not get themselves to believe that the 'sin' of the ban was not attributable to a single person, but had been an unanimous decision by a very varied Executive Committee. Such an extreme case was the Professor of

Anthropology, C. Garth Sampson, of the Southern Methodist University in Dallas, who wrote to several of my colleagues saying:

> Ucko has banned all the South African archaeologists participating in the IUPPS next year in England. He did this without consulting the IUPPS, and made it seem in his letter to the South Africans ... that he was acting according to the wishes of 'numerous organisations' – when in fact these were local left-wing pressure-groups ... If you were planning to go to these Meetings, I urge you in the strongest possible terms to *withdraw*. The most casual analysis reveals that Ucko's actions are self-serving, underhand, and aimed at a defenseless group whose position on racism is unimpeachable. Organisers who attempt this kind of manipulation should be given no support. I beg you to take this very seriously. If you know of others in your area who are planning to go, please try to dissuade them.

A most surprising resignation, in view of her remarks just a few weeks previously, was from Associate Professor Conkey, who now wrote a letter of resignation 'which perhaps came as a surprise given my lack of concern and mumbling on the phone'. More understandably, and much more worrying, was Dr Tim Ingold's dismay at losing two of his sub-theme organisers, as well as his own opposition in principle to the ban. Long discussions with Tim and others were very time-consuming and very depressing. Equally depressing were letters such as one received from Wales, which claimed that the overthrow of the present South African apartheid regime would almost certainly lead to worse and more savage racial repression than existed at the moment.

It was becoming clear that the more the attacks that were mounted against the WAC, the more the Executive members felt that we had to stick together as a united group. In this way we all knew that we must compromise from time to time. In view of later comments it may be worth recalling my own approach at this time. I considered all the matters under discussion from two points of view, one as a Director of the Company running the WAC, in which context I was prepared to follow Derek Hayes' lead and remain exclusively pragmatic, and the other as a member of the WAC Executive Committee, in which context I was by now determined to have the WAC seen to be pro the Third World and against South Africa's apartheid regime. Rather reluctantly, and very influenced by comments by David Harris, I therefore, unfortunately, made no strong objections to John Evans' purely factual and pragmatic statement which was to be included in all copies of the Final Announcement.

A new element had by now begun to come into focus in the form of press coverage of the debate. With all its attendant pressures and phone interviews it was to increase and increase. The press intervention had started innocuously enough with the *Southern Evening Echo* merely reporting the imposition of the ban, and the *Times Higher Education Supplement* and *Nature* carrying factual reports of developments, both stressing comments by John Evans and myself that the South African archaeologists would be sorely missed from the academic debates. This was the first of a series of serious reports by the *THES*. Then, on November 13, *The Times* started what appeared to be a witch hunt against the WAC in the form of a letter from J. Mandelstam (Microbiology Unit), G.A. Harrison (Department of Biological Anthropology), Schuyler Jones (Pitt Rivers Museum), and R.J.P. Williams (Inorganic Chemistry Laboratory) from Oxford:

> The International Congress on Archaeology, due to be held in Southampton next September, faces dissension and perhaps disruption because its organising committee has surrendered to an academic boycott initiated by the local branch of the Association of University Teachers (AUT), the Students' Union of Southampton and the Southampton City Council ...
>
> They seem to have failed totally to realise that a congress of scholars or scientists differ in kind from, say, the Olympic Games. At the former, individuals attend as *individuals* and make their contribution to the furtherance of knowledge in their subject; there are no 'winners', no flying of flags, no playing of national anthems. It is a glaring error to treat individual scholars as national representatives.
>
> On this occasion, the error is compounded by the fact that at least one of the 'dis-invited' participants, like many other South African academics, has been a consistent and outspoken critic of racialism and apartheid ...
>
> Committees of learned societies and the AUT should make it clear that it is not their function to monitor governments and to enumerate those whose subjects may attend a meeting ...
>
> If they fail to do this, they will promote by default the erosion of international scholarship and while doing so, they will, incidentally, tear themselves apart in the way that the International Congress of Archaeologists is doing now.

These correspondents had simply not done sufficient homework. IUPPS Congresses traditionally invited national delegations, its Permanent Council had national representatives who might be proposed by governments, and the AUT's *national* policy for a total academic ban on South Africa was positive and clear. I could not really get upset by this sort of attack, all the more when the same member of the Pitt Rivers Museum later claimed that UNESCO's policy was also wrong, and that the ban was both petty and would be ineffective. Such assaults did nothing but stiffen my resolve.

Nevertheless, I did gain heart when a letter from the national AUT was published making it clear that 'moral pressure is clearly essential if peaceful change is to be achieved'. When Dr Roger Ingham, Secretary of the Southampton AUT, was interviewed about this letter from Oxford on Radio Solent I was not all that surprised to hear the Radio Presenter say: 'We also issued an invitation to the signatories of the (Oxford) letter, which ... they declined.' In this interview Roger Ingham said:

> ... I'm very surprised at the wording of this letter and it is unfortunate that none of the four writers was willing to come and discuss these points in person or even over the telephone, but the point is the AUT, as I say, is a fully

democratic and representative body of University teachers – the Students' Union is similarly fully democratically organised and Southampton City Council, of course, has been democratically elected. So, to call any of these groups 'Pressure Groups' seems to me to be trying to belittle them by the use of some rather clever language on behalf of the writers. What we did was not dictate or threaten, we tried to persuade, and we tried to persuade on moral grounds, that the long-term future of South Africa was almost certainly better dealt with through an isolationist policy in all regards, and most countries have agreed this in economic terms; our own country is wavering a bit! UNESCO is firmly committed to this, and these three bodies, which are mentioned in the letter, agreed that an isolationist policy is the right one. We persuaded the organisers of this view and clearly there are some people within the organisation who are not happy with this view ...

As the November date for the national Executive Committees grew closer, so the press coverage grew, with Paul Lashmar of the *Observer* writing the first of many pieces on the Congress, and posing the question as to whether the WAC would be cancelled. In this article, Lashmar quoted Professor Tobias' view that this was the first time that such a ban had been 'formulated by academics and enforced against fellow academics', an essential point of principle which seemed to me to be far better than using a device such as the holding of a conference in a country where visas would not be issued and where the academics would merely shelter behind government regulations. *The Times* really excelled two days before the Executive meeting. It published a letter from Professor T.E. Hall, a member of our own National Committee and Director of the Research Laboratory for Archaeology and History of Art in Oxford, and one from the Namibian Deputy Minister of Education. The former spoke of widespread anger against the ban in academic circles and demanded that the WAC should be cancelled, and the latter referred to howls of indignation at our action. Throughout the development of this affair, the *Times* continued to be strongly against us and rejected many letters in support of our actions, including one from the President of the Southampton AUT and another from Dr Higginson, the new Vice Chancellor of the University of Southampton, who wrote:

My personal opinion, and that is purely a matter of conscience, is that the Executive Committee took the right decision, insofar as any decision could be 'right' in this case.

During November there was evidence both of further withdrawals and also of further support for the Congress and (or despite) its ban, from Yugoslavian archaeologists, the Prehistoric Society, the National Institute of Adult Continuing Education, the Secretary-General of the Commonwealth and many others including, of course, the anti-apartheid groups and the City of Southampton. Yet it was incredibly difficult to assess what might happen at the Executive and National Committee meetings on the 20th, for we continued to be attacked by Americans (some of whom were threatening a general boycott of the Congress), Western Europeans, Israelis, and South Africans in letters and articles in the local and national British press. Both *Science* and *Nature* published long articles, 'Archaeology Congress Threatened' and 'Impaled on Morton's Fork' respectively, which were both very negative about our position. Some of the complexity of the world situation was brought home to us when we flew Dr Patay from Hungary to Southampton to discuss the details of Hungarian participation in the Congress. Although keen to accept our special arrangements for East European participants, and despite the Hungarian official government policy towards South Africa, Dr Patay was unhappy that such a policy should be taken to apply to academic interchange.

As the meetings grew closer and closer it was Colin Renfrew in particular who was obviously having second thoughts. These varied from suggestions that the ban should be removed and the Congress held in another country to a repeat of his previous suggested compromise. There were three resignations from those who had been appointed to the Honorific Committee at the meeting in 1983, but there were also fascinating contributions to the debate by two of the other remaining Vice Presidents. One of these, Professor Christopher Hawkes, previously of the Institute of Archaeology, Oxford, wrote to me with a suggested procedure for the National Committee which impressed me so greatly that I made use of it in a document which I had decided to prepare for the morning meeting of the Executive, in the fear that Colin might split the Executive Committee apart. Several of our session organisers, such as Dr Mark Leone, were not answering our letters, and he in particular was being pulled one way by Carmel Schrire and the other by Peter Gathercole. In Jean Combier's case he had to think of his own future, for Professor de Lumley was writing official letters of complaint and was also trying to focus the debate on the individual qualities of Professor Tobias. Clearly many people, both in Britain and overseas, were waiting to see what happened on the 20th before revealing their own hand.

I was in any case very apprehensive about a Colin-David axis at the Executive Committee meeting also scheduled for 20 November and totally unsure about the mood of the National Committee. Then, unbeknownst to anyone except my staff, the bombshell came, in a telephone message from Peter Addyman, that Mr Anthony Gaynor would be representing Heritage Projects Ltd at the National Committee meeting and would be announcing the withdrawal of the York sponsorship of £150,000 unless the ban on South Africa was lifted. It was clear to me that in the present situation the Executive Committee would have no choice but to cancel the Congress, for if Heritage Projects Ltd withdrew its promised £75,000 (leaving aside the question of the £75,000 already received) Derek would have to advise us that we could not proceed. Eventually my mood of utter despair lifted a little and I arranged an urgent meeting that evening with Councillor Whitehead. We had got to know each other very well by now, and this was not the moment for false optimism or idle promises; Alan was as aware as I was that he had to find £150,000 by the Wednesday morning, or the Congress would be off, with all the consequences that that would bring. On the next day he cancelled his engagements, and at 5:30 pm on the day before the Executive and National Committee meetings he was able to tell me that if no South Africans were allowed to attend the Congress, then the Greater London Council would not only provide the Royal Festival Hall free of charge but would also give a grant of £150,000 towards Congress activities as they referred to London. Written confirmation of this arrangement was supposed to reach us from Mr Bill Bush, the Head of Majority Party Office at County Hall, in a few days time. Somehow Alan, Jane, Paul, Caroline and I found the way to breathe a little again, and I settled down to work all night to produce, and copy, the four-page memorandum which I intended to table if the Executive Committee meeting went as badly as I was predicting it would.

This memorandum was, in the event, not tabled at the meeting, but I quote it here in full for it serves well as a summary conspectus of my thinking at that time, summarises Colin's 'compromise document', and incorporates some of Professor Christopher Hawkes' suggestions about the publication of South African contributions:

> The Executive Committee/Directors of the Company came to a pragmatic and unanimous decision to ban participation by South Africans/Namibians. This decision is now retrospectively under threat from those who feel that the 'academic free speech' stance (hereafter A) needs to be upheld *even if this means cancelling the WAC 1986.* This wish to reverse the corporate decision appears to be being discussed and canvassed privately by certain members of the Executive Committee.My own view coincides with a large number of people and organisations such as the Prehistoric Society who not only also believe in the principle of academic free speech but who also believe that the WAC should *not be cancelled.*
>
> If the Congress is in fact aborted, there will, obviously, be no 'speech' (of any kind) whatsoever. Colin Renfrew's current suggestion for a 'de-nationalised' group of South African participants apparently aims: 1. to keep the WAC 1986 going; 2. to prevent major defections by Western Europeans and Americans; 3. to quieten those with real aims to *act* on anti-apartheid sentiments (hereafter B); and 4. to fall within the international IUPPS rubric.
>
> These suggestions are somewhat similar to those that Colin telephoned to the Executive Committee on a previous occasion (and which were rejected by the Executive). He previously agreed to the rejection of them. I believe that they should be rejected once again, because: (a) although the act of 'de-nationalisation' is not supposed to be a hidden one, it will be seen as a purely deceptive strategy and will, I believe, be almost certainly rejected by B, accepted by A, and scorned by all; and (b) will therefore fail to protect the WAC 1986.
>
> I would therefore have to vote against Colin's suggestion.
>
> Colin's suggestions *do*, however, stress that the Executive's current stance is a firmly pragmatic one. The Executive, I guess, could only be unanimous *on* pragmatic grounds; I feel that such unanimity is very, very important. As I do

not believe that Colin's suggestions have any chance of removing the opposition by B, his suggestion that South Africans/Namibians *should* be allowed to attend the Congress is based on a matter of principle *and is no longer a pragmatic argument* about which the Executive is likely to be unanimous.

To adopt his suggestion would, I guess, *inevitably* lead to resignations from the Executive and possibly even the cancellation of the WAC 1986. Before the Executive disintegrates and the WAC 1986 is cancelled I would ask the Executive to seriously consider its own conscience.

1. I was told in 1981 by Colin and John Evans that the main reason for Britain being asked to host IUPPS 1986 was to ensure a really world-wide Congress;

2. the British members (who attended Mexico) of the International Permanent Council assured me (in answer to one of my 'conditions' of taking on the position of National Secretary) that: (a) finances were assured from within the City; (b) that the assured budget would allow meaningful participation by Third World/Developing Countries; and (c) that they would support a thematic treatment for (part at least of) the Congress to allow meaningful Third World/Developing Countries participation.

Indeed the Minutes of the 1982 and 1983 meetings of the National Committee continually stress the *essential participation of Third World/ Developing Countries* ('... that every effort should be made to involve participants from the Third World' and '... for this particular Congress the attendance should be less European dominated and that attendance should be encouraged particularly from the Developing World'). My academic programme (always submitted to and approved by the Executive) has continually attempted to effect this stated aim. My years of fund-raising activities (which were, unfortunately, forced upon me) have been essentially devoted to raising monies to realise these stated aims of the IUPPS offer, and Britain's acceptance of it.

Like it ('in principle'), or not, the Executive has been forced to recognise that in 1985/6 it is impossible to hold a 'total' *World* Archaeological Congress if there is to be South African/Namibian participation. At best the International Permanent Council of IUPPS was ignorant in its 'request' to Britain by not foreshadowing how Britain could concentrate on world participation under IUPPS ... 'rules' and, at worst, culpable and deceptive. At best the British members of the International Permanent Council were hasty in offering this country as host to a world-wide meeting without considering the 'South African problem'. The Executive has no excuse; I alerted members to this problem at my first meeting with Executive members and formally alerted the Executive to the Pan African Congress resolution in December 1983.

During 1982-84 I hoped that we were making a strong enough statement of principle by removing the word 'delegate' from all our documentation and letters and only allowing 'participants' in the Congress. I introduced and enforced this action. I used this argument in all my 'confrontations' with B people throughout 1985. What has been revealed by the events of 1985 is simple – those who are applying pressure to achieve the peaceful overthrow of South African apartheid are no longer willing to accept the convenient distinction between 'delegate' and 'participant'. (Colin's proposed resolution only confuses the issue.)

I personally believe that John Evans, David Wilson and Colin Renfrew 'took on' IUPPS 1986 – to be based on world-wide participation – for 'the glory of

Britain' without considering any of the concomitant points of principle, and then unsuccessfully devoted their attentions to problems of finance. On pragmatic grounds alone, they *should* therefore stick to the twice repeated and unanimous Executive decision to ban South African/Namibian participation. If they now wish to 'defect' I think that they should seriously consider resigning from the Company and let others get on with running the announced Congress.

If we are to follow Colin's *belated* attempt to move the Executive's decision away from the pragmatic we come up against what are, I believe, two incompatible points of principle (represented by those called A and B above). I need not rehearse the complex arguments here; I am sure we have all been debating them (certainly Colin and I have). A can only be accommodated with regard to B if the South African situation is deemed to be 'outside all normal principles and regulations' (Press Release – 19 September 1985). I wish to 'give heart' to any Executive members who feel totally pressurised by those of our academic colleagues who are exclusively stressing the 'free speech' aspect: – there are many *democratically-elected* institutions and organisations, as well as British and foreign reputable governments and organisations, who have been prepared to say that South Africa *is* an exception and that cultural interaction with South Africa should be curtailed, prevented, or banned. These include, for example, the British Government and the Commonwealth, the national Association of University Teachers, and the City of Southampton Council. Internationally they include the United Nations, UNESCO, and several academic bodies such as the International Association of Applied Linguistics, the Pan African Association on Prehistory and Related Studies, and the International Council for Adult Education. The number and quality of such democratically elected groups is impressive and their silent support for a ban on South Africa should be weighed against the number of individuals who have written in to resign (14) or to protest against our current decision (16).

Most of all, given the above, how *could* a Congress which aims to be as world-wide as possible, and which has always had as a major thrust the involvement of the Third World/Developing Countries, possibly *not* ban South Africa when the 'legitimate representatives of the South African people' (the ANC), as recognised by the General Asssembly of the United Nations, UNESCO – and the UN Commission on Human Rights, themselves ask us for such a ban? The ANC calls on the World 'to isolate South Africa in the economic, political, diplomatic, military, educational and cultural fields'.

If the Executive *does* feel that it should move away from a purely pragmatic stance – which is what Colin is suddenly pushing for – and if a compromise *is* needed, let me suggest one which, I believe, is not only honest *but could also be successful*:

1. the Executive Committee reiterates its abhorrence of the South African/Namibian regime based on apartheid and feels that this regime 'places South Africa outside all normal principles and regulations'. It therefore follows organisations such as the United Nations, UNESCO, the International Association of Applied Linguistics, etc and refuses to allow physical participation by South Africans/Namibians in the WAC 1986;

2. the Executive Committee reiterates its belief in the principles of free academic interchange of ideas. It therefore declines to follow those such as the West African Journal of Archaeology, etc who refuse to publish works by South Africans/Namibians and it will accept precirculated papers authored

by those resident and employed in South Africa/Namibia (as well as manuscripts for oral presentation to be read out *in absentia*).

I recommend the above motion to the Executive Committee. I would hope that it would enable the Executive Committee to remain unanimous; I believe that the pragmatic argument is covered by such a resolution, that it honestly highlights the points at issue, and that it may offer just enough to groups A and B above, to grant-giving bodies, and to the International IUPPS to keep the Congress viable.

The following morning we all arrived in time for the 8.40 meeting of the Executive Committee at the British Museum but, early as it was, we had to pass through a peaceful demonstration outside the main gates, a demonstration which I had been half expecting, and we were each handed leaflets headed 'To All Visitors to the British Museum' on one side and 'To All Members of the WAC 1986 National Committee' on the other. Both had, as I discovered much later when I had time to read them properly, clear and sophisticated messages, but they caused Colin Renfrew to pass into a white rage of 'That does it, now I know how to vote; if I was undecided before, my mind is now clear', and so on, as he and I went into the Gents. Derek Hayes and John Evans, however, seemed more amused than disgruntled, while David Wilson and Leslie Alcock were busily reading the leaflets. David was rather pleased that the British Museum was the focus of such attention. My reaction to the picket was, I must admit, a mixture of pride in the student body of Southampton, London and elsewhere, and admiration for those who had managed to organise the Southampton students and local South-ampton archaeologists to be there so early in the morning – I knew that one of my own graduate students, Nick Winder, had played a leading part, that Paul Crake had also been involved and that there had been all sorts of problems about paying for the hire of a minibus.

I had done some lobbying with John before the meeting, and he had agreed to the presence at the National Committee meeting of editors, and likely editors, of post-Congress books, the Student Liaison Officer, Peter Stone, together with Anthony Gaynor of Heritage Projects Ltd and Roger Jones of Allen & Unwin. There were no objections to their presence from the members of the Committee. The main business of the meeting was, of course, to settle how the National Committee meeting should be run, but first came my announcement of the substitution of GLC money for York money, and then Colin Renfrew's *'mea culpa'*. I quote from this part of the Minutes of the meeting:

One member of the Committee, while admitting his previous, and twice repeated, participation in a unanimous Executive view, voiced his disquiet on two issues, and urged the Executive to follow him in reversing its previous unanimous decision or at least to accept his tabled compromise. After considerable discussion of Professor Renfrew's compromise document, and in the light of an alternative suggestion by the National Secretary, Professor Renfrew's suggestion was seen to be unacceptable to the Executive Committee both on ethical grounds and on pragmatic ones (because everyone believed that it would be both unacceptable to all those opposing apartheid and also to all those who were supporting the 'free speech' issue).

The National Secretary reminded the Executive Committee that he had warned them from 1982 onwards that the South African issue was likely to become an explosive one if the Committee was serious in wishing to promote a Congress which had meaningful Third World participation; it was for that reason that the word and concept of 'delegate' had been replaced by individual participation, but it was a fact that no such Congress could take place if South African/Namibian participation was allowed. The National Secretary stressed the point that this was an argument which should be handed back to the International IUPPS Executive.

Discussion made it clear that at least one member of the Executive Committee was no longer able to maintain unanimity even over the question of whether or not the Congress should continue. All other Executive members urged him to refrain from 'threats' of resignation and to attempt to maintain unanimity in the context of a National Commmittee meeting which would engage in open, and no doubt vigorous, debate. It was agreed that individual members of the Executive Committee would not initiate points of principle during the debate of the National Committee unless these points of principle were not raised from the floor; if any member of the Executive Committee chose to 'break ranks', it was agreed that any other member of the Executive Committee would have an equal right to make counter-points of principle during the National Committee debate.

The meeting had been tense and yet open and very respectful. I was suddenly summoned to the phone to be confronted with an example of well-meant irrelevancy, which was quite shattering to me. Jonathan Benthall, the Director of the Royal Anthropological Institute, was suggesting that the whole issue could be resolved if his institution invited Professor Tobias to lecture on the place of archaeology and anthropology in South Africa. With some difficulty I remained cool. I simply pointed out that I thought events had moved too far by now for any such action to be positive or relevant to the issue of principle which was being discussed. We then moved to the room for the National Committee meeting. None of us, I suspect, knew what was likely to happen at it. There were 53 people there, and a great feeling of expectancy. As agreed, Derek Hayes started off the proceedings by explaining the nature of the IUPPS British Congress/WAC in terms of its charity status. He also explained that the National Committee meeting was there to advise the Executive Committee/Board of Directors. John Evans then tried to distinguish the roles of the International IUPPS and the UK Executive Committee. I then reported that the Final Announcement had now been circulated to the 2,718 people who had previously registered, and John gave a summary of the pragmatic reasons only why the ban on South Africa had been imposed.

Then the debate was open to the floor. I summarise the main points of the contributions and discussion in the order that they arose:

– Foreign Office policy is to discourage all contact with South Africa except where such exchange will lead to the ending of apartheid. We should recognise that the moral issue of apartheid is more important than the very important issue of academic freedom.

– If the South Africans participate then others seem to feel unable to participate. The British Executive were not authorised to vary the mandate given by the IUPPS.

– The principles involved in academic freedom are so important that we should be giving a lead to others; the Congress should be cancelled. Otherwise we are on an extremely slippery slope.

– It is the political situation in South Africa that puts us in this situation where we are asked to think about freedom of speech. We are forced into this situation and we have a moral duty to exclude South Africans. The only way to support the opposition to the South African situation and to support the policy of the opposition in South Africa is to boycott contacts of all kinds. To go against the Executive decision now would be a blatant support of South Africa.

– The Congress has done its best to get members from the Third World but bringing in South Africans would mean that Africans would not attend. The only way is to cut off all relationships with South Africa. It would not be fair that a few South African academics come while the rest of South Africa suffer.

– We are playing practical politics. We have to support the Executive Committee.

– Many people have made considerable efforts to make the Congress known all over the globe and to cancel the Congress at this time would be a very retroactive step to take.

– This is the one chance for bringing pressure to bear on the destructive system of apartheid and it would be morally wrong to take any other step.

– It is very difficult to think of the argument only in terms of South Africa – what about other countries? Should we not simply restyle the Congress and have it as a Congress of our own limited company?

– The Executive's decision is the only one which is practical and which corresponds to the maintenance of a stand of principles.

– If we are realistic in the world as it is, then we cannot have total academic freedom of association and therefore need to have as much as possible and we shall be having more if we exclude South Africans.

– The biggest misunderstanding, especially in the States, is that the ban is directed against individual South African prehistorians. We need to give reasons why this decision was taken and we need to emphasise that it is *not* directed against individual South African prehistorians, for there are movements in America to bring pressure on the Congress from the National Science Foundation and the Society for American Archaeology to stop grants. We did not point out as strongly as we might have done the moral arguments. The Americans' misunderstanding is becoming rife.

– We should not really concentrate on the pragmatic reasons for the decision and we also need to dissociate the South African government and policies from our colleagues in South Africa.

– The South African regime has used history and prehistory to legitimise its regime. South Africans working in archaeology undermine that regime and we therefore offer them our moral support and are certainly not going against them as individuals.

– The Executive's decision may help to change the situation in South Africa at this particular time.

– The Executive Committee has issued two statements which were entirely contradictory. One was moral, one was pragmatic. The Executive cannot have its cake and eat it.

– The Executive could not have taken any other decision and it would be most unfortunate and counter-productive to weaken at this stage. It is particularly important that a much clearer statement of the issues be issued to all potential participants in the Congress as soon as possible.

– The decision of the National Committee, which is based on moral grounds, needs to be made clear to all participants.

John Evans then announced the resignations of three of the five Vice Presidents – Glyn Daniel, Stuart Piggott, and J.G.D. Clark – who were not present, and stressed that C.A. Ralegh Radford, a former Secretary to the Organising Committee of the London 1932 Congress and former Director of the British School of Archaeology at Rome, was present at the meeting and that a written suggestion and support had been received from Christopher Hawkes, who had also been one of the 1932 Secretaries. He then read out Anthony Gaynor's letter:

> You will recall that Heritage Projects Limited agreed to make available to the WAC the sum of £150,000 principally to ensure that delegates from third and fourth world countries should be able to attend. Our wish was that the Congress should be available and accessible to all archaeological specialists irrespective of their financial circumstances. We could think of no better way in which we could demonstrate our genuine wish to assist world archaeology.It would appear that the original concept of the Congress as being an apolitical gathering of academics has now radically changed. A political dimension has been introduced. Heritage Projects Limited is a non-political company which made the very substantial sums of money available on the understanding that financial assistance would be made available to all, and not subject to external pressure. Indeed we were not informed of developments in this regard and this has heightened our concern.
>
> I write to inform you that unless the initial conditions of the grant support are maintained, that is to say the free access of all delegates from all countries irrespective of race, colour, creed or political persuasion, then our support will be withdrawn.
>
> In view of the impending decisions to be made by the council of the Congress you should know that unless the pre-conditions are honoured, not only will the £75,000 previously agreed to be paid to you on 1 April 1986 not be forthcoming, but we will require the full repayment of the £75,000 already paid to you.

Mr Gaynor then refused to comment on the question put by Dr Robert Layton:

> Given the apparent contradictions in this letter, and in view of the debate so far, can Mr Gaynor clarify the motivation that led him to encourage participants from Third and Fourth World countries in the first place?

A few other matters were then considered but these were of relatively minor importance. The Executive was keen to reconvene, which it did at 1.20 pm with no one dissenting from the view that the National Committee meeting had been all-but unanimous that the WAC must be preserved. The Executive also decided on a press statement for immediate release and decided that one would be prepared to reflect the National Committee's support, and to show that the pragmatic reasons for the Executive's initial decision were strongly defended on moral grounds by the National Committee. It also left me to continue negotiations with the GLC and with Heritage Projects, all of us having noted with proud astonishment that the National Committee had appeared to brush aside the financial threat from Heritage Projects when making its views known to us.

This National Committee meeting created a feeling of euphoria, for throughout December, session organisers such as Drs John Gledhill and Barbara Bender of the Department of Anthropology, University College London, Peter Stone, the Student Liaison Officer, and individual participants, including many who had been at the meeting, went on the counter-attack and were busy composing letters to their participants and to the press in an attempt to nullify the round-robin appeals by those like Professors Schrire, Leone and Desmond Clark in the USA, and the accusatory articles and letters which continued to appear in *The Times*, and the critical reviews which seemed never-ending in *Nature* and *Science*. Peter Stone also prepared and circulated a Special Student Booklet about the WAC, for we were determined to involve the young and junior as well as the old and established in the proceedings of the Congress. To this end Paul Crake and I operated a 'hardship' grant budget to enable those like Charlotte Cane, of the Field Archaeology Unit of Birmingham University, to attend because of her particular interests in archaeology and education.

Paul Mellars, apparently as morally committed to the ban and as unflappable as ever, came to Southampton to stay the night, discuss eventualities and plan possibilities. He prepared a joint letter with Clive Gamble which was sent out to all participants in the Pleistocene sessions. Later in the month, Paul also came to my Buckinghamshire cottage, for events were moving fast with regard to participants in the Pleistocene sessions, and we still had to find replacements for several of the organisers of specialist meetings. We had our normal frank discussions of all events, and mulled over what the next day's Executive meeting might bring. The next morning I left for London, while Paul remained in the cottage to phone several possible replacement session-organisers, and I returned in the evening to find his notes, which updated me regarding the responses. He had left the cottage at about twelve to return 'to the wife/dog etc', and planned to phone Professor Jim Sackett of the Department of Anthropology of the University of California, who was one of the American members of the IUPPS Permanent Council, on our behalf that evening. It was to be the last time that Paul Mellars and I were to share our normal close relationship.

In Australia, things were moving fast too, for Professor Jack Golson had rung to be brought up to date with events, so that the meeting of the Australian Archaeological Association at the end of November could debate the whole situation. To my enormous relief, the meeting effectively left it to individual members to decide what they wished to do. A motion regretting that the WAC had had to impose the ban was narrowly defeated, and a move to use a stronger term such as 'deplore' got nowhere. Those who voted for the motion included the pragmatists and those totally against the ban. It was an important decision for me personally. I would have considered the WAC without major Australian participation to be only a shadow of what I had planned. Now it was up to my individual Australian friends and colleagues to come and support us. By now the press was really full of discussions about the Congress, ranging from assurances in the *Mail on Sunday* that the Congress would not work, to reports in *Science* which coupled an account of the decision by the Society for American Archaeology to condemn our decision with criticism of me, to the accurate reporting of the current state of affairs in the Council for British Archaeology's *Newsletter*, and on to the extremes of the letters in *The Times*, whose pinnacle must have been reached with a joint letter by the Presidents of The British Academy and The Royal Society which was picked up by the *New Scientist*. According to John Evans the original draft of the President of the Royal Society had been even more censorious! The Presidents wrote:

> We write to express our profound concern at the decision by the British organizing committee of next year's WAC at Southampton to exclude scholars coming from South Africa.
>
> International science and learning are a precious and sensitive area in which political considerations should have no place. It is an indispensable condition of holding an international conference that *bona-fide* scholars should be admitted irrespective of nationality, domicile, or politics.
>
> The committee's deplorable decision may well lead to Britain ceasing to be regarded by bodies such as the International Council of Scientific Unions as a fit place to hold an international congress.
>
> The organisers were forced to their decision by intolerable pressures exerted from three directions. It is bad enough that the City Council of Southampton should subordinate academic to political values; it is far worse that the students of Southampton's university should have leant what weight they have to the suppression of free speech and academic exchange.
>
> Most serious of all are the threats by the local branch of the AUT, a body which should above all things resist attempts to use research and scholarship as levers for a political purpose.
>
> It is of course all the more depressing that a result will be to ban South

African scholars who have striven over the years to resist apartheid at home
only to find themselves confronted by apartheid in Britain.

The Times then did us a service, for it published a rebuttal by Professor
Thurstan Shaw of the two Presidents' view, placed on the page immediately
preceding a letter by the three of our own resigning Vice Presidents who had
failed to appear at the National Committee meeting, despite having said
that one at least would do so. These letters give a good indication of the
nature of the debate.

First, from Professor Thurstan Shaw:

There are few academics who do not espouse the cause of academic freedom of
association and internationalism in scholarship, which a number of your
correspondents (November 13, 16, 18, 21 and 27) have championed with such
righteous passion, in connection with the decision of the British organising
committee of the WAC to exclude South Africans.

However, it is seldom that a moral 'good' is absolute, and it is so in this case,
where the unequivocal support of much more fundamental freedoms for the
majority of the South African population – and the opportunity to give
practical backing to that support – must have precedence over a moral
principle, excellent in normal circumstances, but which must take second
place in the face of the totally immoral principles at present enshrined in the
laws and Constitution of South Africa.

It must be remembered that a decision to admit South Africans in the name
of academic freedom would have been a decision to exclude a far greater
number of scholars from a large number of other African countries – because
in that case their governments would have withdrawn funding, and even
permission, to their nationals to attend.

It is no good adopting a Pontius Pilate attitude and saying, 'That is nothing
to do with us': it is a fact of life today, arising from the depth of African
sentiment on the subject, which has been poorly represented in your columns.

Perhaps I have more right than your other correspondents to speak on this,
since I have not only pursued archaeology in Africa for many years (with my
first excavation there in 1938 and my last one in 1978) but also for many years
lived and taught alongside African academic colleagues.

It is unrealistic for those writing from the dreaming spires of Oxford or the
pinnacles of the ivory towers of the Royal Society and the British Academy to
imagine that total freedom of academic association is possible in the Africa of
today; those with their feet on the ground know that it is not.

If, therefore, we cannot get total academic freedom, we want as much of it
as it is possible to get: on that calculation there is no doubt that we shall get
most, not by admitting a small number of scholars from South Africa, but by
receiving a larger number from other African countries.

It is sad that this means excluding courageous South Africans who, by their
work, have indeed helped to undermine the theoretical basis of apartheid.
Such scholars are, as it were, underground resistance fighters; but in the last
war underground resistance fighters were sometimes killed by the British and
American bombs supporting them.

Second, from Professors Grahame Clark, Glyn Daniel, and Stuart Piggott:

We have separately and independently resigned as vice-presidents of the WAC due to meet next year at Southampton University. We are unable to share the notion that delegates to a congress ostensibly concerned with the prehistory and protohistory of man should be limited by the political ideologies of the states to which they happen to belong.

We deeply resent the pressures brought to bear on the distinguished scholars forming the executive committee and deplore the fact that these have apparently been brought to bear in the context of a university supported by public funds.

Despite this sort of press coverage, and the growing number of resignation letters (many from Americans who pointedly marked out copies to Professor Carmel Schrire) which reiterated, some with a considerable degree of venom, several of the points already reviewed in this chapter, the euphoria did not abate, and, indeed, it was transformed into dogged determination to succeed.

The National Committee meeting of November had clearly also inspired John Evans for he had written the required Executive statement by himself in the form of the following President's letter, which I found an outstanding statement, and which was sent to all 2,718 registered participants:

The ban on participants from South Africa and Namibia at the WAC 1986 has naturally aroused mixed reactions and led to the receipt of much correspondence. I am concerned that there seems to be a fairly widespread misconception that it is aimed personally at the individuals affected by it. This is not so, as was made clear in the letters which the National Secretary sent to those concerned, and elsewhere. We are well aware that individual South African archaeologists have been among the outspoken critics of apartheid, and that collectively they have been instrumental in dispelling the mythology which is used in support of it. We value them as colleagues and are distressed and unhappy at having to exclude them on this occasion. The ban has been accepted by us only on the basis that it is a protest against the explicitly racialist political system in South Africa and the inequitable society it has created, not against individuals.

It has also been queried why we did not cancel the Congress rather than bow to pressure, and there have been a few calls for us to do this. We did, of course, consider this alternative. One major reason for rejecting it was that, with the encouragement of the IUPPS, we had made strenuous efforts to attract truly world-wide participation, and these seem likely to be notably successful. We feel that this made it exceptionally important to ensure that the Congress should be able to take place and fulfil these expectations. We felt that it would still have great value and, while regretting the denial of access to scholars of South Africa and Namibia, we recognised that their presence, on this occasion, could lead to the absence of many other countries.

On the 20th November we explained our decision to a meeting of the United Kingdom National Committee and took their advice. This well-attended meeting of over 50 people not only overwhelmingly supported our decision, but many members went beyond the UK Executive's position of acceptance under duress and felt that the ban was also morally justifiable. In reaffirming our earlier decision, following that meeting, we were therefore strengthened in our view that we had correctly appraised the state of feeling among people in this country, and that the decision we took was the appropriate one in the circumstances, however distasteful in its interference with the freedom of academic interchange between individual scholars.I hope that in the light of what I have said above, you will feel able to participate in the Congress.

The Executive meeting in November had ended with the clear decision that John Evans would immediately telephone Secretary-General Nenquin and, as President, summon an International IUPPS Executive Committee meeting for 13 December at 9.30 am at the British Museum and that, at that meeting, the WAC Executive would be invited as observers in order to fully brief the International Committee. Our UK Executive Committee was to meet again formally later on the same day.

4. The Build-up to Paris

It is difficult to conceive how such clear instructions could have been bungled to the extent that they were. Had someone other than John Evans been President of the IUPPS at that time it is unlikely that the international dimensions of the conflict would have developed in a similar way. Much as I had sympathy with him on many occasions the fact is that he was in a position of high authority in England with regard to learned societies, in control of grant-giving committees, and director of a huge archaeological Institute. It is therefore difficult to believe that he was simply not aware of his role at this time. John's struggle to come to terms with his position was later revealed in his television interview on *Heart of the Matter* (Chapter 10).

There was one occasion when it was very easy to feel sympathy for John Evans. This concerned his Presidency of the Society of Antiquaries of London. This is the same body which had decided in 1983 to contribute £2,500 to the WAC each year for the four years 1984-1987. I had been elected a Fellow of the Society of Antiquaries in April 1970.

Before one of our Executive Committee meetings John, David, and Colin had been discussing what might happen at the Society's next meeting, for the ban on South Africa/Namibia had been put on the agenda. I took very little notice of the part of the conversation that I overheard, but when I dined with John one evening in November 1985 I discovered that almost all his concentration and concern was focused on his future role if the Council of the Antiquaries, to which the matter had been referred, were not to vote in our favour. Whatever else we had to discuss that evening always came back to John's acute misery about the Antiquaries. He, as President, was going to press the Society's Council members either to condone our difficult decision as the correct one or to say it had been wrong and therefore cancel their financial support for us. He would threaten to resign from the Society unless it took the former course of action.

I was acutely worried by all this for we could ill-afford to lose John Evans' figurehead at this point, and I had the horrible feeling that the Antiquaries meant more to him than did either the Third World participation in the WAC or even the South Africa issue.

Council of the Society of Antiquaries met on 12 December and, as recounted to our Executive Committee meeting, the next day, by John Evans himself, he made his promised speech and then vacated the Chair, and the room, and went to sit in the Library. In his absence, therefore, 'the eventual decision, by a majority vote was that the following resolution should be passed: The Council of the Society of Antiquaries deplores the exclusion of South African participants from the WAC 1986, since this contravenes the principle of the free interchange of ideas. Although it accepts that this action of the Executive Committee of the Congress was taken unwillingly and under duress, and solely in order to avoid the cancellation of the Congress, it has decided to withdraw the Society's name from the list of sponsors of the Congress and to make no further financial contributions. The Society's future support of such international events will be conditional upon an undertaking by the organisers that the principle of the free interchange of ideas will not be contravened'. None of us could believe our ears. To vacate the Chair could have been considered a piece of English Gentleman's fair play, but to leave the room during all the subsequent discussion , and to be absent from the vote was simply suicidal.

The well-being of our Chairman was terribly important, and I therefore took action the next day. By dint of a day and evening telephone marathon by Paul Crake, who had been taken on full time by the WAC since May, twenty signatures had been obtained for a letter addressed to Evans as President of the Antiquaries. This letter, which requested that an Extraordinary Meeting of the Society should be called prior to any implementation of Council's recent decision, was hand-delivered to the resumed Antiquaries Council meeting of 19 December.

Under the Chairmanship of the Vice President, Professor John Coles from Colin Renfrew's Department, who had been against the holding of the Congress right from the beginning, and who was to spend the next months encouraging organisations to withdraw their support from the WAC (see page 93), 'it was agreed that [our request for an Extraordinary Meeting of the Society] was premature as no formal notification of Council's decision had yet been made to the interested parties, and to the Fellowship'. As matters developed, John Evans never did have to relinquish his Presidency for, by the time that the Society's General Secretary was willing to have the matter considered again in February, he had resigned from the WAC.

Before this episode had finished unfolding, the Executive Committee had indeed met, as agreed, on Friday 13 December, but not in the context of a briefing of the International IUPPS Executive; for our President had apparently not done what he had previously agreed to and there was no meeting of the International IUPPS Executive Committee on that day.

It was almost impossible at the time to make much sense of what had transpired between the two members of the International IUPPS Bureau, President Evans and Secretary-General Nenquin. It appears that John Evans had indeed talked to Jacques Nenquin the day after the November Executive meeting and had agreed with him that 13 December was too early a date to make the necessary arrangements for an International Executive Committee meeting. Instead, they had agreed on 10 January 1986 at the British Museum. Meanwhile, also unknown to us at the time, Professor

Henry de Lumley, who had been the National Secretary of the 1976 IUPPS Congress in Nice, but was not a voting member of the IUPPS International Executive Committee, had written to Jacques Nenquin requesting an immediate meeting of the International Executive Committee. This letter was sent to all members of the International Executive Committee except John Evans and me. It both referred to the ease with which he had accommodated South Africans, Senegalese, Israelis and Algerians at Nice in 1976, and threatened to call an independent meeting of interested prehistorians in Paris if Nenquin did not call the Executive together. By 2 December, President John Evans had apparently agreed to a different place for the IUPPS meeting – Paris instead of London – and possible also to a change of date, to January 17. When David Wilson heard this, he exploded in writing:

> I am entirely distressed to hear that the meeting of the Executive Committee of the IUPPS has been moved to Paris. It is, I am sure, a great tactical error.
>
> In the first instance, it is much better to have such a meeting on your own ground so that you are host and people have to be less rude. As President you can summmon the meeting wherever you wish and I think you ought to summon it in London. Tell Nenquin to jump in the lake.
>
> Secondly, I am sure that the day should be set so that the whole National Executive can appear before the Executive Committee of the IUPPS and you as President have the power to invite them to do so. The 17th January is a date on which both Colin and I are in Athens and for my part I cannot possibly move that date. I would therefore urge you to call the meeting towards the end of January at a date convenient to Colin, you, Peter, and myself, that the meeting be held in London and that you summon us to appear to give evidence to the Committee. Nenquin is the paid Secretary of the Institute, he is not the boss, you are, and I think that you are on a hiding to nothing if you do it on foreign ground, Paris is far from being neutral territory.

Apparently shifted by this blast, as well as by telephone calls of dismay from at least Colin, John Evans returned to his original position and wrote to Secretary-General Nenquin:

> ... I must repeat the view which I expressed to you in our earlier telephone conversations that this meeting ought to take place in London. If the Comité Executif is really going to make a serious investigation of this matter, it is most important that they should hear the views of *all* members of our Executive Committee. If the meeting is here, those who are not members of the Comité Executif can be invited in for this purpose, and asked to leave again while a decision is debated. I regard this as most essential if the Comité Executif is to be properly informed for its deliberations.

What is quite remarkable about this incident is the handwritten covering letter which John Evans wrote to his friend Jacques Nenquin, for it was not in any way influenced by the Executive, and entirely conforms to what he said when banning the South Africans (page 85) and totally contradicts what he was later to claim on television (page 223). He wrote, inter alia:

> I quite realise that there is a lot of feeling about the exclusion of the South Africans. But there are also many people who realise that we must nevertheless face the reality of widespread feeling in favour of even academic boycott ... I believe that one cannot just brush this aside by re-affirming the right of freedom of academic association. It is going to be with us for a long time to come, unless the South African government changes its policy.

Given Jacques Nenquin's later claim to be 'in total agreement ... that the South Africa apartheid regime is hateful, and unspeakably degrading [and] that there [should be] no misunderstanding where my sympathies lie', John no doubt hoped that his letter would have some effect. As far as I know Jacques Nenquin never responded at all.

John Evans continued his letter to him:

> If we are to be a World Congress rather than a basically European one we shall have to reckon with the feelings of the other non-European countries on the Permanent Council, and maybe eventually of some European ones too! At all events, I think the Comité Executif should take this matter seriously, and try to find out from our UK Committee (who after all are responsible people, not naughty schoolboys) as much as they can of the details of the situation before taking any decision.

By the time our Executive Committee meeting took place on December 13, matters had gone one stage worse. Professor de Lumley had now written direct to me and all other members of the International Executive Committee, as host of the proposed 17 January meeting, saying that the main business of the day would be to decide what action to take 'in the face of the unacceptable decision taken unilaterally by the Organising Committee of the 11th UISPP Congress', and expressing the hope that 'wisdom and the sense of international responsibility would be brought to bear at the meeting and that important decisions would be taken'. Nothing could have been more certain to infuriate Colin Renfrew and David Wilson than this action by someone for whom they in any case had little respect and who, in addition, was not even a full member of the International IUPPS Executive Committee. Furiously they took charge of our Executive meeting, employing legalisms as well as openly revealing their contempt for the International Executive Committee. Although I had every sympathy for their mood I myself was anxiously aware of the numbers of potential voters which the Executive controlled, at least from Western Europe, and I could vividly imagine the response which our Executive's suggested missive would evoke. I also feared that Colin and David might be underestimating the skill of European, and particularly Jacques Nenquin's, powers of manipulation.

Our Executive agreed that the President should request the Secretary-General to call a meeting of the International Executive Committee in Ghent, Belgium, which was the official seat of the IUPPS Bureau, on 18 or

27 February, dates chosen to allow sufficient time for Third World members to attend. The President was to invite the UK Executive to attend as observers 'in order to assist the International Executive to reach a fully informed decision'. Our Executive Committee was equally uncompromising about the Nenquin/de Lumley proposed meeting for 17 January. The Minutes record that if it did take place 'despite being unconstitutional, the President will not attend. The National Secretary will however represent the WAC Executive and will attend the meeting with a lawyer'. For the first time we also looked quite closely at the legalities of the IUPPS Statutes and accepted Colin's view that the venues of a IUPPS Congress could only be decided upon by the IUPPS's Permanent Council (not by its Executive Committee). We decided that if the International Executive Committee did decide to throw us out, the President should exercise his right to call a special meeting of the Permanent Council and that he should do so in a Third World country 'in view of the cost of travelling to such a meeting'.

No one was sure that John Evans would do what he had just agreed to do. Caroline had to take down endless versions of the proposed telex and then find Nenquin's telex number, and the President sent the 600 word telex there and then. The telex ended:

> In my view any meeting held in Paris on 17 January would not be a properly constituted meeting of the Comité Executif.

A few days later a French version of the same long telex was sent to all members of the International IUPPS Executive Committee.

The rest of the Committee meeting was quickly over. It was decided to obtain legal advice on the IUPPS Statutes. It was simply noted that finance from York was almost certain to be withdrawn and I described the meeting that I had had the day before with the GLC, and reported that money was still a possibility, but now dependent on the legal situation regarding the GLC after the date of its proposed abolition. Some of the implications of putting back the date for the receipt of precirculated papers were considered. While this had been going on Colin had been drafting an answer to a further letter from Jacques Nenquin, the first mention of IPCHS's future role in the whole affair. John first lost the draft for several days but then did indeed sign and send it off – it read in part:

> The statement by ICPHS in its booklet that 'ICPHS is subject to no ideology', like any absolute statement does not have a universal application in at least one field. For the WAC, if truly international, must express itself firmly as against *apartheid*. We do indeed wish to discuss our difficulties with you and the IUPPS Executive. To quote p.7 of the ICPHS booklet: 'This of course requires due consideration and friendly understanding.' This is not an easy matter, and the UK Executive, if I may say so, is concerned that you, as Secretary-General, and some of the Executive Committee, appear to have taken a firm position without full discussion with us of the problems.

Towards the end of this meeting my mind, as it always had to and did, started to move forwards to the next stage, for I did not really think that we would be able to avoid the Paris 17 January meeting. Over the weekend I was beginning to think out the strategies for such a meeting, but by Monday when I went back to London to assist with the translation into French of the telex to Nenquin and the Executive, everything was becoming more obscure regarding the IUPPS Executive Committee meeting, for Secretary-General Nenquin now informed everyone that letters from him of 22 November to all members of the Executive had been 'delayed in the post'. In that letter, of which he now sent everyone copies, he stated that the President had agreed to the meeting on 17 January in Paris, called by five duly-appointed voting members of the IUPPS Executive Committee who were asking for this meeting on that date (in accordance with the Statutes). So far the President had claimed that he had never agreed with Nenquin to the 17 January date, wherever the place of the meeting, but now he admitted to me that perhaps he had also agreed to the date.

There was nothing to do but to accept that both the President and I should go to the Paris meeting and our Executive Committee reluctantly had to change its previous decision and agree to this, each of us stressing that the reason for the President to attend was so that, if everything went against us, he would summon a special meeting of the Permanent Council. A £66 telegram was dispatched by the President, having been drafted by me, agreeing to the Paris meeting.

At that time, John Evans was in possession of another communication from Jacques Nenquin which he did not choose to tell me about. In this letter of 5 December Professor Nenquin started by complaining that the National Committee's November press release made no mention of his own protest against the ban on South Africa, continued by claiming that he was receiving telephone calls and letters all the time 'all protesting against the ban, from South Africa of course, but also from the United States, from Sweden, Germany, Switzerland, Holland, France, etc' – all but one from the countries we had expected! He then complained that in the Final Announcement the 'provisional *academic* calendar' did not mention the dates of the IUPPS Executive and Permanent Council meetings, and he continued:

> ... the fact that the[ir] programme and theme have been published exclusively in English is bound to provoke remarks, again ...

The letter also included a somewhat personal attack:

> One gets the impression, more and more, that Peter wants to go it alone, and is pushing us as far as he dares. He certainly seems to have split the Union wide open, from what I hear, and this is very bad indeed. I am personally very unhappy about this, especially as I have your country so very much to thank for, and my admiration for England and things British amounts – so my friends tell me – almost to Anglomania!

Nothing genial here, and he appeared to be totally unaware of the existence of the points of principle at issue in the worldwide discussions of the ban.

When I eventually saw this letter I wrote to John saying:

> I am deeply shocked by his letter which certainly changes my 'view' of him as a satisfactory Secretary-General!
>
> Have you ever answered him? If so, could I have a copy? If not, could I suggest that you do so, pointing out at least that his comments ... refer to British Executive Committee decisions (even the amount of French used in the Final Announcement!).

John said that he would answer it. But if he did, he never sent me a copy of his answer.

The so-called break at Christmas and New Year was the time for concentrated work in preparation for the Paris meeting. Very fortunately for me David Bellos came to the cottage and to Southampton during this period, and I was able to get him so involved that he agreed to act as interpreter for us, should he be needed in Paris. There were endless people who had to be brought up to date by telephone and in person and, most important of all, Paul Crake and I set out to establish which international academic organisations had policies about South African participation in their affairs. We discovered that few, except those explicitly African in character, had imposed their own bans. However, what had been happening was that such academic international organisations had evaded the issue by choosing locations for their meetings in countries whose governments had banned South African contacts. Very significantly indeed, ICPHS itself had allowed such meetings of its own constituent members. What was just as revealing, and potentially even more significant, was that Secretary-General d'Ormesson of ICPHS had written to Secretary-General Nenquin of IUPPS that at its meeting a little more than a month before in Istanbul, ICPHS had formulated its policy that:

> No South African shall play a part in the decision-making structures of constituent members of ICPHS.

Meanwhile some of the press coverage was building to an apparent climax, for reporters sensed that that was what the Paris meeting would be. *Nature* argued that what we had done was 'not cricket' and urged us to cut our losses and run. *The Times* pursued us right up to the date of the Paris meeting by publishing another letter from four academics, 'all from Christ Church Oxford', led by Martin Biddle and John Coles, who urged all archaeologists to resign from the Congress in order not to subordinate scholarship to politics. A few resignations were in fact still coming in, from the USA, Belgium, Switzerland and France, almost all referring to the leads given by Professor Schrire or others. There was also bad news from the Wenner-Gren Foundation for Anthropological Research, of which I had always secretly had high hopes. The letter received by me talked of 'a very trendy kind of censorship' and announced that there would be no assistance until 'participation in the meetings were unrestricted'.

We needed to ignore these pressures and concentrate instead on our second strand of actions which needed time and extra money from somewhere and concerned the voting members of the International Executive Committee. Was there a way to win the Paris battle by forcing a vote? Caroline and I settled down to find out from letters, personal contacts of the members, and direct telephone calls to them, but first I had to get help. I pointed out most strongly to both the City of Southampton and Anti-Apartheid that their apparent victory on the South African stand would be enormously reduced if participants failed to turn up to the Congress because it was no longer the XIth Congress of IUPPS. Forcibly it dawned on them that they had everything to win by trying to ensure that the Paris meeting did not expel the WAC. I was assured that letters would be written to appropriate people, both from the ANC and the French organisation 'Mouvement contre le racisme et pour l'amitié entre les peuples' and even to governments of the countries that concerned me, and I was told by Alan Whitehead not to worry about the costs of telephone calls or travel involved in trying to get Third World Executive members to the Paris meeting.

The telephones burned hot day and night (because of time differences). Equally urgent was to get the legal advice already authorised by the Executive because, despite Jacques Nenquin's bland remarks in Madrid (page 51), a vote might be desperately needed in Paris. And if there was a vote, who under the Statutes had the right to vote? The Statutes were self-contradictory about my right to vote as National Secretary, and obscure about the President's. They were, however, unambiguous that the Secretary-General did not have a vote. The Statutes were totally silent about proxy voting or written votes. Gradually the legal opinions came in; there was no doubt that I had the vote and almost no doubt that John Evans could insist that he also had the right to vote. There was much less certainty about proxies, and this whole situation was made even more obscure when we discovered that it was not even clear whether the IUPPS Statutes should be considered to operate under French or Belgian law.

As far as we could guess, and from copies of letters, there seemed little real point in trying to contact the Western Europeans, an impression quickly confirmed by telephone calls, although it was almost inconceivable that Scandinavia could be against such a ban. But what about Yugoslavia and the USSR, both of which had strong anti-apartheid commitment? Were their representatives coming to Paris, and which way would they vote? Telephone calls by David Bellos from my cottage to Moscow revealed the situation very clearly – Professor B. Rybakov of the Institute of Archaeology in Moscow was too busy to attend but he totally supported our boycott of South African/Namibian participation and would telegram Secretary-General Nenquin to record his opinion. Yugoslavia was much more of a problem for of the three members on the Permanent Council, Professor M. Garasanin, the Yugoslav on the Executive Committee, happened to be the only one who might perhaps vote against the ban. The other Yugoslavs were supposed to talk to Professor Garasanin, and the ANC also wrote to him. In the event he did not arrive in Paris.

India is a country with a splendid anti-apartheid record and one which had been taking especially strong action since the South African State of Emergency. However, I knew Professor Asok Ghosh of the Department of Anthropology, Calcutta University, of old, and was less than surprised that a letter to me showed his stance to be equivocal. We tried to reach him by telephone and via other Indian archaeologists, and the ANC tried also, but to no avail. Robert Knox spent hours on the telephone trying to get hold of Professor Ghosh at a conference which he was thought to be attending and via the Director General of Archaeology in India. Reports which came back suggested that Asok Ghosh might indeed vote against the ban. In the event he did not attend the Paris meeting.

I knew nothing at all about Professor J. Lorenzo of the Department of Prehistory in Moneda, Mexico, who had been the National Secretary of the Mexico Congress in 1981, but it was difficult to believe that Mexico could be against the ban and indeed John Gledhill, organiser of the session on 'Violence, coercion and consent', reported great support for the ban from the Mexican archaeologists with whom he was in contact. Robert Knox also had some Mexican contacts and we were worried by their reports that Professor Lorenzo was an individualist. In the end, John Evans, who was at this stage as keen as I was to 'win' the forthcoming battle in Paris, and who knew Lorenzo, rang him only to discover that he was determined to vote against the ban and had every intention of attending the Paris meeting. In the event he also did not materialise in Paris – maybe he had been convinced by a letter from the ANC or, as a result of a number of telephone calls to the British Ambassador in Mexico, by a word from his Foreign Minister!

From the reactions to the ban by my British colleagues, I knew that opinions on the South Africa apartheid issue crossed all normal political allegiances and I had learned how difficult it was to predict anybody's stance, however well one knew them in other contexts. But the review to date was almost unbelievable, for it was as if the IUPPS International Executive Committee consisted of almost the only archaeologist in each of the countries concerned who might not support the ban.

Robert Knox had told me that Professor A.J. Dani from Pakistan was probably retired, if still alive, and that there was little point trying him. By the time I discovered that it was much easier to ring Islamabad than anywhere in India, Professor Dani had just left for Bangkok. We failed to track him down there, despite strenuous efforts, but caught him on his return to Pakistan on 11 January as he was on the point of leaving for a conference in India the next day. He seriously considered trying to change all his arrangements but in the end said he could not possibly manage it, but he did send a telegram of support for the ban. He was not the first to say that he had not yet received any notification of the 17 January meeting in Paris!

I knew of Professor Cheikh Anta Diop's work in Senegal for he was in charge of the only Radiocarbon dating laboratory in Africa, and he held extreme views about diffusion from ancient Egypt. I did not know that it was easy to ring Senegal whereas it was almost impossible to get through to Nigeria. Professor Thurstan Shaw and Dr Alex Okpoko, who joined John Alexander to organise the session on 'Iron-Using Peoples in Sub-Saharan Africa' (which he himself had taken over from David Phillipson), both spoke to Professor Diop in the hope that he would be able to come to Paris after a visit to Cameroon. He was about to leave on the day that we rang, having just returned from Paris. He was totally in favour of the ban and authorised us to repeat this as his firm view in case he could not get permission to travel overseas again so soon after his arrival back in Senegal. In the event he could not get the permission, and he spoke on the telephone to President John Evans in Paris to reiterate his support of the ban and his fury that notification of the Paris meeting had reached him only on that day.

On 13 January the University term had begun again with the welcome reappearance of Peter Gathercole to do some of my teaching. We had by now taken on a new full-time person in the Congress office, Aileen Ross, who had been employed in Peter Stone's Archaeology and Education MSC team for the previous year, whose broad Scottish accent and total cheek was to keep me relatively sane up to, and during, the Congress itself. Ail started on the day that, again, I had to go up to London, not only for further talks with John Evans, but to confront the Annual General Meeting of the Council for British Archaeology, which had previously supported the WAC by establishing six bursaries for students and amateur archaeologists to attend the Congress. It was now faced with a motion from Martin Biddle, author of one of the previous letters to *The Times*, and Professor John Coles, who had long been opposed to the ban, that it should withdraw its support from the WAC. After a lengthy and lively debate which, apart from Biddle's tone, was open and friendly, the Biddle/Coles motion was lost (34 to 29), much to my pleasure, for it gave relief to the CBA's Director, Henry Cleere, who was a session organiser. Meanwhile, there was news from the GLC for the long awaited letter arrived from Mr Bush, saying:

> We have been able to establish that there is a legal route for the GLC to assist this Congress by using our power to promote conferences in London. I have asked for the preparatory work to be undertaken, but ... we have a major problem. With abolition now less than three months away, staff numbers are dropping fast, morale is low and the need to deliver a great deal in a very short space of time is such that it is impossible to rush this report through.
>
> The best that we can hope for (and I stress hope) would be for the absolutely

key legal work to be done in the last two weeks of February with the report being taken to committee in very early March. It is literally impossible for us to do that legal work before then.

It may be that even this timetable cannot be adhered to, as the situation is likely to continue to deteriorate. However, we do intend to seek to keep this project alive because of the importance we attach to it.

I am sorry I can't be more optimistic.

As all this information was coming in, so I started to get messages about the possible role of Professor Jim Sackett of the USA. Jim Sackett was said to be taking his position seriously and to have spent considerable time on the telephone to Colin Renfrew and others in England, and also to his colleagues in the States. According to Colin, Professor Sackett, though 'not well disposed to our position', might 'be open to argument'. For reasons obscure to me, but presumably based on the sorts of rumour and abuse in many of the letters received by me, I was not supposed to know anything about Professor Sackett's interest in meeting a group of British archaeologists as he passed through London on his way to the Paris meeting. Nevertheless, I did know all about it and in fact advised on which of 'our' group should spend time with him. I urged that it should be made up of Paul Mellars, Steve Shennan, David Harris, and Thurstan Shaw for all were organisers of academic sessions, very reasonable and respected archaeologists, and all persons of integrity. All reported back more or less negatively, for Jim Sackett had merely reiterated how sad the situation was, and had apparently produced a set of unrealistic so-called compromises (page 108), but at least he was said to be a reasonable person who was prepared to listen to other views. I was told that he was completely out of touch with Third World conditions and appeared unable to realize that the American furore against the ban would at least be matched by the withdrawal of Third World participants if the ban was removed. It was possible that Professor Sackett might meet me in Paris before the meeting began as he had apparently been reassured by 'our' group that I was not, after all, a far-left communist extremist!

As if on cue, Professor Carmel Schrire descended on Southampton and succeeded in upsetting not only Peter Stone, the Student Liaison Officer, who met her with Paul Crake, but also Councillor Whitehead who described her as the rudest person he had ever met in his life. Carmel's approach with me was much more demure, but, even so, it cut no ice at all as I had known her for many years. It was an unhappy occasion and I remember suggesting to her that it might be best that she left. But before she left she pointed out that I must have wanted, at some level, to accept the anti-apartheid line, otherwise I would have stood out against the pressures even if it had meant a disrupted Congress. To the extent that we could have settled for just another Western European IUPPS Congress and could have had participants escorted in by police, if necessary, she must have been right. I have never heard from Carmel since, although I did, dutifully, send her the factual information which she had demanded – despite her role in lobbying against the Congress.

While all this was going on, Paul Crake had gone to the airport to collect the one Third World voting member of the IUPPS Executive Committee who was definitely coming to Paris, Professor Richard Nunoo of Ghana. The plan was that Paul would drive him to see Thurstan Shaw in Cambridge so that he could be well briefed by someone he had known for years, before flying to Paris with John Evans, Caroline and myself. But, as Paul discovered belatedly in Cambridge, Richard, who reported that he had not received any notification of the Paris meeting from Secretary-General Nenquin and had not been thinking of leaving Ghana before we had reached him just in time by telephone, had not been able to get a French visa in Accra. The arrangements were switched and it was decided that Paul would drive to London with Professor Nunoo to get the visa early in the morning and then meet us at the airport.

5. Western European Manipulation and Presidential Timidity

Caroline and I flew to Paris the next day, without Professor Nunoo because, although he and Paul had been both to the Ghanaian Embassy and to the French visa office, they were still without a visa. They found us at the airport but decided to return to London for one last try, rather than risk getting on to the plane and being refused entry on arrival in Paris. We were also without John Evans for he had gone to Paris a day earlier, in order to meet with Professor Nenquin, and later was said to have called on Mr Palmer of Legal and General on his way to the airport. Caroline and I were staggering under the weight of the mass of files which we thought might conceivably be needed. We were met at Charles de Gaulle Airport by David Bellos, who had flown in direct from Manchester. The three of us took a taxi to the hotel, eager to discover what John Evans had found out from his meeting with Secretary-General Nenquin, but there were no messages awaiting – nothing from him at all. We then went out to eat, and discussed what the next day might bring.

The following morning it had been arranged for Professor Jim Sackett, the American member of the International Executive Committee, to join me for breakfast. I had been expecting a lot from this breakfast meeting, but my hopes were soon dashed. Though he appeared to be pleasant enough he made no significant contribution either to the debate or towards deciding what should happen at the meeting, which was steadily growing nearer and nearer. Although he stressed that he was against apartheid, and indeed said that his son was at that very moment walking the streets of Los Angeles with anti-apartheid placards, his only contribution was that there must be a 'compromise position', but when asked what that position might be, he simply repeated what we had already heard from him, through other people. When all the shortcomings and impracticalities of his suggestions were pointed out to him, he became silent on that subject and switched to an attack on the supposedly anti-American nature of the IUPPS International Executive Committee from which he had apparently wished to resign several years previously. I was by now more or less convinced that he would be ineffectual at the meeting and, if it came to a vote for or against us, would be against us.

Meanwhile Caroline had been in contact with Paul and Professor Nunoo, who was still in London and just about to make his last effort to get a visa to enter France in time for the meeting. It was arranged that if all else failed he would ring through to the meeting room from London later in the morning. Caroline had also managed to find John Evans and eventually we managed to get him to speak on the telephone to Professor Diop in Senegal, who repeated what he had said from the beginning – that he was in favour of the ban on South African/Namibian participants, and that it was disgraceful that such short notice of the Paris meeting had been given to Third World members of the International Executive Committee.

John Evans then told us that, at his meeting the day before, Jacques Nenquin had shown him a copy of a letter sent to all members of the International Executive Committee, in English and French, from the Southampton Local AUT. The letter urged the Committee to 'consider most seriously the important moral issues involved in this debate, and to give (their) support to the courageous stand taken by the British Executive Committee'. John Evans also showed us, with evident glee, a telegram that had been waiting at the hotel from the 'Mouvement contre le racisme et pour l'amitié entre les peuples', urging the Executive to support the British ban on South Africa/Namibia, and two other telegrams which had reached him in England, one from the French equivalent of the AUT also supporting our stand, and the other from the Irish Federation of University Teachers which referred to the United Nations' policy and urged the non-attendance of South Africans at the Congress.

As we left for the meeting I tried to determine how he, as President, intended to handle the meeting. The last thing I reminded him, as we entered the famous old Institute of Human Palaeontology, was of the legal advice we had received that if things went badly, he, as President, could call a special meeting of the Permanent Council and that that was what the British Executive Committee expected him to do. I received no clear response from him.

Inside we met Professor Henry de Lumley, Head of the Institute (and author of the letter which had made members of the British Executive Committee so angry). He led us to where members of the International Executive Committee were collected. The first person I caught sight of in the crowd was the South African archaeologist Professor Philip Tobias (what *was* *he* doing here?), and the second, Professor Desmond Clark, the outspoken and vehement critic of ours, whom I had not seen for some fifteen years. Soon we were all ushered towards the meeting room, and I noticed that John Evans was talking to the Secretary-General and was clearly agitated. He had warned us that Secretary-General Nenquin was going to refuse to allow the presence of Caroline and David Bellos at the meeting. I then witnessed one of the only two attempts by the President to exercise his statutory authority, as John Evans attempted to argue that Caroline was only there to help me find things in the numerous files (if that should become necessary), and that Professor Bellos was there only as interpreter and could be used by anyone who needed such assistance. Secretary-General Nenquin refused to give ground, and I then questioned his right to challenge the President on these matters since the Secretary-General was, after all, only the junior half of the Bureau. Professor Nenquin remained unbudging except to say that if an interpreter was needed there was one available in the Institute. I asked where he or she was, but received no reply. John Evans had clearly given up the argument and, as people passed us on the way to the meeting room, I pulled Professor Henry de Lumley towards us and said:

> The Secretary-General is trying to refuse entry to the meeting of both my secretary and the interpreter whom the President himself had asked me [on 10 January] to bring to the meeting.

De Lumley too seemed upset, and tried to reason with the Secretary-General, but to no avail. Professor Nenquin argued that the Statutes made no allowance for the presence at meetings of anyone who was not a member of the Executive Committee. I pointed out that Caroline had been at the Madrid meeting throughout its deliberations in the previous year. I turned to the President expecting him to support my requests but he seemed unwilling to confront the Secretary-General and made no ruling. Very reluctantly I agreed to Professor de Lumley's suggestion that Caroline should stay in a nearby room, and that she could be called in if I needed assistance in finding materials from within her filing system. The battle over the interpreter continued (David Bellos having already gone into the meeting room). Even Professor Evans pointed out that to conform to the Statutes everyone had to communicate in French, and that this would not be possible if any member did not speak French and if there was no interpreter. I was also arguing the same case, especially for those Third Worlders like Professor Nunoo who knew no French at all, and who (I still hoped!) had come so far and with such trouble to attend the meeting. It was left to the Committee itself to decide this issue.

This whole unpleasant affair was useful in one way, for it alerted me, and should have alerted the President, to the lengths that the Secretary-General was prepared to go in order to have things his own way. I was reminded forcibly of the Madrid meeting the previous year, when remarks by John Evans and myself that English was at least as widespread as French in the 1980s, and that the Statutes were unnecessarily out-of-date in insisting on French usage only, were met by two classic remarks from the Secretary-General. The first was that all UNESCO/ICPHS organisations had to opt for one official language only (which is in fact untrue) in order to avoid unnecesary arguments; the second, much more significant, was that there was a IUPPS tradition not to vote on any matters, even on issues such as language (a ludicrous situation given that the rules about voting are about the only area of the Statutes which are quite precise). The Madrid discussion had also been heated, with Secretary-General Nenquin receiving explicit support from the French and Spanish members of the Committee.

His obsession with this language question – he himself is marvellously fluent in English and, of course, French – had led to an absurd interchange of letters with John Evans – who also speaks good French – about where and when the special Executive meeting should take place. In December Secretary-General Nenquin accompanied an official letter in French to his friend Professor Evans with the following remark, 'Sorry about the French, but I'm afraid in the present circumstances one has to be formalistic about this – which is silly', to which John Evans replied in English with an accompanying note saying, 'I enclose a reply to your two letters – I'm afraid it's in English, but hope that will be OK. I hadn't time to put it into French.' Silly, certainly, but also an example of pettifogging bureaucracy.

An unfortunate result of the first skirmish about the secretary and the interpreter at the present meeting was that I missed the beginning of the meeting, for by the time I had found Caroline her nearby room, and had asked her to try to find out about Professor Nunoo's movements, the meeting had begun, and I arrived to find Professor Evans seated as President, but with the Secretary-General obviously running the meeting. As I nodded greetings to old friends on the Executive Committee, and tried desperately to find papers in Caroline's files (which, of course, I had not inspected before as I had assumed she would be with me), I saw that Professor Desmond Clark (though not Professor Tobias) was seated at the table, as well as several others I had not seen before and was not introduced to.

The debate about the interpreter was already underway. Once Professor Desmond Clark (who, it turned out, would otherwise have had great difficulty in communicating throughout the meeting) had agreed that David Bellos should be allowed to stay, even Secretary-General Nenquin had to give way, albeit with rather bad grace. David was instructed to interpret only, without giving his opinions, and told that matters were confidential. He pointed out that he was a professional interpreter, and therefore of course knew all the rules. He explained the various ways that translations could be carried out – by leaving gaps for his translations to be heard by all, or by a simultaneous 'whispering' technique. It was a minor triumph for us that, over lunch, David was congratulated by almost all present for the remarkable job he had done, even by those who had originally argued against his presence.

The interpreter problem settled, the meeting passed to the first of the routine agenda items which the President had previously agreed with the Secretary-General could be included for discussion. These items were quickly resolved while I continued to struggle with files on a side table, and tried to catch the eyes of some of the Executive members whom I knew best in order to assess their mood, but with surprising lack of success. I had no time to do more than glance at the batch of papers which had been placed on the table in front of each person.

I do not know what, if anything, had been agreed before I came into the room but, as we moved closer to the agenda item which was so vital to us, it became only too obvious that the President was there in name only; it was Secretary-General Nenquin who, in practice, presided over the whole, extraordinary, ritualised meeting. There was a possible clue to this situation in one of the tabled documents. Professor Desmond Clark had written (on University of California letterhead) to the Secretary-General, on 13 January, claiming not only that he himself had the right to attend the Executive Committee meeting, but that:

> Since Professor Evans is both the President of the IUPPS and the Chairman of the British Organising Committee whose decision is under review, there would seem to be a conflict of interest in the present situation. I presume, therefore, that you will already have made arrangements for an alternative Chairman for the meeting on 17 January.

Formally, or informally, John Evans handed the Presidency to Professor Nenquin, and Professor Desmond Clark, although not a voting member of the International Executive Committee, through continual interruption, effectively took over as 'President' Nenquin's collaborative Secretary-General.

It was at this point that I had almost my only success of the meeting, for, against Secretary-General Nenquin's wishes, Professor Ripoll-Perello, from Spain, supported my insistence on a run-through of all those present at the meeting. The unknown people, as well as Professor Desmond Clark, were apparently present in their capacity as Co-ordinators of Special Projects (in Desmond Clark's case, the Atlas of African Prehistoric Industries). All in all there were seven voting members present: President John Evans (according to our legal advice – but *would* he vote?), Bertha Stjernquist of Sweden, Hans-Georg Bandi of Switzerland, Kurt Böhner of Germany, Eduardo Ripoll-Perello of Spain (which had just made a bid for the next IUPPS Congress), Jim Sackett of the USA and myself. That represented, at best, a vote of four against us, one possible USA abstention, and presumably only myself and the President from England, and Richard Nunoo from Ghana (whenever he arrived) in favour. Among the missing voting members we had received written or telephoned support for our stand from Pakistan, the USSR and Senegal, and evidence of a vote against us from Mexico, and possible abstentions (or even votes against us) from Yugoslavia and India. It would obviously be a very close thing indeed if there were to be a vote.

But there was also someone else who was, apparently, to be present at the meeting – the Secretary-General of ICPHS, described in Secretary-General Nenquin's subsequent Minutes as 'having been invited by the Bureau' – although John Evans had told me (on 10 January) that Secretary-General Nenquin had done this off his own bat. The Secretary-General of ICPHS had, of course, no more, or less, right to attend the meeting than Caroline who, at least, would not have been there to speak.

A list of apologies was read out by Secretary-General Nenquin. I added that Professor Nunoo was hoping to get to the meeting shortly, having especially flown all the way from Ghana, and also that the President had spoken to Professor Diop that morning from Senegal, and that Diop had also previously given his views of the situation by telephone to England.

The cards seemed to be well stacked against us, with ICPHS *and* five non-voting, retired executive members of the IUPPS all being wheeled in for this meeting. Should I object to the presence of ICPHS, just as Secretary-General Nenquin had objected to Caroline's presence? In the seconds I had available, I decided against following the tone set by the Secretary-General. I was interested to see how Mr d'Ormesson, the Secretary-General of ICPHS, would handle the situation, since ICPHS was supposed to be opposed to having South Africans on the ruling bodies of its constituent members.

By now Secretary-General Nenquin, was insisting both that the only matter to be discussed by the Committee was whether or not we had broken the IUPPS Statutes, and that no views of absent Executive Committee members should be heard. Subsequently Secretary-General Nenquin recorded in the Minutes that the Committee had agreed to these two demands. In fact, both were hotly disputed, both by Professor Sackett and myself, and there was, in the event, no Committee consensus or view. It struck me that Jacques Nenquin's extraordinary determination not to allow any discussion of the principles involved was not because he was indifferent to them but because he was in fact deeply disturbed by the whole South Africa issue.

John Evans made his introductory, and almost only, remarks in which he stressed that the British Committee(s) had never tried to deny that they had broken one of the Statutes, and that this had been clearly stated in the President's letter to the Secretary-General of 19 September 1985. However, the British Committee hoped to convince the Executive that to do so had been the correct thing to do. Several of the non-voting members present at the meeting replied that there could be no situation in which a ban could be correct. I was then asked to add any further points and I explained some further details of events. Professor Desmond Clark remarked that this was the most brilliant speech in defence of the ban that he had ever heard and asked me to prove that I had been equally as eloquent in speaking on the academic freedom issue prior to the ban. I said that I would be pleased to do so, but at this point Paul and Professor Nunoo telephoned from England having still failed to get a French visa. Since it was impossible to interrupt the Executive meeting at this point I asked them to ring back later on.

By this time the Secretary-General of ICPHS, Mr d'Ormesson, had arrived, to the evident acute embarrassment of Professors Nenquin and de Lumley, who clearly did not want him to have to sit there listening to the current debate without being asked to give his statement. In the event he did have to sit there for some considerable time. Professor Desmond Clark claimed that Secretary-General Nenquin had not known about any problem connected with South African participation in WAC until he heard about it many weeks after the British Executive Committee decision. While Professor Desmond Clark was speaking Secretary-General Nenquin was heard to mutter, 'This isn't true.'

Before anything could be taken further Secretary-General Nenquin turned to Mr d'Ormesson and asked him to speak, insisting that since Mr d'Ormesson had been waiting for so long he should now be permitted to give his address.

For some ten minutes Mr d'Ormesson outlined his own organisation's philosophy of free academic interchange. To adopt any other philosophy or policy, he argued, would mean confronting problems such as those of China and Taiwan, or Israel and Arab countries. Secretary-General Nenquin then tried to thank Mr d'Ormesson for his address, and to move the meeting on, but I insisted on challenging Mr d'Ormesson to explain three specific points. Secretary-General Nenquin tried to refuse, but in the end I stressed that as he had invited Mr d'Ormesson there must have been a purpose, and I asked Mr d'Ormesson the following questions:

1. Was it not true that ICPHS, the intermediate body between IUPPS and UNESCO and through which IUPPS finance was derived, had a policy that no South Africans should be on ruling Councils? This being so, was he aware that the Permanent Council of the IUPPS had up to four such South African representatives (who, incidentally, could be nominated by government) and that two of these places were, in fact, currently filled?

2. Despite his bland remarks about everyone being allowed to attend Congresses, was it not true that ICPHS had sanctioned the meeting of the International Congress of African Studies, one of its constituent members, in Ibadan in December 1985, knowing full well that Nigeria would not issue visas to South Africans, and did he not agree that this, unlike the British action of openly banning South Africans, was dishonest?

3. Was he aware, and if so why had ICPHS taken no action, that one of the Associations affiliated to the IUPPS was the Pan African Association on Prehistory and Related Studies which had, since its Jos meeting of December 1983, adopted a policy against any contact whatsoever with South African institutions and colleagues?

With Secretary-General Nenquin trying to move the meeting on and Professor Desmond Clark starting to intervene, Mr d'Ormesson replied that I was correct about the first point and that he was embarrassed by IUPPS practice. He also admitted that the second point was correct and that the British move was explicit and honest whereas the ICPHS stance was:

a case where pragmatism had to take precedence over principles.

I quickly replied that I thought that pragmatism was always supposed to be an English characteristic. There was some hollow laughter from those who had followed the interchange, and who remembered that one criticism of the reasons given for the ban in the first British press release had been that they were essentially pragmatic.

Secretary-General Nenquin was beginning to look desperate and insisted, again, that we were not supposed to be discussing any matters of principle, but merely whether the British had broken the rules. However, Professor Desmond Clark was unstoppable, and broke in:

> The Pan African Congress meeting consisted of 75 per cent Nigerians and only 24 or 25 Europeans, who all abstained in the voting, and the meeting therefore cannot be described as a meeting of 'savants' and should be ignored by this Executive meeting.

I could hardly believe my ears. Here, for the first time, was a quite explicit statement, and I immediately objected to the remark, waiting for a reaction, or at least a Presidential ruling. I waited, of course, in vain. Professor Sackett merely intervened to say that he thought we should indeed be discussing the principles involved (as if this was not in fact the most fundamental point of principle), that he did in fact want to hear what other Committee members, present and absent, had to say, and that he was seeking some compromise between the IUPPS position on academic freedom and the real political situation of South Africa throughout the world. I missed my chance to point out that I knew that at least one white person had not abstained in the voting in Jos.

Secretary-General Nenquin, however, once again refused to allow views from those not present at the meeting, even while Paul and Professor Nunoo were ringing in yet again, to report that the French visa had been finally refused.

I called Professor de Lumley over to me at the telephone and pointed out to him that the Ghanaian member of the Executive Committee was sitting in England and was prevented by the French Embassy from getting a visa for this meeting. Henry de Lumley, still appearing to be totally friendly, said he could deal with the problem, but in fact he went back to the meeting table and did nothing whatsoever.

I was left talking to Paul on the telephone; Henry made no mention whatsoever of Professor Nunoo waiting at a telephone kiosk in London – I repeated twice to the International Executive Committee that this was the case and I then interrupted proceedings again on a point of order that they should take a communication from a voting member of the International Executive Committee. That point of order, like everything else which occurred, was not dealt with by the President but by the Secretary-General. He said that he could see no reason to listen to any absent member of the International Executive Committee, and refused to admit such opinions on the grounds that other members of the International Executive Committee *had* managed to get to the meeting. If people could get to the meeting from

Los Angeles and San Francisco, he said, then the others should have been able to do so also, from Africa, Russia and so on.

There followed some ten minutes of hostile confrontation, during which I pointed out that his letters inviting people to the International Executive Committee in Paris had not allowed Third World members to even hope to get here, let alone actually get here, and that he obviously had no conception of how difficult it was for Third World participants to get permission and visas to attend meetings at such short notice. I also stressed the point that the meeting had been arranged at the worst possible date, as far as the Christmas and New Year mail delays were concerned. I suggested that it was an indictment of the IUPPS organisation that he appeared to have no understanding of the problems involved in Third World participation. Professor Sackett then came to my support, repeating his previous sentiments that the absence of Third World members, both in terms of geography and age, around the table, made the meeting both ill-informed and irrelevant. He also insisted that any Third World views telephoned to the Committee should be noted and considered.

At this point Secretary-General Nenquin went behind a table and brought out some large files, insisting that if any communication from an Executive Committee member was to be mentioned, tabled, or presented at the meeting he would insist on reading all the letters in his large files, which would take, he said, at least until Sunday night. I therefore insisted that only the communications received from members, or at least voting members, of the Executive Committee should be read or communicated to the meeting without reference to all the other letters that Secretary-General Nenquin might have in his files. Secretary-General Nenquin refused to do so unless all the letters were read out. The President made no ruling whatsoever and Professor Desmond Clark, as he had throughout the meeting, led away from the item under discussion.

Again, Secretary-General Nenquin repeated his demand that nothing was to be discussed at this meeting except whether or not the British organisation had infringed the IUPPS Statutes. Again, I pointed out that nobody from Britain had ever denied that we had broken the 'rules' but I also stressed that the Statutes included none of the wording used by the Secretary-General in his letter to Professor Evans; that ICPHS had not denied that it had, effectively, also broken the rules by allowing meetings in countries where it knew that visas would not be issued to South Africans, and that the IUPPS itself included an association which itself had banned South Africans. Professor Sackett tried to demand that Secretary-General Nenquin should no longer be allowed to force the discussion before the Committee as simply being one of 'yes' or 'no' with regard to whether the British Committee had infringed the Statutes, and stressed that the matter was a complex one which needed sympathetic consideration and that he (not formally but for discussion) suggested three possible areas of compromise. These were:

1. That there should be a change of venue within the UK for the 1986 Congress to somewhere where there could be a change of policy regarding the exclusion of South Africans;

2. That the Third World's position of total opposition to any South African presence should be disregarded. However, he was now convinced that this was not a viable area of compromise but he wished me, as National Secretary, to be given the opportunity to document the opinion of the Third World in the absence of any Third World members at this International Executive Committee, and in view of the adamant refusal by the Secretary-General to allow any reference to the opinions of absent members:

3. That all participants who wished to do so (including, by definition, any South Africans) should register in the Congress as members of the 'international community'. Given such a situation he said that he would himself refuse to register as an American, but would insist on being registered within such an 'international community'.

Secretary-General Nenquin responded in a predictable way, insisting that none of the points raised by Sackett were relevant, since there was 'nothing to be discussed' except whether or not the British organising committee had or had not infringed the Statutes. I was not given the opportunity to present the evidence which showed that the Third World participants would not attend the Congress if South Africans participated. Secretary-General Nenquin now insisted that each Committee member should make his or her views known. Professor Böhner (representative of Germany) started his speech, which was interrupted almost immediately at 12.30 pm by another telephone call from Professor Nunoo, still from England. This time the President came to the telephone to document Nunoo's contribution to the meeting, since it was now clear that he would not reach it in person.

While John Evans listened to Professor Nunoo I repeated the question as to how the IUPPS had intended major Third World participation in the WAC while at the same time allowing South African participation. I was answered by Henry de Lumley (the man reported to have said, during a discussion about the ban of South African participation at the WAC, that the Western media were exaggerating the situation in South Africa). He maintained that there was no problem, since at his 1976 Congress in Nice he had had archaeologists of all countries, including Israel and Arab countries, South Africans and Algerians, together in the same room. I pointed out that the situation in 1976 was totally different from 1986, and that South Africa (especially since the State of Emergency) was a unique situation. I also added that in Nice there had only been very few from most of these non-European countries, and that these were symbolic and senior representatives, whereas the WAC was determined to have meaningful participation by those involved in active work in the Third World countries.

Acrimoniously, and with the President still taking down the telephone message from Professor Nunoo, the meeting closed for lunch. While waiting for Evans to finish with Nunoo (whom I heard Evans assure that his message was perfectly clear and that he would have it translated and read out in French to the meeting), I had time for a short discussion with Mr d'Ormesson before he left the meeting for good. He ridiculed my statement that it was becoming clear that the WAC and the British Committee were about to be thrown out of the IUPPS, saying that that was totally unthinkable and impossible. Over lunch I told Caroline what had been happening and suggested that now that Richard Nunoo had finished ringing up there was no point in her waiting around, and that we would see her back at the hotel. I told her that I was certain that we were about to lose. Meanwhile, Professor Tobias talked to all the Committee members (except me). I do not know who John Evans talked to at lunch or what he did, but I was pleased that our paths did not cross.

The meeting reconvened at two o'clock. I was horrified, but no longer surprised, to see that Professor Evans made no effective attempt to get Professor Nunoo's message heard, in spite of the enormous efforts this full voting Executive Committee member had made, first to attend and then to telephone his message to the meeting. Instead Professor Desmond Clark repeated his claim that Africans and Indians would attend the Congress whether or not South Africans were present. Again I rebutted the statement, and again explained the level of Third World participation which the WAC was aiming for.

At this point Secretary-General Nenquin again requested that all those at the table give their views, and as I listened my heart sank, especially as my worst fears of Jim Sackett, our only possible ally, were confirmed. There would clearly be no point at all in trying to force a vote of those present. By this stage in the proceedings I had no idea even what John Evans would actually do if faced with a vote.

Professor Desmond Clark, in a final statement, claimed that he knew, better than anyone else, the real position of the Third World. He then requested, and received, Professor de Lumley's views of the current state of African sentiment about apartheid, which would not, he said, preclude black Africans from sitting round the same table as white South Africans, while I tried, quietly and without success, to get our President, who was supposed to be Chairman, to demand a meeting of the IUPPS Permanent Council.

As the meeting was obviously staggering towards its climax, I demanded a hearing and repeated the three main points I had made earlier, insisting that it be made absolutely clear to me whether any Executive Committee view reached at this meeting would be a recommendation or a decision.

At this point Secretary-General Nenquin said that discussion had gone on far too long, and that a resolution must be reached. Without further ado, he began to read from a document, obviously prepared before the meeting, which stated that:

> The Executive Committee appreciates the great efforts made by the National Committee organising the Congress at Southampton.
>
> Refers to paragraph 3 of the Statutes [which] states that the aim of the IUPPS is 'the collaboration of scholars of all countries in enterprises contributing to the advancement of prehistoric and protohistoric sciences';
>
> Refers to the commitment, taken by all countries inviting the IUPPS to hold its Congress in its country, to guarantee the participation at the work of the Congress of all *bona fide* archaeologists, irrespective of their origin or of their philosophical, political or other convictions;
>
> Recalls the tenet of the ICPHS which is to 'total independence from politics and to academic liberty'; and which has always taken the position that scientific congresses are open to all, without distinction of race, religion, or belief.
>
> The Executive Committee regrets the decision taken by the Organising Committee to exclude from the XIth Congress of the IUPPS scholars working in South Africa or in Namibia, for political reasons.
>
> The Executive Committee, guardian of the traditions of the IUPPS, cannot accept any meeting where participation is subjected to non-scientific considerations as being organised under the auspices of the Union.

I began to pack my files away, and could see John Evans and David Bellos also packing things away, as the final nail was hammered in:

> Therefore, the Executive Committee refuses to recognise the Southampton meeting as the IUPPS Congress.

I addressed the Executive Committee briefly, and for the last time, pointing out that if that was the case I was no longer a member of the Executive Committee, being a member solely through my position as National Secretary. I left the room with David Bellos, and John Evans apparently following behind. Outside the door David and I waited for John Evans, the British President, to join us, but we waited in vain. Downstairs David remembered he had left his coat in the meeting room and went back to fetch it. When he returned he told me that Secretary-General Nenquin looked as though he had been crying – and that John Evans was back seated at the table.

We joined Caroline, who was clearly extremely upset by our news, in her hotel room, and waited for John Evans to appear. He and I were to leave on the quarter to ten plane to London, and David was flying straight back to Manchester. Only Caroline was staying on in Paris for a few days' holiday. David and I brought Caroline up to date with events, including Professor Desmond Clark's remarks about Nigerian archaeologists (an episode confused in the Minutes of the meeting). David and I also planned a press conference, drafting what we would say, and deciding which of David's Parisian contacts we would get in touch with. Before anything could be finalised we would need to talk things over with John Evans.

He finally arrived some two hours later, confirming that Secretary-General Nenquin had indeed broken down, had pleaded for Evans to stay with the Committee, which he had agreed to do, but as a co-opted member, not as President. We were all shocked into silence. John Evans went on to tell us that Professor Böhner had offered to stage the IUPPS Congress in Germany, on the same days as ours in Southampton, and that he had been appointed IUPPS President, in Evans' place. Visibly upset, John Evans told us that the International Executive Committee had given us an ultimatum. We had until 15 February to reverse our policy and allow South African/Namibian participation in the WAC. A postal vote was to be taken from the members of the Permanent Council in which they could agree or disagree with the actions of the International Executive Committee and Professor Evans himself had agreed to count the votes, together with Professor Böhner and Secretary-General Nenquin. These votes had to be in by 15 February, allowing a mere four weeks for letters to be sent out to all members of the Permanent Council, to reach their destinations all over the world, and for responses to be returned to Ghent, Belgium, where the Bureau of the IUPPS is located. Any lack of response was to be counted as a vote in favour of the actions of the International Executive Committee.

For John Evans, the ordeal was almost over. For me, it was nowhere near the end, whatever the self-satisfied group we had been ejected from might think. I wondered whether I could bear to travel back in the same plane with our President, but he was so obviously distressed, now miserably saying that he ought to resign from both the International Executive Committee and from the WAC, that, in fact, we did eat together and returned to England on the same plane, making idle conversation as though the momentous events of the day had never occurred.

*

A week later Professor Evans 'regretfully' resigned in writing from the International Executive Committee referring in his letter to the 'very emotional end' of the Paris meeting and giving his reasons:

> ... first that I continue to feel that it was very unfortunate that the CE [Executive Committee]'s decision was taken in the absence of members from any country outside Western Europe and the United States, or consideration of the opinions submitted by some of them, and secondly that I feel sure that, as was said at the meeting, the time allowed for replies from the members of the Permanent [Council] to your letter announcing the resolutions is not sufficient to ensure a representative vote. One of the points made by Richard Nunoo in his statement which I was not allowed to read was that letters take three or four weeks to reach Ghana, and I am sure that this is by no means unique. For these reasons I feel sure that the decisions arrived at are bound to be regarded in many quarters as biased.

Nevertheless I am told that a count did indeed take place (though on a different day and in front of a different German representative from those agreed by the Executive) and that Professor Evans, no longer a member of the Executive, was in fact present. The result was that (of the 208 existing members of the Permanent Council) 41, predominantly from Western Europe and North America, voted in favour of the Executive's action, 8 were against it , and 11 wrote to say that they effectively abstained. 148 (over 70 per cent) remained silent, a good indication, and true reflection, of the failure of the IUPPS to communicate with its members on this as on other matters.

6. Cancel and/or Be Damned

The first thing that had to be done was to let the British Executive Committee members know what had happened in Paris – a lengthy business, by telephone, leading to much discussion about what should happen next. I also sought reactions from as many members of the National Committee as possible; many were gloomy about carrying on, though not as gloomy as the Executive. Obviously there had to be meetings of both groups, as soon as possible, to discuss the implications of the Paris meeting – and we also had the 15 February ultimatum, reported to us by John Evans, to consider. A meeting of the Executive was arranged for the evening of Saturday 25 January and it was arranged to hold a National Committee meeting on Saturday 1 February, with another Executive meeting before and after it.

I spent a great deal of time trying to let as many people as possible know the up-to-date situation, including the Vice Chancellor of Southampton University and the University's Conference Officer, John Hiett, who first urged me to continue with the Congress whatever happened, and then suddenly switched completely and demanded that it be cancelled. As the news spread, some people simply assumed that the WAC would now have to be cancelled. One of the most significant to do so was Peter Addyman, who wrote to me from the York Archaeological Trust, refusing to support the attacks by Martin Biddle in *The Times*, and saying:

> ... my very sincere sympathy for what must be the most appalling outcome after so much work. I can't imagine a more total loss to everyone concerned. I think I speak for everyone here in saying that you have our commiserations and best wishes. I don't doubt that the problems of wrapping up the debris and disposing of it will be horrendous too, and we wish you strength and the very best of good wishes.

Throughout all this time it was fortunate for me that Peter Gathercole, having agreed to teach several of my university courses (paid for by the Congress, an early foresight by David Wilson), was therefore in Southampton every week. Throughout these months he and I had discussed all the events and complications as they occurred and, on this occasion also, Peter was both a source of comfort and of erudite understanding and stimulating suggestions. There were many others with whom I talked and discussed developments – apart from, as always Jane, Caroline and Paul at any time of day and night – including, especially, Dr Alex Okpoko. Looming up, however, was the meeting in London of the Council of the Royal

Anthropological Institute which I had been asked to attend for its debate on whether or not to withdraw its own (and the Esperanza Trust for Anthropological Research's) sponsorship of the WAC.

In between teaching some courses and administering my Department, I tried to consider the situation from all points of view. I desperately needed time to get to my Buckinghamshire cottage to be alone. I was irritable at home and at work, and the telephone never seemed to stop ringing. Each Executive Committee member was clearly trying to decide whether we should cancel the Congress, or 'go it alone'. The local and national press were full of it all, and I became pretty sure that the cancellation argument would win on the 25th unless I could come up with some other solution. The *Times* archaeological correspondent misled everyone by announcing on the 20th that the Congress had been moved to Mainz, a piece of misinformation then repeated in *Nature*. Some people were saying, 'All that work for nothing, all that enthusiasm wasted'; others, 'All that money wasted'; some, 'To cancel now would be seen as a major blow to the anti-apartheid lobby, to the City of Southampton and even to the University'. The telephone never stopped ringing and ringing. A few more letters of resignation trickled in.

January 22 was an important day, and a chaotic and traumatic one at that. It started with a notorious leader in *The Times* entitled 'An Academic Retreat' which seemed to smear the WAC by claiming that if the IUPPS had not moved its Congress to Mainz, Southampton would have been:

> ... left to host a rump congress attended by a disreputable group of British Communists and 'Third World' archaeologists ... As a world gathering the ... congress would have been a sham.

This attack was coupled with a threat to the AUT, that:

> ... its pusillanimity should not be forgotten when the professors make their high, idealistic arguments for more public funds.

Throughout the following months I never heard a single archaeologist, of whatever persuasion regarding the ban, express anything except profound disgust at this *Times* leader.

I had been feeling guilty about being unable to find the time to do more than telephone Roger Jones of Allen & Unwin to keep him up to date, and now, at last, we could squeeze in a working lunch. As usual Roger was contained, supportive and apparently without qualms about the trust that he had vested in me as Series Editor. I left reassured but still dreading the next assignment, the Council meeting of the Royal Anthropological Institute.

I should say that the RAI has a very special place in my affections, for not only was I the youngest person ever to have become one of its Fellows, but I had published my first article in its *Journal*, and my first book in its

Occasional Papers series, and, later, I had even been considered for its Directorship. Above all, the kind of anthropology for which the RAI stands, encompassing social and physical anthropology as well as archaeology, is very similar to the whole concept of the WAC.

After a debate which reflected many of the points already reviewed in this book, the RAI Council, chaired by its President, Jean la Fontaine, decided that:

(1) The RAI will not in future support any conference unless it is assured that no individuals will be excluded on grounds of their nationality, residence, colour or creed.

(2) The RAI, in seeking to further the understanding of all humanity, opposes all discrimination, whether based on colour, ethnic identity, religion, citizenship or sex. It affirms that there is no justification of a social system based on such discrimination, like that of apartheid in the Republic of South Africa. The Institute also insists on the distinction between individual scholars and the representatives of government regimes. Among scholars there should be free circulation of ideas, whether in publications or in international meetings. While recognising that national delegations or government publications may sometimes be unacceptable to the academic community, the Institute cannot support the exclusion of individuals whose contribution to knowledge is of merit.

(3) Financial support for participation of Third World scholars in specific seminars in the WAC (£1,000 made available by the Esperanza Trust for Anthropological Research) will not be withdrawn.

(4) The RAI applauds the attempts that the WAC has made to encourage the participation of Third World scholars.

(5) The RAI should withdraw its sponsorship of any intended WAC to be held in Southampton if the exclusion of South African residents is maintained.

This is a series of decisions which reflect poorly on President Jean la Fontaine's subsequent published statement that:

In political circles (anthropologists) may be charged with unwillingness to sully their pure academic hands with the dirt of policy decisions ... It is no longer enough for anthropologists to offer an understanding of 'other cultures' as their sole contribution to creating a less prejudiced society. We must confront the problem directly, in research and in what we write.

In spite of this I am still reluctant to relinquish my RAI Fellowship, for I have consistently argued to others that resignation is an inappropriate response to this particular set of incompatible principles, and because the RAI has given the WAC largely sympathetic coverage in its *Anthropology Today*, and has stressed the complexity of the issues.

I left the meeting upset and shaken, and dashed across London to the house of someone who I thought might be able to influence Government to assist us financially. I argued that, with the recent Nassau agreement that there should be 'discouragement of all cultural and scientific events except those where these contribute towards the ending of apartheid', and the threatened withdrawal of sponsorship by Heritage Projects Ltd (York), the WAC's ban on South African/Namibian participation was exactly in line with Government policy and would be an excellent way for the Prime Minister to show that, although determinedly against economic sanctions, she did indeed mean business regarding those points of the Nassau agreement with which she had agreed. I pointed out that the WAC had already played a significant part in the successful departure of Professor Khazanov from Russia to Israel.

My visit did not prove successful. I rushed on to the Athaeneum to eat with Michael and Micky Day and Professor Eric Sunderland, Secretary-General of the IUAES. We discussed details of the WAC's situation, the *Times* 'rump' leader, the RAI's decision of a few hours (or was it days?) earlier, the way the IUAES' Inter-Congress in Alexandria had been abandoned (because of the Egyptian academics' belated refusal to allow the Israelis, who had already arrived in Alexandria, to participate), and the possibility that the IUAES' main congress scheduled for August 1988 in Yugoslavia might be affected by the South African situation. The IUAES Executive Committee was one of the few bodies to have supported the WAC in its effort 'to resist the cancellation of its meeting' (see pages 145 and 146), support which was later endorsed by the IUAES Permanent Council without demur.

I slept fitfully through much of the train journey back to Southampton but suddenly found myself wide awake and again thinking about what once had seemed a possible solution. (It had also been suggested by Dr Robin Derricourt, an archaeologist working for Cambridge University Press whom I had known a little in the 1960s, and who had subsequently worked in southern Africa.) Was it conceivable after all, and even at this late stage, that the South Africans might be persuaded to withdraw voluntarily from the Congress, in order to save the archaeological world community from division? This suggestion had already been put to the South African Association of Archaeologists, just before the Paris meeting, but their Executive Committee had replied that it 'did not think it was able to speak on behalf of the Association on this issue and that a postal vote would (have been) necessary'. Regretfully, I could see no way of gaining sufficient time to try again. To Professor Michael Day and myself, insistence by South African archaeologists, such as Professor Tobias, to attend international meetings, has always appeared the most curious of situations, for such insistence goes directly contrary to the ANC's position. In addition such insistence on attendance, when it is clear that it may well wreck a congress, seems a strange way to support academic freedom.

Through sleepless nights over the next few days my own position was becoming clearer and firmer. I would not be able to live with myself if I let down our Third World colleagues at this stage. I would not let myself be used to give the pro-South Africa lobby further ammunition, and I would not be beaten by a group of elderly Western Europeans and an American in Paris who had refused to listen to, or debate, any of the important issues of principle. Was there anything at all that could be done? I had under a week to come up with something.

It seemed to me that everyone involved should be able to agree, academics and politicians alike, if only the WAC could become a forum for significant archaeological discussion as well as provide an opportunity for *explicit* anti-apartheid action. If the Congress were cancelled, no one (except those in favour of apartheid South Africa) could be happy. The way to get the best academic archaeological meeting would be to remove the ban – and yet still get the Third World to participate. The only way to achieve an effective and public action against apartheid, by the Congress, would be for the WAC to remain within IUPPS so that this action could be taken at the scheduled meetings of the Permanent Council. To make such action possible the Third World members of the Council would have to attend in order to vote. Was it even a possibility that the Permanent Council would, at its meeting during the Congress, either throw South Africa off the ruling Council and/or ban individual South African participants from the Congress? Was this possible public action, with all the press attention it would attract, enough of a carrot to persuade the anti-apartheid movements to remove their pressure? Was it worth a try? Was it too much of a compromise for me to stomach? As usual I discussed all the ins and outs with Jane.

It was worth pursuing further; if only there were more time ... I needed to test the idea against some yardsticks, but also to keep the matter totally confidential until it had been authorised by the Executive. I contemplated the Executive members. There was obviously no point in discussing it with John Evans, for at about the same time as finally resigning from the International Executive he had written (20.1.1986) to all the British Executive saying:

> The WAC is now on its own, and we shall have to meet as quickly as possible to decide its future. Either it must be cancelled, or continue without IUPPS sponsorship. If the decision is to cancel, I will stay with the Committee to help wind up its affairs; if, on the other hand, it is decided to continue I shall have to resign from the Committee and the Company. My acceptance of the ban on individual participants from South Africa was in order to save the IUPPS Congress, and if it is not to be that, I do not wish to continue.

John Evans was obviously not the person to be approached for an objective reaction. I presumed that our Honorary Treasurer, whose primary aim was to control finances, and was basically probably against the ban anyway, would welcome anything which would maximise the number of participants in the Congress. What about the others?

I decided to use Colin Renfrew as my litmus paper and, during a long telephone call, he was enthusiastic – saying that he saw such a move as potentially unifying. He also stressed that we had nothing beyond John Evans' incomplete report of Secretary-General Nenquin's ultimatum, and he agreed to ring Nenquin to discover the exact wording of the International Executive Committee's decision. He wished me luck ...

With regard to the National Committee, some of the older and more reactionary members would no doubt sense a victory. The younger, more radical members would have to decide whether cancellation of the Congress was really preferable to the compromise (if there could be one) with its promise of public debate and probable public action over South Africa. I discussed the situation with my old friend David Harris, who was seen (rightly or wrongly) to be middle of the road and somewhat establishment. He greeted the suggestion with joy and relief, but with strong disbelief that I would be able to convince the various pressure groups involved to come up with any commitment on paper. Michael Day and Peter Gathercole also urged me to go ahead and try.

Normally I would also have rung Paul Mellars but, in a phone conversation with one of his Cambridge colleagues, I had gained the impression that Paul might, despite all the evidence to the contrary, be having doubts. I had rung him, to discover that there were indeed problems and we had agreed to meet in London as soon as possible. As it turned out, this would also be the occasion for me to discuss my new ideas about negotiations with the ANC.

When we met, Paul repeated again and again that he had not wanted me to hear about his 'change of heart' from anyone but himself, and he claimed that it had happened on his drive back to Cambridge from my cottage (see page 83). I was, for once, deeply and emotionally affected, for Paul Mellars had come to represent to me much of what I considered exceptional and good about the Congress: consistency, hard work, and innovation, all combined. I was especially shattered because the picture that I had formed of Paul over the last few years of close association was so very different from my initial reaction at our first meeting (see page 34). We did, in fact, manage to discuss the tentative plans to try negotiation with the ANC, and I was both pleased and sad that this would have brought Paul back into the Congress, for I knew that if these plans came to nothing, Paul was lost to us. I was not able to hide the sense of hopelessness that began to close in on me, for as we parted Paul said: 'If *you* give up, then I will never believe in any human being again!'

Could I persuade the Southampton AUT, the Southampton Students' Union, the Anti-Apartheid Movement, and the ANC to state publicly that the WAC should be an (or even *the*) exception to their normal policies? Paul Crake, Caroline Jones and I dropped everything and began to count and phone, and count again. Yes, we thought we could promise that a vote at a September meeting of the Permanent Council would throw South Africa out. Yes, it was possible that individual South African/Namibian participants would be banned – although this was much more difficult to predict and certainly impossible to 'promise'. I put it to the City, to the AUT, and to Anti-Apartheid, contrasting the public debate and subsequent public humiliation of South Africa with the humiliation and criticism which would follow cancellation of the Congress. They all said they needed time to think and confer, but it was clear that for two of them nothing was going to be really possible without ANC agreement. In any case, I was sure that I myself could not live with the situation unless the ANC made the Congress an exception.

Meanwhile Paul Crake approached the Students' Union, which agreed to debate the issue again. I agreed to stand by if called to address such a meeting. For the first time I called an open meeting in my Department to discuss the suggested 'compromise'. Until this moment I had determinedly kept the WAC affairs as separate as possible from my Department's affairs and had never called for a Departmental view, either from staff or students. In fact I had no idea of the attitudes of several of my staff, and was very surprised as their different views became known to me as the months went by. Likewise, I had been too busy to find out the views of the student population but now, with a Student Union debate imminent, I judged that staff and students alike must receive as full a briefing as possible. I am told that reactions were very mixed, some at least seeing the suggested compromise as a sell-out. I had no idea what would happen at the Union meeting.

How was I to approach the ANC? I decided to ring their office in London and asked to speak to the only contact whose name I knew. With pounding heart I heard him reply that the suggestion had some merit as long as the issue would really be a live one at the Congress itself, and so long as the parent body of the British ANC would also agree. My contact stressed that I had been given a personal view only, and that I should ring again the next day. I drove to the cottage and sat up all night writing a document which I hoped all parties would be able to sign, and planning a public debate on the South African-academic freedom issue for the Royal Festival Hall.

Next morning my ANC contact told me that he had 'worried all through the night'. I read him my draft statement, which he liked, and he gave me his blessing to go ahead. He also thought that the ANC might help with persuading African countries to attend the Congress, and he said that he would be talking to his superior on Monday 27 January. I telephoned Alan Whitehead and gave him my news; his response was that if Anti-Apartheid agreed to my document he would be prepared to take such a recommendation to his Policy and Resources Committee also on the Monday. I spoke again to all the other groups involved and I also started talking to those who I thought might be willing to join the Executive Committe if the so-called compromise document was adopted and if existing members of the Executive Committee resigned as a result. David Harris and I had long and detailed discussions of my document by phone.

On Saturday I was almost too late for Caroline to type up my document before the Executive was convened at 7 pm. Exhaustedly I noticed that the Executive accepted without comment my tabled Matters Arising document which laconically (but in fact irritably) merely reported, without comment, that the President had not, at the Paris meeting, called for a meeting of the Permanent Council, and I heard David Wilson say that he had only that day (viz 25 January) received Secretary-General Nenquin's letter of the 17th stating that the International Executive Committee had thrown us out. If it took a week to reach England, what hope had the Third World to respond by the 15 February deadline? John Evans read out Secretary-General Nenquin's ultimatum which demanded *written* guarantees from the City of Southampton, the Students, the AUT and Anti-Apartheid that they would not interfere with the Congress if held with South African participation. This drew the question whether the suggested alternative organisers in Mainz, West Germany, had also been asked to supply such written guarantees. Colin Renfrew was worried that Professor Nenquin's letter to members of the Permanent Council made no mention of the possibility of the WAC still remaining as the IUPPS XIth Congress, if the South African ban was removed.

The meeting continued with the assistance of a tabled document from Derek Hayes, and the Minutes state that four possible options were discussed in detail: (1) cancellation of the Congress, (2) continuing with the Congress outside of the IUPPS, (3) readmission of South African/Namibian participation, and (4) calling for an emergency meeting of the Conseil Permanent. The financial implication of the first two options were outlined in detail and discussed by the Executive Committee. The fourth option was discounted as being impracticable and possibly unobtainable.

It was clear to me from the discussion that the Congress was about to be cancelled and I had no other alternative but to table my document which read:

The UK Executive and National Committees reaffirm their abhorrence of the South African apartheid regime. However, in view of the recent decision in Paris by the International Executive Committee of IUPPS it has no option but to allow South African/Namibian participation in the WAC 1986, if it is to remain within IUPPS. It has therefore discussed this new situation with the Southampton AUT, NUS, Anti-Apartheid Movement and the City Council.

The Paris decision was taken by a membership of the International Executive Committee exclusively derived from Western European countries and the USA. It has allowed no reasonable time or conditions for true ratification by the Permanent Council of the IUPPS.

1. IUPPS is governed by a Permanent Council which includes South Africans. This is against the policy of its parent organisation, ICPHS.

2. Members of the Permanent Council may be national representatives 'suggested by government', thereby making any IUPPS public stance that it is only concerned with individual scholars, patently dubious.

3. IUPPS is officially affiliated to the Pan African Congress (now, Pan

African Association on Prehistory and Related Studies) whose policy is 'censorship of colleagues and institutions maintaining links with South African institutions', thus rejecting the International Committee's claim that the UK's decision to ban South African/Namibian participation would be breaking new ground.

The UK Executive and National Committees therefore remove their ban on South African/Namibian participation in the WAC 1986 because it sees this as the only possible way in the forseeable future for the whole archaeological world to effectively debate the above matters both within the academic programme of the Congress and at meetings of the Permanent Council of IUPPS scheduled to take place in September 1986.

The UK Committees therefore urge all those – individuals, organisations, and governments – who have declared their refusal to attend the Congress if there were to be South African/Namibian participation in it, to make the WAC 1986 an exception to their normal principle, and they urge them to participate.

The UK Committees have considered the implications of the Paris decision to discriminate between the Pan African Congress and the WAC regarding South African/Namibian participation. They recognise that to hold the WAC 1986 without South African/Namibian participation as well as a IUPPS Mainz/Frankfurt Congress with such South African/Namibian paticipation, threatens to divide western archaeology and to isolate it from the rest of world archaeology. These matters deserve full public discussion at meetings of the Permanent Council and General Assembly of the IUPPS at a time and place when the real worldwide presence of archaeologists can be assured, namely at the WAC 1986. For this reason the UK Executive and National Committees, the Southampton AUT, NUS, Anti-Apartheid Movement and the City have agreed that the Congress will be open to *bona fide* scholars 'of all countries' (IUPPS Statute 3) irrespective of nationality, philosophical conviction or religious faith.

John Evans remarked that the document was 'very remarkable and would put a bomb under IUPPS'. The Committee unanimously agreed that it should be put to the special National Committee meeting on 1 February. Miraculously, the WAC was still just alive and still part of the IUPPS.

Next day, Sunday, I read the draft document to as many people as possible including Professor Barry Cunliffe (my foe-to-be of a live BBC debate – see page 139), who said that it was 'masterly', and to Peter Gathercole who had sustained me so often during the previous months. He also approved of it.

John Evans also rang me that Sunday to discuss a few changes of wording to the document and to suggest a preamble, which I readily agreed to. I thought that by now I had suffered all that the President might come up with, but on Tuesday, like all members of the Executive, I received a letter from him written the day before announcing his resignation from the Executive Committee. In the letter he said that he had not had time to consider my document properly at our Executive meeting (despite the fact that the meeting had lasted three and a half hours) and that he now thought the proposal cynical, although:

the proposed arrangement appears to offer the possibility of running the Congress at Southampton as a IUPPS event, and under conditions which, in theory at least, could attract participants from all countries, and with all shades of opinion on questions of academic freedom and the appropriate response to *apartheid*.

I could not help ruefully remembering his letter to Nenquin about 'naughty schoolboys' (page 90)! This time no one on the Executive could bring themselves to plead with him to reconsider or at least to defer his resignation until after the scheduled meetings of the Executive and National Committees.

Back in Southampton, negotiations with the Anti-Apartheid groups and the Students' Union were continuing apace. Peter Stone had addressed a special meeting of the Students' Union, called by the President, which passed on my document to the Administrative Committee with the recommendation that it be accepted but, even if the ANC would also agree to it, the Congress would be charged full rates for all use of rooms and other facilities. The City could not formally ratify any decision before its Council meeting on 12 February, just three days before the IUPPS had to have the City's written statement. Alan Whitehead also needed some strong indication to show to his Committees that real action would be taken during the Congress against South African participation. On 3 February I could supply him with a resumé of the actions we had already taken, and would continue to take, to increase the number of Permanent Council members by more than double to the full potential of 485, both by getting representations from the 49 countries with no member and by bringing the complement of each country up to their full strength of four per country, as well as a preliminary analysis of likely voting patterns, and finally a letter to the IUPPS Bureau from Associate Professor Les Groube, the representative for Papua New Guinea on the Permanent Council of IUPPS, who happened to be in England at the time, which read 'I hereby give you notice that in accordance with the procedure outlined in the Statutes I am seeking nine signatories by other members of the Permanent Council for the following resolution to be debated at the next meeting of the Permanent Council and/or General Assembly:

> That the memberships on the Permanent Council of IUPPS of South Africa and Namibia be withdrawn while the current South African government policy on apartheid prevails, even if this action requires alteration or reinterpretation of the Statutes [and that] the separate issue of the participation of individual scholars from South Africa or Namibia (regardless of their countries' representation on the Permanent Council) should also be debated at the Permanent Council and the General Assembly meeting in September.

As Councillor Whitehead said, 'We seem to have a runner.'

Somehow I got away from the office, knowing that Paul and Caroline were coping despite the crises all around, to meet Ian Skipper and Anthony

Gaynor of Heritage Projects Ltd (York). Ian was, as usual, absolutely clear. If the 'compromise', which I explained in detail, became effective, we could count on his continued support (the promised additional £75,000) but if it did not he would do everything in his power, however much it might cost him to do so, to get back the £75,000 already paid to the Congress.

I promised, and duly carried out my promise, to make it clear both to the Executive and National Committees that his sponsorship of the WAC had been in the expectation of being associated with a 'joyful' international event. The meeting was very cordial and, as usual, I thoroughly enjoyed Ian's company (although Anthony's disapproval was self-evident throughout). As his parting shot, Ian offered to reserve the £150,000 (later reduced to £75,000 in correspondence) for any good project that I would suggest, in a few months time, to Anthony, Peter Addyman and himself to consider as a joint undertaking. I informed both John Evans and Derek Hayes, but I have never mentioned Ian's last point to anyone then connected with the Congress.

Meanwhile, meetings were taking place at various high levels, for example between the National Secretary of Anti-Apartheid, and Alan Whitehead, with the suggestion that the local Anti-Apartheid should be left to follow the Congress' lead while national Anti-Apartheid would concentrate on raising consciousness to ensure that South Africa would definitely be thrown off the Permanent Council in September. The local press was beginning to get wind of some possible developments. If all went well Councillor Whitehead would call a meeting of local Anti-Apartheid, the local NUS and the local AUT, and all these groups could shelter behind a City Council statement that they would not object to South African participation in the Congress along the lines of my document but that they abhorred the South Africa regime, and they would also make criticisms of the apartheid regime.

By now it was clear, therefore, that we could not hope to get formalised agreements as early as the very beginning of February and, with telephoned agreements from the Executive Committee, the National and Executive Committee meetings were scheduled for 8 February. The document was circulated to all members. It was headed in bold type:

Confidential draft of a text tabled by the National Secretary at the meeting of the Executive Committee on 25 January 1986.

The Executive unanimously recommended that it should be considered at a National Committee meeting. NB At this time none of the following groups have endorsed it: Southampton AUT, NUS, Anti-Apartheid Movement, City of Southampton, National Committee.

It caused some immediate reactions, as predicted, amongst those who saw the possible removal of the ban as a 'sell-out', and less predictably by Dr Ian Glover, who resigned from the National Committee and participation in the Congress because the WAC as 'a forum for attacking the inconsistency of other international bodies towards South Africa ... (would be) a gross distortion of the purpose of an international academic conference'.

In November 1985, after the ban on South African/Namibian participation, Dr Glover had silently handed me a letter informing me of the cancellation of the widely publicised issue of the journal *World Archaeology* of which he was editor, and which was to have had a special number devoted to the WAC (with a background article written by me). Later he did in fact attend the Congress and was a formal discussant during the session on plant domestication and early agriculture.

Every archaeologist in Britain appeared to be discussing the document. Several members of the National Committee, including Vice President Ralegh Radford, contacted me to suggest relatively minor changes to wording of the document. It was impossible to assess the likely outcome of a vote at the meeting which would depend for many on whether the Third World, particularly Africa and India and countries such as the USSR, would agree to participate if the ANC supported the Congress in spite of South Africans being present. It was clear to me that a high-powered delegation would have to travel fast to various countries to explain the situation in person. I started to think of suitable people and to make tentative contacts with those who could introduce me quickly to people such as Lord Carrington and Edward Heath. Colin Renfrew phoned Secretary-General Nenquin to alert him to the possibility that his ultimatum might be met; he reported that Jacques Nenquin was not enthusiastic about a possible solution, appearing to be firmly wedded to a Congress in Germany which would rival Southampton on the same dates.

Then, on the 6th, I was told that the national Anti-Apartheid movement would not agree to the plan after all. Apparently the ANC had changed its mind on instruction from Lusaka, and Anti-Apartheid was not willing to go it alone. Once again the Congress seemed doomed.

The Executive convened on 8 February at 10 am at the British Museum with David Wilson in the chair, and I informed them in detail why the suggested compromise document could not be proceeded with. It was clear that Colin Renfrew, at least, thought that this was the end of the matter, Colin having made it clear to me in earlier discussions that he would support Mainz if the WAC was not the official IUPPS Congress. Only Derek Hayes and I were quite sure that we should go on anyway, with David Wilson apparently vacillating but supplying the news that Dr Konrad Weidemann, the new German 'IUPPS National Secretary', had told him that he would attend the WAC anyway and confirming that Mainz would not take place until 1987. We broke up five minutes before the National Committee meeting, having briefly discussed the procedures to be followed.

There were 45 people in the room as David Wilson, Derek Hayes and I brought the Committee completely up to date. The issue was quite clear, for there were only two options: to continue with an independent Congress (with a break-even point of 1,000 participants if the insurance policy was invoked) or to cancel (with an immediate deficit of some £28,000). Each member of the Executive was asked to speak.

Colin Renfrew attacked the Victorian self-righteousness of some of the views in leaders and letters to the press and said that he had not yet finally made up his mind; Leslie Alcock stressed the amount of work that had gone into the Congress and what a wasted investment it would be if the Congress were cancelled; and I claimed that the WAC could continue to be academically important and that we should continue both on financial and moral grounds. None of the other Executive members wished to add further comments.

Thirty-two other people spoke from the floor, some of them on more than one occasion. It was an exemplary discussion, sober and polite throughout, with views more or less evenly divided, ranging from those of Dr Ian Hodder, who strongly supported continuation, to Professor Teddy Hall, who decried continuation as a disaster and morally indefensible, and others much less clear with many stressing the divisiveness of any continuation. Much of the debate reflected the range of views of people who had written in to say that they could not attend the meeting. There were some shocks, particularly to me, and some nasty confirmations of withdrawals. Even so, on a quick count and assessment of the implications, it appeared that it was mainly the specialist meetings which might have to be cancelled. The most upsetting resignation was that of Dr Mellars, with the threat that that produced to the meeting on the Pleistocene. The most unexpected reaction, in view of his total support for continuation a few days earlier, was from Dr Robert Chapman who pulled out together with his colleague, Dr Richard Bradley, also of Reading University. There were some very welcome strong voices in favour of continuation – enough, I guessed, to form a respectable new membership of the Executive Committee if that were needed, and a forceful speech from Professor David Bellos, who gave his assessment of the International Executive Committee as a group of people totally cut off from the reality of the world.

The Chairman closed the meeting at 12.45; and, having thanked Paul and Caroline at the beginning of the meeting, he now thanked me. It seemed terribly obvious that this was to be the very last meeting of the National Committee – members were to be informed of the Executive Committee's final decision after 15 February (in order to allow negotiations with the insurance companies to take place with the Executive Committee in the strongest possible position) and there was to be no press release before then.

There were twenty minutes before the Executive was to reconvene. We stood around talking to National Committee members. None of those who talked to me had any doubts the Congress would be cancelled by the Executive Committee. I was caught by old Ralegh Radford who wanted to explain again why he and Professor Hawkes would now have to resign as Vice Presidents: they could not get themselves to proceed outside of IUPPS despite their superb support of the Executive over the period since the ban on South African participation.

The beginning of the Executive Committee meeting was informal and charged with regret. David Wilson appreciated that the views of the National Committee were about equal and stressed that many who wanted the Congress to continue had clearly put an enormous amount of work into it, but he now felt that we should cancel, because he could see no other way to act, and he feared the divisiveness of continuation. Colin Renfrew agreed, stressing the complexity of the whole situation. Derek Hayes thought that there would be no Congress in Mainz if Southampton did not go ahead. Leslie Alcock agreed with Derek but appeared to believe that we should cancel for the long-term good of archaeology.

I argued against cancellation for three reasons – (1) to show support for the Third World, (2) to show that we did not have to be a 'rump' Congress, and (3) for financial reasons.

By 2 pm David Wilson was beginning to suggest that he, Colin and Leslie should resign and that Derek and I should continue to run the WAC, but Colin was adamant that there should be a vote to cancel the Congress. We all looked at each other in despair, and all of us took food and drink. We went on arguing, again and again, over the same points of principle; some of us drank on. Each time that it appeared to be about to come to a vote, I tried desperately to get them to reconsider and to let the Congress continue. On one occasion I turned to Paul and Caroline to ask them if they wanted to continue or whether it had all become just too much. Despite their total exhaustion, and for different reasons, both argued in favour of the Congress proceeding. I do not remember the details of that anguished afternoon meeting, just a few highlights. I remember David Wilson suddenly exclaiming 'the Congress has fallen apart and so has the world' and I remember him on one occasion having to leave the table hurriedly to avoid his tears becoming obvious. I remember that Caroline and Paul sat white-faced and at one point tried to find relief in washing-up. I remember Derek Hayes keeping calmly supportive, and Leslie Alcock losing track of the details of the argument. I remember, just before 4 pm, that the Chairman said he could take no more of it and was now going to put the matter to a final vote but that he would give me one last chance to try to convince the Executive not to cancel the Congress, if I wanted that one final opportunity. I said that I would think about it as I went out of the room. At that moment I really thought that I had no chance of convincing the Executive, and I was so emotionally drained that I did not think that I could plead once again. On my return to the meeting I caught sight of Caroline and Paul's faces and knew that I must make one more attempt. I have no idea what I said, nor for how long. There was anagonising silence when I finished. David Wilson, Leslie Alcock and then Colin Renfrew resigned from the Executive Committee and the Directorship of the Company. Derek and I did not have to vote to continue.

Peter Stone had hung on to hear the decision, as he was to address the Young Archaeologists' Conference in Lancaster the next day about the WAC, a decision which it then fully supported. To our amazement we were told that Paul Lashmar of the *Observer* was also still waiting for our meeting to end. Despite the previous decision not to talk to the press at this time, a decision which had been based on the assumption that the Congress would be cancelled, some of us went to him and issued the following Press Release:

> Three of the UK Executive Committee (Sir David Wilson, Director of the British Museum, London; Professor Colin Renfrew, Disney Professor of Archaeology at the University of Cambridge; and Professor Leslie Alcock, Professor of Archaeology at the University of Glasgow) of the WAC resigned today on the basis that they considered that, with the withdrawal of the IUPPS affiliation, the Congress as planned cannot be as they had originally anticipated. However, the remaining members of the Executive Committee are continuing to organise a Congress in Southampton with substantial Third World and Eastern European participation.

Lashmar had to rush away to meet his paper's deadline but not before David Wilson had told him:

> This has been one of the most difficult decisions I have ever had to make in my life.

7. Public and World Reaction

There was little time to relax after this traumatic day, for now, even more than ever, the WAC had to be a resounding success. Derek Hayes and I had to find new Directors of the Company as quickly as possible, especially as the Congress programme needed to be reconsidered. In choosing new people to join the Company one thing was essential – that the new Board must be, and must be seen to be, at least as strong as the old Executive Committee, and there must be no possiblity for *The Times*, or others, to claim that our Congress was a mere 'rump'. We needed a blend of seniority, establishment acceptability, conviction, youth, acknowledged academic excellence, commitment to the WAC, and above all, courage – for the following months, as well as the Congress itself, were unlikely to be without extreme pressures. I worked through correspondence, statements made at the National Committee meeting, and my earlier list of possible Executive Committee membership, and weighed up the pros and cons of each individual. Some people were obvious candidates but there were others, such as Peter Gathercole (who in any case volunteered the information that he would be too busy), about whom I had to make a considered choice.

One person I had no doubt about was Thurstan Shaw. Back in January – which seemed so long ago – he had summarised his reactions to my report on the Paris meeting in the following words:

The meeting of the so-called International Executive Committee of the IUPPS, in Paris on 17 January, was composed entirely of West Europeans and one American. (Two representatives from Africa were prevented from attending, and the committee refused to allow their communications to be read out.) The committee condemned the ban on South Africans attending the Southampton Congress on the grounds that this was a violation of academic freedom. European science has long cherished this principle, arising out of the struggle against the authoritarianism of revealed religion, and, more recently, against the restrictions imposed on scientists by some East European governments. Only two or three members of the committee had any experience of working in Africa, none had lived in Africa in post-colonial times, none had had the experience of being grossly and insultingly discriminated against and totally disfranchised because of colour. In other words, the Europeans and American, in considering the African ban, quite literally did not know what they were talking about: apartheid to them was an academic matter, not one of experience. The result is that the Committee's upholding of the 'holy principle' of academic freedom is seen by Africans as just one more example of the hypocrisy of Europeans, who put their hands on their hearts and say 'We are against apartheid' but who by their actions give comfort to the apartheid government of South Africa.

Thurstan readily agreed to join us.

Within my own Department, I had received nothing but fantastic support throughout from Tim Champion and Steve Shennan, the latter, contrary to Professor Desmond Clark's claims about the non-voting whites present at that meeting, having fully supported, with at least one other white archaeologist, the resolution of the Pan African Association in Jos in 1983 to ban South African/Namibian colleagues (see pages 37 and 206-7). Both agreed to become Directors. Ian Hodder, a strong supporter from Colin Renfrew's Department in Cambridge, also accepted the challenge, especially since he had been against the compromise and was eager to make the Congress a success. We also needed representatives from London, so that it could also be seen to be with us (preferably through the British Museum and the Institute of Archaeology). I was delighted to find that David Harris, from John Evans' own Institute, was willing to come in with us despite having been in favour of the aborted compromise document, and also Dr Michael Rowlands, Reader in Anthropology at University College London, who had been against the compromise. I thought of asking Juliet Clutton-Brock, of the Natural History Museum, but deferred asking her, in view of the courageous stand which she had already made against her husband, Professor Jewell (see page 63). From further afield, I knew that Andrew Fleming, in Sheffield, was right behind us, and he readily agreed to be a Director.

I was left with the critical choice of a Chairman and, after intense consideration, I approached Michael Day. Not only did he have the standing and commitment that was vital, but he was also a representative of early hominid studies, from which there had been many defectors from America and elsewhere. He also happened to be a personal friend of Professor Tobias. Above all I had been impressed with the strength and purpose of his written suggestion to the National Committee that it should, among other things:

> ... inform all who have enquired, or registered, that those who take part in the IUPPS XIth Conference (at its alternative venue at Mainz/Frankfurt) will be doing so in the company of South Africans contrary to the declared policy of UNESCO, ICPHS, the Pan African Congress and many other organisations (and) inform those participants whose studies are based in countries opposed to the South African apartheid regime that by taking part in the IUPPS XIth Congress at Mainz they may risk their opportunities to continue work that depends on Government research permits and access to collections or field sites in those countries.

He agreed to become a Director and at its first meeting on 13 February was duly elected Chairman.

Subsequently we gained two further Directors and these were officially ratified in March. I had telephoned Juliet Clutton-Brock to see if she intended to continue to organize her academic session without her husband. We met at my cottage to discuss her position further. When I described the new Board of Directors she jokingly said that we obviously needed a 'statutory woman', a remark which gave me the chance to ask whether she would like to join us. We included her with pleasure. The other late addition was Leslie Alcock, who had written to me on his way back to Glasgow after the National and Executive Committee meetings, admitting that he did not really know why he had ever resigned.

The new Board of Directors, at its first meeting on 13 February, issued a press statement that the WAC would continue as planned, in the conscious knowledge that a furore was bound to follow. The next day I called another open meeting in my Department to update the University staff and students. I wrote to Ian Skipper bringing him up to date and urging him to change his mind and to rejoin us (a move which he declined a month later). We decided to drop the battle with the Society of Antiquaries for an Extraordinary Meeting now that the IUPPS decision had again affected the situation.

A few days later our Board circulated all 3,000 potential participants with a lengthy Notice which explained the events of the preceding few months, and con

1. The WAC will take place in the first week of September 1986 at Southampton, without South African/Namibian participation.

2. We now expect, therefore, that, as originally intended, there will be a very wide representation of archaeologists from almost all over the world, including those from the Third World and from Eastern Europe who would otherwise have been unable to attend. We would remind you that a significant proportion of the registration fee is to secure grants for participants from the Third World and Eastern Europe.

3. Dr Weidemann has informed (20 February 1986) our Secretary, Peter Ucko, that the 11th IUPPS Congress in Mainz will now be held in September *1987* (with a programme yet to be determined), in order to minimise possible conflict between the two Congresses.

4. We envisage that our academic programme will proceed as planned although some changes may be made; however we anticipate that the major theme meetings will be largely unchanged. Details of any amendments will be sent by the end of March. All those who have already completed Congress Announcement forms will be given a place in the academic proceedings.

5. We have already begun negotiations with several archaeological organisations, both overseas and in Britain, in the hope and expectation that the World Archaeological Congress 1986 can be held in formal association with them. *In fact the Pan African Association on Prehistory and Related Studies has just announced (19 February 1986) that it 'fully supports and associates itself with' the WAC 1986, and that its 'members will fully attend the Congress in Southampton'.*

6. We look forward to welcoming you in Southampton in September 1986.

These were brave aims, but to translate them into reality many strands needed to be followed up with speed and energy. Not least of these, yet again, was the question of finance, and at this stage it became essential to know whether or not the Greater London Council would in fact provide funds, since this would affect when and where part of the Congress would be held. One of the biggest challenges Caroline and I faced was how to adjust our schedule regarding precirculation of papers, and yet still allow sufficient time for them to be received and read before the meeting itself. Paul entered into long and complicated negotiations with the printers and, by March, was ready to circulate a new schedule to all organisers of precirculated paper sessions. Equally important was to produce a revised academic programme, and this could not be done until it was known how many new resignations would follow the dissociation of the WAC from the IUPPS.

At this first meeting the Board had taken the vitally important decision that the academic programme should not only, as far as possible, be kept as it was, but should also contain at least one additional academic session to show that the WAC was not merely being reactive.

Not surprisingly, perhaps, the worst problem was again the Pleistocene, that meeting and subject which was totally reliant on professional specialists for its success. A considerable number of American and Western European archaeologists had withdrawn from this session, and Clive Gamble now joined Paul Mellars in withdrawing from organising their Themes on the Pleistocene period. Both were afraid of the divisiveness of the issue and Paul stressed that this might affect their own work with American and European colleagues. The same argument regarding their European colleagues could, of course, have been advanced by those involved in the Medieval sessions which had also lost a considerable number of participants, but they did not do so; on the contrary, the Congress now gained the participation of Professor Philip Rahtz, of the Department of Archaeology, University of York, and Dr David Austin, of the Department of Geography, University of Lampeter.

I needed to clarify the situation regarding the organisation of the Pleistocene sessions as soon as possible, so that this part of the academic programmme could be reworked. After long discussions, and frank assessment of the characters and expertise of the available Pleistocene specialists in Britain, it was decided that Robert Foley, who had recently left his position in Durham to return to Cambridge, (though not to the same Department as Paul Mellars) should be approached by both David Harris and Ian Hodder, who knew him better than most of us. Robert Foley's role was potentially a very important one, not only because of the resignations of both Clive Gamble and Paul Mellars from the organisation of their sessions, but also because of the previous resignation of IUPPS members such as Henry de Lumley and Alan Bryan, who were, supposedly, to have organised the specialist Pleistocene sessions on Europe and the Americas, as well as the probable large-scale loss of American and European participants from the sessions. Meanwhile Michael Day agreed to continue to organise the session on fossil hominids despite the withdrawal of the IUPPS member as his co-organiser. Rob Foley, to our delight, eventually agreed to take on most of these sessions, but only if he could do so in collaboration with another Cambridge colleague (who happened to be actively working with Clive Gamble in Greece).

With some trepidation David Harris and I travelled to Cambridge to talk to this potential duo, to return convinced that it was unlikely to work. The potential collaborator declined to join in the task, and Rob Foley joined Michael Day in organising the sessions on the early periods of the Pleistocene. Throughout all these negotiations both Clive Gamble and Paul Mellars were more than helpful and co-operative, coming up with positive suggestions and even drafting letters for me to sign. I discussed alternative session-organisers for the later periods at some length with Clive, for he himself could not face taking on the organisation of his own session again, having visibly anguished about the whole affair for months and months, and I did not try to pressurise him. It was a strange situation which was to become even more peculiar, for while I was again discussing possible names of substitute organisers with Arthur ApSimon of my own Department, he himself volunteered to take on the whole responsibility. I realised, at that point, that my policy of having kept Department and Congress as separated as possible meant that I had gained no idea of Arthur's views of the ban. I also had not realised that he had known Richard Nunoo (see pages 98 and 111), many years before, at the Institute of Archaeology in London, and was himself deeply committed to his Third World colleagues. I accepted Arthur's offer with deep gratitude and relief, and flew Dr Janusz Kozlowski over from Poland, to see if he would remain associated with this Pleistocene session, as co-organiser with Arthur ApSimon. This was a somewhat embarassing position for us all to be in, for Janusz was also working with the Cambridge team and Dr Gamble on the same Palaeolithic site in Greece! Eventually it was agreed that Arthur would organise the session alone but that Janusz would contribute a paper, probably chair a session, and would participate fully in the Congress! Meanwhile we still awaited a decision from Jean Combier, of the Centre National de la Recherche Scientifique in Paris, as to whether or not he wished to continue as an organiser within the Pleistocene sessions. Originally, Jean had considered the ban to be only of local British concern, but now he also resigned. The problem of substitute organisers was acute and the main burden of the continuing changes and adaptations of the academic and non-academic programmes fell on Caroline. In my own case, I was beginning to feel that I would never be able to get back on top of things in time to handle the arrival of participants.

I was becoming seriously worried about both Caroline and Paul and their ability to cope with the unremitting workload in the run up to the Congress, let alone the Congress itself. Caroline was, by this time, unable to stop work without getting severe headaches, which were only alleviated by acupuncture. I determined to try to force both of them, and Ail, to take some time off. My chance came at the end of March, when the revised academic programme was almost ready to be despatched and Caroline could be ordered to take a short skiing holiday. As Paul, in a note typical of their spirit and attitudes, wrote to Caroline for her return:

> The revised academic programme has been sent out to everyone (copy attached). The version sent out had an error (!), the word 'PEOPLES' missing from one of the subtitles ... this has now been corrected and all of the new versions have the word inserted. Also, there is a new session (on USA, on the attached copy), with two organisers. Also, and missing from this version because no one told me, there is a new co-organiser for Tilley's session ... I think that's all you need to know (except that we broke three different xerox machines, including our own, trying to get it all copied ...).

In fact during Caroline's absence we had only managed to complete the massive job of typing, copying, collating and envelope-filling because of the unique spirit in the Department whereby undergraduates, graduates, some academic staff, Sue, the Archaeology and Education team, as well as Jane and some unsuspecting visitors, all joined in throughout the night.

The revised academic programme proudly announced the new formal association of the Indian Archaeological Society and the Indian Society for Prehistoric and Quaternary Studies with the Congress. It also reported that, as of April 3, some 300 out of 3,125 people (from 104 different countries) had withdrawn because of the ban, and that over 1,700 people had already applied to give papers at the Congress. The Cultural Attitudes to Animals theme remained unchanged except that the day-session on art and animals was to be organised by Mark Maltby and Dr Howard Morphy, Lecturer in Ethnology at the Pitt Rivers Museum in Oxford. Howard had very courageously agreed to take on this role in defiance of the vast majority of his Oxford colleagues, particularly in the Pitt Rivers Museum, and his newly-structured section incorporated the previously announced specialist meeting on rock art which had now lapsed as a result of 'Hage' Bandi's withdrawal. All the other major themes remained essentially unaltered except for some changes in organisers. Many of the specialist meetings also continued unchanged, and others had been taken over by other experts, the 'Copper and Bronze Ages of the Old World' session by Dr Ruth Whitehouse, Lecturer in the Department of Classics and Archaeology in the University of Lancaster; the 'Archaeology and Ethnology in Iron Age Europe' session by Dr John Barrett, Lecturer in the Department of Archaeology in the University of Glasgow; the 'Problems and Developments in Medieval Archaeology (400-1400 AD)' session by two of the original Executive Committee, Leslie Alcock and David Wilson, and the 'History of Prehistoric and Protohistoric Archaeology' session by Professor Antonio Gilman of the Department of Anthropology, California State University who took over this topic from Colin Renfrew and Professor J. Sabloff of the Department of Anthropology, University of New Mexico, Albuquerque. Only two specialist sessions were cancelled because of resignations – those dealing with data management and mathematics, and with physical and chemical dating techniques.

Meanwhile, we had gained one new, all-day session. Ian Hodder had phoned from the SAA meeting in New Orleans (see page 142) to say that Russell Handsman, Director of Research of the American Indian Archaeological Institute, and Assistant Professor Randall McGuire, of the Department of Anthropology of the State University of New York, would organise a meeting on 'Material Culture and the Making of the Modern United States of America'. As a result, without me knowing exactly how, Paul set his mind to creating some grants for American Indians, such as Cecil Antone from Arizona and Jan Hammil of 'American Indians Against Desecration', who were to participate in this session.

Following the February meeting and the decision to continue with the WAC with an enlarged Board of Directors, the problem of the Congress's image locally, in the national press, and internationally, became even more important than before.

Southampton's local newspaper, the *Southern Evening Echo*, was the first to follow the *Observer*'s scoop with details of the story of the new situation, reporting that the Congress organisers now had:

> three new weapons to ensure the event is a success. They have (a) announced a new team of 11 directors, (b) received the backing of an influential African organisation of archaeologists, and (c) been assured that the rival official congress will not take place in Mainz, West Germany, until a year later.

From that time onwards I said in all press interviews that I expected the number of participants who would attend the WAC to be closer to 1,000 than to the 2,000 that we had anticipated. In another report the *Southern Evening Echo* repeated Martin Biddle's alleged statement to the *Observer* that control of the conference had been 'wrested from (the British organisers) by local activists', a view which I was correctly quoted as having described as 'utter tripe'.

At the same time, however, John Hiett, while writing to the *Southern Evening Echo* in his role as University Conference Co-ordinator, was also commenting publically as Chairman of the Southampton Tourism Group. It seemed from an *Echo* report that he was concerned that if the WAC was held successfully in Southampton the pressure groups would then be able to argue that Southampton's reputation as a conference city need not be harmed by the exclusion of South Africans.

News began to filter through that the University was about to reconsider its financial contribution to the Congress, and John Hiett was demanding advance payments of deposits for food and lodging. In March he published comments on a piece that had been written for the University's *New*

Reporter (based on my letter to all participants) in which he claimed that:

> Southampton had lived since 1981 on the prestige of hosting a major international conference. In 1985 we lost it.

All this led to unpleasant confrontations with a senior University committee which attempted to renege on its prior financial commitments to the Congress (see page 21), a series of sores which were only healed when the Vice Chancellor convened a sub-committee of Council in May which overruled any attempt at renegotiation of prior arrangements.

Meanwhile Alan Whitehead was staunchly defending the City's position both on local radio and in the local press, stressing that a substantial Congress would still be taking place in Southampton despite the withdrawals of some participants. In a public statement Councillor Whitehead said:

> One of the main reasons for the strong support given by Southampton City Council to the WAC was that for the first time ever it centred around Third World archaeological themes. We felt it was high time that archaeology broke clear of its obsession with Europe and were pleased to back the first-ever Congress truly capable of being called a worldwide event.
>
> It was naïve of some archaeologists who are now complaining about the course of events to believe that it was possible to arrange such a Congress without addressing the South African question.
>
> We are sorry that the largely European-based international executive of the IUPPS has failed to follow the principled lead of the British section in backing the decision of the British organisers to exclude South Africans from the Congress. However, I am confident that the worldwide support this stand has obtained will ensure the success of a significant conference in Southampton in September this year. As far as the City Council is concerned, we will be taking every step possible to ensure that such an event takes place and is a great success.

Elsewhere he also stressed that any local authority has to balance principle against economic expedience. In addition to the incredible support that Alan Whitehead gave to the Congress through thick and thin, he also tried desperately again to raise major funding on our behalf from the Greater London Council, before its final dissolution, to cover such things as transportation of participants to London, any special sessions held in London, and possibly for advance programme printing. I too had been involved in these bizarre negotiations for some £150,000 – £250,000, both before Christmas and now, again, during the death throes of the GLC. Each time success seemed imminent, however, the negotiations were blocked by legal challenges to the whole financial operation of the huge and struggling Council.

Meanwhile, at the national level, some of the press, including at long last a new reporter for *Nature*, were beginning to become more reflective, and to see the implications of the Congress' ban. By far the most encouraging coverage was by the *Times Higher Education Supplement* (21.2.86) which not only carried a factual report by David Jobbins but also published a perceptive editorial, under the title 'South Africans in Southampton':

The controversy generated by the planned exclusion of South African scholars from the WAC to be held in Southampton in September is now many months old. But the important issues of principle, and of practicality, that have been raised remain unclarified. The moral commitment of the supporters of the ban has been answered by the moral outrage of those who oppose it. Neither side it seems has made much effort to understand the opposing view, nor maybe to examine critically the logic of their own view. Too many people have argued the issues in absolutist terms.

The supporters of the South African ban deny that there can ever be business as usual with that country until the evil regime of apartheid has been overthrown. They may admit that their stand is unfair to many individual South Africans who oppose the regime as vehemently as they themselves. The may even admit that their stand is contrary to the principles of academic freedom. But in their view both are minor offences that must continue to be committed if the much graver offence of appeasing or offering comfort to South Africa is to be avoided. Their model is the exclusion of South Africa from international sport under the terms of the Gleneagles Agreement, although the parallel is not exact because nations do not field 'teams' of scholars and scientists nor is it clear that acknowledged academic prowess is as important to the South African white supremacist psyche as success in sport.

The opponents of the ban argue that however abhorrent the South African regime academic freedom must not be abridged. This is not simply because bans divide and impoverish particular disciplines but because the free pursuit of knowledge, unaffected by any national, religious or political tests, is an absolute condition for the preservation of a free society. Once ideas and their expression come under a ban the slide to totalitarianism begins. Their favourite model is that of Galileo threatened by the Inquisition. Again it is not an exact parallel; it is the participation of South Africans not the production of South African scholarship that is the issue at the Southampton congress. But small sins can lead to big crimes. In their view absolute vigilance is the price that must be paid for preserving intellectual freedom.

The clash of these two strongly held moral views has split world archaeology. The IUPPS has withdrawn official recognition from the WAC. The union now intends to hold its annual meeting in West Germany. Many archaeologists have said they will not be coming to Southampton, and some of the most distinguished members of the organising committee like Sir David Wilson, Director of the British Museum, have resigned. Despite these pressures the ban on the South Africans, 24 white and two black archaeologists, has been reaffirmed and the congress will go ahead.

Both sides of this dispute must ask themselves some hard questions. The supporters of the ban must be clear why South Africa is different, why it is in an immoral category of its own. After all the state of affairs in the Soviet Union offends most liberal principles, while there are many people who disapprove of the policy of Israel towards its Arab neighbours, and there may even be some foreigners with a question or two for us about Northern Ireland.

Yet everyone would recoil from the idea of a ban on Soviet or Israeli scholars. Nor is it a totally sufficient answer to say that in South Africa higher education, and so scholarship, is compromised by its collaboration with apartheid. All systems of higher education reflect the character of their societies, vice and virtue. In any case South African universities have often acted as a focus of opposition to apartheid. The opponents of the ban must accept that we do not live in a perfect world and that these imperfections mark scholarship too. The choice is not between a nasty discriminatory ban that arbitrarily and unfairly excludes some scholars and some ideal situation in which all scholars commune together regardless of race, religion, colour or class. In sad practice the choice is often between inviting South African scholars or scholars from the Third World. Only rarely can both be invited together. It is this rock that the Southampton congress has struck. Academic freedom is a fine ideal but nowhere can it be absolute. It is always conditioned by external circumstances, legal, economic, social, political, cultural. In all free societies abhorrence of South Africa is a powerful external circumstance. The moral pressure that it exerts on the organizers of events such as the WAC is entirely legitimate; it cannot be dismissed as some politicized irrelevance. It has to be recognized that academic freedom is only one of the essential freedoms on which a liberal civilisation depends – freedom to vote, freedom of movement, freedom from racial discrimination, freedom to participate in the making of the laws that govern us. All these freedoms are denied to the majority of South Africans. The exclusion of South African scholars from the WAC is certainly cruel but in a crueller world it may be necessary.

Even more striking, perhaps, was the fact that this edition of the *Times Higher Education Supplement* was also devoted to several major feature articles, written by academics from Cambridge, Durham and Glasgow, on 'Casualties of the State of Emergency', 'A determined, ruthless police force backed up by fear' (which began 'The controversy over the archaeological conference at Southampton has raised again a question which white South Africans, incensed at international criticism, persistently ask: "Why pick on us?" '), and 'Britain's legacy and the drift into chaos'. For me at least, this was the most convincing answer possible to those not only from the press and radio, but also from among my friends and colleagues, who had scoffed at the possibility that a ban imposed by an academic conference, about archaeology of all things, could have any effect on anyone, let alone the South African Government. On the contrary, it was apparent that, at the very least, the ban was raising the public conscience within Britain, and far exceeded the bounds of the archaeological profession.

Michael Day replied (14.3.86) to the *THES* Editorial:

You ask both those who support the ban (however reluctantly) and those who oppose it (however vehemently) hard questions. You ask 'supporters' why South Africa is different, why is it in an immoral category of its own, among the nations of the world?

My answer to that question, is that in South Africa, and in no other state in the world, a majority of the citizens of that state have no vote and suffer educational, economic and social discrimination, on grounds of race alone, by the law of their land. Racism is institutionalised in the Republic of South Africa.

The white minority are responsible for this state of affairs, regardless of the fact that some of them are doing their best to change the situation from within. In a democracy, once the elections are over, the government represents the people. White South Africans cannot escape the fact that the present government represents them (it certainly does not represent the black majority) and they, like the rest of us, must live with the consequences of their own government's actions. Only in this way are we all spurred to bring about social change through the ballot box.

There may indeed be injustice to some of the 26 South African archaeologists denied access to the WAC but perhaps this is a small price to pay for the benefits to archaeology as a whole by the attendance of many hundreds of participants, particularly those of the Third World, who otherwise could not have come.

In a piece on 'The WAC Updated; an archaeologist's view' Tim Champion had begun to discuss, in the University of Southampton's own newspaper, the view that Professor Weidemann (see pages 47, 51), and others, had been suggesting in response to our academic programme for the WAC:

Despite the objections from some quarters that the WAC has split the archaeological world, it has in fact brought together a much larger part of it than ever before. And there are signs that some permanent good may come out of the heartache of the last six months. The Mainz congress has been postponed until 1987, so it will not clash with the WAC. There is the beginning of a recognition of a need to establish a forum for European specialists, and another within which themes of world interest can be discussed. If it happens, it will be a major step forward.

Not surprisingly, of course, Professor Tobias did not share these views and he wrote (1.3.86) from the Department of Anatomy of the University of Witwatersrand, to the *South African Medical Journal*, stressing his position on the ruling Permanent Council of IUPPS as a representative of South Africa, saying that the IUPPS:

... in reaffirming that its meetings must be open to scholars from all countries is a landmark in the history of the fight for the freedom of science.

In other parts of Africa, however, no one appeared to agree with Tobias' remarks. A well-informed piece by Akwe Amosu in *West Africa* (17.3.86) was particularly interesting, for it concluded:

Whatever happens in Southampton, it is clear that the issue of academic boycotts against South Africa is not going to go away. One leading member of a London medical school could cite other rumbles currently intensifying in his field and was in no doubt that the issue is rapidly entering greater prominence.

The overseas service of the BBC also became interested in the debate and the Producer of its Science Magazine tried for months to get the agreement of one of the Oxford correspondents to *The Times* to enter into a broadcast debate with me, but without success. In the end I suggested Professor Barry Cunliffe, and the debate was recorded in May with Paul Lashmar of the *Observer* setting the scene, and Nobel Laureate Professor Maurice Wilkins commenting on the discussion, which was presented under the title 'Does academic freedom come before politics?' It was courageous of Barry to agree to do what all his Oxford colleagues who were so ready to write letters to *The Times* had refused to do, and I do not suppose he enjoyed the experience. There were various crunch points during the debate, of which I quote just a selection:

Cunliffe: Apartheid as a problem, as an evil, really didn't come into our consideration and positively didn't, because I believe that the issue is one of complete freedom of anyone who wishes to come to a conference to be able to come, irrespective of that regime. There are many organisations, many countries around the world that I would very much like to ban for what they're doing to their people politically and morally, but none the less, I think there should be no ban on anyone to an international congress. And it's an absolute, very simple, perhaps over simple, absolute to believe in, but I firmly believe in that, irrespective of the apartheid question.

Chair: So would you have preferred, for example, Peter Ucko to write to people and say, 'We want to defend academic freedom, but there will be these disruptions. What are you going to do about it? And give them, as it were, an option to withdraw – would that have been the tactic?

Cunliffe: Had I been in his position – and I don't know all the facts, I think it's only fair to say – but had I been in his position, had I come under that kind of pressure of threats of disruption and so on and threats of withdrawal, I would, I think, have forced on the conference in terms of its original brief to be a truly international conference open to all, and faced the consequences. Now if at any stage it had looked as though the consequences were going to be so serious, I would have rather cancelled the conference totally.

Ucko: There have been a few fringe elements who have actually written to say they're in favour of apartheid, but I fully take Barry Cunliffe's point that that does not in any way refer to him and many of our archaeological colleagues. However his absolute distinction is I think terribly over-simplistic. We can all accept, I think, that most of the people like Barry say that they are against apartheid, and I'm quite sure they mean it. But what he's saying is he's not strongly enough against apartheid for it to overrule what he's suddenly invented as an absolute, which is something he hasn't told us what it is yet. I happen to believe that there is no such realistic freedom, or whatever he's going to call it. I think it's something we can strive for. But when it comes up against a totally incompatible thing like we want the Third World present and apartheid is a disgraceful system which is infringing the individual rights of individual human beings, I personally, and many of my colleagues, think that's more important than his abstract idea of total freedom of speech, which is an impossibility anyway.

Chair: I just want to clarify your respective positions. Peter Ucko, you seem to be saying that academia, although we might talk about academic freedom, academia can't really divorce itself from real world political issues. You take that point, you go along with that point, Barry Cunliffe, but you do seem to be saying that the search for an objective truth is all important and OK, we live in an untidy political world, we'll just have to live with that?

Cunliffe: Yes, that's a fair comment, that given the situation in which we live, the only rule that I think I can abide by is to get as close to complete freedom of choice as I can manage.

Chair: But are there any circumstances, and you've got to realise Peter Ucko's position – he's a man faced with pressures – are there any circumstances – here's a little thought experiment for you – where you might feel that a boycott is justified?

Cunliffe: Not, I think, in an international congress. I don't think it happened in 1938 when the Nazi regime was developing ... I can't conceive of an instance, where the ideal – OK, golden-haloed ideal – Peter, of academic freedom, should be overtaken by any short term political event. We can see that as archaeologists. Apartheid has got a few years to go and then it'll be gone, finished, forgotten. Not forgotten, but gone and finished.

Ucko: What you're saying is, you hate the regime, you therefore feel for the people there. They are asking you to do something as an academic, probably the only place you can actually do something useful about apartheid, and you're refusing even to do that.

Cunliffe: Yes, Peter.

Ucko: Well, that is where I don't follow you.

After this interchange, Barry and I looked with excited anticipation at Professor Wilkins, whom neither of us had ever met and to whom we had not had the chance to speak. Neither of us had any idea what he would say.

Chair: I wonder whether listening to what's been said, Professor Wilkins, there's going to be a revolution in scientific conferences now. Is this setting a trend do you think?

Wilkins: I hoped that there would be, but I'm not too hopeful, because I think the way the discussion has gone is rather sort of taking the problem too narrowly in terms of ban or not to ban and in terms of somewhat conventional views of what academic freedom is. We have to face the fact that we live in a world of great violence today and suppression of freedom, and just as much as no man is an island – I mean, science and scholarship can't be isolated from all that violence. And so what do we really do about it? Some people would say, 'Well, ideals about academic freedom and so on, these ideals are impractical in this a very imperfect world, they're not appropriate to it.' I would take the opposite view that we should give considerably more attention to these ideals and look very much into what these things really represent.

I don't think you can separate one kind of human freedom from another. And academic freedom is only one aspect of all the other human freedoms. And I think you see that there's a certain amount of smugness and hypocrisy in the world of scholarship and science today in their attitudes towards academic freedom. It is, I believe, somewhat dishonest and smug to be satisfied, as most scholars and scientists have been, with their vision of the way in which academic freedom has operated in the past, where they ignore the fact that contributors from small, poor countries – in general the door was open to come to the conference, but they didn't have the money to do so. What sort of freedom is that if you can't participate?

If we don't look at the wider implications, we're going to get into more and more difficulty. And I think the world of scholarship and science in the past has looked at things too narrowly. They have made a sharp division between scholarship, science and politics for example. This won't wash any more. I think we've got to get to grips with this sort of problem. And I think that this particular congress is of very great interest in so far as it has made an attempt to come to grips with these problems.

I think the community of scholars and scientists, all these international unions and so on are taking a much too narrow and conventional and, I think, outdated view of what academic freedom is.

Chair: Even the distinguished Royal Society?

Wilkins: Certainly. They just have a fixed idea of what academic freedom is. What they ought to be doing is enquiring into its nature. All sorts of knowledge, values and so on are evolving and changing with time. And I think what they want to see is what underlies certain sorts of formulae about do you invite or don't you invite, this sort of thing. Why is freedom a good thing? How is freedom related to creativity? How is creativity regarded [in relation] to their intellectual activities? How is it related to being a human being? How is creativity related to life itself?

Barry and I were given the last words:

Cunliffe: I don't disagree with any of that and I think that's absolutely fascinating. But I do believe you've got to start somewhere, and to me the simplest point to start is to say that all men can meet and discuss things.

Ucko: I think the problem with that is that in the case of South Africa, freedom of speech in the way that we've been talking has not stopped a totally disgraceful system from coming into being and operating.

The Board of Directors of the WAC was particularly concerned about the situation in the USA, not only because of the number of withdrawals, but also because many of the individuals concerned were considered reasonably critical for the success of particular academic sessions. Even worse, there were rumours that various grant-giving bodies in the States would no longer consider requests for assistance to attend the WAC. The influential SAA, which had condemned our ban in December, was due to meet at the end of April, and Ian Hodder had long planned to attend it. American IUPPS International Executive Committee member, Professor Jim Sackett, had written to me after the Paris meeting to say that 'Since then, my energies have been directed toward America's future role in the IUPPS (if any), and I've organised a general public discussion of the business for our SAA meetings ... in New Orleans.' In this same courteous letter, he said that he would not be coming to Southampton because '... to be truthful, I do come down on the opposite side of the fence to you, regardless of the fact that my position (and surely my sentiments) are probably closer to those of many on your side than on mine ... I hope you show us all wrong, at least to the extent of having a successful congress ...'.

In March the Board decided, despite its acute lack of funds, to make a special effort with regard to this meeting of the SAA, for the SAA's notice to members stated that 'the World Congress issue has generated a great deal of debate and controversy. So that SAA members may have information, and consider the impacts of the issue on further international archaeology meetings, an informal get together is scheduled ... Discussion leaders will be James Sackett ... and Don Fowler.' Accordingly I wrote to the SAA secretary as follows:

> I write to you on behalf of the Executive committee of the WAC with two requests which I hope that you will find acceptable. Our concern is to foster an interchange of views and to heighten informed debate of what is a complex issue.
>
> (1) Would you be prepared to pass on [a] ... statement from the Executive Committee to all your SAA members as they register for your 1986 April meeting?
>
> (2) Three members of our Executive would wish to attend your meeting (Professor D. Harris, Dr Tim Champion and Dr Ian Hodder) and we would be grateful if one of them might be granted the same 'discussion leader' status as accorded to Professors Jim Sackett and Don Fowler for the 25th a.m. 'informal get together'.
>
> We make the above suggestions in the hope that they will foster mutual understanding and the relationship between our two groups.

Both requests were refused by the SAA and ill-tempered phone calls took place between myself and the SAA office, culminating in a telegrammed message from Dr Don Fowler, the SAA President, reporting that all his polled Executive were against our request, and two letters written by Professor Sackett, one addressed to me and the other copied by him to me, which presumably reveal much about his stance in Paris (see page 99), and were strikingly different in tone and attitude from what he had written before. To me, he wrote:

The session is to deal primarily with the many problems the Southampton business has raised here in America and the many issues that the affair has raised regarding America's future role in the IUPPS. This might not exclude my making some personal comments about the affair to my consituency, but this is again American business.

To Don Fowler, he exploded:

The principal end of the meeting is to discuss America's future role in the organization. We very possibly have 50 per cent of the world's archaeologists capable of participating actively in such an organization, and yet we don't play – nor, perhaps, are encouraged to play – a role commensurate with our numbers. My personal view is that we should either get in on a large scale or get out, and this involves discussion of such issues as our current representation (including my own role), whether USA ought to bid for the next world congress, and many other matters …

In short, it was my intention of our devoting the little time we have scheduled largely to America's future in the IUPPS. The pros and cons of the Southampton congress now constitute antiquarian business as far as I am concerned, the propagandists on both sides have had their say, and I am not going to waste any more of my time in a goddamn debate over the goddamn congress. We have more important business that concerns us and we had better get at it. This is American business and it would be entirely uncalled for to have a British representative on the platform; his presence would be inappropriate, irrelevant, and could only serve to distract the meeting from the issues that should be discussed.

This letter was in sharp contrast to one that, early in January, Don Fowler had written to me:

Should you wish to meet with our Executive Committee and our members at the April meeting in New Orleans, you are welcome. We will extend to you as a matter of course all the considerations and courtesies we have always accorded all scholars from all nations. If you wish, we will provide a conference room for you to meet with people to discuss the Congress.

Not surprisingly, it was the British paid-up members of the SAA, such as David Harris and Tim Champion, who were most disgusted with this American jingoism. Regretfully, we cancelled the plane reservations for David Harris and Tim Champion, and Ian Hodder was left to confront our American colleagues on his own. I did not envy him, for the same letter from Don Fowler had continued:

If you do come, you should be prepared for peals of derisive laughter from many. I'm afraid the view here now has shifted to the one expressed to me yesterday in Albuquerque by a colleague from a third world country: 'How do they think they can reconcile the absurd post-hoc mock-morality stance they've taken with the money they're getting from all those corporations with South African ties?'

If there was any encouragement from the USA, it was in the formation in January of American Archaeologists Against Apartheid, a group whose representatives, Thomas Patterson and Philip Kohl from the Departments of Anthropology at Temple University and Wellesley College respectively, published a letter in *Science* which was in sharp contrast to the preceding letter in the same journal from the President of the South African Council of Scientific Unions, and which urged American archaeologists to ignore the SAA Executive Committee's statement against the WAC and, instead, to attend the Congress. Also hopeful was a letter (5.2.86) published in the American Anthropological Association's *Newsletter*, from Michael Blakey of Harvard University, which added a significant new point to the overall arguments, suggesting that:

> ... any vote against the ban represents a statement in support of apartheid...and under the current circumstances opposition to the ban could not be read any other way in the Third World where we work ...

It was at this point that Rob Foley was again placed in a strange position. Having now accepted his organiser's role within the WAC, and taking it very seriously indeed, he had to decide what to do about his prior acceptance of an invitation to deliver a paper at 'a gathering of archaeologists in Berkeley to honour Professor Desmond Clark, one of America's most distinguished archaeologists'. I refrained from giving any advice, and Rob, although he knew of others who had refused to participate given Desmond Clark's role in Paris, decided to attend and 'face the music'. On his return he reported that although Professor Clark and others had made a huge point about the free association of scholars at this meeting (which did indeed include both South Africans and some other Africans), the whole meeting had been kept very low key, with participants removing their lapel badges as they moved around the campus, in case anyone learnt on campus that the meeting was indeed taking place with South Africans participating.

Matters were hotting up in Australia also. My own friends there were being remarkably quiet – and I often wondered what their personal lines would be – but the debate was obviously raging in some quarters, for the Australian Rock Art Research Association suddenly devoted two pages of its *Newsletter* to a ballot of its Membershp seeking their opinion on the WAC's position.

Worried by the international situation, I came home exhaustedly one night in May, and collapsed in front of the television to watch the news. Dimly I heard that Bishop Desmond Tutu was in Britain, and thought I heard that he was to preach the next day in Ireland. Eager to trace him, I rang all my contacts there, but no one had heard that he was coming to Ireland. The next news, at 11.00 pm, announced that he was in fact coming to Wales to take part the next morning in a meeting of the Welsh Council of Churches. It was too important an opportunity to be missed. I knew that American Archaeologists Against Apartheid had tried to reach Bishop Tutu while he was being awarded an honorary degree in the United States, but that he had not made a public statement about the Congress. We needed to get to Wales before morning, but I was much too tired to drive through the night. Jane thought I was mad to try anything at this late stage, but I was determined to go.

Thus, some time after midnight, having extracted a somewhat reluctant phone authorisation from Michael Day, I set off by taxi with Jane, still complaining, to track the Bishop down. By dint of various calls to Paul Lashmar of the *Observer* from telephone booths on the way to Wales we learnt that the meeting was to be at Builth Wells. We caught up with Bishop Tutu eventually the next morning, a minute figure in a very large field surrounded by an enormous number of clergymen, and he unhesitatingly gave our Congress, and its ban, his blessing. Later, part of his message was included in documents prepared by the Southampton AUT, and quoted by me in a letter to participants. It was featured in another excellent article in the *Times Higher Education Supplement* (20.6.86), and was referred to in the television programme *Heart of the Matter*. Jane grudgingly admitted that my 'madness had been right after all', as we slumped back exhaustedly in the back of the taxi, to return to the hectic activity that the day in Southampton was sure to bring. The trials of the day would not seem so heavy after all, for the Bishop had said to me:

This is the only way to make people who are otherwise quiescent and compliant stand up and do something positive.

Throughout all this period of expressions of opinion from all sides, I was quietly worrying whether certain of the Eastern European countries might not be able, or even willing, to participate in our Congress now that it was no longer affiliated with the IUPPS. I decided to get in touch with the Russians again, and particularly with Dr R. Munchaev of the Institute of Archaeology in Moscow, to whom both Steve Shennan and David Bellos had spoken on various occasions. Telephone calls with Professor Kohl were reassuring about Dr Munchaev, who was currently in the States. However, Dr Munchaev would not discuss matters in detail, let alone explain what had happened to the long overdue papers for precirculation, unless we came to Moscow to see him. As a result, Michael Day and I were authorised by the Executive Committee/Board to try to go to see him (although, in the event, Michael was unable to come with me).

There had been one other important international reaction, as the Congress grew closer and closer. The Executive Committee of the IUAES had met in June in Stockholm, and had resolved that:

(1) The IUAES affirms that it supports the free interchange of *bona fide* scholars across international boundaries for the proper purposes of scientific and cultural exchange, without interference from national governments or from groups of their citizens; (2) Where, subsequent to the organisation of a meeting, the free interchange of *bona fide* scholars across international

boundaries is limited by circumstances beyond the powers of the organising committee to control, then the organising committee will, nevertheless, do all in its power to prevent the cancellation of its meetings, so that the sciences of Anthropology and Ethnology will not suffer, and that those who attend may still benefit; (3) The IUAES Executive Committee supports the efforts of the WAC to resist the cancellation of its meeting in Southampton in September, 1986, but regrets that the cost has been to restrict attendance of individual scientists, on political grounds.

The IUAES, also a member of ICPHS, was to become an important element in future developments, for Michael Day was on its Executive Committee and it was to be represented at our Congress by another Executive Committee member, Professor Mario Zamora of the Department of Anthropology in the College of William and Mary at Williamsburgh, Virginia, in the unavoidable absence of its Secretary General, Professor Eric Sunderland (page 198). The IUAES's own Alexandria Inter-Congress in January 1986 constituted an unfortunate example which belied Professor Tobias' oft-repeated claim that the WAC was the first group of academics to impose a ban on colleagues. At Alexandria it was the academic staff and students of the university and not the Government of Egypt who cancelled the Congress in order to avoid Israeli participation.

Back at home there was a new and worrying development which reappeared on each agenda of the several Executive Committee/Board meetings held in the run-up to the Congress. Some people were trying to claim back their registration fees because they no longer wished to attend the Congress, because of the South African/Namibian ban and/or the dissociation from IUPPS, and others because the programme was no longer exactly the same as originally planned. The Board was forced to refuse such repayments until after the Congress had taken place and a profit established. Not only were there no available funds from which to do it, but Derek Hayes argued further that any such repayments could undermine the legal point of principle that the WAC was the same Congress that had always been planned, and that changes of name or affiliation, or indeed of particular Directors, made no difference to this essential point. Derek had argued consistently, throughout the period before and after the decision to impose the ban, that the insurance policy (see page 15) was bound to cover us, on the basis of this argument. There was no doubt that Derek felt much less at ease with this new Board of Directors of those he called 'dreamers' than with the previous one which he considered was made up of 'doers', and he had to battle his case on numerous occasions, but he always won through. In one or two instances proceedings were started in the Law Courts against the Congress.

There was also concern about the £150,000 (£75,000 already in hand) from Ian Skipper's organisation, without which we would be unable to proceed at all on the scale envisaged, and certainly not with the major Third World participation which was so fundamental to the Congress.

1. Four members of the initial British Executive Committee outside the British Museum after the official launch of the WAC. *From left to right*: Professor Colin Renfrew, Professor Peter Ucko, Professor John Evans, and Dr (later Sir) David Wilson (see page 48)

2. Professor Barry Cunliffe, Emeritus Professor and Nobel Prize winner Maurice Wilkins, and Professor Peter Ucko after their debate 'Does Academic Freedom Come Before Politics?' broadcast by the BBC in May 1986 (page 139). Photo: BBC

3.   Joanne Rappaport and Antionio Males at Maiden Castle (pages 164 and 173). Photo: Giles Gardner

4.   Aspasia Gould and Don John, members of the Local Communities Committee, during the evening of 'Music, Drama and Dance from All Over the World' (pages 174 and 176-7). Photo: Giles Gardner

5.   Jane Hubert and Makkhan Lal discussing arrangements for the next interview of an Indian participant (pages 155 and 163). Photo: Giles Gardner

6.   Paul Crake receiving his present at the Plenary Session (page 165). Photo: Lydia Maher

7.   Caroline Jones in the WAC office (page 169). Photo: Lydia Maher

8.   Adebisi Sowunmi sharing a secret with Michael Day, Chairman of the WAC, with Clare Golson standing behind (pages 129, 158 and 206). Photo: Lydia Maher

9. Police guards and barbed wire at Stonehenge in 1985 (page 32). Photo: Frank Martin

10. Professor Jack Golson and Professor Daniel Zohary in animated discussion during the WAC (pages 158 and 160). Photo: Lydia Maher

11.   The WAC Plenary Session formal speakers (minus Professor Bassey Andah (Pan African Association on Prehistory and Related Studies) and Professor Mario Zamora (IUAES). *From left to right*: Professor Jack Golson (IPPA), Professor Klavs Randsborg (IUPPS), Professor Michael Day (WAC), Professor Dharmpal Agrawal (Chairman), Dr Ian Hodder (Convenor), Dr S.P. Gupta (Indain Archaeological Society), Jo Mangi (independent archaeologists from 'small countries'), Dr Valentin Shilov (Institute of Archaeology, Academy of Sciences, USSR), Professor Peter Ucko (Secretary) (pages 187-8). Photo: Giles Gardner

12.   Sir David Wilson and Professor Peter Ucko guarding participants' luggage outside the British Museum (page 184). Photo: Lydia Maher

13. Members of the WAC Steering Committee after their first meeting at the St Thomas' Hospital Medical School. *From left to right*: Jack Golson (Australasia and the Pacific), Bassey Andah (anglophone Africa), An Zhimin (east Asia), Peter Ucko (Secretary), Jan Hammil (indigenous minorities' interests), Michael Day (western Europe), Charlotte Cane (women's interests), Dharmapal Agrawal (south Asia), Dena Dincauze (North America), Mario Sanoja (Latin America), (not present, Valentin Shilov (eastern Europe) (pages 226-7)

14. Jo Mangi and Peter Ucko attempt the barn dance at the evening of 'Music, Drama and Dance from All Over the World' (pages 165 and 177). Photo: Giles Gardner

15.   Jan Hammil and Robert Cruz speaking at the Plenary Session (pages 204-5). Photo: Lydia Maher

16.   Professor Wu Rukang at Waterloo Station before going on to the British Museum (page 214). Photo: Lydia Maher

Again, Derek was adamant that there was no case to be answered, for the Congress was the same as had originally been supported by the York organisation. After all, had there ever been an international conference in which the programme remained completely unaltered, and all the originally advertised excursions took place exactly as announced?

None of this made for a feeling of security, and the Board watched anxiously as the estimates of numbers attending waxed and waned. Quite apart from my deep desire to repay Ian Skipper if we possibly could (though we had written to him saying that we were not able to repay him at this time and that there was no legal commitment for us to do so) our financial situation in general was, of course, a major worry. With the energetic help of Professor Henry Ettinghausen of the Department of Spanish in the University of Southampton, we tried all sorts of last-minute approaches, but all were reported as unsuccessful to the Executive Committee/Board meetings in March and May, sometimes accompanied by the news of withdrawals of previous support (financial and otherwise).

One such case was the Council for British Archaeology which, at its General meeting in January, had voted to support the Congress (see page 96) but, at the direction of its then President, it had then balloted its Membership and now, on the basis of a 36 per cent return of its Membership, it withdrew all of its previously offered support of various kinds, and left Henry Cleere to continue his support of the WAC without the backing of his own organisation.

Another strange example was that of the Prehistoric Society which had first offered an annual grant to the WAC in 1983, reaffirmed its support for the WAC in November 1985 after the ban on South Africa, and then discussed the whole matter again at a Council meeting in February 1986 after the WAC and the IUPPS had parted ways. There, the Congress's old opponent, Professor John Coles, Past President of the Prehistoric Society, tried to get all support removed from us – as he had done elsewhere – even threatening to demand an emergency meeting of all members. This attack was apparently stoutly resisted by Colin Renfrew and Ralegh Radford, and the matter was deferred for reconsideration in May. Now the Prehistoric Society had decided to refuse formal association with the WAC but it established two Fellowships with particular reference to Third World scholars, and it 'invited the WAC to supply (it) with appropriate names of those who might be assisted'.

At the Institute of Field Archaeologists' Council meetings in January and February 1986, John Coles, this time in his capacity as Chairman of the Institute, again tried to influence decisions to withdraw support from the Congress. This time his defeat on Council led to his resignation, but the matter was taken up again by Martin Biddle at the Institute's Annual General Meeting in July where his demand for support for the WAC to be withdrawn was defeated, as was his subsequent call for a postal ballot of the Institute's membership. The IFA, although not formally associating with the WAC, continued to finance bursaries for attendance at the Congress.

The British Academy had provided the initial £5,000 in 1982 for preparatory expenses for the Congress, with the expectation, and then agreement, that the same amount would be forthcoming in each of the following four years. On the same day (25.11.85) that its President wrote to *The Times* (pages 83-4), the Academy wrote to John Evans:

> At a recent meeting, the Academy's Council received a report on the events that led up to the decision by the Executive Committee of the Congress to exclude participants from South Africa. You, will, I am sure, understand our concern, as one of an international community of Academies, to defend the principles of free interchange between scholars of whatever nationality.
>
> The members of Council appreciated the intolerable weight of the pressures on you in coming to your decision and expressed their sympathy. They fully recognised that your decision had been taken unwillingly and under duress, and solely with the aim of ensuring that this major scholarly Congress, on which so much time and effort has been expended, should take place.
>
> They agreed that in these circumstances the Academy ought not to withdraw the financial support already made, and we will be willing to consider one final application for grant next year. Nevertheless, members were united in deploring the fact that open access to an international scholarly meeting was being denied to scholars from a particular country. Had the Academy known that such a restriction would be imposed it would not have been willing to commit itself in support. Indeed, Council proposes to adopt a rule henceforth that all Academy Conference Grants will be conditional upon observance of the principle that participation by scholars from all parts of the world will be free and unfettered.

In February, Colin Renfrew advised us to apply for the outstanding £5,000 in the name of the new Executive Committee members, making it clear that the WAC was no longer under the auspices of the IUPPS, and he added that he would argue at the relevant meeting that the grant should be paid. By April we had been told that the relevant sub-committee had recommended a reduced grant of £2,000 for the year and that this had been approved by the British Academy Section. Then, in May (and see pages 225-6), the whole application was rejected by the Council in a letter which referred to the lack of IUPPS sponsorship and the Academy's adhering to open participation in international scholarly meetings.

The success, or otherwise, of our various financial appeals would, among other things, determine the nature of activities in London (including the possibility of special events at the Horniman Museum and the Commonwealth Institute), as well as the location of the Plenary session. The situation regarding London-based finance was now even more obscure than before, the only hope appearing to be some swift action by those chairing GLC Committees, possibly in collaboration with certain London boroughs, but all these moves were surrounded by legal problems and questions. While Alan Whitehead was going frantic over this whole GLC situation, our WAC Board had to plan for all possible developments, as well as working out the details of distribution costs of precirculated papers in the changed circumstances produced by the inevitable delays to the original schedules.

Throughout all these events, decision-making, and adaptations, the archaeological and other academic communities continued to discuss and debate. Allusions to the Congress and the ban appeared in editorial prefaces to books, in special numbers of journals, and in the press. It is interesting to note that archaeological opponents of the ban continued to maintain their 'coy' behaviour, for the *Archaeological Review from Cambridge* (5:1) reported that it had 'invited four people opposed to the ban to contribute to the debate on these pages but unfortunately they had been unwilling or unable to do so'. Meanwhile Ian Hodder published the paper he had given at the SAA meeting at New Orleans in this *Review*, and Tim Champion and Steve Shennan jointly contributed a piece entitled 'Why the Congress had to go on', which they concluded with the sentence:

> Archaeologists must be sensitive to the wider issues of the world, they must pay attention to the meaning that will be ascribed to their actions, and, if they wish to promote archaeology on more than a local or regional level, they must seek a forum which does not dictate either the academic purpose or the conditions for attendance in terms appropriate only to narrow European and North American perceptions of the past and of academic activity.

In the same *Review*, Thurstan Shaw wrote a long piece about the nature of so-called academic freedom, a contribution which is destined to become a classic. In his article, Thurstan examines the concept of academic freedom in greater depth than most other works which usually accept the concept uncritically as both self-evident and as paramount moral 'good'. The article also weighs the principle of academic freedom against moral values such as human rights, and is a striking follow-up to the views of Professor Wilkins in the BBC discussion between Barry Cunliffe and me (page 141).

These members of the Executive Committee/Board took some of the pressures off me, for I had neither the time, nor the peace of mind, to settle down to write any considered articles. Tim also plunged into the local University debate, contributing articles to Southampton University papers – articles which deserve a far wider readership. He also confronted the scientists in their claim that they were somehow different from those who pursued the humanities or social sciences, and I observed with a detached amusement how close colleagues and friends were discerning a new depth and quality to the Tim Champion whom they had known before. Later, after the Congress was over, when the right moment came to enter into direct negotiations again with Ian Skipper (at the specific suggestion of Peter Addyman), it was to Tim that we turned, and he skilfully undertook this delicate mission, returning with the news that Ian no longer threatened to take us to court and might indeed be prepared, at some stage in the future, to play a part in furthering the course of world archaeology.

Meanwhile, almost unnoticed by me, there was enormous activity going on in connection with what was featured in the WAC Programme as 'the Archaeology and Education Open Events', for which I had given approval some time before (provided it would cost the Congress nothing!). This activity was being spearheaded by Peter Stone and Kate Wilson-Barnes, with other members of the Department's Archaeology and Education MSC team. Kate also adopted the mantle of Press Officer. From time to time, long and detailed memos between Paul and Kate would flash across my table, from which I gathered that there were plans for some fifteen educational displays and presentations, all to be mounted and staffed by the same MSC team, in a large room very near the theatre where the education academic sessions were to take place. There were also going to be educational 'Open Events', evening activities primarily organised by Robert MacKenzie. As I began to focus on all their activities, so I began to realise that they had carefully planned things to provide a bridge between the formal Congress sessions and more general educational concerns. As our Press Officer, Kate was already making arrangements, none more important than for a programme which BBC television would be filming during the Congress, and in which Bishop Trevor Huddleston, President of the British Anti-Apartheid Movement, would feature (pages 237 and 241).

As these and others worked valiantly to support our independent Congress, determined that it should be a success, some Oxford academics continued to write letters about 'truth', and the inevitable failure that the WAC would be. Other journals such as *Science* and the *New Scientist*, continued to fulminate against our iniquities. At the same time some close friends, such as Peter Gathercole, joined Paul Mellars in a 'change of heart'. However, Peter did not think of deserting the (sinking?) ship. Once again, just as with Paul Mellars, I discovered Peter's 'change of heart' almost by chance, in this case by picking up a subdued and rather evasive tone from one of our frequent phone calls. As far as I could gather, Peter had been discussing a draft of what he wished to write about the ban, at a Darwin College dinner, and a colleague had 'convinced' him that his support for the ban was wrong. It was difficult to discover any more than this, though Peter seemed tormented by his own change in convictions. Even during the Congress itself, where he had intended to first reveal this devastating conversion through his precirculated paper presentation, the reasons he gave appeared both obscure and naïve. His overall state of mind during the Congress manifested itself in an unpleasant, and totally unwarranted, attack on David Wilson who, he claimed, 'had no right to be [t]here'! Another problem was the unexpected defection of Robert Knox of the British Museum, who had been liaising on our behalf with the Indian Archaeological Service and who had spent many hours discussing the whole issue with me. I still have no idea what lay behind his change of stance.

Deeply distressing as these individual cases were to me personally, I never at any stage considered that they should colour existing friendships, and I was able to appear surprisingly unconcerned about them in public. I maintained to all that the matter was indeed a difficult and contentious one, and that I myself, having had to work out my own stance on the whole complex matter, fully understood how someone might in all good conscience decide against the WAC's actions. When confronted with a genuine case of agonising and introspection, I felt none of the anger and bitterness which many, including Jane, appeared to feel. However, I was not so mild about those who did not even recognise that there was a complex issue, and who actively campaigned to destroy the Congress!

I felt no rancour whatsoever against Colin Renfrew and David Wilson for their parts in the whole drama, and the positive assistance they had given since their resignations meant an enormous amount to me. Their behaviour was far removed from the unexplained *volte face* of those such as Paul Mellars, Clive Gamble, Robert Knox and Peter Gathercole. Even with these, however, the matters were certainly not as clear as they might have seemed. Clive, for example, though he would not continue to organise his theme – apparently because, at various times, he variously thought that the Congress should be cancelled, or that the ban should not be lifted even if the ANC agreed to such a move, and finally that the nature and extent of withdrawals from his session would have made it both divisive and of a poor academic standard – he was nevertheless prepared to participate in the Congress. Peter was also keen to continue to organise his sessions and to be the editor of a post-Congress book, and he apparently intended to keep his views private until the actual Congress meeting itself. Only Paul Mellars and Robert Knox intended to boycott the meeting. Robert's withdrawal was in one sense particularly annoying, as he had appeared in the revised academic programme as the organiser of the session on 'Chalcolithic, Bronze and Iron Age Cultures in South Asia'.

But it was Paul's refusal to commit himself even to coming to the Congress that caused me by far the most personal distress and, given his activities and role throughout the whole creation of the Congress, his many intimate meetings with me, his travels abroad on behalf of the Congress and his many confrontations of conviction with extremists such as Professor Binford and others opposed to the ban, it was, and still is, almost impossible for me to understand his vacillation at this time. Previously Paul had tried to get the best of both worlds, and had actually suggested that, despite having resigned as an organiser, he should nevertheless be a co-editor of the post-Congress volume(s) on the Pleistocene period, and yet by April he was still leaving Arthur ApSimon dangling without telling him whether he would agree to chair a session at the Congress. I wrote to Paul at length at the end of April, including the remark:

Unless I am going mad, one thing was clear in our last meeting which was that the deferral of the Mainz meeting to 1987 removed the *necessity* of people like you having to make any invidious choices ... As I said to you from the very moment that you asked to be an editor of the post-Congress volume this would be inconceivable to me with regard to someone who was not even intending to participate ...

Paul declined to be a session chairman or to attend the Congress at all, by phone on May 8. I did not debate his decision.

Over the course of these chaotic months I had mentally adjusted to considering the Congress a success at various, quite different, levels. There were times when I would not have been all that surprised if it had consisted of only one meeting per day, and that comfortably located in just one average-sized meeting room. At this level I felt it would be successful if it produced even one or two good post-Congress books. Another possible aspect of success would be if discussion of the ban retained a high national and international profile, and resulted in some change in the South African situation, or in attitudes towards that situation. Some evidence of this sort of success came in April with a letter to *Nature* from three South African academics who wrote that they felt:

> ... a great deal of sympathy with those people abroad who are attempting to bring about change in this country through the application of boycotts [including academic boycotts] ...

However they argued that instead of a blanket boycott, South African conference-goers should be made to sign anti-apartheid statements. They concluded that:

> It is important for the academics who have a commitment to the future of a non-racist, democratic South Africa to unite against apartheid policies.

Also in April came the news that Irish anti-apartheid protestors planned to disrupt a major conference on Computer Science in Dublin 'unless the organisers banned South African delegates to the meeting.' Meanwhile the *South African Archaeological Bulletin* seemed oblivious to what was going on in the world, and simply continued to follow the Tobias line and his attack on 'the violation of academic freedom'.

By June it was clear that the numbers of participants would not be as low as I had sometimes privately predicted to Jane. Indeed, as I pointed out to her, the nature of the Congress had significantly changed, and was becoming much more the kind of meeting in which I was interested, since almost all of those whom we were still expecting were actually contributors to sessions, and the working ethos of the Congress was therefore largely assured. Session organisers, as well as Caroline and I, were frantically busy trying to get in, by telephone and telegram, overdue papers for precirculation. I will never forget my first telephone conversation with Pekka Aikio, a Sámi from Finland, who pointed out that the deadlines for these papers simply had to take second place to his calving reindeer.

The time had now come to get back in touch with the participants, despite the huge amount of extra work that this would entail for Caroline, Paul, Ail, Peter Stone and his staff in the Archaeology and Education Project, Sue Stephenson, and Departmental students. On the 19 June, I sent out the following letter:

I use the occasion of the payment of our 1,000th registration to bring you up to date about the WAC (1-7 September 1986).

I enclose copies of the contents pages of the precirculated paper volumes which will be circulated free of charge, to those who have registered and have indicated their choice of topic, in early July. They look excitingly varied and we are indebted to our principal publishers, Allen & Unwin. Any additional late papers (of which there are already a considerable number) will be precirculated during July/August to authors presenting papers in the same sessions, and will be tabled for all participants within that Theme at the meeting itself. So, *please send your paper in to us, as soon as possible*, if you are not one of the majority who has already done so. At this time the USSR has agreed to the participation of 25-30 archaeologists in the Congress, and their contributions will be precirculated when they are received.

As previously announced, all sessions of the congress will be tape-recorded and cassettes will be available for purchase. Copies of relevant sessions will be provided free of charge to those whose contributions have been discussed, but the main aim of this facility is to enable all those attending the Congress to acquire a permanent record of the Congress debates at a specially reduced rate. As previously stated in the Final Announcement, this 'will be the only way for participants to have a full record of all the proceedings of the Congress, because post-Congress books will not include reports on the final discussions.' *Please*, therefore, *complete and return the enclosed order form* to secure the discount for any tapes which are ordered in advance.

The Plenary Session devoted to the future organisation of World Archaeology will now be held in the Southampton Guildhall on the afternoon of Saturday 6th September, co-ordinated by Dr Ian Hodder of the University of Cambridge, and will be followed by a Reception, hosted by the City of Southampton. We have therefore transferred all accommodation arrangements for Saturday night from London to Southampton. On Sunday all participants will be provided with free transportation to London.

At this stage we need to know whether or not you wish to attend the free Concert and Firework Spectacular given by the London Symphony Orchestra (programme includes Handel's Water Music Suite and Elgar's Enigma Variations) on Friday evening at 7:30 at Broadlands ('the magnificent Stately House of Lord Mountbatten'). *Please return the enclosed slip as soon as possible* so that we can reserve your seats.

An important exhibition of Lepenski Vir art objects will be mounted to coincide with the Congress in the Southampton City's Art Gallery. Unfortunately the planned exhibition on Stonehenge has not been completed in time: in its place there will be a special exhibition about the vast megalithic site of Avebury, based on Gray's 1905-1932 and Keiller's 1934-1939 (previously unknown) photographs in Southampton City's God's House Tower Museum. In addition, the University of Southampton's John Hansard Gallery will be mounting 'Museology', a special exhibition of Richard Ross' photographs, which will open on 1st September to co-incide with the WAC. Ross aims to 'record not only the object but the environment, the light, the smells and sounds as well'.

The special free excursions on Wednesday 3 September to Stonehenge, Maiden Castle, Danebury and the Andover Museum, will, of course, take place as previously detailed in the Final Announcement. On our return from these excursions the members of the Local Communities Committee of Southampton are inviting us to 'An evening of music, dance and drama from five continents' [subsequently called An Evening of Music, Drama, and Dance from All Over the World], an evening which aims both to entertain us, and to demonstrate the nature of multicultural life in a city like Southampton.

Those of you who have not yet paid your registration fee should do so now (and definitely before the beginning of August) if you want to be sure of: (i) getting the kind of accommodation you require; (ii) receiving the set of precirculated paper volumes before the Congress begins; and (iii) not suffering inconvenience to yourself when you try to register on Sunday 31 August in Southampton.

I know that you will be as pleased as we are to learn that the following eminent bodies have now formally associated with the WAC:

The Historical-Archaeological Research Centre, Lejre, Denmark
The Indian Archaeological Society
The Indian Society for Prehistoric and Quaternary Studies
The Ministry of Culture, People's Republic of China.
The Pan African Association on Prehistory and Related Studies

I have, personally, received particular encouragement from Bishop Desmond Tutu's recent statement to me in which he said 'I applaud the stand taken by the Congress with its ban on South African/Namibian participation, and I hope that other similar organisations will do likewise while the current apartheid regime continues'.

I look forward very much to meeting you in September.

Despite the optimism of this communication, the question of numbers, and therefore income to be received, was obviously of major concern to Derek Hayes and the Executive Committee/Board.

At its meeting in late June, the Board adopted a budget now based on 1,750 participants (738 participants having firm registrations) and accepted all the necessary revisions to various items in the budget and prepared for the worst by discussing further possible savings. Sadly, it was announced that Martlet had decided to cancel all of the post-Congress tours, but the Board members were cheered by the fact that the first six volumes of bound, precirculated papers were available for them to inspect and take away. The GLC finally had to be discounted as a source of finance, and Peter Stone's and Michael Day's attempts to get the Commonwealth Institute to produce funds at least sufficient to cover the costs of participants' travel to London had also not led to anything concrete. The Board, therefore, adopted Steve Shennan's suggestion that the London end of the Congress should only consist of travel in a special chartered train, a cultural bus tour of London, and a free visit to the British Museum exhibition. Even at this late stage, however, we had not totally given up the hope that more money would be forthcoming from somewhere. The national AUT was to insert an appeal for funds in its *Newsletter*, and the City of Southampton had agreed to an additional grant of £25,000 to the Congress. The Board hoped that the formal association with the Ministry of Culture of the People's Republic of China would result in increased participation from China. It was also announced at this meeting, to everyone's relief, that Dr Makkhan Lal, a Visiting Fellow in Cambridge, had agreed to take over the organisation and badly-needed restructuring of Robert Knox's South Asian sessions.

A month later the Board met again, chaired by Derek in the absence overseas of Michael Day. The situation had again changed, and there were now 816 firm registrations (with 246 of the participants who had submitted papers for precirculation having not yet paid registration fees). We still knew nothing about a further 2,458 people who had filled in First, Second, or Final Announcement forms. The precirculated papers, although already copied, had not yet gone out to many participants and the hoped-for spin-offs from them could not yet be apparent. With this information, the Board decided to continue to operate a budget based on 1,750 participants, but it earmarked potential savings which would allow a break-even budget on 1,500 participants. It was clear that we would only discover whether the Congress would reach such dimensions on the first day or on the Sunday before, when participants who had not yet registered might arrive out of the blue. The task of trying to allow for such last-minute eventualities, and of preparing for all contingencies, would fall particularly on Caroline and Paul and on Martlet who had now, rather belatedly, appointed a new person to handle the Congress. Finally, the Board considered Ian Hodder's revised plans for the Plenary Session and its final details were entrusted to him, together with Michael Day and myself. We were not to meet again until the morning of 28 August, by which time we hoped to have a clearer idea of what would be happening at the Congress itself, not least about participation from the USSR, as Jane and I had at last received visas to make a quick visit.

In Moscow, at the Institute of Archaeology of the Academy of Sciences, Drs R. Munchaev and V.P. Shilov greeted us warmly and reassured us about the number of participants coming to the WAC from the USSR, despite the IUPPS's removal of its support for us. We found it difficult to communicate some of the reasoning behind the chosen themes of the Congress, and we failed to get precirculated papers from Dr Munchaev. In Leningrad, however, it was a different matter for the Institute staff appeared to realise the full implications of a Congress focused on discussion, and they handed over all their contributions for us to precirculate at least to participants in the relevant sessions if not, at this late date, to all participants in the overall themes. Throughout our week's stay we were treated with immense courtesy and the Russians were obviously looking forward with great anticipation to the Congress – the first time that several of them would come to England. On our last evening in Moscow, we were able to tell an astonished Philip Kohl that the WAC was now formally associated with the Institute of Archaeology, Academy of Sciences of the USSR.

The next three weeks were a chaos of hectic activity as Paul and I attempted to operate within, and between, the very different potential budget levels, and all the last minute arrangements had to be finalised. Fortunately Alex Ross of Martlet was now focussing solely on the Congress. In addition, the Final Programme was beginning to come into being, with the local printers standing by, waiting to add this rushed, vital and final job to the huge and successful one of the precirculated paper volumes. Paul continued to fill me with amazement, for the greater the work the more he appeared, at least on the surface, to relax. One of his main areas of responsibility was organising grant aids for participants in need, but it was impossible to demand that he update grants and drop everything else, as so much depended on him not dropping anything at all! I remember seeing with astonishment that he and Kate had apparently come to some complicated arrangement to mount an exhibition of Indian Rock Art by Dr Yashadhar Mathpal! I wondered what else would be there at the Congress about which I knew, or remembered, nothing ... Paul also had to arrange the printing of the catalogue of the Avebury Exhibition which Peter Stone had suggested as an alternative to the aborted 'Stonehenge Observed'.

There were times when the growing sense of excitement was overladen by exhaustion and anxiety. On the morning of 24 August, when my spirits could not have been lower and I could not summon up the strength to start the day, one man suddenly changed the whole situation for me. Neal Ascherson in the Observer devoted his column to 'Apartheid divides the archaeologists' coming down very firmly on the side of the Congress in a highly perceptive article, which accurately criticised many of the weaknesses already reviewed in detail in this book. Mr Ascherson, whom I have never met, nor spoken to, seemed to have mastered all the incredible complexity of the past year. He concluded:

> The WAC is the first body to face the challenge which will soon face most international scientific bodies. It has lost some dignity, but managed to take the right course. The late Sir Mortimer Wheeler used to say that 'Archaeology is not a profession, but a vendetta'. Those – American scholars especially – who pile abuse on Professor Ucko should remember that. Academia is not a temple but a battle field in which final victory may require tactical retreats.

However, lying in bed that Sunday morning, it was not the overall quality of the article, nor its conclusion, that made me weep as I tried to keep reading it aloud to a staggered Jane, but an earlier passage which read:

> It seems to me that Professor Ucko has been right all along the line, for all the humiliations and scolding he has suffered as a result ...

Later that day, ironically, I stopped all further expenditure on grants, and awaited the Board meeting on the 28th. At this meeting Derek Hayes predicted that the Congress would incur a loss of about £118,000; I reported that the blocking of grants could save about £13,000, and that there were a few further minor possible savings. The Board concluded that losses would be about £100,000 and, in view of the uncertainty about how many would actually register at the beginning of the Congress, adopted a budget based on 1200 participants to cover that potential loss. Despite the financial situation, and because the Board had already taken so many steps to minimise any loss, it authorised the payment of £3,000 of the blocked £13,000 of grants, having scrutinised and assessed the academic importance of each of them. It also considered the necessity for simultaneous interpretation facilities at the Plenary Session, for which I had obtained a quote of £3,500 for interpretation into four languages for 1,100 people, 'given the heightened interest in the proceedings compared to a month ago due to national and international press coverage and the major importance of the Plenary Session for the future of world archaeology'.

The Board agreed the expenditure on the grounds that it was:

> a crucial facility for the Congress and that it would be left open to serious criticism if the Plenary Session was conducted only in English.

We had just a few days to finalise this contract and to accept the offers by Marianne Dumartheray, Cecilio Mar Molinero, Ilona Bellos and Kathy Judelson to undertake simultaneous interpretations of French, Spanish, Russian and Chinese, together with a professional team, all to be co-ordinated by David Bellos. Through the haze of this activity I realised that the Congress was upon us.

8. The World Archaeological Congress

I don't know whether I was alone in praying that Sunday morning, praying that it would not rain! It did not, and the whole week was blessed by the most marvellous autumn sunshine. The University campus looked beautiful, and it was a pleasure to move from meeting place to meeting place.

There was so much that could, and no doubt would, go wrong – both academic and organisational. I already knew, of course, that financially we would almost certainly be relying on our insurance policy. But the main thing in my mind that morning was – who would really turn up?

As things turned out I was totally unable to keep in touch with all that happened during the Congress: there was simply much too much going on and in almost all cases I did not discover what happened in academic sessions until they were over. My best chance to know what was happening was to listen in to the walkie-talkie system and stay glued to the Viewpress visual message system. This is exactly what I was forced to do, in any case, as I was the final arbiter for any problems about grants which Paul and his helpers could not deal with themselves, as well as the long-stop for organisational problems as they cropped up via Martlet or Caroline. I therefore spent almost all the time tied to my own room as I was besieged by people wishing to meet me, and the problems poured in – from participants from India who had turned up with no money and no approved grant, to faulty television cables between Halls of Residence. Sometimes those who reached me caused mixed emotions; thus, my old friend Professor Daniel Zohary from the Department of Genetics in the Institute of Life Sciences, Hebrew University, Jerusalem, arrived – as I had always known that he would – despite having never answered any of the letters from the session organisers, and then attacked me savagely for over an hour over the South African ban. Then there was Bozidar Slapsak from the Department of Archaeology at Ljubljana whom I had met during my visit to Yugoslavia (page 49) and who, since then, had been so firmly behind the ban and had worked hard to make the Congress a real international success by encouraging other Yugoslavs to participate. Occasionally I managed to take a walkie-talkie walk or drive around the campus meeting places, bumping into old friends, particularly those from Australia including the President from my former Institute and Jack and Clare Golson, and marvelling at Paul's continuing unruffled charm to all and sundry and Caroline's apparent total control over everything. Even Martlet staff seemed infected with a glowing spirit of co-operation which made any previous problems with them fade into insignificance.

Whenever I came across a session organiser, I bombarded them with questions as to how it was going, who had not come, had people read precirculated papers, were the recordings working and technical staff coping, and so on.

* * *

David Harris:

'Like many others, my first reaction – back in 1983 – when Peter Ucko first asked me what was I going to contribute to the Congress, was to say: but I don't like *large* meetings. Previous experience of conferences, as participant and organiser, had convinced me that it was the small focused meeting that was academically worthwhile. After all, the Wenner-Gren Foundation had long since shown – at Burg Wartenstein – that this was what really produced the intellectual goods ... So no, I wasn't planning to organise a session at the Congress, indeed I was not at all sure I would even go to it (when the alternative might well be another fieldwork season in northern Australia).

'But then my preconception of what a IUPPS Congress was likely to be, began to be eroded. One crucial event in the chain of circumstances that led me to Southampton was a chance encounter in my room at the Institue of Archaeology in London. Peter Ucko was arranging to meet Jeremy Sabloff of the Department of Anthropology, University of New Mexico, Albuquerque and asked if he could use my room for a rendezvous. They did, and we got into one of the first I remember of many discussions about the novel structure of the London/Southampton Congress: it was to be a mix of major themes, and symposia based on some of the long established IUPPS Commissions. What should the major themes embrace, and what more focused symposia were really worth organising?

'I had thought for some time that a new look – in world perspective – at the old question of plant domestication was overdue: much new evidence had become available in the two decades since the topic was last examined internationally, and ideas about the processes involved in the beginnings of agriculture had also changed radically. So I took the plunge, and offered to organise a symposium at the Congress which would be loosely based on IUPPS Commission 13(1) (Origin of Domesticated Plants). But there were to be three conditions; first, as with the themes, it would have to consist, on the day, *only* of discussion, based on papers circulated (and read!) before the Congress; second, I must have the freedom to invite a nucleus of leading botanical and archaeobotanical experts whose contributions would form the core of the symposium; and third, that I should invite my colleague Gordon Hillman to join me in organising the symposium. Peter Ucko agreed enthusiastically to all three propositions, and I was committed. Happily,

Gordon agreed to share the job with me, but of course neither of us realised what we were letting ourselves in for.

'So, three years later, after Gordon and I had both been through a long, mind-clarifying and heart-searching process over the South African issue, we found ourselves, on the evening of Sunday 31 August 1986, contemplating a dauntingly deserted room in the basement of Boldrewood, seemingly remote from where the 'real' Congress was likely to happen, on the main campus of the University. 48 hours later, after two days of engrossing and unremitting discussion, that room felt as familiar as home. It had provided us with the perfect combination of isolation and intimacy; a blend that was much more difficult to achieve in the formal lecture halls on the main campus. And this had happened despite the fact that far more people came to our sessions than we ever intended or expected.

'We knew that the symposium had suffered relatively little erosion over South Africa, although we had, to our great regret, lost a few key participants. We thought we knew who to expect on the Monday morning, but there were some surprises in store. For example, Tom Markey, a linguistics scholar from Michigan, previously unknown to us, had offered to contribute what promised to be a fascinating paper on the connections between Indo-Europeans, pre-Indo-Europeans and the beginnings of agriculture in Europe. We had pursued him by letter and cable as he flitted from one continent to another, following his own academic trail in the months leading up to the Congress, but eventually we almost lost hope of his appearing. Then, on the Monday, he arrived, replete with 50 copies of his paper, and was soon happily chatting to Congress participants in – as it seemed – most of the languages of Europe. There was an even greater surprise in store. Daniel Zohary was one of the botanists who from the first we were determined should come. He had so much to contribute to the symposium. But ... no reply was ever received to any of our letters in the two years preceding the Congress. Other potential participants from Israel had withdrawn and there seemed little prospect of Daniel attending. Peter was not convinced. In fact, he bet me a bottle of champagne that Daniel would appear, and at 9 am, just as I was about to open the symposium, I lost the bet. Daniel burst into the room clutching a cluster of copies of his paper, and apologising for being late! It had an electrifying effect on Gordon and me, and from that moment we never looked back.

'We were absolutely determined not to allow anyone to read a paper, and to devote all of the 15 hours designated for the symposium to discussion. The first session was going to be critical. Could we pull it off and check everyone's natural inclination to give a paper (not to mention show their slides)? We arranged all the authors of first-session papers in a semi-circle at the front of the room, summarised the themes we had selected for discussion, and plunged in. By the first coffee break I knew we had 'won'; the challenge was no longer to get people to discuss freely, but to steer the vigorous discussion in the most fruitful academic directions. As each of the first-day sessions proceeded, and those friends we had persuaded to join us in the task of 'creative chairmanship' took up their successive roles, Gordon and I began to realise that an extraordinary academic event was taking place. Archaeological and botanical colleagues from all the inhabited continents, many of whom had never met before, were engaging in animated discussion, even showing signs of re-considering long-cherished views about plant domestication and the processes by which agriculture began. Our symposium had apparently achieved the unlikely, if not the impossible: two days of sustained academic debate at a frontier of knowledge, in the midst of a vast and unprecedently diverse international gathering. Boldrewood had become our Burg Wartenstein, and yet all the world was there.'

*   *   *

Over in the Congress office Ail was ringing to say she could not stand being isolated there and wanted to join Caroline and Paul in the registration area; and off she went, leaving behind a nervous student and Jane's totally unflappable niece to hold the fort.

I had to discover how much English the Chinese really knew and whether or not they needed interpreters – a delightful group of individuals who were, each and every one of them, fully in control of what session each intended to attend. The Russians also – did they want to move around as a group or were they going to be free to attend sessions individually? Professor Vadim Masson, Director of the Institute of Archaeology in Leningrad, made his normal voluble entry, speaking an extraordinary mixture of English, French and, no doubt, Russian words at incredible pace, took one look at the chaos of my room and the people waiting for me to get free, said 'You are too busy' and took over the Seminar Room as his office for the remainder of the week. From there he wrote papers, instructions and Plenary Session addresses, with frequent forays into my and Sue Stephenson's rooms when he could see that there was a gap in the queues. He was a joy to have around throughout the week. He also showed us all how to move in on a situation and take it over completely!

From time to time Jane came in or phoned to tell what was happening from her vantage point, and where she was. Often, during that week, I found myself marvelling at her qualities, at her extraordinary capacity for empathy with all sorts and kinds of people.

*   *   *

Jane Hubert:
'I was in Australia when Peter was first asked to become the National Secretary of the Congress. Over the telephone he warned me that if he took it on it would take over his life, and mine too, if I chose to be there. He was right. For almost five years the Congress dominated our life.

'To most people it was, until it exploded into the atmosphere and sent vibrations into all corners of the world, an unobtrusive and unformed dot of time somewhere in the future, something to look ahead to, but without having to worry about how it would come about or the logistics of how it should be run. For me, it was quite different right from the beginning; I was, as it were, caught in the epicentre of the Congress, caught up and swept along with it over these years, without being directly involved in the work that went into it, but inescapably part of it, and, and as the storm began to break, at first locally, and then gradually swirling across every continent, those of us at the centre clung desperately together, determined not to be dragged apart, nor to let go of what had become the vital issue – a truly international World Archaeological Congress.

'There is no point in reiterating the arguments that raged, and still rage, about the relative value of free academic speech and cultural boycotting of South Africa. For me, although I could see the arguments against it, there was no doubt which was the more important, and I therefore escaped the agonising periods of decision-making that many others suffered. But it was easy enough for me. I had nothing to lose by supporting the ban, I could stick to my well-worn, untested and untried principles, without risk of sacrificing my career or reputation. For Peter, the situation was quite different. Not only did he have to make an agonising personal decision about his own position in relation to a South African ban, but having made it, he faced another equally unbearable decision – whether or not he should act on his belief, and support the imposition of a ban by the Executive under John Evans. There were many endless discussions far into the night as the everchanging implications and consequences of the possible courses of action emerged at each stage of the drama.

'The local representatives of the AUT and Anti-Apartheid Movement, at one of the most crucial moments, stunned us by suggesting that the issue might, after all, be got round in some way. They were obviously unprepared for the seriousness with which their moral arguments were being considered, and they were alarmed at the effect that the personal confrontation of these issues was having on Peter. I felt, then, that they had never really considered the possibility that an international congress of this stature would actually ban South Africans, and that they had only intended to make a protest at this stage and then, when the Congress took place, organise a programme of disruption. They had misjudged their victim. The debate continued, and the ban was imposed.

'This single act changed many things. As the factions closed ranks old enmities were fanned into renewed life. On the other hand, some long-standing friendships flickered and died, though others grew stronger day by day, and new bonds formed in new and unpredicted directions. Each day presented new problems, new defections. Worst of all were the times when friends whose support had seemed indestructible and unquenchable, suddenly, and often silently, crept away in the night, taking away, with their support, yet another fragment of the confidence of those who remained.

'It was too late, though, to destroy the Congress. The closer it came, and the more bitter the attacks became, the more inevitable was its success. In spite of the constant struggle to survive, the planning and organisation had continued relentlessly, adjusting and adapting to the constantly changing situation. As the first participants arrived, the Congress Secretariat miraculously seemed ready for them.

'Like everyone else, I had been given work to do throughout the week. My brief was to record interviews with as many people as possible, especially those from the Third World, to find out why they had become archaeologists, what had first made them interested in their past and so on. But on that first day there was no time to do anything except try to help those participants who were lost or confused. Some had no money, others could not speak or understand English. The leaders of the USSR group had not been booked into a hotel, and a frantic search began to find them somewhere suitable to stay. Eventually I was sent off with them to a bleak and distant hotel. It compared very badly with the impressive hotel block in which visiting academics to Moscow are housed. But I need not have worried – one of the Russians, as we drove through some of the least imposing areas of Southampton, blew kisses from the car window, calling out 'Beautiful architecture!' to the shabby pre-war houses. I left them in their hotel, handing them each a bunch of damp autumnal flowers in a vain attempt to match their own hospitality to us.

'That evening, the sprawling rooms of the University Staff Club were filled with a company more diverse and spectacular than had ever been seen there before. There was an undercurrent of excitement and of triumph, which came to a head in a speech by the Vice Chancellor, whose courageous support for Peter, and for the South African ban, had persevered from the first rumblings of trouble, right through to the end. He reaffirmed his support, in this speech, and spoke of his admiration for Peter, for the stand Peter had taken, and stuck to, in spite of the attempts to discredit him, and to smear his name and reputation. It was sad that the speech was not relayed to participants in all the rooms, for it meant that some of them never came to know how much support the Vice Chancellor gave to their controversial Congress.

'The euphoria of the first day never really left the Congress. I managed very few interviews, but each one that I did – with American Indians, Japanese, Cameroonians, Nigerians, Papua New Guineans, and others – brought home to me the unique importance of this Congress. Kathy Emmott, also interviewing, emerged from an hour with two of the American Indians with tears streaming down her face. None of us was prepared for the emotional impact of the stories these people had to tell, stories which made our own trivial preoccupations pale into insignificance. Apart from the sheer lack of time, it was not easy to find people who were free to be interviewed. Everywhere groups of participants were locked in discussion which it was easier to join than to disrupt. There were almost none of the normal Conference drinking sessions, nor the bartering of jobs that often turns conferences into glorified cattle markets. Everyone seemed to be there to work. During the day very few people spent any time not in a session – and when the formal sessions were over each day, the discussion and debate continued, often over Chinese, or Indian, or Greek meals provided by the local communities in Southampton.

'On the day of the excursions, three of us dogged the footsteps of those participants who chose to visit Stonehenge, to discover what they thought of the monument, as the icy wind whipped around them – and also round the microphone, obliterating almost all of the recordings. On the bus, Kathy stretched out and immediately fell asleep, having spent the night showing some of the more intrepid participants the night life of Southampton; a group of Nigerians laughed and chatted, mainly in Yoruba, but with occasional lapses into English; on the lap of Antonio Males, the Quichua Indian from Ecuador, a Sámi child was engrossed in my daughter's Turkish puzzle ring. As the ancient yellow double decker bus rattled and jolted its way along the narrow roads an Indian couple marvelled to each other at the greenness of the Wiltshire hills. An exuberant American related to us how, in order to get to the Congress, she had taken the cheapest flight she could find out of New York, regardless of where in Europe it was going, and had then gone by bus across the continent, arriving in Southampton penniless but happy, where she was now staying with an hospitable local family.

The Plenary Session [see next chapter] was both nerve-racking and exhilarating. It soon became clear that not only had the WAC succeeded in being a world event, including full and active participation from the Third World and Eastern Europe, but it had also re-directed the course of archaeology, irrevocably, into a new direction. Whether IUPPS decided to be involved or not there would, it was now clear, be a World Archaeological movement continuing on the basis of what had happened in Southampton during this historic week in September 1986.

'Peter's speech, which outlined the course of events leading up to the Congress, ended with a simple personal statement:

'The British Executive Committee in 1985 had no other choice but to either ban South Africa/Namibia from its Congress *or* to abandon the Congress. I am convinced not only that the Executive Committee was correct in deciding to continue with this Congress but I am also convinced, unlike my initial stance, that to ban South African participation was, and is, morally correct.

He sat down amid deafening applause.

'By now most of the people on the platform were familiar figures, but as they spoke I was aware of them not only as the friends I had come to know during the past week, but also, at this point, as representatives of huge areas of the world, which would, through them, learn about this Congress, and participate in future ones. At the end of the table Jack Golson (a friend for some twenty years) sat, as ever, with his glasses pushed up into his hair, or perched precariously at the end of his nose, shuffling the pages of his notes and inevitably mixing them up. Dr Shilov sat beaming throughout, captivated by the simultaneous translation provided (through his earphones) by Kathy Judelson, who in addition to being indispensable as Russian interpreter, had found her house becoming a second home for the twelve Russian participants. All the speakers were confident and determined. The small figure of Jo Mangi from Papua New Guinea, as he stood to give his impassioned speech, was an unforgettable sight, with his mass of dreadlocked hair around his shoulders. The mood of the participants who filled the hall was overwhelmingly positive, with only a few apparent exceptions.

'Finally, the Congress staff and helpers were presented with gifts, including, for Caroline, a baby rabbit, because her old one was thought to be dying (though in fact it was only shamming, and the moment Caroline had time to pay it more attention, it completely recovered); for Paul, a bicycle wheel to replace the succession of them that had been stolen from his bicycle as he worked late into the night, and for Sue, an aptly-named Conference Pear tree, which, according to the tag tied to its branches, would bear rich and plentiful fruit within two years ...

'Michael Day, in thanking Peter for all that he had done, joked that he had risked his lungs and liver to do it – a remark that was nearer to the truth than any of us knew, for within a week Peter had almost collapsed from what proved to be diabetes.

'The last formal meeting of the Congress was over. Throughout the meeting Peter, pale and tense, had listened to the accolades and to the spirit and determination of all who spoke, fully aware, I knew, that this was only the beginning of the struggle, and that he, once again, would have an agonising decision to make – whether or not he should take a major part in what was to come.

'The Plenary Session over, there was the Mayor's Reception. It was not surprising, I suppose, given the atmosphere that had dominated the Congress, that after a short period of civic dignity the participants promptly sat down on the ground in the marquee, and took up their discussions where they had left them earlier that day, or yesterday, or at any time throughout the Congress.

'The visit the next day to the British Museum was the last official activity of the Congress. As we waited to see The Great British Archaeology Exhibition word came that there was a skeleton on view, as well as the famous Bogman. The North American Indians turned tail, and crossed London to seek out the Museum of Mankind instead.

'For the participants, the Congress was over. Peter stood, as he had all day, shaking hands with the queues of people who waited to thank him for the Congress and to say goodbye. Gradually the incongruous mountain of suitcases under the great pillars of the Museum grew smaller and smaller until, in the end, the last one was gone.'

* * *

On the first night I chose to go to the lecture by Professor Allan Wilson of the Department of Biochemistry of the University of California, Berkeley, on 'People: their differences and evolution'. I knew then that the Congress was going to be a real success of the kind always envisaged, for the theatre was full, and the lecture electrifying and fascinating in its implications for the beginings of humanity, a beginning which he derived from one black African woman. Later Allan Wilson was to refuse to participate in a meeting in Cambridge (see page 236) which Paul Mellars and Christopher Stringer insisted on putting on with South Africans invited and participants including many of those who had refused to attend the WAC because of the ban. The dreamlike quality of the first day continued until two o'clock in the morning as a small group of us, including the *Observer's* Paul Lashmar, sat in the Professor of History's room, miraculously commandeered by Sue for our Chairman, drinking and discussing Allan's paper with him.

Back home that early morning I heard story after story from Jane and Jack and Clare Golson about what had been happening. It all seemed beyond belief. Throughout the day I had heard that the session on 'Material Culture and the Making of the Modern United States: Views from Native America' had been an extraordinary occasion with the room proving too small, and the audience reduced to emotional pulp by the level of discussion and by the American Indian participants. Later in the week I met three of the American Indians for a pub lunch. I saw immediately not only why their impact had been so immense but also why I had invested so much of my past five years in mounting the WAC. It was people like these, and my Aboriginal friends and colleagues back in Australia and at the Congress, who had made me decide to continue with the Congress even if the ban had meant that only they and I, instead of a thousand, had actually turned up for it. These were the people who lived archaeology, suffered from it and yet needed it at least as much as anyone else.

* * *

Jan Hammil:
'We were in the middle of a fierce battle with the archaeologists from the SAA, at their annual meeting in New Orleans, when we noticed that the attention of the archaeologists was diverted from the main issue of the Plenary Session, reburial of Indian remains, to the debate currently raging in England involving the exclusion of South Africa from the WAC and the question was raised as to whether the American archaeologists should

attend the Congress in Southampton.

'I was invited to it and the WAC offered to pay my fare. Robert Cruz from the Papago nation, who was acquainted with international travels, asked to participate in the session. After many attempts to raise funds for his travel Jackson Brown, the pop singer, agreed to sponsor Robert, and we made plans for American Indians Against Desecration's first efforts to address our concerns on an international level.

'At the welcoming reception on the first evening one thing became clear; this was not going to be like any other archaeological conference we had attended as we listened to all the different languages surrounding us.

'The next morning all participants of the session, in which I was to be the first speaker, had arrived by nine o'clock and the room was filled to capacity. I had never seen such a mixture of peoples – Chinese, Indians, Africans, Russians, Sámi, etc. As the session started, I began to explain how the storage of our ancestors and desecration of sacred sites was affecting American Indian people and their religious practices. With the theme repeated by each of the American Indian participants, the serious effect of archaeologists on the people of the Third World began to be absorbed and understood by all present, and was extended throughout the six days of the Congress. As the session drew to a close, it became clear that for many in the audience there was shock and surprise as they learned of the effect of their science on the lives of American Indian people. Our point was emphasised by Steve Moore, an attorney with the Native American Rights Fund, who listed numerous examples of discriminatory practices applied while relocating cemeteries where both Indians and Whites were reburied, describing how the bodies of Indian people were placed in cardboard boxes, paper sacks and plastic bags, and taken to a museum, whereas the bodies of non-Indians were treated with dignity and respect as they were reburied.

'As Robert began his presentation, I suddenly remembered that I had forgotten something of great importance – but what was it? Then I knew what, for the audience suddenly fell totally silent as Robert began to discuss 'bone lickers', common terminology for archaeologists, used by the Papago and other Indian peoples from Arizona. The term, never meant as an insult, was the result of Indians observing archaeologists in the arid deserts of the South West using saliva in the normal course of their work during excavations.

'The enthusiasm and emotion generated as a result of our session extended throughout the Congress, resulting in a request to repeat the session, to participate in additional sessions, and to address the Plenary Session where I was eventually co-opted onto the Steering Committee [see next chapter and page 227].

'The solidarity of Third and Fourth World participants grew as mutual experiences were shared concerning the world-wide effect of desecration of sacred sites. At the request of the South American Indians a fantastic private meeting was arranged with us, at which they talked to us through interpreters, with a Papua New Guinean archaeologist joining in.

'The second formal meeting on reburial took place in the evening later in the week and was quickly extended to include input by participants from South America, Africa, Papua New Guinea and Australia, indicative not only of the international perspective of the issues involved, but the success of the WAC in involving Third and Fourth World participants within a profession from which they had previously been excluded. At this meeting we showed a video of burials publicly displayed in the State of Kansas and the whole discussion became very strongly emotional.

'On returning to the United States, we realised that although little effect may have been achieved within the SAA, the extreme frustration by Indian peoples at working with archaeologists had now been replaced with a realisation that not all archaeologists were the enemy of the American Indian peoples. The experience of the Congress had made all of us much more aware of the need for us to be in control of our own cultural resources.'

* * *

Cultural resource management was also the topic of a three-day session on 'Public Archaeology and Cultural Resource Management' at the Congress. Those like Jan Hammil who care so deeply for their own lands and their cultural heritage should be the natural allies of the archaeologists in the proper protection of sites and land. The WAC discussions focussed on the levels of administration and legislation, and the Director of the CBA, Henry Cleere, writes:

> The sessions on public archaeology represented a new departure for an international archaeological congress, in that they brought together archaeologists whose main concern was not with research but rather with the identification, protection, and conservation of the archaeological heritage. The papers dealt with the history and development of archaeological heritage management, archaeology in legislation, government, and planning, and the training of archaeologists for heritage management. The authors of the papers presented came from fourteen countries, from all parts of the world, one international agency, and one international non-governmental organization. Contributors to the lively discussions brought the total number of countries represented to nearly thirty.
>
> The undoubted success of the sessions lay in the fact that such an international gathering had never been held before. Many of those present became aware for the first time that the problems that confront them in their own countries – pressure on the finite stock of sites and monuments from development of all kinds, inadequate legislative protection, shortage of resources, both human and financial, etc – are not unique but recur in every country of the world, and that there is a variety of solutions worthy of consideration. There was considerable enthusiasm expressed for more frequent and better structured facilities for the interchange of information between archaeological heritage managers at regional and international levels, and these sessions will be seen in the future as marking a new phase in this vital field of 'applied archaeology'.

Most of the week, between the chaotic chasing about, brought me moments of sheer reflection and wonder. Most concerned individuals and, in particular, those from Australia. Some like Athol Chase from Griffith University and Nancy Williams from my old Institute were full of support for the Congress and the ban, others like Alex Barlow and David Horton, also from the Institute, did not make their views known, whereas Rhys Jones from the Australian National University, and others, were against the ban and had come because of the exciting Congress programme and personal allegiance to me. I also wondered at the courage and steadfastness of my two French friends, Jean Clottes and Michel Lorblanchet, of the 'Direction Régionale des Antiquités Préhistoriques de Midi-Pyrénées' and both experts on Palaeolithic art, who had stood out against the overwhelming French withdrawal from the Congress, and who had each contributed important precirculated papers to the Congress proceedings.

From time to time Paul and Caroline, usually late in the evening, would come and collapse in my room so that we could catch up with each other's news and experiences. What had I done to these two extraordinary people, both young enough to be my own children and both with whole futures to follow? What would they do later, what on earth could possibly keep their interests, and test and extend their capabilities after the last years of the Congress? How would I have been able to cope if it had not been for these two? I remember wondering whether their relationship was based on hatred, mutual respect, or love, or what combinations of all these elements. I remember feeling how strange it would be when they had gone. Caroline looked white and ghastly, Paul slightly mad with extraordinary sticking-up coloured spikes of hair!

Caroline had been an extraordinary gamble, looked at with total disbelief by those consulted before my decision – a decision supported at the time by Sue, my Departmental secretary who had struggled so nobly during 1982 with all the extra work, which she did in evenings and at weekends. Caroline was awkward to interview, but at the same time she was obviously quick and bright and had excellent typing and shorthand speeds. She also struck me as someone who might give up a few years of her life to something which really caught her imagination. She was plunged straight into the deep end and she attended both the Congress Official Launch and the National Committee meeting (see pages 19 and 47) even before we knew that she had successfully passed her secretarial exams.

By the time of the Congress she actually knew the registration number of each participant by heart! She had also learnt a great deal about archaeology and archaeologists and about the emotions of battle and compromise. If the whole programme was working, despite all the changes which we had had to introduce in 1985, just a year ago, it was due to a very great extent to Caroline.

* * *

Caroline Jones:

'In September 1984, as I was just coming to the end of my secretarial course, I went for an interview and, one week later, I was attending the Press Launch of the WAC as secretary to its National Secretary. It was only after this 'initiation' that I was actually given the position (one that I wanted very much but which my father tried to warn me away from) of Secretary to the National Secretary of the WAC.

'The next two years of my life belonged to the Congress – morning, noon and night. There were all night stints when there were deadlines to meet, numerous journeys to London for meetings, trips to Europe to sort out the organisation of sessions (and the fate of the Congress), whole weekends in the office – Paul and I never seemed to stop. Towards the end our diet consisted solely of pizzas 'delivered to the door' (of the office) and jars and jars of coffee.

'Finally, a week before the Congress was due to begin our first participant arrived from India! He came into our office laden down with all his luggage – and none of us knew what to do!

'One of my main duties was to be in charge of the distribution and sale of additional precirculated Congress paper volumes. On the Saturday before the Congress, Nick Bradford (one of the Department's technicians) and I spent almost all day transporting the volumes from the printers, some five miles away, to the University campus. That evening people were arriving at the University from all over the world on a series of buses and coaches from Heathrow and Gatwick airports. As I left that night at half past eleven, people were still being bussed in, with the last bus due to arrive at some unearthly time in the early hours of the morning.

'On Sunday morning in the Registration area in the Students' Union there were staff and helpers milling about everywhere, desperately trying to get everything ready and working. The television engineers were still trying to sort out the Viewpress system to ensure that their messages would be relayed to the thirty television screens set up all over the campus, and there was an expectant air of anticipation.

'At eight o'clock registration was officially open and soon participants were beginning to appear, as if from nowhere. One couple arrived having driven all the way from Poland in order to take part in the Congress. My precirculated paper desk was due to open at half past ten, but people were already queuing up long before that and I decided to open early. We were still distributing and selling volumes at six o'clock that night, and by then our stocks of volumes were beginning to look a little depleted.

'Since I was in charge of the volumes of papers that were already printed and bound everybody seemed to assume that I was also responsible for those papers that people were bringing to the Congress with them – some of which we did not even know existed. I was expected not only to receive them, but also to place each one in the correct sub-session of a theme or Commission meeting, which involved trying to find the organiser of the relevant session – itself an impossible task, particularly as I had often no idea what they looked like. I also had to make sure that enough copies were made for every participant in the session to receive one (a formidable task, carried out by a dedicated team of xeroxers, collators and staplers in the Congress office).

'Monday seemed to be just as busy as the day before. People were still arriving, and those that had arrived late the previous night (too late to register) were already congregating in the registration area to collect their packs before making their way to sessions, due to start at nine o'clock.

'Towards Monday lunchtime panic began to set in. Professor Allan Wilson, who was lecturing that evening, had not been seen and no one had heard from him. He finally arrived at the University, ready to give his lecture before flying off for Crete very early the next morning (which he somehow managed to do in spite of very late discussions after his paper).

'Throughout the week the *Southern Evening Echo* was covering the Congress, and enough copies of the paper were delivered to the University each day for every participant to receive a free copy. On Wednesday the paper confirmed the rumour that the London Symphony Orchestra concert scheduled for Friday evening had been cancelled by the promoter. With the cancellation of the concert two problems were solved – how to get the Russians away from the Concert before the LSC started playing 'Stars and Stripes' (not our choice!) and how on earth to feed and transport five hundred participants to Romsey in the hour between academic sessions ending and the concert starting. But, what were we going to programme for the participants in its place? We were rescued by Dr Sara Champion, Senior Visiting Lecturer in Peter's Department, who stepped in and arranged an instant party and disco for all participants instead.

'Since the first day of the Congress, Olivia Harris had spent all her spare moments, between translating both in and out of sessions, trying to arrange for one of the participants to fly from Bolivia to attend the Congress. She had raced up to London on Monday evening expecting Carlos Mamani, an Aymara Indian, to arrive at Heathrow the next morning, only to find that he was not on the flight. She went back to London again very early on Wednesday morning and Carlos finally arrived at the Congress on Thursday.

'I arrived in the office on Saturday morning to find that there was an article about the Congress in *The Times*. I was horrified by what I read. Not only was it an attack on the Congress but it was also a personal attack on Peter. I got no further than the first column, not wanting to read any more.

'On Saturday, the day of the Plenary Session, Ail and I spent all morning typing up Motions and speeches that were to be presented that afternoon. Every time we thought we had finished someone would rush in to the office with a new, handwritten script desperate for it to be typed up.

'During the Plenary Session someone from the floor suggested that there should be a secret vote on the Motions. We had not been prepared for this and so about ten of us spent the next half hour tearing up sheets of paper and frantically scrawling 'yes' and 'no' boxes on them. But there was no need – the votes were overwhelming, and carried with a show of hands.

'At the end of the Plenary Session Paul, Ail, Sue and I were called up on stage to be given gifts. I had to make a supreme effort not to burst into tears as I went up the steps and was presented with a huge hutch inside which I later found a baby grey rabbit.

'The next morning I travelled up to London with all the participants on the specially chartered Congress train. I hoped to distribute the cassettes of the academic sessions that had not yet been collected by participants and so I boarded the train armed with a box full of tapes. However, it was absolutely impossible to move along the train, crowded as it was with people and suitcases.

'I slept through most of the two-hour bus tour of London, but I do remember being shown the South African Embassy at which there was bemused laughter.

'We arrived at the British Museum to be met by the Director, Sir David Wilson. Soon the portico of the Museum was covered with suitcases as members of the Museum staff acted as left luggage attendants. Peter seemed to spend much of his afternoon acting as a lost property person with numerous participants having left coats and hats on coaches and on the train.

*   *   *

My Wednesday morning started with a rare disaster of which I was the first to become aware. It was a day dependent for its success on an early start (eight o'clock), for buses would be leaving for places such as Stonehenge and Maiden Castle, to return in the evening in time for the Southampton Local Communities Committee cultural evening. I reached my room in the Department at half past six to discover that our television screens were still relaying yesterday's messages – no mention of an early start or where to find the buses. I dashed to the control room – empty. I dashed to the Hall of Residence to discover that the early breakfasts had, by mistake, been prepared for the day before and nothing had been done for this morning, and the Viewpress staff did not see why they should start work without any breakfast... The local bus companies were magnificent – they scrapped the detailed scheduling and filled buses according to where people wanted to go, and then simply set off when they had a full load. Shivering, unshaved and in shirt sleeves from seven until ten o'clock I witnessed the extraordinary sight of hundreds and hundreds of people arriving dressed in the most fantastic variety of clothing, often greeting each other and me as old friends whom they had known all their lives, dashing to collect their lunch packs and piling into the rows and rows of buses. Later I learnt of the friendships and contacts cemented on this day of international sightseeing.

I again thought of David Wilson and ruefully remembered his initial insistence on at least one day of sightseeing between all the academic work, and how he had really wanted me to schedule two days. I met Colin Renfrew and Rosemary Cramp, both English Heritage Commissioners, as they left Southampton for a meeting in London, and I knew from Colin's face that he was genuinely happy – at least at this moment – that he had agreed to resign in order to let the Congress continue (page 126). I thought of Barry Cunliffe and our secret meeting at Waterloo Station when we battled away over the South Africa issue, about his incapacity to say to my face that he had resigned over it, to our BBC discussion with the Nobel Prize winner (see page 139). It was particularly heartwarming that Barry was even now waiting at Danebury to give personal guided tours to our participants. I thought of Geoffrey Wainwright who had supported us throughout in our association with English Heritage, and who had gone through so much regarding the choice of Maiden Castle for an excavation in 1986, and I remembered Jane, Geoff and I clambering up to Beacon Hill in the snow and ice as we reviewed the possible sites.

I drove a lady who was feeling ill from the buses back to her Hall of Residence, to discover as I deposited her there that she was Professor Marija Gimbutas from the USA, whose work I had strongly criticised in print! There I saw Olivia Harris about to depart for Heathrow to collect a late Indian arrival from Bolivia, and thought back to how much she had contributed to the success of the Congress by virtue of her consultations on our behalf with Latin American Indians. Both she and Joanne Rappaport, whom I had first met at the IUAES Congress in Canada (see pages 28 and 29) spent the Congress not only contributing academically but always unobtrusively at the side of anyone who needed help with Spanish translation. I saw Les Groube staggering around looking for a member of the Department's Archaeology and Education team whom he had been supposed to meet on one of the buses, but he could neither remember which one, or for which destination, and I remembered his disgust at the way the Paris International Executive Committee meeting was handled and his subsequent letter of protest to the IUPPS Secretary-General. Jane, with her daughter Olivia, drove up and screeched to a halt at the side of the departing buses, late because she had had to collect a Russian and had forgotten her tape recorder. I saw her engulfed in a huge African embrace from someone I did not recognise but thought was from Cameroon.

It is hard for me to describe the Wednesday evening and all that it represented, especially to me, but also to many others. The 'Evening of Music, Drama and Dance from all over the World' was the result of the original dream and, I feel, it reflects much about my own involvement in the whole Congress as well as much about Councillor Alan Whitehead, Leader of the City of Southampton Council.

From the very beginning I had seen the Congress as a unique chance to involve the local communities, a chance for overseas participants to see what it was like to live in England in 1986 having come from a different cultural background, and a chance for a new spirit of real community to be developed in Southampton. In addition I had always seen the Congress as a chance to break down the barriers between City and University. From the beginning I was determined that the local Southampton communities should become more than merely the source of exotic foods, but I knew that I would have a huge task in creating genuine interest and a community spirit for the diverse constituency which is the City of Southampton. My early, and at that stage unsuccessful, attempts to raise money from the City, local government and Chamber of Commerce, had merely confirmed the enormity of the task ahead of me.

Alan Whitehead had fallen for the first and only trap that I ever laid for him! He responded to an attack that I made on the City of Southampton in the local press, in which I pointed to the lack of City support for the WAC; and he responded, typically for him, by coming to see me in person. From that very first realisation that we 'clicked', Alan played a wide variety of roles in my life and in the life of the Congress, as instigator of the ban on South Africa/Namibia (see page 56), confidant on late evenings of despair, money raiser (see pages 75 and 148), but, most important of all, the supporter of my ideas about the local community involvement and the bridging of the gap between the City and the University. Alan was the one who introduced me to Don John, the Community Relations Officer, who became the Chairman of the Congress's Local Communities Committee, which was made up initially of friends of mine, like Jack Richardson who had first been a neighbour, then friend and later a colleague in work in Crete, people I knew I could count on for involvement, informality, and work. Other members were suggested by Don from the Hindu, Muslim, Chinese, Greek and other local groups. Eventually, from these beginnings, the Committee grew bigger and bigger, and Paul became the anchor man, as I took a background role through lack of time. It was perhaps the most difficult of all the jobs that I gave to Paul, for I doubt whether he had ever before dealt with people from other cultural backgrounds, and his type of efficiency and hard work did not make it easy for him to accept other styles of activity. He gained the admiration of all the Committee.

*   *   *

Paul Crake:
'Even without the political furore the Congress would have been a huge organisational task. There were times when I was certain that the whole edifice would crumble, and others when I was equally convinced that it was unstoppable. Every time things went well another crisis would loom, threatening the end of everything we had worked for. The only thing to do

was to try and keep our wits about us, thinking up new ways to tackle problems.

'With the apartheid storm-clouds gathering in mid-1985 I was certain a crisis could be avoided. But more and more pressures were put on us, and suddenly the anti-apartheid groups threatened to overwhelm us. Like many others, for the first time I was forced to consider the whole issue of academic freedom and apartheid. With much soul-searching I was convinced that the ban was the morally correct course of action. I needed that conviction to support me over the next year. Caroline and I, later joined by Ail, forced ourselves to keep going. Caroline was astonishing: whenever situations occurred which seemed impossible, situations which then somehow contrived to get worse, Caroline just dug in and worked harder. As Peter piled on impossible pressures (but which didn't really compare to those he was under), Ail proved to be indispensable. Her awe-inspiring sense of humour was vitally important to all of us in giving us a sense of proportion.

'One of my main duties was to organise the Congress's grant-aid system, designed especially to help Third and Fourth World participants. As time went on and my grant-aid budget was cut again and again, despite Peter's attempts to protect it, it increasingly became a matter of scrabbling around, trying to raise paltry sums of money from different sources which, when cobbled together, might make the difference between someone being stuck at home or able to come. Always, the demands for grant-aid money were greater than our capacities to supply them. And there were extra pressures. Paying for travel tickets meant dealing in many different currencies. I was constantly gambling on movements in the money markets, trying to stretch the money as far as possible. A bad day could have wiped out large chunks of our budget.

'The logistics were complex, with last-minute demands to fly Papua New Guineans, Easter Islanders, Inuit, Sámi, Chinese and Russians to the Congress, all for the cheapest prices but in ways that would not be too traumatic for the travellers.

'We lived in a whirlwind of impossible crises that, somehow, seemed to get dealt with. Always my concern was that the participants should feel welcome, and that their stay should be as easy as possible. I bullied, cajoled and pleaded with colleagues to do just *one* more impossible job that seemed to be absolutely crucial. I remember hours spent late into the night riding on the Congress's buses, trying to help participants get where they needed to go.

'Before the Congress, alone one night in the strange quiet of the office, I had wondered if it would all be worth it. I need not have worried. It was a fabulous experience, and one that transformed my life.'

*   *   *

We linked the Local Communities Committee effort to Peter Stone's

Archaeology and Education MSC project by offering two academic papers to the 'Young People and the Past' session of the Congress, based on the work of Fyona Suffield (then an undergraduate in my Department) and Kathy Emmott (one of Peter's staff) who had consulted local Southampton parents and children about their different perceptions of the past and how they did, or did not, differ according to cultural backgrounds. Through this activity of consultation we hoped to add a strand, and academic status, to the local communities' involvement in the whole Congress. Meanwhile cultural activities had been planned, foods were being prepared, interpreters had volunteered, hospitality in private houses had been offered, the Guildhall had been offered free of charge, and Jack Richardson had mounted displays there of cultural and educational interest.

The trouble was that no one could gauge whether anyone would turn up, despite the publicity of the free evening put out in local papers and on buses. Was the nature of Southampton too heterogeneous for it to work? Was the division between City and University too wide for us to have successfully bridged it? Would the Congress participants be too tired from their excursions to turn up? I was really nervous, a state not helped by the latest prediction by someone or other of a few hundred people if we were lucky, and by others that the National Front might turn up and that the police had been alerted. That day someone had plastered the University with anti-Mandela notices. I was also nervous about the whole production, for my idea that Councillor Whitehead should not only formally open the proceedings but should then act as linkman to each cultural performance (Chinese Lion dance, Greek dancing, Barn dance, Indian music and dancers, break dancing, Polish dancing, Cameroonian poet, etc) had been overruled. Someone I did not know was to link the performances, and I was worried about the tone which he might adopt.

I got to the Guildhall very early and simply could not believe my eyes! There were already hundreds of people from the City there, adults and children from all the local communities, seated at small tables on the floor of the Guildhall. An area of the floor was reserved for the performers, and the displays were up on the stage and along the walls. And more and more people came, more and more children mingling excitedly with each other and more and more Congress participants interacting with locals. The bars opened and people rushed to take drinks back to their tables – one I remember, especially, crowded with the official Chinese delegation of senior archaeologists happily ensconced with local Chinese restaurateurs. Pig tailed Indian children from the city sat crowded together with the children of my academic colleagues, outside the circle reserved for performers. The noise and spirit was indescribable. The crush was also incredible; disapproving City employees informed me that the doors would have to be closed for there were far too many people – a view quickly and efficiently overruled by someone higher up in the City hierarchy.

Alan Whitehead hit the right note in opening the occasion and the performances began with the crash of the Chinese Lion and continued throughout this fantastic evening with a vitality which shook everyone there. Only I knew what my Cretan friend, Aspasia Gould had had to accomplish to get the Greek Cypriot dancers on stage, who performed so beautifully, for I had approved payment of the dry-cleaning bill for the Greek costumes which had not been taken out of cases for many years. Flash lights were going off everywhere. Patrick Mbunwe-Samba, the Cameroon poet, could only just be heard but he looked splendid in his robes, and still people were coming and coming.

The brilliance of the choice of linkman was proved, not only by his insistence on the seating arrangements at separate intimate tables and having the performance area on the floor of the main hall, but by his introduction of the barn dance at various times during the evening. Children started to be taken home about half past ten but the rest of us danced and danced, talked and talked, laughed and laughed, until we had to leave at two o'clock.

The same previously grumpy Guildhall official who had threatened to close the doors came up to me with a huge grin and said that he had never seen anything like it in his life, that the Guildhall had become a changed place and, most important of all, that life in the City could never be the same again. There is pressure on Don John and Alan Whitehead to do something to follow up this breakthrough in community relations. Later we learnt that over 3,600 people had participated in the 'Evening of Music, Drama and Dance from all over the World'.

Thursday was the day that I really had to organise myself so that I could at last attend some academic sessions, not least that on 'The Politics of the Past: Regional Emphases: Africa and North America' in which my own paper on 'Another case of irreconcilable issues?: the fate of "culture houses" in Zimbabwe' was to feature. The day had started well with me getting to the early start of the overall session, a showing of the recent video on Stonehenge and the battles between police, so-called hippies and Druids. I stayed on for part of the following academic discussion, but I was restless and left. I was immediately caught up in various problems and in the interview arranged by Press Officer Kate with the BBC's External Radio Service for a special edition of their programme *Discovery* devoted to the Congress. I returned to the session just in time for my own contribution in the session which was superbly chaired by Maori-Irish Stephen O'Regan who had, I was told later, started off the session with a Maori song of welcome, which had been 'answered' by several members of the audience!

I decided that a part of my overall plan had failed, in this thematic session at least, for we were all asked to give short summaries of our precirculated papers, rather than leaving all available time for discussion. At another level, however, the whole thing was working superbly as planned. My precirculated paper was about problems in setting up what are called culture houses in Zimbabwe (see page 3). There was time for only about ten minutes discussion of it but that discussion involved an archaeologist and an ethnographer from Papua New Guinea, one a native Papua New Guinean and the other an expatriate, a British archaeologist who had worked in West Africa, British and expatriate Botswana educationalists, and a Zimbabwean, as well as our Maori Chairman. I felt privileged to be able to receive such a wide ranging and informed set of comments. This experience also demonstrated another success of all our planning and our eventual insistence on keeping £7,000 in the budget for our tape-recording contract, despite all our financial problems. When I came to revise my paper for a chapter in one of the Allen & Unwin post-Congress books, I could not remember the details of the discussion. Gerry Bass's recordings gave me them, as well as recreating the atmosphere of the occasion in an unrepeatable way, and Mr Taka Mudariki's three interventions in the discussion, recorded for posterity, caused me to make four major additions and changes to my paper.

As I left the session I remember wondering whether other sessions were also witnessing this level of academic excellence, as well as the unique international flavour. Later reports to me indicated that indeed they were. Tim Ingold, the co-organiser of the overall theme, 'Cultural Attitudes to Animals', wrote to me about his session entitled 'What is an animal?':

> The purpose of this session was to address the problems surrounding the definition of animality, whether inclusive or exclusive of humanity, from a number of different personal and disciplinary points of view. The papers introduced a wide variety of perspectives, from philosophy, psychology, biology, anthropology and semiotics. They generated an exceptionally vigorous and sometimes heated discussion, in which many of the most fundamental assumptions attending 'Western' or 'scientific' conceptions of animality were exposed and criticised. Though the discussion moved on a fairly high level of abstraction and generality, and was sometimes diffuse on account of the diversity of opinion expressed, the session made a vital contribution to the success of the entire theme on 'cultural attitudes to animals', both in getting it off to a lively and exciting start, and in drawing attention to major issues that repeatedly surfaced during the subsequent sessions, and to which participants had frequent occasion to refer. Academically, the session demonstrated very clearly that the problem of understanding man's relation to animals of other species, both past and present, is one that unites not only archaeologists and anthropologists, but scholars of many other disciplines as well. In bringing them together, foundations have been laid for their future, more effective collaboration.

Juliet Clutton-Brock was the organiser of the session on 'The appropriation, domination and exploitation of animals', which ran for almost two full days:

> As planned the session was divided into four sections covering discussions on the domestication and exploitation of animals, pastoralism, hunting and collecting, and the interaction of human and animal behaviour. The majority

of the contributors were able to attend the Congress and there was a total of 34 discussants who had provided precirculated papers.

The sections were unique in their world-wide coverage of the subjects and in the combination of archaeological evidence with modern practices, whilst the session as a whole was highly successful in the aim to examine the processes and patterns of domestication and the exploitation of animals rather than reporting on case-studies in archaeozoology. There were wide-ranging discussions on a diversity of topics from fishing in ancient Tasmania to ancient and modern pastoralism in South America, Lapland, the Ukraine and Africa.

The third sub-theme lasted for a day. It was run by Roy Willis, who, like Tim Ingold, is a social anthropologist. He wrote to me at some length and I quote a part of his report:

It was an unprecedently crowded session that attracted contributions from all five inhabited continents and from a wide variety of theoretical perspectives. Consequently, there was an abundance of ethnographic material and insightful observations but little or no sustained common focus. In quality, the contributions covered the whole spectrum from the obviously brilliant to the patently abysmal. Extracting value from all this is a certainly viable but a certainly demanding editorial project. While some papers were written in the 'ethnographic present' of traditional anthropology, others belonged to the domain of history or prehistory. One contribution, [which] represented an intensively researched theory of the origins of human religiosity in emotional attitudes to certain fearsome animals, could be said to have epitomised the catholicity as well as the ambition that animated the more outstanding contributions. Controversial arguments enlivened much of the presentations, including one on the evidence for remote Palaeolithic animal and human 'sculpture', another on a postulated universal mythic association of menstruation and the serpent image, and myself on the meaning of the snake.

Superlative ethnographic detail distinguished three of the South American contributions in particular. A careful and empathetic study of the Gorgona theme in Cretan art also provided much food for thought.

J. Olowo Ojoade, of the University of Jos, Centre for Development Studies, on the Nigerian cultural attitude to the dog, electrified the gathering with his combination of rich ethnography and superb showmanship.

Finally, a paper on the idea of fish in Icelandic society, written from a Marxist perspective, and one on Ojibwa-Cree food and animal categories, threw light on the social dynamics of historical change in animal images in two very different societies.

The final session on 'Learning from art about the cultural relationships between humans and animals' proved to be a happy combination of two previously separate sessions (see page 133). As Howard Morphy, one of the co-organisers, said:

The session focussed both on the ways in which animals are represented in art and the meanings of animal representation in art. It included people who approached art from a wide variety of perspectives: art history, anthropology and archaeology, linking them together through the discussion of common themes. Perhaps the most exciting thing to emerge was just how far the study of prehistoric art had left behind simple evolutionary models and just how much archaeological data the study of art now produces. Without the deadweight of a rigid evolutionary schema a cross-cultural perspective becomes much more useful in suggesting alternative ways of interpreting art in particular contexts. In the session, papers on living arts from Australia, Africa and North America encouraged new ways of looking at prehistoric art systems from Europe and Central America, and the papers dealing with prehistoric traditions encouraged people to think of the place of art in the origins of human consciousness and of the way in which changes in art might reflect or be part of the processes of social and political change. In the Australian and North American papers in particular the productivity of a multi-disciplinary approach was clearly apparent. The use of ethnography in combination with formal analysis, quantitative methods and the wider archaeological record was shown to produce exciting insights into the process of the transformation of regional artistic systems over time. The three papers on the Kakadu region of Northern Australia, where the artistic record stretches from 20,000 years ago to the present day, provided an encouraging foretaste of what the future has in store. The overall feeling was that the study of art is an area which is becoming both more varied and more unified, varied in its potential as a source of information about human cultural creativity and ideational systems, and unified as a discipline or area of interest that has a sense of direction.

On Thursday evening Alan Whitehead had arranged a public meeting on 'Southampton and Apartheid' in the Guildhall, to be addressed by Bishop Trevor Huddleston and a representative of the ANC. The City Council had received considerable attack in the local press because of its decision to fly the ANC flag above the Civic Centre during the week of the WAC. One of the striking things about the evening was the large number of Congress participants who turned up for this meeting, not only those who had sat at the feet of 'Father' Huddleston, at least in spirit, some thirty years ago, but also many who were still in doubt about the ban, and who, in any other circumstances, would not have even considered attending what really was an Anti-Apartheid meeting. It was, therefore, even more moving when, at the end of his speech, the whole audience rose to its feet in a standing ovation – the people of Southampton, Congress participants from all over the world, the committed and the waverers.

*   *   *

Philip Rahtz:
'I was one of the real fence-sitters in the months before the Congress. I was impressed by Philip Tobias' paper, but I was also under heavy counter-persuasion from several of my colleagues at York. I had not had to make up my mind as I hadn't actually enrolled, so I only had to have a theoretical stance. I was however forced to come down on one side or the other when the CBA after a referendum withdrew its support – and I was up for election in July as their next President!

'I was rather dismayed at the CBA decision and I was firmly booted into touch by Peter Ucko, who asked me in a characteristically fierce letter 'how could I possibly stand for president of a body which could behave ...'. We considered the possibility of overturning the referendum at the July Annual General Meeting of the CBA; this proved to be constitutionally impossible, given the formalities and length of notice required. So I got up at the meeting *before* I was elected and made a short speech accusing the CBA membership of supporting apartheid etc; any passion I might have put into this was uncharacteristic, as I am rather an unpolitical animal. My speech was greeted with a deadly silence, and then there were a few antagonistic comments from those who were clearly regretting the choice of this fellow as their next President. I was suitably relieved when there were whispered approbations at tea-time, so I'd done the right thing. Peter liked my speech and said *"Come"*. So my wife and I dropped everything and came.

'I was to chair some sessions on medieval archaeology in "Settlements and Societies". Leslie Alcock was the principal chairman in this, and we arranged the programme to include my participation. On arrival at Southampton we were however swept into the amazing scenes in the afternoon and evening of registration; there was an air of being born again, an excitement of newness which is sadly lacking from British archaeological conferences.

'I found the medieval archaeology sessions rather descriptive and particularistic. Its exponents tend to be like this; modern theoretical archaeology has made little inroads here. However I was stuck with it, the more so as some of the listed speakers had not turned up [including Konrad Weidemann (see page 124)].

'My wife, however, was free to be a "floater", and she met me each break with tantalising reports of mind-boggling papers and discussions on subjects of real relevance to the study of the human past, such as objectivity, cultural attitutes to animals, and the rights of the human dead and their descendants. I did get to the splendid sessions on cultural resource management concerned with Stonehenge; here we were regaled with videos of police confrontation with neo-hippies, the secular Arch-Druid, the ley-liners, and the debacle of the English Heritage representative. He was putting over a very dull idea of how to make Stonehenge more attractive, but was swept aside by Peter Addyman with Heritage Projects' plans of what *they'd* do to Stonehenge, based on the experience of the enormous success of the Jorvik Viking Centre in York.

'There were however also the evenings and lunch-breaks, where one could talk to Sámi reindeer hunters, Innuit Esquimaux, and an Indian who wanted to relate all European history and archaeology to Hindu texts. There was a splendid lecture by Chris Chippindale on Stonehenge, prefaced by the building of a model of Stonehenge in bricks, which he and Andrew Saunders, the Chief Inspector of Ancient Monuments, accomplished in ten minutes.

'There was ethnic food, and a most exciting evening of multi-ethnic entertainment in the Guildhall. In this, rather to everyone's surprise but gratification (especially the beaming Ucko), the local communities got together – would they ever have done so except by the stimulus of the Congress?

'We went on excursions to Maiden Castle, where we were properly received by Geoff Wainwright and his team, and to Danebury where we were given an excellent talk by Barry Cunliffe, the more welcome since he had pulled out of the Congress earlier. We were saddened to hear that those who went to Stonehenge got *no* reception, and saw, or did not see, the monument in all its sordid present reality. English Heritage might at least have been on hand to let our visitors *touch* the stones.

'The whole experience was overwhelming and we came away from the Congress feeling that it was one of the most exciting weeks that archaeology had ever brought us. In my 25 years of academic teaching, I'd felt restricted by the parochial nature of most undergraduate teaching, forced on us by the limitations of an English degree, and by the Europo-centric, if not actually Anglo-centric, predilections and experience of our undergraduates. World Archaeology is the *only* subject, and was much reinforced by the Southampton experience. It was especially important to me, as I retired at the end of that month and needed to have my interest in archaeology, and its importance in the modern world, made manifest in the (last) retirement stage of my archaeological life. Our perceptions too were changed; how much we had taken our own value-systems for granted as the only right ones, until we were brought hard up against others!

'It remains to be seen whether we can contrive to uphold our "western rationalist" attitudes to ley-liners, Glastonbury witches, metal-detectors, and neo-druids; or shall we be more inclined to accept them, or be accepted by them, as part of the wider spectrum of world anthropology which the Congress represented?

'Direct knowledge of the Southampton event is bound to be limited to those who were actually there; it is difficult to explain to others what they missed and why it was significant in the history of British and world archaeology. I shall do my best by writing and giving seminars where I can – I'm just off to Canada to give one now!'

*   *   *

Leslie Alcock, the co-organiser with David Wilson of the sessions on medieval archaeology, found them rather less dull than as described by Philip Rahtz. He reported to me after the Congress:

Apart from an innovative paper on urbanisation along the Kenya coast, the papers in the sessions on the 'Problems and developments in medieval archaeology, 4th to 14th Centuries AD' came entirely from Europe. The largest single group was from Eastern Europe (Czechoslovakia, Hungary,

Latvia, Poland and Yugoslavia) and the second largest from the UK; but the Scandinavian countries, France and Germany were all represented. The presence of a significant number of Slav archaeologists, both those reading papers and also non-[paper-readers], brought important new discoveries to the attention of western scholars. There were also very interesting contrasts in theoretical stand-points, by no means along simple Marxist : non-Marxist lines. Another important series of papers dealt with recent developments in human skeletal and demographic studies.

Despite obvious language problems in sessions where German was often the preferred language of discourse, the exchange of information and ideas was reinforced by a high degree of enthusiasm and mutual friendship. As a result, in addition to the high academic value of [the] sessions, a very real sense of community was generated between archaeologists from diverse nations.

On Friday the session on 'Indigenous perceptions of the past' began. I considered this one of the most crucial themes of the whole Congress. If this were not a success, then, for me, the Congress would have been at least a partial failure. In the event it was a huge success, as the organiser, Robert Layton, reported to me later:

> The 'Indigenous Perceptions' session provided an unparalleled opportunity for representatives of many cultural traditions to meet. Participants were able to demonstrate a common interest in studying the past, to share ideas, and yet to learn from each other about the intellectual and moral problems raised by the practice of archaeology in contexts arousing diverse cultural expectations. The respect shown for competing views was exemplary and the great majority of papers were of a very high standard, fully justifying the organisers' faith in funding the travel costs of Third World participants.

However, not every academic session depended for its success on major Third World participation. For example, Leslie Davis and Brian Reeves reported to me about their session on 'Communal Land Mammal Hunting and Butchering':

> Sixteen persons from six countries (Canada, United States, Argentina, United Kingdom, Denmark and Italy) presented papers in our symposium. Two others were submitted for presentation. The symposium was organised topically by the types of mammal hunted. Subjects covered included mammoth, bison, antelope, red deer, llama, guanaco, reindeer, ibex, communal hunting representations in Upper Palaeolithic cave art, and contemporary variation in communal hunting patterns.
>
> The symposium was well attended. From the participants' view it was extremely successful in bringing together for the first time at an international congress researchers from different countries and backgrounds interested in communal hunting strategies. Exchanges of views between participants in the symposium, as well as with and between members of the audience both formally and informally, was most productive and our view and understanding of the significance and problems associated with communal hunting strategies expanded. Particularly fruitful was the exchange between researchers from North and South America, who were dealing with patterns of

the historic natives or those of the recent past, and European Mesolithic and Paleolithic specialists from both western and eastern Europe.

The format of the symposium – prepublished papers and sufficient time for discussion – was extremely beneficial. In all, it was the best of the congresses we have attended.

Things were inevitably drawing to a close but there was still the formal Plenary Session to come (see Chapter 9), followed by our Congress train journey to London with its cultural bus tour and the special opening of the British Museum.

The following day, Sunday, was the day of the Congress train ...

As I left for the railway station I met Alex Ross of Martlet. A few years earlier he had wanted nothing more than to be left behind his desk in Brighton with his computer. Now he was quite overcome: 'I have never met such a lovely group of people; I can't bear to think of going back to just organising conferences for businessmen and doctors'. I felt proud of the Congress. I even felt proud that we had our own train!

Chaos hit us at Waterloo station, for the representative from the London office never appeared and there was no sign of the queue of buses which should have been waiting for us. Our participants wandered aimlessly about as Jane, Caroline and I tried, in the end successfully, to find someone in charge of buses. On Waterloo station there is no point assuming that any non-white is a Congress participant! It was a shambles... It became even more so when the first bus had to be emptied of participants and all the luggage unloaded because the driver/owner had come without a public address system and the guide therefore refused to work on it. The queue got longer and longer, but I did not hear a single complaint; the Congress spirit lived on as if in a different world.

Caroline apparently slept through the whole of the cultural tour; Jane, on another bus, fumed throughout. I thought it terribly funny – at least I did after my first embarrassment, for the London which was chosen for display was one of famous hotels and restaurants, shops where Princess Diana bought her clothes, and somewhere in Knightsbridge where members of the royal family 'took tea'! Again no one complained, and those who were still awake did, I suppose, get a chance to see buildings and monuments such as Westminster Abbey, Piccadilly Circus, and the side of Buckingham Palace.

The farce continued. Our bus stopped at the side of the British Museum (right on time) with the driver and guide apparently totally oblivious to the fact that our participants had heavy luggage which they could not be expected to lug round to the front entrance. Bus loads of our participants had been deposited at the locked back entrance which was not due to be opened until the public were to be let in, an hour later. I got our bus load off and in through the guards at the entrance where David Wilson – bless him – was waiting for us and then I dashed in a taxi to the back entrance. The scene was indescribable but, again, no one was furious, even as they beat on the Museum's locked doors! I persuaded the hundred or so stranded archaeologists to abandon their luggage and to walk round to the front (to get in to their private viewing of the 'Archaeology in Britain' exhibition) while I spent two and a half hours and £15 on taxis, ferrying the luggage to the front. Professor Jayne Botscharow of the Department of Anthropology, Northeastern Illinois University, wrote to me later:

> Not only was the Congress interesting, it was also fun. I shall not forget the image of a mountain of luggage piled up on the steps of the British Museum, all very efficiently taken care of while we were inside. It sums up for me the lengths to which all of you went to make us comfortable.

9. The Plenary Session

The Plenary Session took place in Southampton's Guildhall on 6 September 1986 from 2.00 until 6.15 pm. Over five hundred people from 62 different countries participated, an extremely high proportion of those who had taken part in Congress academic proceedings throughout the preceding five and half days. It was presumably no accident that *The Times* chose that morning to publish an article by Conor Cruise O'Brien, which I quote in part:

> Obviously, the implications of this affair go beyond the boundaries of archaeology or any single discipline. They may reach into every branch of intellectual life in Britain.
>
> My former colleague, Neal Ascherson, last month in the *Observer*, defended the decision to ban the South African archaeologists. As Ascherson's account establishes, the original decision to ban, made by Ucko and his colleagues, appeared as a result, not of any determination to strike a blow against apartheid, but of a simple intimidation, through the threat of a double boycott.
>
> Southampton city council, the Anti-Apartheid Movement, the local students' union and the Association of University Teachers declared that they would not accept the presence of South African scholars at the congress. They would withdraw financial support and accommodation. They would demonstrate.
>
> At the same time, most African participants made plain that they would boycott the congress if the South Africans attended ...
>
> So Ucko and his colleagues caved in. Having caved in, Ucko has been giving him himself retrospective ideological airs ...
>
> ... The new Ucko argument is even more disreputable than the decision it is designed to defend, or glorify. The whole idea of 'damaging the regime' by excluding archaeologists from a congress is ludicrous ...
>
> Though I respect Ascherson, I was dismayed to find him in such company ... As I read him, I came to feel that a certain kind of rot in British intellectual life has gone further than I would have believed possible, and is affecting people whom I would have assumed to be immune to it ...
>
> ... Personally, I am off to Cape Town, accompanied by my black son, now aged 18. I am going to teach at universities there for five weeks. I did not accept the university's invitation to demonstrate solidarity. But I shall be glad to have my visit taken as a demonstration of solidarity with the staff and students of the University of Cape Town. Also as a gesture of defiance against an intellectually-disreputable attempt to isolate what I know to be an honest, open and creative intellectual community ...

For those who had read this article before the meeting it only served to emphasize how big a gulf there remained between the realities of the past week and the preconceptions of those allowed or chosen by *The Times* to comment on the Congress.

The organisation for the Plenary Session had been entrusted by the Executive Committee to Dr Ian Hodder. His plan had originally been to include at least one representative of the IUPPS but both Professor Nenquin, the Secretary-General, and Professor Weidemann, the German 'National Secretary', declined to attend. He had originally asked Professor V.N. Misra of the Department of Archaeology, Deccan College, India, to chair the meeting but when he was unable to attend the invitation was extended to Professor D.P. Agrawal of the Physical Research Laboratory at Navrangpura, India.

The Congress package handed out to participants as they registered contained an announcement of details regarding the Plenary Session including a Motion proposed from the dais:

That a temporary Steering Committee be set up to be charged with (1) discussing the views of the Plenary Session with the IUPPS at its meeting in Mainz, through members of its Permanent Council and/or in direct meetings, and (2) considering the formation of a new world archaeological organisation in the event that joint discussions should prove unsuccessful.

Other Motions would be accepted for discussion if handed in by the scheduled tea break during the Plenary Session. Many people asked to contribute to the Plenary Session, and as a result of various informal meetings held during the Congress, such as a women's group and a minorities' group (page 167-8), various other matters had been prepared for the Plenary Session. Other motions emerged from programmed academic sessions, such as that on 'Public Archaeology and Cultural Resource Management'.

Ian Hodder, Michael Day and I had numerous snatched meetings during the Congress in which we hurriedly discussed how best to organise the proceedings given the necessarily extremely restricted time available on that Saturday afternoon. The Plenary Session was forced to end at 6 pm because the Mayor's closing reception, which was to follow it, was scheduled to begin at 6.15 pm. As the Congress proceeded, so the numbers grew of those wishing to contribute to the Plenary Session.

The first formal part of the proceedings consisted of speeches from those on the platform. I began, giving the history of interactions between the IUPPS and the WAC. Then followed Professor Andah of the University of Ibadan, Nigeria (speaking as Secretary General of the Pan African Association on Prehistory and Related Studies), Professor Masson of the Academy of Sciences, Leningrad, USSR (speaking on behalf of the Soviet participants), Dr Gupta of the National Museum in New Delhi, India (speaking as General Secretary of the Indian Archaeological Society), Mr Mangi of the University of Papua New Guinea (speaking on behalf of the new group of independent professional archaeologists from 'small countries'), Professor Golson of the Australian National University (speaking as a former President of the IPPA), Professor Zamora of the College of William and Mary in Virginia, USA (speaking as a member at large (and on behalf) of the Executive Committee of the IUAES), and Professor Randsborg of the University of Copenhagen, Denmark (speaking on behalf of the IUPPS).

Simultaneous translation took place for the whole of the Plenary Session (English, French, Spanish, Russian, and Chinese), a facility arranged at the very last moment in view of the obvious importance of the meeting, and the desire to keep faith with the overall Congress insistence on meaningful participation and communication between the various peoples of the world. That it took place so successfully was due in no small measure to the generous assistance of multilingual friends and residents of Southampton.

What follows are the main relevant presentations given at this closing session of the WAC.

*

CHAIR: PROFESSOR D.P. AGRAWAL (INDIA):

In the course of this afternoon, you will get to know more about the tumultuous conditions under which the Congress was born. That the decision to hold the Congress was correct has been vindicated by its success and the magnitude of global participation. Belonging to a developing country, as I do, it is heartening to see such a large participation from the African, Asian, Latin American countries, and also from the socialist bloc. I have talked to a large number of delegates and there is consensus that the IUPPS can, and should, be made a more representative body in which developing countries, the students, the women's organisations should find adequate place. Perhaps the constitution should be changed to make it more democratic. Most people think that a delegation from this Congress should meet the IUPPS functionaries and convey the concern and the fears of this Congress, so that our aims are achieved without a clash or a confrontation. On both sides of this unfortunate divide, I am sure the scholars owe allegiance to the cause of world archaeology, and this should go a long way in avoiding a split. This task of negotiations has to be performed by a Steering Committee. In such a large gathering we thought that a panel of names for a Steering Committee should be proposed from the dais for your approval. It is a temporary body which will dissolve itself after discharging its mandate, given by you. If you feel there should be more representations on the Steering Committee, it will have the power to co-opt. I thank your organisers and you all for asking me to chair this session, and for your co-operation. This World Congress has taken place in an atmosphere of bonhomie, cordiality and harmony. In this last function we should conduct ourselves in the same cordial spirit and conclude this function on a note of friendship and love between people and nations.

DR IAN HODDER (BRITAIN):

I wrote to Professor Jacques Nenquin, the Secretary-General of the IUPPS, and Dr Weidemann, of the Mainz Congress, asking them to attend this meeting. They said they were unable to, but Professor Nenquin wrote a letter to me which he said could be read at this meeting as a statement. It is a long letter and I will only read the part that is directly relevant to this afternoon's theme. He says:

I wish to make this very clear: what I am writing to you should be regarded as informative, or as personal opinion, since I have received no official instructions from either the Permanent Council or the Executive Committee to speak on this matter.

The point which is now being emphasised by some members of the Southampton organising committee seems to be that the non-western world is not adequately represented in 'existing world archaeological bodies'.

This criticism seems odd to me, coming from an organisation (the Southampton World Congress) which has recently excluded from its activities all scientists working in two non-western countries, and coming at a moment when non-western participation in the IUPPS is the largest since the Union was established. Without going into details, I would point out that at this moment professional archaeologists from more than sixty non-western countries are members of our Permanent Council, out of a total of some hundred countries represented, and, as is clearly mentioned in our Statutes, the Permanent Council is the main governing body of the Union. As regards the Executive Committee – which is responsible to the Permanent Council – a distinction must be made between the elected members, and the 'ex officio' members, who are 'invited' to the reunions of the Executive Committee, and who do not vote. At this moment (1986), six of the members elected by the Permanent Council are from non-western countries (two from Africa, two from Asia, two from the Americas). When the Executive Committee was first established, in 1950, only one non-European member was elected. It is true that most of the 'ex officio' members of the Executive Committee come from Europe. This is due to the fact that the Presidents and the Secretaries of the organising Committees of the IUPPS Congresses automatically become members of the Executive Committee, and most previous Congresses have taken place in Europe. The main reason is, I think, that organising an international Congress can be an expensive business, and because of this it has been difficult to elicit a congress-invitation from a non-western country. May I also point out, that it is the Permanent Council which decides upon the date and the venue of the IUPPS Congresses.

The IUPPS has accepted the affiliation of a number of international organisations working in one particular geographical area, or in one particular specialisation. Among these organisations are the 'Pan African Association on Prehistory and Related Studies', what used to be the 'Far Eastern Prehistoric Association', and the 'Union Internationale d'Archéologie Slave'; – specialities are the 'International Council for Archaeozoology' and the 'Association Internationale de Paléontologie Humaine'. They all have their own internal organisation, they all hold their own congresses, and they all work either on a continental or on a world scale. I do not think any of these bodies can be accused of discrimination against non-western participation ...

Some 350 professional archaeologists are active in the twenty or so Commissions working within the framework of the Union, with Commissions and sub-Commissions on the pre- and protohistory of Africa, Asia, the Americas, the Pacific World, the Near East, and so on; needless to say, here again participation by scientists from all over the world is considerable, indeed essential. This is of course equally true for the several Special Committees co-ordinating initiatives of international importance, such as the Committee for the 'Atlas of African Prehistory' and the 'Inventaria Archaeologica'.

In view of all this, I think you will agree with me that the suggestion that 'the non-western world is not adequately represented in existing world archaeological bodies' cannot be true for the IUPPS.

That ends the part of the letter that I am going to read.

PROFESSOR V.M. MASSON (USSR):

As this Congress draws to an end, we can say that we are very satisfied with what has been achieved. The various tribes of archaeologists have been for this short period united in a chiefdom skilfully led by Professor Peter Ucko. During the preparations for the Congress numerous problems had to be overcome as you all know only too well. Soviet archaeologists support the position adopted by the organiser of the Congress. We were asked to lay particular emphasis on this point by the Director of the Institute of Archaeology of the USSR Academy of Sciences, Professor Rybakov who is Vice-President of the IUPPS.

International archaeology today has come to embrace an ever-growing number of rapidy developing centres and national schools, and this is an indisputable fact. The bringing together of various archaeological centres in a harmoniously balanced macrosystem, the streamlining of its infrastructure, and adjustments to improve the mechanism of the ties within it are important functions of such congresses. As we see it this Congress has been successful in these tasks.

While acknowledging as we do the successful work of this Congress that has brought together archaeologists from all continents, we now consider it essential to consolidate these achievements in the organisational and administrative sphere. As an initial step in this direction, a temporary

Steering Committee needs to be set up with the participation of representatives from all major regions of the world.

The organiser of this Congress compiled a most apt Academic Programme. Thanks to this programme our attention has been concentrated not only on new information coming to light in a haphazard way but on series of important theoretical and also practical problems. A most important part of the Programme was the session entitled 'Objectivity in Interpretation'. Gone are the days of romanticism, when precious objects were exhibited to an audience, preferably gold ones, in order that the beholder might be dazzled not merely by ancient cultures, but also by the archaeologist who had found the objects in question. This has been replaced by a more scientific approach, by archaeology using analysis that involves procedures on many different levels, a system of reconstructions and the thorough revelation of the information potential in archaeological material. In this connection the link between archaeological artefacts and the phenomenon of ancient culture is very important. An ancient culture is objective reality and archaeological materials are samples of that ancient culture. An important feature of this Congress was the interest shown in developed social systems referred to in the Programme as 'Complex Societies'. These are in essence societies in which social differentation has reached the level of a system of classes or was at least foreshadowing the latter.

It was also most significant that the work of the Congress confronted questions relating to the link between archaeology and the topical issues of our times. This applies to the sessions on firstly 'Public Archaeology and Cultural Resource Management' and secondly 'The Politics of the Past', to name but a few. When confronting these questions archaeologists became directly involved in spreading culture, in education and most important of all they leave their mark on the psychology of the society in which they work, and in its turn this involvement brings many problems in its wake. Sometimes the priceless legacy of the past perishes under the caterpillar wheels of bulldozers sent in by ignorant technocrats. The greed of an individual antique-hunter can sometimes inflict fatal wounds on the cultural heritage of the developing countries. There are times when evil minds attempt to use monuments from the past to fan ill-will between nations. Historical and archaeological experience however has shown that cultural progress has made particularly rapid strides in those places where cultural ties and contacts have been actively fostered. This experience should provide a valuable lesson for the politicians of today. In the USSR the protection of monuments and their utilisation in work to spread culture has been the state policy supported by the whole people. According to the constitution of the USSR all land belongs to the state, whose task it is to protect that land while making use of its resources. The tangible manifestations of the implementation of this task is the legislation to consolidate this principle. In 1976 the Supreme Soviet of the USSR passed a law 'On the Protection and Utilisation of Historical and Cultural Monuments'. Similar laws have been passed in all the republics of the Soviet Union.

Our delegation must now express its profound gratitude to the organisers, to the University of Southampton and to the City of Southampton. To bring together archaeologists from scores of different countries, to organise their attendance and work at the Congress and supply them with all the necessary information is a tremendous task, that can well be compared to the construction of Stonehenge! The work of the Congress has proceeded in a business-like and friendly atmosphere. In this connection we might do well to recall the Eastern proverb, 'Those who sail in the same boat share the same fate'. We archaeologists know all too well how difficult it was to build that boat, with first a stone, then a bronze and finally an iron axe, and our task is to do all we can to ensure that the ship of civilisation should continue to sail across a peaceful ocean with progress as its lodestar.

PROFESSOR BASSEY W. ANDAH (NIGERIA):

The African participants at this WAC have agreed on the following:

> That the organisers of this Congress be congratulated for successfully organising a truly WAC. Our feeling is that this has been a most meaningful Congress because the organisation has: (i) achieved truly worldwide representation; and (ii) addressed themes of worldwide interest and relevance. With these achievements, it is clear that the WAC has made a breakthrough in discussing and finding solutions to the practical problems of man understanding fellow man.
>
> It is therefore this kind of Congress we would want to see in the future. The Plenary Session should therefore be discussing how to sustain this WAC, to give it a structure and what form this structure should take. The kind of body we want to see is one that avoids the situation that now exists within the IUPPS. We want a body in which the Executive Council will have elected representatives so that the principle of democracy is maintained. Such representation can be along regional lines.
>
> Secondly, members elected to such an Executive Council should serve for a limited period rather than permanently. Our suggestion would be that a new Executive Council be elected after the holding of each Congress.
>
> Thirdly, we would want membership of this body to be open to all practising scientists engaged in the study of man. Membership should be open to societies, institutions and individuals, including students.
>
> Fourth, we recommend that a membership fee be introduced. The IUPPS is dependent financially on Governments and other bodies for funding. The introduction of a membership fee would avoid total dependence on such funding. Subscriptions should vary acording to the different categories of membership. Money from such subscriptions, paid annually, would then be used for organising future Congresses, rather than depending entirely on registration fees. At the same time, the elected Executive Council will be expected to engage in soliciting funds from various sources.

Fifth, we suggest the setting up of a permanent secretariat of this world body which will, among other things: (a) collect and disseminate information to the membership; (b) organise fellowships; and (c) work out meaningful programmes for the development of archaeology and related disciplines in member countries. For us in Africa, a major advantage of belonging to such a body would be: (1) obtaining assistance in areas of training of personnel for our institutions and establishments, and the development of relevant cultural resource management institutions; and (2) to assist African members to travel to Congresses abroad and within Africa to facilitate contact and links among ourselves.

We would want this meeting to therefore look ahead to ensure:
  (i)   the achievement of a new world society
  (ii) planning of the next WAC
  (iii) ironing out details of a Constitution
  (iv) that there is no going back, because this would undermine the fundamental question of the dignity of man. The loss of personal or academic friendships should, in our view, be subordinated to such important questions. Going back now would put us Africans in the subordinate position that we have always been. It would also undermine the commendable and courageous decision that the organisers of this WAC have taken to hold this Congress, despite the various pressures.

Lastly, we want to see the immediate setting up of a temporary committee. Our mandate for such a body is not necessarily to negotiate with anyone, but rather that this body ensure the directions we have outlined, ie: (i) to draw up a constitution along the guidelines indicated; (ii) to solicit for funds from various organisations; and (iii) to work out details of the next Congress regarding its venue and other issues.

On our part, we give our assurance that such a Congress will have the full support of all our Governments. We undertake to do all in our power to mobilise total support for such a Congress in our continent.

DR S.P. GUPTA (INDIA):

Today is perhaps historic; after all it is the first time that the world organisation of academics engaged in the study of man have openly stated that in the society of man no other principle can be greater than the principle of human rights. The banning of the entry of South Africa and Namibia has been an historic decision. It is also in conformity with the stand taken by India and more than a hundred non-aligned countries of the world. However, some of our most valued colleagues have opposed this stand on the grounds of academic freedom. Personally I do not see any contradiction between the two, since the ban is temporary and for a very specific purpose.

To my mind the significance of the present Congress lies in the fact that what was so far almost exclusively a club of the Europeans and Americans has become a centre for researchers from all parts of the world. I have attended such congresses in the past but I do not remember that in any one of them the Africans, the Indians, the Sri Lankans, the Chinese, the Russians, the Pacifics and others participated in such an active manner. While some of the countries were not represented at all, others had only marginal representation. In the IUPPS these countries had practically no voice. In fact, at no time an attempt was made to involve the Third World closely or intimately as equal partners. In other words, the IUPPS was a world organisation without two-thirds of the world properly represented. Not that the constitutional provisions were not there, not that some countries of the Third World were not represented, but it was more a case of having a vote than in really influencing factors. We welcome the efforts of those who fought their own colleagues for a cause which may have been very small in the beginning but which has now become far-reaching in consequence. Asia, Africa, Latin America and the Pacific can now look forward for meaningful participation as equals.

A word about the choice of subjects for seminars. In the past there was a tendency to select topics for general discussion which were specific to European archaeology. We were very happy to note that the theme for general discussion this time has been 'Cultural Attitudes to Animals', which is universal in its scope. I hope that in future also, while choosing subjects for seminars, it will be kept in mind that the subjects are universal in scope so that scholars from all over the world can actively participate.

Which brings me to some of the constitutional conclusions of the IUPPS in which most of the members of this Committee are not elected. This is hardly in complement with the democratic spirit of today. Similarly, all of these countries are, according to the constitutional provisions of the Union, represented in the Council by four members. Many countries of the Third World are not represented. Sri Lanka, for example, is still not represented, although it has an age old department of archaeological services. So is the case with China. There are many such anomalies and I hope every effort will be made by us to introduce reform in the constitution of the IUPPS in order to make it a really democratic body, and a body in which all the countries of the world are involved.

As far as we know there is neither formal membership nor a permanent secretariat of this world organisation. Hence it could not become a movement. It could never involve large numbers of people to dedicate themselves for the cause of archaeology. Like the governmental elections in many countries they suddenly become active during the fifth year of the following Congress. Although some projects were undertaken by a few groups in the past, they had very little impact. In other words this world organisation never played any active role in the dissemination of knowledge gained by its members. An active permanent secretariat could be able to do this job.

Therefore I suggest that two types of membership could be introduced: national, in which each country is represented by two to four members; and individual, including students and other bodies. I would suggest that an ad hoc small body be formed which shall convey to the IUPPS the wishes of those who have assembled here on this historic occasion. The world organisation must change its constitution in the real spirit of democracy. We should also tell them that wherever human rights are infringed we will raise our voice since there cannot be anything more sacred for human beings than the liberty of human beings themselves.

So let us hope and pray to God that our friends and colleagues in the IUPPS will see our reasoning and allow a world archaeological movement more united and more responsive than what it has been so far.

MR JO MANGI (PAPUA NEW GUINEA):

It is a privilege to talk on behalf of the independent archaeologists. I would also like to address this Congress on behalf of ethnic minorities. The question before us is, there is a need for a world archaeological organisation dedicated not only to the idea of maximum world participation but also to taking decisions to ensure that idea. I would like to address that by looking at what has happened in this Congress so far, particularly in the section 'Objectivity and Interpretation'. It is a pleasure to know that the hobby of the middle upper crust Europe of collecting and writing about their hobbies, the pastime of the middle upper class of Europe is gone. It is a pleasure to be here and to say that archaeology has finally changed, thank God.

In the session 'Objectivity and Interpretation', it has finally come out that the archaeology and scientificness of it are two different issues. Methodology is scientific, interpretation is subjective. Therefore, it has finally made me realise that archaeology is not *the* interpretation. I have heard many delegates talk about other possible interpretations and equally valid ones. What we do in the name of science and the advancement of humanity, the understanding of our past, from a strictly archaeological perspective, need not be the only way that we see and view the world. I can finally stand up and interpret my data in peace, I can address issues like reburials and others in peace because the audience, particularly my colleagues from the northern hemisphere, have become very receptive, and are beginning to respect the whole issue that the world is not seen in one form alone. I would like to thank the Congress for arranging it so it has been possible for people like us to come up and air our views. Coming from Papua New Guinea, you sit down there, there is no chance of ever being heard. It has also exposed me to cultures which have been similar from other parts of the world, from other minorities, ethnic minority groups, when they are faced up against the professional archaeology. And in that sense I would like to come back to the whole idea, to the theme behind this session, of the IUPPS.

I would like to say that membership to the IUPPS – they seem to be having a rather dubious means of appointing membership – but by whatever means that is agreed upon, membership should be extended to two groups. The criteria should be two: academic per se, and local authorities. I would like to say that the membership should be extended to indigenous groups, ethnic groups, so that they can also have a much louder voice in an issue which involves human beings.

PROFESSOR JACK GOLSON (AUSTRALIA):

I speak to the business of this meeting, to the fitness and the appropriateness of the IUPPS to act as a world body for our discipline, in the light of my experience as the Australian delegate for some years on that body and also from long years of involvement with a regional organisation which has many of the problems which the international organisation whose performance we are discussing is heir to.

IUPPS, of course, claims that it is organised in such a way that it is capable of responding to the needs of the discipline on a worldwide basis. My experience, and I think the experience of my organisation [IPPA], is that its very structure makes this impossible. Its main governing body is a Permanent Council consisting of four delegates about whose nomination we have heard, from every affiliated country. We are also told that there are at present something like 100 countries affiliated to IUPPS. This makes a governing body of some 400, a totally unwieldable organisation, practically, to advance on a day to day, year to year basis, the affairs of our discipline.

Since it is a body which is impracticable to convene, the Permanent Council, which governs the organisation, must continue to be dominated by representatives of those countries closest to the traditional seat of operations. Consequently, the Executive Committee of that Permanent Council is elected by a small number of the Permanent Council and itself serves to perpetuate an imbalanced situation. The situation is such that the Congresses of IUPPS, when they are called, are structured in such a way as to inhibit easy discussion on a general basis across regions and across specialities. The Congress I attended in Nice ten years ago was to a large extent a Congress of regional European prehistory, and the rest of us from the far parts of the world were compelled to organise ourselves in the same way. Since IUPPS Congresses have this character, they increasingly fail to attract the interest or commitment of other parts of the world, and the problem as a result becomes permanent.

The conclusion must be that if we are to continue to have world organisation and world congresses, they must deal with world issues and be fully representative of world interests, as this Southampton Congress has set out from the beginning to be.

How is this to be achieved organisationally? Now I would like to draw on the experience of the IPPA, with which I and many other delegates at this conference have been associated for some years. We attempt to cover a very large territory, from India to New Zealand, from Japan to Australia. Not in terms of the individual prehistories of particular countries, but the common and overlapping themes and interests of a distinctive region. On our Council, therefore, we have abandoned representation by country and operate through representation by region. There are, after all, too many countries really to cater for all. Countries, we have discovered, are not the most appropriate units for either organisation or study. And regional organisations have sprung into existence, throughout that region, reflecting the realisation that prehistory crosses national frontiers and that there are distinctive regional traditions which can be represented by such organisations. And it is on the basis of existing regional organisations in our area, that the IPPA has been established. I would therefore suggest for the attention of the Steering Committee which it is the purpose of this meeting to establish, that the Council of any international archaeological organisation be represented by regions and not by countries.

There is a very important second point stemming from our experience with the IPPA. This is that an organisation means nothing to the members of the discipline apart from their possible periodic attendance at Congresses, if we operate solely through representatives from regional organisations. In addition there must be individual membership. Subscriptions to IPPA enable it, even though it is a small and widely scattered organisation, to produce a newsletter and the bulletin which maintain the links between individuals and organisations in the intervals between our Congresses.

Congresses in any case can never be attended by more than a small proportion of its membership. In order to make IPPA Congresses more meaningful, it has adopted the policy of moving them around the region. This is a policy which has certain implications. It means, for example, that a different part of membership is catered for on each individual occasion, so that the newsletter and the proceedings of those conferences become all the more important in communicating back to the many people who are not able to attend. There is also a very important academic function, however, which these moving congresses can fulfil. This is to stimulate discussion of general issues raised by the prehistory of any of the regions where a meeting is held.

Many parts of the wider world with whose participation in world archaeology we are now concerned are unable to host Congresses on the scale that has become conventional for IUPPS, and indeed on the scale of this present Congress. Even at this Congress, which has broken new ground in putting forward a thematic approach to the study of the past and the comparative study of human history, despite the advances, the decisive break which has been made with tradition, many of my colleagues and myself have felt frustrated at being unable to attend more than one, or a limited number at any rate, of the very important themes which have been canvassed and which have been developed. I ask, therefore, the Steering Committee to consider this proposition. Can we have future world Congresses aiming to bring the professionals together to discuss matters of general interest, which are organised on a less complex basis? There are a number of ways of doing this. My suggestion is that periodically we remove ourselves to a different part of the world, and sitting down in that part of the world, we attempt to look at the major issues in prehistory, through the individual distinctive experiences of the peoples in the part of the world where we happen to be meeting. I think this would be a vital and stimulating experience for all of us and would also be a feasible proposition for those areas of the world which are not large enough or not developed enough infrastructurally to put the large congresses on.

PROFESSOR MARIO ZAMORA (USA):

Mr Chairman, Mr President Dr Day, Mr Secretary Professor Ucko, the man behind this revolution, distinguished colleagues from all parts of the world, especially those who were not here before, I also represent a minority in this Congress, and that is the non-archaeologist. We are many here, I think. There are statisticians, cultural anthropologists, historians, ethnohistorians and we have been very happy to be with the archaeologists today.

On behalf of Dr Eric Sunderland, the Secretary-General of the IUAES, and in my capacity as an elected member at large of the Executive Committee of this IUAES I wish to congratulate the officers of this Congress for a very interesting, pleasant, fruitful and successful conference. I have been to many congresses worldwide in the past twenty years. I rate this Congress as the best. It is not only international, it is also interdisciplinary. It also involved the community, where we danced with them the other night.

I would like really to commend the officers and members of the Executive Committee for their admirable courage and wisdom in maintaining the scientific dialogue at all cost, and keeping the integrity of this Congress in the face of ceaseless pressures involving issues of crucial concern to people who believe that apartheid should go, and those who defend the right of all scientists to attend conferences.

The IUAES' Executive Committee, in a meeting in Stockholm, Sweden, on 17 June 1986 passed, by a majority vote, a resolution supporting the WAC in its serious and successful efforts to prevent the cancellation of this Congress:

> The IUAES affirms that it supports the free interchange of *bona fide* scholars across international boundaries for the proper purposes of scientific and cultural exchange, without interference from national governments or from groups of their citizens. Where the free interchange of *bona fide* scholars across international boundaries is prevented, subsequent to the arrangement of a congress, by circumstances beyond the control of the IUAES, then it will do all in its power to prevent the cancellation of its meetings, so that the sciences of anthropology and ethnology will not suffer, and that those who may attend still benefit. Finally, the IUAES supports the WAC in its efforts to resist the cancellation of its meeting in Southampton in September 1986, while regretting that some scholars may not be attending.

The IUAES, through its Secretary-General welcomes serious and substantive proposals for co-operation and dialogue between the WAC through a proposed Steering Committee and the IUAES Executive Committee.

PROFESSOR KLAVS RANDSBORG (DENMARK):

As a member of the Permanent Council of the IUPPS, I have accepted to speak in support of the Union, although this organisation, in my opinion, is responsible for the unhappy situation we are in today. As I myself voted against the movement of the Union concerning South Africa, I cannot defend the organisation on this point either. What I can do, however, is to outline the present structure of the Union and to give you, and the Union, a few suggestions for a necessary modernisation of the rules and therefore also of the structure of our Union. I find it to be of the utmost importance to maintain the IUPPS as a framework for our international co-operation and solidarity with fellow scholars.

The Union has been dominated by those countries where the research on the pre- and protohistorical periods was developed early and where institutions are well-established. In view of the larger stage now being set for our subject it is pertinent to broaden participation in the affairs of the Union. It must now be ensured that the very many non-European members of Permanent Council participate actively in the organisation. Because of this and some recent happenings, the time certainly has, I think, come to revise the rules and therefore also the structure of the Union. If we modernise, we must also be willing to put more money into the business. But let us first outline some of the basic needs of the world archaeological society, and thus of the Union:

(1) Firstly, we need more information on the archaeology, in particular of

the pre- and protohistorical periods, in the various countries of the world. The information should concern issues such as education of archaeologists and others, museums (a special organisation for museums, ICOM, is already in operation), research institutions, publications, relations to the general public, archaeological research projects, etc.

(2) Secondly, we need better and freer communication on several levels, between institutions in different countries. One necessary step is the establishment of a larger and more permanent secretariat which, among other things, can undertake the publishing of statistical material on the archaeology of the countries of the world, and of a regular newsletter.

(3) To provide for this, some sort of paid membership of the General Assembly of the Union must be established. Whether we should also change the membership-rules of the Permanent Council is another question. The basic issue is not only the fact that the Permanent Council is self-elective, but also whether we want to give up the one country-four votes structure. Personally, I am certainly not against a democratisation here, although I realise that this would not have an effect on all countries. Also, paid membership by individuals, institutions, etc, might be a problem for some members, especially in countries with currency regulations. In short, involvement of all archaeologists of the world in the Union is not only a question of votes, but also of economy, and in particular of information.

At any rate I will personally recommend that the Union revises its rules in the light of the current developments. What particular steps will be taken must be left to the discussions in the Union and between institutions in the various countries. No doubt the rules for other bodies affiliated with the UNESCO can serve as models for the upcoming revision.

Finally, and as a personal statement, I should like to stress the importance of giving individuals free access to communication with fellow scholars and with institutions in other countries. We, and the world as a whole, are facing a great number of political problems. And as we are almost all paid for our work by the government we cannot ignore the wider politics of the country, the region, the world we are living in. What we can do, however, is to maintain a right, also in the future revised rules for the Union, to free communication on the individual level and to claim this right vis-à-vis whoever is denying it to anyone.

In conclusion I should like to address myself to the leadership of the Union and urge them to revise their stand on changes in the organisation. As I see it, they have no other choice left than to negotiate and compromise.

*   *   *

This was the last formal speech from the platform. Participants who had requested time to speak from the floor were now invited to do so.

*   *   *

PROFESSOR AN ZHIMIN (Chinese Academy of Social Sciences, Beijing, PEOPLE'S REPUBLIC OF CHINA):

This conference has been a victorious and a successful conference. That nearly a thousand archaeologists and enthusiasts from so many countries have gathered in the beautiful town of Southampton is a pioneering event for archaeology's outlook and future, for exchange of experience, for advancing friendship and deepening understanding, and the conference itself. We the Chinese representatives feel extremely honoured to be able to participate in such an important international meeting. We have met several old friends at the meeting and have formed many new friendships, but most importantly we will be conveying the deep friendship and newly acquired knowledge of all the participants back to our country to pass on the considerable achievements of this meeting to our Chinese colleagues.

There is a saying in China, 'Within the four seas all men are brothers', which means that between the peoples of all the world's countries there should be neighbourliness, peaceful co-existence and shared progress. We strongly oppose any racial discrimination because it is not in keeping with the historical trend of progress. We strongly oppose the apartheid government of South Africa but we do not oppose those anti-apartheid scientists carrying out research in South Africa.

Mutual exchange and shared effort amongst the whole world's archaeologists is needed before any significant results can be achieved. The most effective path, apart from the exchange of published materials, is the energetic promotion of this type of international meeting. The proposal to hold international archaeological meetings at regular intervals in future in order to increase interchange, promote friendship and encourage the development of world archaeology, to embark on a new phase, is I think a hope shared by everyone present.

Like that of every country in the world, China's archaeological development changes with each passing day and is especially fruitful since the founding of New China. At present, workers engaged in archaeology in China have various organisations; apart from the Archaeology Research Institute of the Chinese Academy of Social Science and the Vertebrate Palaeontology and Anthropological Research Institute of the Academia Sinica, each province has research institutes, museums and university archaeology departments doing a considerable amount of work. The eleven of us attending this conference came from the various organisations listed above, however we are all here in our own name and do not represent a particular Chinese organisation. As for an academic organisation of national character, that is the Chinese Archaeology Institute where Xia Nai, who passed away last year, held the chairmanship of the Council. More than once he expressed a wish to participate in this conference and it is a great pity that he was never able to do so. It is a tremendous consolation to

Xia Nai's last wish that today, at last, Chinese archaeologists have participated in this conference.

PROFESSOR SENAKE BANDARANAYAKE (SRI LANKA):

The Sri Lankan participants at the WAC congratulate the organisers of the Congress for bringing about a most successful meeting of archaeologists from countries representing a most significant cross-section of the international archaeological fraternity. Archaeology, like all other academic disciplines, has national, regional, and international dimensions, and it is important to assign the correct degree of priority to each of these aspects. We have seen here the immense value of international academic and scientific contact and exchange. This is perhaps the first meeting on this scale, especially devoted to archaeology and related disciplines. The momentum generated by this Congress for the establishment of wide international links, should not be lost. We sincerely hope, therefore, that the current problems of organisation within the international community of archaeologists can be speedily resolved, taking into account the high level of international representation achieved at this Congress. We support the formation of a Steering Committee, whose mandate will be to work towards this objective. We believe that the most important principles in international academic relations are those of equality and mutual benefit. Thus, the fullest representation of all countries is important, and this should be expressed through institutions which will combine two compatible concepts: representation on a country as well as an individual basis, while at the same time taking into account recent developments in the discipline, realities in the sphere of international relations, and the values and aspirations of the countries and peoples of the world.

PROFESSOR DENA DINCAUZE (USA):

I am addressing you today as a private citizen, and my remarks are not authorised by the SAA. I think, however, that many of my colleagues in the United States and Canada and elsewhere in the western hemisphere would share my feelings.

Like all human endeavours, archaeology has its political aspects. The more diverse its practitioners, the more opportunity exists for contrastive, even contradictory political agendas among them. Differences of such kind have both energised and threatened this Congress. Ideally, as students of the human past, archaeologists should strive to transcend politics. To achieve penetrating understanding of that past and of the human condition in all its manifestations, I believe in that goal.

Because of that belief, I maintain that we all need each other. We need to seek out and to cherish the widest possible range of perspectives on the past. We need to submit our own work to critiques from those who may be expected to agree and those who may disagree with our perspective. Only through openness to diversity can we rise above the particular social, economic and political perspectives that are given us by our own cultures. Only through openness can we come to terms with the intricate complexity of the social world. We need each other.

Therefore I think we need a worldwide archaeological organisation that is protected from both the threats and the realities of external politics. An organisation that cannot be held hostage by any faction or factions. We need an organisation that will sponsor, foster and protect free and frank discussion of archaeological issues, political or otherwise, an organisation that is open to dissent. Such an organisation must be truly representative of the diversity of modern societies and of modern research. It must be all this in order to provide opportunities to consider the work of others, and thereby to reconsider our own.

My hope is that archaeology can find or create this sponsor for worldwide communication, that is fully representative, that is truly universal. With its help we might ultimately contribute insights that will help construct a new world order, dedicated to diversity and justice.

PROFESSOR KRISTIAN KRISTIANSEN (Ministry of the Environment, Copenhagen, DENMARK):

The majority of Scandinavian archaeologists present here in Southampton, and many not present, do not agree with the decisions taken by the Executive Committee of the IUPPS to withdraw support from the WAC in Southampton and arrange a new world congress in Mainz. Since our representative on the Executive Committee of the IUPPS voted for these decisions, we want to make it clear that this was not, and is not, a position shared by many Scandinavian archaeologists.

We believe it necessary to look forward now. The wide international representation and success of this Congress indicates that the IUPPS was not in accordance with the opinions of world archaeology when they decided to withdraw their support from Southampton and arrange an alternative congress in Mainz. We further maintain that the Executive Committee's decision was unconstitutional. The failure to act in accordance with the needs and the realities of world archaeology is in part due to the structure of the organisation and especially the rules of self-election. The first objective must therefore be to revise the Statutes and the organisation of the IUPPS to ensure a representation that is elected according to the rules of election of each country.

The second objective, we believe, is to withdraw official support from the Mainz Congress. The reason for this is that it is the participants in the

Congress who decide about proposals from the Executive Committee and the Permanent Council representing the permanent members of each country.

Since the participants at the Mainz Congress, in all probability, will not be representative of the member nations of the IUPPS, it is important that the Mainz Congress is not an official IUPPS world congress. Otherwise there is little hope that the decisions taken will help to solve our problems. If neither Southampton nor Mainz is the legal World Congress, decisions about a reorganisation will have to be taken at the first World Congress after Mainz. This will give time for negotiating and preparing proposals for necessary reorganisation of the IUPPS. The Mainz Congress could then become a bridgehead. There a decision should be taken to set up a working committee with representation of the next official World Congress.

If such a moderate and stepwise strategy for fulfillng our objectives cannot be accepted by the IUPPS, we think that the Steering Committee set up here today should proceed to make proposals for a new international organisation.

Finally, since the IUPPS is an organisation linked to UNESCO, contact should be made with UNESCO, both by the Steering Committee and the representatives of each country present here, to forward our objectives.

The Scandinavian participants in the WAC 1986 in Southampton call upon the IUPPS:

(1) to withdraw their unconstitutional and unjust decision to arrange an alternative World Congress in Mainz in 1987;
(2) to revise the Statutes and the organisation of the IUPPS to adjust to the needs of present day world archaeology.

To fulfil these goals we support the proposal to set up a committee representing the participants of the Southampton WAC to negotiate these objectives with the IUPPS.

*   *   *

There followed a short tea break and the meeting was then opened to the floor, with directional microphones taken to anyone who wished to speak.

*   *   *

MS JAN HAMMIL (USA):

On behalf of American Indians Against Desecration and the International Indian Treaty Council [formed in 1974 with representatives from some 97 Indian tribes, and now with non-governmental UN status] we should like to thank the WAC for inviting us and for allowing us to participate in this Congress.

I think it has been very important to us, as well as to you, that we have had the chance to have input into your profession. We have tried to emphasise, as have many others throughout this Congress, that your profession is making a difference in the way that we live – in our religion, in our culture – and we believe that we have the right to have some input, and it is for that reason that for the last five years American Indians Against Desecration has tried to have that input into the profession of archaeology in the United States for all Indian peoples and for all red nations of the western hemisphere. So we appreciate having been here but we hope and we encourage that the Third World nations, all of the brothers and sisters, are allowed to have input into future Congresses. We believe that this is of utmost importance for if we are to survive as a people, all of us, the red, the white, the black and the yellow man, then it is important for all people to learn to live together.

There is one thing in particular that we think is of utmost importance, and that is that discussions of the Steering Committee, and in fact we would suggest the entire Congress, emphasise the rights of women, of young archaeologists, and of ethnic minorities in the future.

We also look at the composition of the Steering Committee and we hope that it will be kept in mind that even though some of us are not archaeologists, and some of us are not anthropologists, that we have an interest, that we have a need, that we can be more than just your collections, your specimens and your objects of antiquity.

We wish to have that input just as we have tried to have that input in our own nations. We cannot rely upon other organisations to do the work of the international community. We know of the problems when the international community does not pay attention to what is happening in the Third Worlds, entire nations have been wiped out of the American Indian because the other people allowed that to happen.

Within the United States today national Indian organisations, the Tribal Councils, the legal representations, the Indian Commissions from throughout the United States, have tried to work with the SAA. That is our problem. But we may close the door on those communications, we may shut off those communications, then it is everybody's problem and it is going to affect us, it is going to affect them, and it is going to affect all of us. And by having a group that we can be part of, that we can participate in, I think that that will relieve a lot of tension.

Thank you very much for allowing us to be part of your Congress.

MR ROBERT CRUZ (USA):

I thank the Creator for letting us be here and thank the Committee here. I propose the following resolution:

Whereas the WAC recognises the profound desecration that archaeological research has had on the cultures, histories, lands and traditions of indigenous peoples and their nations around the world therefore we resolve that the involved nation states, professions, institutions, and organisations must work together with indigenous peoples and their nations to recognise the desecration and its effects on their ways of life and to solve the issues of: reburial, repatriation, cultural hegemony, protection of sacred sites, religious freedom, sacred objects.

DR NANCY WILLIAMS (Australian Institute of Aboriginal Studies, AUSTRALIA):

I will read a resolution which arose from the meeting following discussion on 'Archaeological "Objectivity" in Interpretation':

that the WAC recognises the genuine and deep felt concerns of communities and cultures in many different areas of the world on the issue of re-burial of human remains. In keeping with that recognition it declares that the power of decision on such matters belongs to the indigenous community concerned or with the community traditionally associated with such burial. And it declares that scholars have a prime responsibility to explain, mediate and negotiate the issues of biometric research prior to reburial or otherwise. And it urges that every effort should be made by the profession to clearly explain the values and relevance their studies can have for the ongoing cultural life of the community under study. And it considers that it is a duty of scholars to formally recognise the contribution of communities to their research and that the training, involvement and consequent participation of indigenous communities should be a major aim.

DR M. ADEBISI SOWUNMI (Archaeology Department, University of Ibadan, NIGERIA):

On behalf of more than fifty African participants attending the Congress:

1. We recognise and commend the uniqueness of this Congress in its worldwide representation which has made it truly a *World Archaeological Congress*, and demand that this new direction be maintained;

2. We hereby wholeheartedly support the courageous move taken by the organisers and participants of the WAC in upholding the dignity of humanity, and particularly their unequivocal condemnation of apartheid;

3. We express our utter dismay at the decision of the IUPPS to withdraw support from the WAC;

4. In view of the worldwide representation and the quality of scholarship that characterised the proceedings, we call upon the IUPPS and its parent body, UNESCO, to accord the WAC the support it clearly deserves;

5. We urge all colleagues and organisations to positively respond to the resolution of the Pan African Association on Prehistory and Related Studies

(taken at its Congress in December 1983), calling on all to desist from any form of scientific collaboration with apartheid South Africa; and,

6. Finally we wish to place on record our profound gratitude to all organisations and individuals who contributed to the success of the Congress, in particular the Mayor of Southampton, the Southampton City Council, the staff and students of the University of Southampton and all sponsors.

MRS CHARLOTTE CANE (BRITAIN):

The 1986 WAC has been unique in recognising the issue of under-representation by country, class and status. We would like to emphasise the need to extend this initiative to women. We note that while approximately 30% of the papers were presented by women, only 12% of the organisers were women. Therefore, the 'International Forum for Women in Archaeology' strongly recommends the following Motions:

1. Broad representation of women at all levels of organisation and planning in all future international meetings;

2. Establishment of fora on women's perspectives and feminist issues; and

3. Future meetings to be structured in such a fashion that informal workshops form an integral part of the programme to enable fuller participation.

MR PETER STONE (BRITAIN):

At the risk of some repetition I feel I must say what a tremendous success this Congress has been and what a wonderful atmosphere of hard work and enjoyment there has been here. And on behalf of the students and the low-paid workers who had the benefit of hardship grants I should like to thank the Executive Committee for their foresight and belief in encouraging us and helping us to come.

I should like to charge, and I use that word advisedly, the Steering Committee set up by this meeting with not forgetting what has happened here, through this week. And I should like to charge them to take this feeling, this atmosphere, this desire for *world* archaeology to the IUPPS. Perhaps a good way to express this atmosphere and desire would be to co-opt members onto the Steering Committee from the three groups that today's discussion has already identified of especial worth: women, young archaeologists and ethnic minorities.

And yet I do not think that that alone is enough. The Committee must charge the IUPPS, or whatever group is created, with working, really working, for interaction and the finance for that interaction, between students and young archaeologists throughout the world; so that those bodies, those groups, can receive the facility of world knowledge, experience and training.

Such work should form part of the work of a permanent secretariat for whatever group takes on the task of promoting world archaeology. It is only if finance is found for such a permanent secretariat, a secretariat that should serve an elected organising committee made up from representatives from all over the world that the ideals, hopes, aspirations all sown and nurtured during this last week, will be able to live and to grow. An organising committee that elects its own members as the Permanent Council of the IUPPS is able to do cannot be seen to be representative of anything other than itself. When I mention finance I think we must face a bold fact. Some of that finance, in part, may need to come from the full membership of a world archaeological community. In other words, Ladies and Gentlemen, yourselves.

As someone asked to speak on behalf of students and young archaeologists I ask the Committee, the Steering Committee, not to forget the future. Their successes and their mistakes will be our heritage.

PROFESSOR MARIO SANOJA (Caracas, VENEZUELA):

I am going to read a resolution signed by the majority of Latin American representatives at this Congress and I am going to make a declaration in my own name and in the name of Iraida Vargas as representatives from Venezuela on the Permanent Council of the IUPPS.

The majority of the participants of South America, Central America and Puerto Rico have deliberated and decided and reached a consensus on the following points:

> We repudiate every political society based on discrimination: social, class, economic, ethnic, linguistic, religious, ideological and others. Especially we repudiate the South African regime based on the system of apartheid.
> Secondly, we support the free participation of scientists coming from different parts of the world in academic circles but, that said, given the unfortunate circumstances which have limited the participation of certain members problems like this should try to be solved in the best possible way to limit breaking up the scientific community.

We wish to thank above all, and recognise the efforts of, the organising committee of this Congress for organising a scientific event which responds to the needs of archaeology in the world. First of all from my interdisciplinary point of view there was a really humanistic and humane character which has allowed a real participation of representatives of the Third World. Discussion of the problems of our peoples as in the case of problems of cultural heritage are intimately related to the sovereignty of individual members and the independance of nations. The rest of us support planning for a modern and democratic organisation of the workings of the IUPPS to ensure a democratic and active participation for the majority of the representatives in all countries of the world as they have done in this meeting so that they can discuss freely all the problems related to science and culture and fundamentally, what is very important for everybody, the advance and preservation of the cultural heritage of the people.

*   *   *

The Chairman, Professor Agrawal, then read out the text of the two slightly amended Motions:

> *That a temporary Steering Committee be set up to be charged with:*
> *(1) discussing the views of the Plenary Session with the IUPPS; and*
> *(2)considering the formation of a new world archaeological organisation in the event that joint discussions should prove unsuccessful.*

He suggested that, in terms of the contents of the discussions with the IUPPS, the temporary Steering Committee should have a general mandate from the meeting, but that it would welcome further documents from interested groups. The Steering Committee would be temporary and set up for a very specific purpose. It would complete its negotiations with the IUPPS in one year, and then dissolve itself to hand over to a properly elected body. He stressed that, in its discussions the Steering Committee would emphasise the rights of women, young archaeologists, and ethnic minorities.

The Chairman finally proposed that the composition of the Steering Committee should consist of regional representatives from the Southampton WAC, and he moved the Motion that the Steering Committee should be: *from Africa, Dr Bassey Andah; from East Asia, Professor An Zhimin; from South Asia, D.P. Agrawal; from Australia, Professor Jack Golson; from Eastern Europe, Dr Shilov; from West and North Europe, Professor M. Day; from North America, Dena Dincauze; and from Latin America, Mario Sanoja.* The Committee would have the mandate to co-opt further members. It was to hold its first meeting within two days of the Plenary Session.

There followed some discussion of the constitution of the Steering Committee, and also about the voting procedure for the Motions put before the meeting. Finally it was Sir David Wilson who urged that the Motions should be put to the vote.

All three Motions were carried with 'overwhelming' majorities.

A suggestion by Professor Frank Willett from the Hunterian Museum, Glasgow, 'that we should give support to the working party by agreeing that none of us who is present here today and has been here at this Congress will go to the Congress in Mainz', was not formally seconded nor put to the vote at the meeting.

Professor Agrawal then asked the WAC Chairman, Professor Michael Day, of the Department of Anatomy, St. Thomas's Hospital Medical School, London, to bring matters to a conclusion.

* * *

PROFESSOR MICHAEL DAY:

It falls to me as Chairman of the organising committee to bring this Plenary Session to a close and to reflect a litle on the past week and the years of preparation that have gone into the first truly World Archaeological Congress that has ever been held. It is my view and that of many to whom I have spoken, that the Congress has been a tremendous success despite all our problems.

During the past week nearly 1,000 archaeologists from almost 100 countries worldwide, have gathered in this university and lived and worked together. Many countries represented here have never before sent a representative to a world congress; many participants have never before left their own lands. The experience has been exiting, not only for them but for us all. People from all these nations and cultures have been able to contribute to the work of the Congress and have done so with great enthusiasm.

The sessions based on precirculated papers followed by discussion alone have been a new departure in world archaeology and one that has been a great success; this format coupled with the choice of 'Themes' has allowed many more to contribute to the discussions than in other congresses that I can remember.

From the twenty volumes of precirculated papers our publishers, Allen & Unwin, have agreed to produce up to 25 books, not just as proceedings but a series of volumes of high quality incorporating only the very best that modern archaeology has to offer. These volumes will represent the 'new' archaeology – not only 'bones and stones' but cultural attitudes, objectivity, complex societies, and technological change. A 'new' archaeology that now requires a new international organisation.

The dominance of Europe and North America and the virtual exclusion of many developing countries from the councils of world archaeology is clearly no longer acceptable to world archaeological opinion.

Four hundred archaeologists withdrew from this meeting over the South Africa issue, but nearly 1,000 came, and it is you, the majority, who are asking for change, asking for an opportunity to take part, asking for our voices to be heard. Let the IUPPS take note of your resolutions and of our success.

When the IUPPS withdrew its recognition from the World Congress *The Times* newspaper said that we would be a 'rump' congress. Ladies and Gentlemen, you are the largest collective 'rump' that I have ever seen!

The World Congress exists – we have had our first meeting; we will not be denied or brushed aside – for if we are, then believe me we will all meet again at the *second* World Congress in a few years time.

I do not wish to say very much about the South African issue other than to reaffirm publicly the position in which we found ourselves. Had the South Africans been permitted to attend, as the IUPPS insisted, then there would have been no Congress here *or anywhere else* in Britain, because of the withdrawals of many nations and the opposition to apartheid shown by university staffs and students alike as well as the National and International Anti-Apartheid Movement and the elected representatives of the people of this City.

The choice was clear: cancel, or go ahead without South Africans. The Executive, supported by the National Committee, refused to cancel.

At this point I and several others were asked to join the Executive, and we determined to go ahead for the sake of archaeology and for the vast majority who wanted the Congress to continue. The result has been as you have seen.

May I reaffirm that I personally support the free interchange of scientists between nations, but where it is not possible, as in thepresent case, then I believe it is the right course of action to proceed with the meeting.

The subject of archaeology spans millions of years, its international progress cannot be stopped by the transient political difficulties of a few of its followers from one nation of the world.

*

Before passing to his final vote of thanks to sponsors and organisations and to those who helped to organise the WAC, Michael Day read a telex from Sir Shridath Ramphal (Secretary-General of the Commonwealth):

I am pleased to send my greetings to the WAC as it begins its session in Southampton with a focus on the archaeology of Asia and Africa. I do so in the general context that the objectives of the Congress are bound to be a further contribution to the store of human knowledge. With so much remaining to be done in adding to that knowledge, so many sites still awaiting the archaeologist's spade, your Congress is itself a service to our civilisation.

But I send you this greeting in the specific context of the decision of your organising committee to bar participation from South Africa. That decision has been greatly welcomed in the majority of Commonwealth countries who view this as a worthy expression of solidarity with those within South Africa who bravely oppose apartheid and wait and work to be delivered from its indignities.

A decision of this kind is not an easy one, and there are some at least who dissent from it on honourable grounds. I am particularly mindful of its implications for those South African archaeologists who are themselves among the opponents of apartheid, but it would not surprise me if, among them, there are many who feel it is a sacrifice they themselves are willing to accept acknowledging that the enormity of the moral issue involved allows of no exceptions.

Your Congress, therefore, sends a signal of much significance to Pretoria's rulers, a signal of the worldwide abhorrence of their system and of the increasing solidarity of the world's scholars. As you proceed with your Congress, you and your colleagues can be mindful of the overwhelming support which exists in the Commonwealth for the stand you have taken in this matter.

*

The Plenary Session was over. The participants moved slowly from the Guildhall to the Mayor's Reception. In all our minds there remained the inevitable question – what now would be the future of World Archaeology.

10. The Aftermath

It is all too easy for significant events such as the WAC initiative to fade away through subsequent inertia. Sometimes it is not so much inertia as lack of time and financial support and, especially in situations such as those described in this book, because the relevant people are scattered all over the world. In this case what happens next depends on exactly what was the nature of the success of the WAC, a success which can, in fact, be assessed at several different levels.

In terms of personal interactions and new contacts forged, the WAC was particularly successful because of its international flavour and the emotional impact of many of its meetings. This can be judged from a selection of letters from those who attended the WAC, which are published in *World Archaeological Bulletin* 1 (see below). Some of these interactions are delightful and personal, such as the exchange of correspondence between Juliet Clutton-Brock of England and Pekka and Marjut Aikio of Finland, in an attempt to establish if the dog in one of the Aikio's photographs was the same as one which Juliet had seen with the Sámi who showed her round in the 1950s. Others are more formal, one resulting in Yashodar Mathpal's unique watercolour paintings of Bhimbetka art having been acquired by the Hunterian Museum in Glasgow, another leading to the holding of an Archaeology and Education conference to develop many of the educational topics discussed at the WAC, and another expected to result in an official scientific exchange between the British Academy and the Academy of Sciences of the USSR. At the informal level, again, postcards and letters are now exchanged between an American Indian, a Papua New Guinean archaeologist, and USSR archaeologists in Moscow and Leningrad.

The overall impact of the WAC, at all levels, has already been described in Chapter 8. The outstanding success with regard to its academic programme, both in terms of its content, and in its dedication to hard work was due, in part, to the fact that almost everyone at the Congress was at least a paper-giver, a discussant, or chaired a session. The real proof of this academic success will be in the post-Congress books which are currently being prepared by a series of editors for publication by Allen & Unwin.

These books include some deriving from Congress themes based on precirculated papers and some based on the more specialist traditional meetings where contributions were given verbally. In the former case the volumes will consist of a selection of only the best papers precirculated at the Congress, all revised in the light of discussions in the academic sessions and, subsequently, with editors, and will include new contributions especially commissioned for these books. In the latter, the presentations have now been written, and the books are more devoted to an up-to-date statement of the present development of a particular archaeological subject. Several of them, such as that on South Asia, review areas and periods for almost the first time. Others, such as that on Early Hominids, include the first published detailed accounts of important new discoveries. In this particular volume, Professor Wu Rukang, the Chinese doyen of world palaeo-anthropologists, publishes the details of the Yinkou skull, which is on the boundary between Homo sapiens and Homo erectus.

The original agreement with Allen & Unwin was for up to 25 post-Congress books. Despite the difficulties faced by session organisers since the ban on South Africa there remains a striking list of 22 post-Congress books which will appear on schedule (see page 42).

WHAT IS AN ANIMAL?
(Editor: Tim Ingold)

THE WALKING LARDER: PATTERNS OF DOMESTICATION, PASTORALISM, AND PREDATION
(Editor: Juliet Clutton-Brock)

SIGNIFYING ANIMALS: HUMAN MEANING IN THE NATURAL WORLD
(Editor: Roy Willis)

ANIMALS INTO ART
(Editor: Howard Morphy)

THE PLEISTOCENE PERSPECTIVE: HOMINID EVOLUTION, BEHAVIOUR AND DISPERSAL
(Editors: Michael Day, Robert Foley, and Wu Rukang)

PLEISTOCENE PERSPECTIVE: INNOVATION, ADAPTATION AND HUMAN SURVIVAL
(Editors: Arthur ApSimon and Simone Joyce)

ARCHAEOLOGICAL APPROACHES TO CULTURAL IDENTITY
(Editor: Stephen Shennan)

THE MEANING OF THINGS: MATERIAL CULTURE AND SYMBOLIC EXPRESSION
(Editor: Ian Hodder)

THE POLITICS OF THE PAST
(Editors: Peter Gathercole and David Lowenthal)

THE EXCLUDED PAST: ARCHAEOLOGY IN EDUCATION
(Editors: Robert MacKenzie and Peter Stone)

WHO NEEDS THE PAST?
(Editor: Robert Layton)

CONFLICTING PRIORITIES
(Editor: Robert Layton)

DOMINATION AND RESISTANCE
(Editors: Daniel Miller, Michael Rowlands and Christopher Tilley)

STATE AND SOCIETY: THE EMERGENCE AND DEVELOPMENT OF SOCIAL HIERARCHY AND POLITICAL CENTRALISATION
(Editors: Barbara Bender, John Gledhill and Mogens Larsen)

CENTRE AND PERIPHERY
(Editor: Timothy Champion)

INNOVATION
(Editors: Sander van der Leeuw and Robin Torrence)

FORAGING AND FARMING: THE EVOLUTION OF PLANT DOMESTICATION
(Editors: David Harris and Gordon Hillman)

FOOD, METALS AND TOWNS IN AFRICAN HISTORY: AFRICAN ADAPTATIONS IN SUBSISTENCE AND TECHNOLOGY
(Editors: John Alexander, Bassey Andah, Alex Okpoko, and Thurstan Shaw)

CHALCOLITHIC, BRONZE AND IRON AGE CULTURES IN SOUTH ASIA
(Editor: Makkhan Lal)

FROM THE BALTIC TO THE BLACK SEA: STUDIES IN MEDIEVAL ARCHAEOLOGY
(Editors: Leslie Alcock and David Austin)

ARCHAEOLOGICAL HERITAGE MANAGEMENT IN THE MODERN WORLD
(Editor: Henry Cleere)

HUNTERS OF THE RECENT PAST
(Editors: Leslie Davis and Brian Reeves)

These volumes which are currently in preparation, demonstrate the indisputable significance of the WAC as a significant academic event. Each individual book will act as a significant stimulus to academic progress in its subject. As a whole, the series cannot fail to be a powerful and unprecedented body of contemporary archaeological knowledge and theory.

As far as the numbers participating in the WAC are concerned, Henry de Lumley and Philip Tobias have claimed that it was not a success, and they soon moved on to attack the WAC in a letter to *Nature* (12.3.87). In their condemnation of the WAC as a failure because of the numbers (850 participating from 71 countries – see Appendix VIII), they conveniently omitted to mention that the last IUPPS Congress, in Mexico – unlike some much bigger, earlier IUPPS Congresses – had had only 400 participants.

Nevertheless it is true that from the point of view of the WAC's finances, the fact that a smaller number attended than had been originally predicted, caused a serious financial loss of some £90,000. However, this figure needs to be seen in the context of an overall budget expenditure of c. £485,000 (see page 14) and the unforeseen withdrawals of promised sponsorship as a result of the ban on South Africa/Namibia (c. £100,000, see pages 146-8). In fact the Congress's finances were handled by Derek Hayes, its Honorary Treasurer, in such a way that there was always total control of the budget, even in the very last days before the Congress when we knew that if the expected late registrations did not in fact eventuate we would be covered by our insurance policy (see page 15). In the event there is dispute whether that policy will be honoured by the insurance companies concerned. By the time this book is published, either the insurers will have made a satisfactory payment or litigation (supported financially by the City of Southampton and others) will be underway.

The question of numbers does, however, raise a very important set of questions regarding the future of at least archaeological/anthropological international congresses, and their finances. If a congress has above a certain number of participants the academic programme is bound to be overburdened so that sessions will have to overlap and run concurrently – thereby creating invidious choices – and contributions will have to consist of the traditional short verbal addresses. For really productive academic exchange of views to be able to take place, and for thematic cross-cultural questions to be seriously addressed, this latter arrangement is quite inadequate. If such themes are really of theoretical and worldwide significance, then the invidious choices which participants are forced to make are very unfortunate. Large international congresses lasting several weeks are clearly impracticable except in highly exceptional situations, such as the one I organised for the Australian Institute of Aboriginal Studies' Biennial Meeting of 1974 (which lasted for 17 days of discussion of precirculated papers and resulted in 8 published volumes: 'a unique statement about the status and development of Aboriginal Studies at that particular period'). Even in this case the overall numbers were significantly less than at a meeting such as the WAC, and the travel and subsistence costs of all those presenting precirculated papers were covered by the Institute.

As Chapter 2 has made clear, the organisation of a meaningful Congress based on a considerable number of discussion topics is a major undertaking which can only be accomplished successfully by dedicated work from session organisers. The WAC was clearly successful in this endeavour, not only with regard to its academic programme and precirculated papers but also in the context of the cassette recording of all the sessions – with free copies given to all contributors – and its efficient Viewpress message system which was also used to alert everyone to any changes in the programme. Even Jacques Nenquin has publicly acknowledged the quality of the WAC's organisation, and the Research Director of the Wenner-Gren Foundation recognised that the WAC's introduction of 'some rigorous concepts' should help to determine the future of large international meetings. The necessary dedication is unlikely unless the aims of the congress concerned are likely to have important academic consequences. Normally large international congresses have, as their primary aim, the facilitating of contacts, and the academic organisation is left to cater more or less for itself (and see page 29). Many leading academics refuse to attend such large and unstructured international meetings, which are often, for this reason, academically of minor importance.

The published figures for the numbers attending an international congress are notoriously difficult to assess. It is usually impossible to tell from them how many are academic participants, how many academic observers, and how many 'accompanying persons'. There is also frequently confusion between the numbers of participant registrations, the numbers paying, and the numbers actually attending. This is amply illustrated by the different numbers of participants quoted for the Nice (1976) Congress. Henry de Lumley and Philip Tobias claim in their letter to *Nature* (12.3.87) that '3,127 participants ... were present'. Glyn Daniel, on the other hand, in his Editorial in *Antiquity* (March 1977) writes 'of the 3,000 whose names appeared on the list of *congressistes* 1,700 assembled ...'. Traditionally in very large congresses it is normal for the number of people attending to be vastly greater than those offering papers. In the WAC there was no such divergence – a very high proportion of participants had contributed papers.

If international congresses are to aim simply for large numbers, without much reference to academic merit, then the costs involved are such that few countries will ever be able to afford to offer themselves as hosts. If the number of participants anticipated actually do come, such congresses can break even, but there must be an enormous financial outlay for considerable periods before the registration fees are received. In almost all cases, now that conference-going has become so complex, a major financial outlay will be for the engaging of a professional conference-organising company with appropriate back-up computer facilities. In the case of the WAC, and quite contrary to Nice and Mexico, where finances derived from municipality and government and were therefore not a problem, all the finances had to be secured through individual effort and soliciting (see Chapter 1). If the WAC had received any governmental back-up it would not have been necessary to impose such a high registration fee – and the involvement of young archaeologists and students would then have been much greater. Without prejudice to the correctness or otherwise of the pressures by anti-apartheid groups on the WAC, had major financial support been secure from the outset for the WAC, the original threat of bankruptcy would not have carried so much weight.

The problems created by the size and numbers of participants at international academic congresses remain acute, and are ones which any world archaeological organisation must face up to. So far the IUPPS has singularly failed to do so. Nor has it formulated any detailed aims for its five-yearly meetings, despite numerous cries of alarm in the past about its lack of international focus, and its exclusive concern for European matters.

S.J. De Laet, Secretary-General of IUPPS from 1952 for fourteen years, published two reviews of the IUPPS (in 1970 in the *Acts* of the Prague Congress of 1966, and in 1985 in *Antiquity*) in which he acknowledged the overwhelming European bias of its origins and development, and stressed that even at the Zurich Congress in 1950 where 'there were 244 participants coming from 30 different countries, the conference still had 'human' dimensions, but in the future, the congress would become more 'mammoth'-sized, which would cause organisational problems'. De Laet urged the IUPPS to concentrate on specialist colloquia where it was possible to have detailed discussions of well-defined subjects. To De Laet, these were 'of greater scientific importance than large congresses, where all the available time is generally taken by short communications and none is left for discussion. This', he concluded, 'is the very important problem of the "giant" congresses'.

Professor de Lumley, in the letter already mentioned (page 216), claimed 3,127 'participants from 94 countries' at Nice in 1976, with evident pride and self-satisfaction. About this Congress, De Laet wrote that the plan at Nice 'proved to be a lopsided answer to the problem. Indeed, of those participants who wished to present a contribution not falling into one of these colloquia, each had three (!) minutes in which to present his work. The result was chaos'.

Just as significant, and disappointing, has been the failure of the IUPPS to carry out its brief as an international organisation. In his published review in *Archaeology* (April 1974) of the 1971 IUPPS Congress in Belgrade, entitled 'The Writing on the Walls of Beograd', John Alexander wrote that:

> To review ... the happenings at Beograd ... is a saddening task, for the Eighth International Congress fell far short of its potential. The primary reason for this deficiency seems to be that whilst prehistoric archaeology throughout the world has expanded and developed, the International Union, nurtured

through its first 30 years by European prehistorians, continues to have its meetings, in spite of wider membership, attended largely by European archaeologists and to be concerned almost exclusively with European problems. This initial bias has been encouraged by the succession of European countries which have generously acted as hosts to the congresses, whilst in the last two decades a growing number of continental and regional conferences held in Africa, Asia, the Americas and Australia have reduced its interest to more distant scholars. No separate European conference has yet been instituted, and this has meant that the congress this year became more noticeably dominated by European prehistorians preoccupied with their local problems. If this trend is continued there will be little relationship between the theoretical union represented by the permanent council of 85 members and the reality of the meeting to be held in Nice in 1976.

At Beograd, the writing was clear upon the wall, for only 14 non-European countries were represented as compared with the 24 present in Prague in 1966. Their reduced number was reflected in the program; no one working outside Europe was invited to contribute to the 'General Reports' issued in advance of the congress in a praiseworthy attempt to improve the quality of discussion, and all non-European papers were delivered in one of the eight simultaneous programs of papers which lasted for only two of the five working days. If we are to judge the content of the meeting at Beograd, it would be better for us to set aside its world role for the moment and consider it a European event ...

It is the world role of the congress which seems most in jeopardy. If it pursues its present course it will become merely a regional conference for those working in or interested in the continent of Europe with a sprinkling of fraternal delegates and observers from the rest of the world. If the International Union decides otherwise, it could become a true Congress of the Pre- and Proto-history for which there is now a very great need and, for that matter, strong international support, especially among the younger workers. To fulfill this role it will have to change its present form considerably, and the following suggestions are offered for discussion: (1) that the European Continental Conference be separated from the World congress; perhaps the Union could hold them alternatively at five-year intervals; (2) that the World Congress be held outside Europe at a crossroads, where communication between the continents is easiest; (3) that the papers accepted at meetings of the World Congress be such that there is a balance between the continents; (4) that there be a greater emphasis on new methods and techniques of considering, as well as of locating, excavating and assessing evidence [sic]; (5) that the 'General Reports' be commissioned and the programs be arranged on grounds other than that of simple chronological regional summaries. Perhaps particular problems such as the spread of iron-use or the utilisation and domestication of cattle or of tubers and rhizomes could be included and discussed across the world; (6) that some consideration is given to the wider implication of the study of prehistory and of humanity as a species, and of the intercontinental problems which followed; (7) that some discussion of the worldwide 'political' problems of archaeology – for example, the wholesale and increasing destruction of evidence, or the illicit traffic in objects – might be regularly undertaken. This would fit well with the Union's representative position as the only archaeological member of the International Council (Philosophy and History) of UNESCO.

Despite these warnings Henry de Lumley, National Secretary for the Nice 1976 Congress, did nothing to improve world involvement in IUPPS academic programmes (see page 196). Far from his Nice Congress of 1976 being a model of academic harmony and success, as implied in his *Nature* letter with Professor Tobias, Glyn Daniel said about the whole of its academic organisation, 'Everything was confusion, and papers did not happen at the right times, or at all'. In their letter to *Nature* they continue by claiming that the WAC did 'grevious harm' to world archaeology. Glyn Daniel, who witnessed the Nice Congress, concluded that, as a result of it, 'we very much doubt whether there will be a Xth Congress ...'.

On the occasion of the Xth Congress in Mexico in 1981, John Alexander hoped for better things than at Nice. However, he wrote in his report of it that:

This year there was every reason to hope for a change; it was the first meeting ever to be held outside Europe, it was in an area as archaeologically rich as Meso-America, in a city easily reached from all parts of the Americas and ... Eastern Asia. It was expected to offer Old World archaeologists a challenge to see and hear much that would be unfamiliar to them and to offer their New World colleagues, especially those not regularly attending the Congress, the chance to meet and hear of the problems of Africa, Asia and Europe. This hope was largely unfulfilled and the development of a genuine World Congress still rests in the future. The reasons for this failure seem complex, but at least four can be isolated:

(1) the absence of all but a few North and South American archaeologists, even from Mexico only a small number attended;
(2) the overwhelming predominance of Europeans working in Western Europe among the participants;
(3) the failure of many of the commissions (groups of academics chosen five years previously to plan the many individual sessions) to choose topics which could be discussed as international problems;
(4) the interpretation of 'Proto-historic' of the Congress's title in such a way that the development of the urban, civilised states of the Americas and those working on the problems related to them were largely excluded from Congress.

These factors resulted, although many excellent papers were read, in a concentration on European problems which made this Congress very similar to previous ones, and even exaggerated previous trends since only small numbers of archaeologists working in Asia and Africa attended.

Reflection on this Congress leads to the conclusion that its future is still at risk and that the high hopes raised by the Mexican offer to become its host in 1981 have not resulted in it becoming the world forum for the discussion of common problems which is needed. It still remains what it has been for the past fifty years of its existence, a European regional conference to which small groups from the other continents come to hold lively but largely separate sessions.

The two plenary sessions, the only meetings in which all participants met, were also very disappointing. Since the Congress is the only archaeologi[cal] representative on the Council of UNESCO, the Congress has an obligation to voice the concern of the profession at the world wide destruction of archaeological evidence, to encourage programmes of cultural resource management, to encourage and advise and support international agencies concerned with the growth of illicit trade in antiquities and with the improvement of museums and conservation service. This opportunity was not taken.

Many of these shortcomings regarding the IUPPS have been seen in this book to derive from a combination of factors, not least the excessive practical domination of its affairs by a blinkered and almost exclusively Western European group of archaeologists with little or no interest in world archaeology. Reflecting this situation, the vast majority of the IUPPS Commissions are devoted to European inquiry, defined by Chronological Period (thus, 'the Neolithic of the Old World', 'the Archaeology of the High Middle Ages', etc). These are exactly the areas where the WAC was least successful. As Ruth Whitehouse wrote to me after the Congress:

> My section [Copper and Bronze ages of the Old World] included some interesting papers and there were lively discussions in some sessions, so it was very far from a waste of time. However, with the wisdom of hindsight I now think it would have been better to abandon the commissions when the IUPPS backed out and to have put together a new thematic session called something like 'New developments in European later prehistory'. This would have allowed us to regroup papers from Andrew [Fleming's 'The Neolithic of Europe'], John [Barrett's 'The Iron Age of Europe'] and my sessions together under headings that related to theoretical approaches rather than the tired old geographical and chronological divisions.

Much the same sentiment was expressed by Professor Thurstan Shaw for the traditional Commission topic of 'Neolithic Africa', and indeed his opening paper to the session at the WAC was a full-scale demolition of the category 'Neolithic' as traditionally applied to African material.

It has been demonstrated, and brought out very forcibly in the Plenary speeches of Dr S.P. Gupta (page 194) and Professor Jack Golson (page 196), that although the structure for world participation exists in the IUPPS its effective control is, by definition, vested in a small and non-representational International Executive Committee. Meetings of that Committee have been almost entirely European affairs. No doubt this in part explains the IUPPS emphasis on European archaeology. But this emphasis also exists because Europe, unlike America, Africa, the Pan Pacific, and India, has no organised European body to cater for this continent's pre- and proto-history. Traditionally, therefore, meetings of the IUPPS catered for its world brief simply by organising meetings of its Commissions on 'Prehistory of the Pacific' or 'The Peopling of the American Continent'. Its few attempts to choose wider-based, non-geographically or chronologically anchored, Commissions have completely failed to 'take off' (eg the 'Origin of Cities', which has remained totally devoted to Medieval Europe) or have been of such a kind (eg 'Physical and Chemical Dating

Techniques in Prehistory') that the practitioners are almost exclusively from Europe, Australia or North America. The IUPPS has no Commission dealing with 'Public Archaeology', although this could be viable within a predominantly European and North American framework, and was indeed discussed at the IUAES's Congress in Canada. This topic, in the international framework of the WAC, formed the basis of a session already described (page 168), which will lead to the book on 'Archaeological Heritage Management in the Modern World'.

But what of the argument, put forward by some colleagues, that the WAC has also been divisive of the archaeological world by its imposition of the ban on South Africa/Namibia? At one level the accusation is largely irrelevant since any such divisiveness, it could be argued, may be necessary for the long-term good of the overall situation. Short-term divisiveness is not necessarily a bad thing if the long-term potential gains are much greater. In actual fact, however, archaeology has gained the respect of the world, and a new world dimension, even if it has for the time being upset some rather narrow Western European interests. Those who make the allegation of divisiveness and obviously feel that this is the case, at least in the short term, are very often those, like the SAA in refusing even to listen to the case being put, who are making the matter so. However, the results of the recent elections for the Council of the IFA, in which two members were elected who represented opposite sides of the WAC debate, do not support this argument, any more than does the successful cooperation of members on the Prehistoric Society Council which includes known protagonists on both sides of the issue. It is also clearly not the case with regard to the book to be published on 18,000 BP which includes papers from the WAC and from another conference to which South Africans have been invited (see page 224). Similarly, that it is not so for all is epitomised by the presence at the WAC of all the original British Executive Committee members except for John Evans. As far as the Mainz congress is concerned, I also have no reason to assume that Colin Renfrew and David Wilson will not attend it, nor that either of them, or Leslie Alcock, consider that they should not attend IUPSS meetings as the British members of that organisation. I am sure that there will be some archaeologists who attended the WAC who will also attend the Mainz congress. Contrary to the divisive decision taken in Paris by the International Executive Committee (see page 111) to hold the Mainz congress at the same time as the Southampton WAC, Professor Weidemann, with the express intention of avoiding rivalry between the two congresses, postponed the Mainz congress until September a year later – a statesmanlike decision.

For me, at least, this vital matter of principle regarding the banning of South African/Namibian participation from the WAC rests on two fundamental points. The first depends on whether the case of South African apartheid is unique in the world today. On this point many would disagree with John Evans' view in the BBC programme, *Heart of the Matter*, that 'I don't think that [South Africa] is different, only in degree, not fundamentally ... [it is a] bad case ... certainly not absolutely unique. [There] have been other cases where [they] try to do same thing'. This claim ignores the *legalised* basis of the South African regime and ignores the appalling reality of a society in which people are legally treated as inferior from birth, on the basis merely of the colour of their skin. Many people, apparently, cannot conceive of even the existence of such a monstrous situation. It is to this South African situation that Thurstan Shaw refers, when he writes in *Archaeological Review from Cambridge* (1986):

> ... very few 'Western' academics have had any personal experience of being denied the fundamental human freedoms; that danger has not entered into their experience ... it makes it very difficult for them to *enter into* the feelings of South African blacks, denied those fundamental freedoms on the basis of colour, or into the feelings of black academics elsewhere, who feel far more threatened by South African apartheid than by restrictions on scholarly freedom.

It is to this facet of apartheid that Trevor Huddleston referred, in *Heart of the Matter*, when he said:

> Apartheid assails human dignity in a way that most whites in South Africa simply have no idea about, as the very nature of apartheid means that they will never witness it.

John Evans' remark, in the same programme, that 'South Africa is just another example of a country where racism exists' was countered by Bassey Andah, who claimed that South Africa alone in the world attempts to divide its black population from its white one as if they were not equally Homo sapiens.

The second fundamental point depends on whether the offence of the apartheid regime against human rights makes it of greater importance than the principle of academic freedom of association. To me, disagreement on this issue is not in itself divisive, unless people choose to make it so. The development of events in connection with the WAC reveals how some of those associated with the decisions became confused. Thus, despite all his actions, his numerous signed messages to Congress participants, and his vote in Committee after Committee in favour of banning South African/Namibian participation, John Evans publicly stated, in *Heart of the Matter*: 'I felt that it was extremely important that academics should have the freedom to assemble and to discuss their findings, and without interference for any reason, and because of that I felt it impossible to accept the principle that we could exclude for a political reason the members, scholars coming from a certain nation.' Yet, he had written in a letter to Secretary-General Nenquin that 'the WAC if truly international, must express itself firmly as against apartheid'.

Archaeologists must now recognise that on some issues they hold diverse opinions. This self-evident remark applies even to the weight given to the importance of the principle of academic freedom vis-a-vis other human rights. Normally such divergences of opinion, as with differences of political or religious opinion which undoubtedly exist among archaeologists, are not considered relevant topics of discussion or debate. If the claim is accepted that South Africa's apartheid regime, which institutionalises racism within its own society and laws, puts it 'outside all normal principles and regulations' – as stated by John Evans in the Executive Committee's first press release of 19 September 1985 – the archaeological world must recognise that, even so, it is not unanimous about what should be done by them about the situation.

Even for those who accept the cultural boycott in principle, there is still room for a variety of individual opinions. In my own case, for example, I see a difference between the physical presence of South Africans/Namibians at congresses with the implicit government backing which the granting of exit visas implies, and the publication and reading of what South Africans/Namibians have written, which preserves what, to me, is the fundamental component of academic freedom of speech, without any implications regarding governmental involvement in the views expressed. In my document of November 1985 I had laid some store by this distinction (page 77-8). In the case of the session on 18,000 BP, the contributions delivered at the WAC were not geographically representative enough, on their own, to constitute a post-WAC volume. I have therefore facilitated the publication of a book consisting of contributions on 18,000 BP delivered at the WAC, together with papers on the same topic which were presented at a conference from which South Africans were not banned and which may, therefore, include papers by South Africans. This book is to be published by Allen & Unwin but outside the Congress Series, and edited by Clive Gamble and Olga Soffer, an archaeologist from the USA who did not come to the WAC because of the ban. My own position vis-a-vis the publication of papers by South Africans/Namibians (as opposed to their attendance at meetings) is an uneasy one. I am fortunate, perhaps, that Allen & Unwin have themselves stated that, if the situation arose they would not publish papers by South Africans/Namibians within the Congress Series, since they felt that to do so would be inconsistent with the policy of the Congress. At the same time I have been made aware that I am a 'Member of Honour' of a French archaeological journal whose policy is to refuse the publication of articles submitted by South Africans/Namibians (as do also a West African archaeological journal and others, mentioned in the May 1987 edition of *Nature*). My own position on this issue is therefore inconsistent.

This issue crosses all political affiliations. No simple correlation between someone being left-wing or right-wing, and supporting or not supporting the academic ban on South Africa, emerged during 1985/86 in the context of the WAC, whatever *The Times* of 22.1.87 might claim (see page 114). The discussion, the dilemma, and the points of view are at a much more subtle level. Some stress that 'academic free speech' (or whatever term is preferred) is paramount, and must not be tampered with *at any time* or for *any reason.* Some refuse to eat South African foods or buy goods from certain stores, while others rely on their governments and organisations to take the appropriate steps to deal with the South African situation. Some follow some variety of the second course and also refuse to visit South Africa on principle (even for academic purposes), while others contribute finance or other assistance to anti-apartheid organisations. A few may even volunteer to fight for the freedom of black people in South Africa. At the other extreme it is to be hoped that few archaeologists would join J Snyder, Secretary of the American Committee to Advance the Study of Petroglyphs and Pictographs, Washington, in his claim to Peter Stone that:

> ... The Soviets would love to divide the West, in order to conquer it the more swiftly and cheaply. This is the motive behind the attempts to isolate S. Africa in its current crisis. The Soviets would love to get control of a Marxist government there, and control the sea lanes around the Cape... J. Edgar Hoover was right that Moscow and its agents are 'masters of deceit'. If and when the truth is finally told, I do not doubt we will find that President Kennedy was the victim of Khrushchev's personal death order.

I am not really surprised that views on the appropriate action to be taken with regard to apartheid in South Africa should differ any more than that they should do so on issues such as capital punishment or nuclear disarmament. There should, however, be no reason why such divergence of opinion, even about the sanctity of academic freedom of association, should be any more divisive than any other of the differences of opinion and belief which normally characterise a heterogeneous group of human beings with diverse backgrounds, experiences, and education. As archaeologists and anthropologists our friendships, working relationships, angers and hopes should be able to encompass and survive differences in emphasis on the various facets and approaches within our own discipline, let alone on the pre-eminence or otherwise of learning and scholarship.

If schism does result from the WAC it will be very largely due, not to the imposition of the ban, but on the one hand to a combination of the actions taken by a number of grant-giving bodies, such as the Royal Society, the British Academy, the National Science Foundation and the Wenner-Gren Foundation, and, on the other, to the refusal by the IUPPS to recognise legitimate world interests in archaeology. If the former insist on funding participation only at meetings where free access to all is permitted, they are effectively imposing their own ban on personal liberties, and restricting their grants to only one kind of academic – in this instance the academic who does not feel strongly enough about apartheid to follow the call to boycott South African academic participation in meetings. The British Academy is now in even deeper conflict with the national AUT. Its President, Sir Randolph Quirk, is personally writing and telephoning those involved in international conferences to stress that Academy support for conferences and individual participation in them will depend on their being open to all. He also adds that:

> *Organisers of international conferences should be aware that pressures to exclude scholars can come from many sources – national, local, and sectional, and it is important to ensure at an early stage that sponsoring bodies will not seek to interfere with the academic policy of the conference or to prevent bona fide scholars from attending.*

One such national "pressure" will certainly be the AUT. At its May Council meeting it instructed its Executive Committee to:

> *(1) Make urgent representations to the Committee of Vice Chancellors and Principals for the purposes of establishing an academic boycott of South Africa.*
> *(2) Provide support so that local [AUT] Associations can organise and campaign in support of a boycott in their own institutions.*

Coercive techniques, such as that of the British Academy, are as out of place in this situation as are the cases reported (but which, for obvious reasons, cannot be specified here) from America, Britain, some Eastern European countries, France and Israel, where staff were threatened with prevention or loss of tenure by their superiors if they were to attend the WAC, or were told that their future research funding would be at risk, or were ordered not to participate in the Congress. Others were simply 'advised' that it would be 'unwise' to attend. In England there have also been worrying indications of potential pressure from the Department of Education and Science against those attempting to enforce the academic ban on South Africa in other contexts.

It is a central aim of the WAC, and its Steering Committee (see page 209), to prevent the schism of the world archaeological community if at all possible. Its primary brief is to pursue negotiations with the IUPPS. However, schism can only be prevented if the IUPPS acknowledges the existence of the fundamental dilemma inherent in the recognition of the principle of human rights in an institutionally racist society versus the principle of academic free speech. It cannot continue to accept its Secretary-General's 'deepest conviction that we should avoid *at all costs* (my italics) having non-scientific arguments influencing the work of the IUPPS'. Academics must recognise that solidarity with such groups as the ANC on the issue of an academic boycott, is necessary in order to show that they are at least as concerned as any other group to try to achieve basic human rights in South Africa.

The Plenary Session of the WAC, attended by 502 people from 62 (not 82 as wrongly stated in *World Archaeological Bulletin* 1) countries, set up a Steering Committee with a one year lifespan (pages 188 and 209). In addition to those elected by the Plenary Session, five additional members were co-opted onto the Committee: Charlotte Cane (representing women's interests), Joseph-Marie Essomba (representing francophone Africa), Jan

Hammil (representing indigenous minorities), Peter Stone (representing students' interests [and later, also, young 'non-established' archaeologists]), and – chiefly because Bassey Andah refused to serve on the Steering Committee unless I would also – myself. I agreed to serve as Secretary only so long as there was sufficient finance to run an efficient secretariat. Michael Day was unanimously elected Chairman. As a result of generous contributions from some Steering Committee members, and a donation from a Congress participant, Caroline Jones was able to continue working for the Steering Committee until the end of February when she went on six months leave.

The Steering Committee has so far met twice, and is ready to meet again in September 1987 if negotiations with IUPPS make such a meeting desirable or necessary. Given the fact that Konrad Weidemann had postponed the Mainz congress until 1987, in the same spirit I argued to the Steering Committee that we should not follow the suggestion made at the Plenary Session (page 209), that no one who had participated in the WAC should attend the Mainz meeting. The Steering Committee considered this matter at length and decided that:

> The Committee would not make any public statement about participation in the Mainz Congress but would leave such participation to each individual's conscience.

The Steering Committee also debated the question of the ban on South Africa/Namibia in detail, and in the context of its negotiations with the IUPPS. It decided unequivocally to follow the stand of ICPHS and to urge the IUPPS to remove South Africa and Namibia from its ruling body, the Permanent Council. It also decided to seek the amendment to the only IUPPS Statute which refers to world participation in its affairs – '… through collaboration with scholars from all countries' – and to demand the addition of 'respecting the principles of UNESCO regarding human rights'. The Steering Committee then agreed that once the IUPPS had approved this and other changes to the Statutes, a main agenda item for its Permanent Council to discuss publicly would be the issues raised by the participation in its affairs and Congresses by South Africans/Namibians.

The *Observer* reported (29.3.87), rather prematurely, that an alternative WAC organisation already exists. By this it presumably meant that the WAC Steering Committee has successfully published and distributed *World Archaeological Bulletin* 1, whose contents include a discussion of Academic Freedom and Apartheid, compiled by Paul Crake from articles and letters, several review articles about the WAC itself, and up-to-date information about the Steering Committee's activities. The *Bulletin* also featured the setting-up of an international forum for women in archaeology as well as planned developments for the future of Archaeology and Education.

The production of this *Bulletin* highlights another of the deficiencies of the IUPPS, for that organisation has never – unlike the IUAES – produced either a newsletter or published reports of its committee activities. By the time that this book is published and the congress in Mainz is held in September, it is hoped that *World Archaeological Bulletin* 2 will have appeared, focusing on another of the crucially important international areas of archaeological activity, the treatment of human remains and the affront to dignity that their excavation and display causes to some of the living peoples concerned (whether they be orthodox Jews or American Indians or Australian Aborgines). This number of the *Bulletin*, financed by the UN's Special Committee against Apartheid, will also explore the more extreme claim by some, that the wishes to be buried in a particular way by any person of any culture, whatever the date of that disposal of the human body, should be considered sacrosanct and the deceased should be allowed to 'rest in peace'.

The WAC Steering Committee has made the question of human remains one of its main points for discussions with the IUPPS and insists:

> that the IUPPS recognise that questions of principle surrounding the study and conservation of skeletal remains are of central concern to the archaeological profession and that human skeletal material should always be treated with dignity and respect. To this end the Steering Committee recommends to the IUPPS: (1) that it undertake to draw up international guidelines or codes of behaviour for the treatment of skeletal remains by archaeologists, and (2) that it ensure the full participation in discussion and consultation of representatives of all those with legitimate interests in such skeletal material, not only the views of professional archaeologists.

One of the main successes of the WAC has been to bring to the attention of archaeologists the way that archaeology affects the lives of others – at a national and a local level. It is this 'humane face' of archaeology which has been strikingly absent from IUPPS affairs to date. The WAC Steering Committee has made this one of its most important suggestions for revision to the IUPPS Statutes, recommending that representatives of Indigenous Peoples should form part of the IUPPS Permanent Council. Archaeologists ignore these matters at their peril and threaten the future of their discipline by so doing. The World Council of Indigenous Peoples, an organisation with observer status at the UN, states in its Declaration of Principles that:

> The original rights to their material culture, including archaeological sites, artifacts, designs, technology and works of art lie with the indigenous people.
> The indigenous peoples and their authorities have the right to be previously consulted and to authorize the realisation of all technological and scientific investigations to be conducted within their territories and to be informed and to have full access to the results of the investigations.

The archaeological profession must come to terms with the aspirations of such organisations and the deeply held beliefs and practices which they reflect.

At issue here is the fundamental nature of archaeological inquiry, a subject discussed elsewhere in this book (pages xv and 23-4). Archaeologists can no longer afford to claim that they deal exclusively with objective facts and scientific techniques. Their discipline is, in this sense, firmly within the social sciences – at least insofar as its findings are socially conditioned, and have social effects which need to be acknowledged and analysed by the profession. Dr Bozidar Slapsak wrote at the time of the Congress:

One immediate issue to discuss is the recognition of the new reality in world archaeology – archaeological scholarship has developed in most countries of the world and there is a necessity that this scholarship be equally represented in international bodies. This Congress showed the importance and strength of this scholarship and obvious consequences should be drawn therefrom.

My own position on the South African issue (and that includes also my understanding of why the Faculty of Philosophy of the University of Ljubljana and the Slovena Archaeological Society decided to give support) is founded upon the conviction that: (a) there is nothing such as neutral social science and that archaeologists, anthropologists and other social scientists, in order to avoid being manipulated and instrumentalised from outside, should better be aware of the fact and try to understand and control their own knowledge in these terms, so that they can act as an independent social power; that, I believe, is a basic prerequisite for the relevance of academic freedom; and (b) being aware that we as scientists are an integral part of culture, that our knowledge is a derivate of culture-bound conceptual tools and often ideology-laden research objectives, but also that scientific knowledge does acquire respectability through adequate implementation of science-specific methods and logical procedures, respectability which finally permits it to act as an independent power, we feel the responsibility towards this culture and a need to act. Numerous instances, on all possible levels, of implementation of this responsibility, have been demonstrated at this Congress. As archaeological, anthropological, social scientists however we cannot disregard the issues of utmost impact and importance; and racism, legally instituted, is such an issue. Today, legal justification of racism is at stake: it is simply unacceptable, it is felt by a vast majority as a terrifying anachronism. The WAC had to react (the more as there might be [a] chance to influence) and fortunately the cultural attitudes of the local community and of national organisations were instrumental in this respect.

I am aware that a number of scholars in South Africa oppose the apartheid policy of their government and that in a sense, to them at least, the decision of the WAC was unfair. On the other hand, their responsibility is greater on this issue and as perverse as it may seem, I think that the decision by the WAC can be understood as a contribution to their position and to their intellectual and moral integrity: speaking of academic freedom, their first obligation certainly is to securing equal legal opportunities to all their fellow citizens to acquire the privileges of it; and actions like this might help the endeavour.

This is why I support the move by the organisers of the Congress to contact the IUPPS Permanent Council and would not oppose a solution which would exclude South Africa from the IUPPS till the apartheid laws are abolished there.

With the acceptance of the fundamentals of archaeological inquiry, may come recognition that world archaeology would be more at home with the IUAES, its co-descendant from the same original world organisation, than with the IUPPS. The IUAES has recently decided that it would seriously entertain an application from the WAC to become formally associated with it.

It is probably not only because of the growing atrocities in South Africa during 1985 and 1986, culminating in the State of Emergency, which led to it being an archaeological congress which took the decision to ban South Africa/Namibia. In part, at least, it was also because of the nature of archaeological inquiry in several parts of the world. As Professor Jack Golson wrote in a report to archaeologists after the Congress:

> One of the many ironies of the situation is that it had been a major objective of the Southampton Congress, announced well before its South African/ Namibian ban and its disinheritance by IUPPS, to promote recognition of the fact that the practice of archaeology is not, as orthodox opinion within the profession would have it, above or outside politics. A central week-long symposium at Southampton called 'Archaeological "Objectivity" in Interpretation' illustrated the reality of this proposition in a number of ways: from questions of conflicting views on 'ownership' and 'control' of sites and their contents, and on the 'right' of scholarly access to them, to more subtle issues of bias in archaelogical aims and interpretations and of archaeologists' evaluations of alternative perceptions of the past. There are real problems here affecting the relationship of archaeologist and indigenous minorities, often focusing on the question of skeletal remains, which we know well from recent Australian experience and which was a prominent matter for discussion in the symposium. There are problems for the profession, too, in respect of Third World countries, where the cultural domination of the colonial era has sometimes been exchanged only for cultural dependency in the era of political independence.
>
> The Congress organisers made special efforts to bring to Southampton people from new nations and from minority groups to speak of the implications of the past and present practice of archaeology for them, and of what they saw as the way ahead. Thus there were speakers from Papua New Guinea and the Solomons, as well as from Africa and Latin America, by some of whom archaeology was seen as a potential tool in nation-building, and contributions from Aborigines and Maoris and American Indians, for whom our archaeological data are the material expressions of their ethnic identity. And lest we should imagine that problematic areas in our professional operations are confined to what we know as the Third and Fourth Worlds, there was a fascinating session on the politics of Stonehenge, and discussions of gender and other biases in the presentations of archaeology in schools, museums and the media in the First and Second Worlds.

As has been made clear in Chapter 2, much of the subject matter of the WAC was incomprehensible to the IUPPS old guard, which Jacques Nenquin, its Secretary-General, denied was 'a group of ancient reactionaries closed to all developments in archaeological thinking, insensitive to all that happens outside their own small specialist world ...'. One aspect of the 'Objectivity' sessions examined the nature of the archaeological record and how archaeologists have attempted to identify 'peoples', 'races', 'linguistic groups' and 'societies' from remains of material culture, which is all that is usually left for the archaeologist to uncover. This is one of the areas where archaeological theory and method are at their weakest and where the various interpretations offered at different times of the same material culture evidence has been abused most often by governments and others. Archaeologists who are involved in such studies should be aware of the intensely subjective nature of much archaeological interpretation. They should also be aware that what is deemed to be an 'ethnic' group at any particular time is the construct of that time, and 'ethnicity' is therefore not necessarily anything to do with the actual archaeological record of past events. The past is therefore very much a concept rather than an actuality. Archaeology teaches us that human societies, at all times and in all parts of the world, have artificially constructed 'types of people' so that they may establish control over them.

It should not be surprising, therefore, to find that archaeologists who recognise these events for what they are, and have been, are willing to take the lead in demonstrating the iniquities of a contemporary system which has actually legalised and institutionalised such a mythical category as an 'ethnic' group (or groups) in order to subjugate the people concerned. To study a situation, and to be aware of a common human practice, should not lead to a mute acceptance of an unacceptable contemporary practice.

The WAC Steering Committee now 'exists' in a wider sense than just as the formal coming together of its members. It has, for example, responded to an invitation from Medicine Men Roger Byrd and Vernal Cross, via American Indians Against Desecration, for me, as the Committee's Secretary, to consult with American Indians about the 'reburial' issue. In February 1987 Jane and I joined Jan Hammil and Robert Cruz in Arizona and travelled through the Indian reservations discussing this issue. Jane will be editing this part of the *World Archaeological Bulletin* 2 which will include details of an Inter-Tribal Council meeting, chaired by Cecil Antone, which discussed the reburial issue. We were also asked to convey messages to the Steering Committee and to all archaeologists from both the Hopi and the Navaho, as well as from several individual American Indians.

The WAC Steering Committee has also been successful in its bid to raise awareness of this issue, and to extend the range of international information available to those involved in this aspect of archaeology whether as excavators of sites or as museum curators, and has also successfully encouraged the Pitt Rivers Museum in Oxford to take the lead in removing skeletal material from its displays, and in getting museums in Britain to come together to discuss the issues regarding the display and conservation of American Indian human remains. The Steering Committee has also obtained the agreement of the Australian National University to welcome Professor Dena Dincauze and Jan Hammil in Australia, and to arrange meetings for them, with archaeologists and Aboriginal groups, to discuss subjects of mutual concern. The Steering Committee is now actively engaged in acquiring funds to enable this exchange of information and views to take place.

Meanwhile the IUPPS refuses to enter into any negotiations with the WAC Steering Committee. Michael Day first wrote to Jacques Nenquin on 5 December 1986, offering him the chance to talk formally or informally with the Steering Committee at its second meeting in January 1987; he received no reply. He wrote again, this time to be told that the Belgian mail system must again be at fault! The answer read:

> It is kind of you to invite me to attend part of your Steering Committee's meeting next month, but I am afraid I must decline to do so. First of all, January is a very busy month here, with much lecturing to be done (it may interest you to know that during the first semester I have to lecture 16 hours per week); and secondly, any discussions could only be on the basis of the resolutions adopted by the Executive Committee and the Permanent Council of the Union, and again recently by the General Assembly of the ICPHS. I enclose a copy of these last. It therefore seems to me that discussion is doomed from the start, since our priorities are clearly directly opposed to one another – scientific vs. political considerations.
>
> May I however reciprocate your invitation and ask you, if you find the time, to come to Belgium: you will be very welcome here.
>
> May I also point out what has been very clear to many of us: that apparently the whole South Africa issue which precipitated this most unhappy affair, is no longer mentioned by the Southampton group, as if it were of no consequence; instead all criticism is now directed against the IUPPS as such, for reasons which I prefer not to understand.

Michael Day answered (24.2.87):

> I am sorry that you feel that our discussions are doomed from the start, since we are determined to attempt to negotiate with IUPPS, in fulfilment of our mandate from the WAC Plenary Session. It gives us little hope that you understand the seriousness of the situation that you face if you take this attitude now ...
>
> The Plenary Session ... gave us our mandate to try and negotiate with IUPPS over a series of issues, only one of which relates to South Africa.
>
> If IUPPS will not negotiate then that organisation, sadly, will be seen to be responsible for schism in Archaeology.

Attempts to involve ICPSH also got nowhere, ending with a letter from its Secretary-General d'Ormesson who simply said that his organisation fully supported Jacques Nenquin's line. As nothing was progressing, the Steering Committee authorised an approach direct to the chief of the Non-Governmental Organisations Unit of UNESCO and it approved a detailed letter from me (reproduced in full in Appendix IX) which was sent on 9.2.87 and read, in part:

The Steering Committee has three major points to put to UNESCO:

1. *South African/Namibian participation*

Our Steering Committee formally requests UNESCO's response to the following two questions: (1) whether the banning of South African/Namibian participation from business meetings is or is not in line with UNESCO resolutions; and (2) whether the banning of South African/Namibian participation from congresses is or is not in line with UNESCO resolutions. Furthermore, it urges UNESCO to consider whether or not such a ban is more in line with its resolutions than are either the practices of ICPHS or of the IUPPS.

2. *IUPPS's decision not to recognise [the] WAC*

It has been brought to the Steering Committee's notice, subsequently confirmed by legal opinions from Britain, Denmark and France, that the actions taken to disenfranchise the WAC as the XIth Congress of the IUPPS infringed the existing IUPPS Statutes.

The list of such infringements is long ...

The Steering Committee formally requests UNESCO to examine the unconstitutional actions of the IUPPS regarding the WAC, here alleged to have infringed its Statutes, and to give the Steering Committee its view as to the constitutional status of (a) the WAC of September 1986; (b) the proposed meeting in Mainz in August/September 1987; and (c) the validity of the decisions taken at the extraordinary meeting of the IUPPS Executive Committee on 17 January 1986 in Paris.

3. *The future*

(a) As already mentioned, we have been put into a situation where we so far have been unable to 'negotiate' with either the IUPPS or with ICPHS.

The Steering Committee, therefore, suggests to UNESCO that the most constructive way forward is for there to be a special meeting of at least the Permanent Council called specifically to discuss significant changes to the organisation including revisions to its Statutes. It urges UNESCO to finance such a meeting in a way that would allow true world-wide participation in such a special meeting.

The main part of the reply (12.3.87) from Georges Malempré to this long, detailed and specific letter was:

As the difficulties raised in your letter are the result of an internal controversy between the IUPPS Executive Committee and the Steering Committee of the 11th World Archaeological Congress, you will certainly understand that the Unesco Secretariat cannot interfere in the solving of this matter. We hope nevertheless that a positive solution to the conflict in question will finally be worked out.

Mr Malempré did not respond to Professor Essomba's several attempts to fix a meeting with him in Paris.

There seems little or nothing left that the Steering Committee can do to try to influence the IUPPS, ICPHS, or UNESCO. These organisations appear to be in conflict with the UN. Meanwhile, Jacques Nenquin is continuing as if the WAC never took place and as if there are no lessons to be learnt from it. He has called a meeting of the International Executive Committee (see page 285), and the Mainz congress programme has been circulated. The programme gives little information about academic matters except to announce that IUPPS Commissions will meet, and it concentrates almost exclusively on tours. The IUPPS is making an unfortunate mistake if it thinks that its Eurocentric mini-world will be able to continue to discuss its local archaeological affairs while posturing as a world organisation, but without reference to most of that world. It was to be hoped that it was a small step in the right direction that Jacques Nenquin invited Professor V.N. Misra of Deccan College – who is neither a member of the International Executive Committee nor one of the Indian members of the Permanent Council – to the May meeting in Czechoslovakia. However, Professor Nenquin telegrammed in April to Professor Misra to say that he was not offering any financial assistance for Professor Misra to be able to reach Czechoslovakia. Nor did he invite the Secretary of the Pan African Association on Prehistory and Related Studies (who was also not invited to the Paris meeting of January 1986 (page 103)).

The WAC has been a resounding success in raising the consciousness of archaeologists throughout the world about the nature of the Western domination of the IUPPS. Two letters from Associate Professor Les Groube, the Papua New Guinean member of the IUPPS Permanent Council, have recently been sent to the IUPPS President and the IUPPS Secretary-General (whoever the legal incumbents of these posts may currently be). Both these letters have had considerable support from many countries of the world.

The first letter, which demands the removal of South Africa and Namibia from the IUPPS Permanent Council while the current policies of the Government of South Africa continue, has been supported in writing by IUPPS Permanent Council members from Australia, Chile, Ecuador, Ghana, Greece, Ireland, Kenya, Madagascar, Mozambique, New Zealand, Nigeria, Norway, Phillipines, United Kingdom, Union of Soviet Socialist Republics, and Venezuela.

The second letter , which sets out in detail (see Appendix XI) those Statutes of the IUPPS which should be amended including the necessity for representation on the IUPPS Permanent Council of young archaeologists/ students, women, representatives of indigenous minorities, as well as archaeologists elected for fixed-term periods (see page 47), has also been supported in writing by IUPPS Permanent Council members from Australia, Chile, Ecuador, Ghana, Greece, Ireland, Kenya, Madagascar, Mozambique, New Zealand, Nigeria, Norway, Phillipines, Syria, United Kingdom, Union of Soviet Socialist Republics, and Venezuela.

In addition, three Danish members of the Permanent Council have written to the IUPPS demanding that discussions should take place

regarding revisions (unspecified) to the Statutes.
Under IUPPS Statute 45:

> ... modifications to Statutes can be proposed in writing by 10 members of the
> Permanent Council who collectively sign the proposal for the revision ... An
> interval of at least one month must elapse between the receipt of the proposal
> and the meeting of the Permanent Council [due in September 1987 in Mainz,
> if the Mainz congress is indeed the XIth Congress of the IUPPS] ... If they are
> accepted it instructs the Bureau [see page 284] to present specific proposals
> for reform to the [International] Executive Committee ... The [International]
> Executive Committee then transmits its suggestions to the Permanent
> Council which discusses them and votes on them during its next reunion [ie
> some 3 years later].

Far more than the necessary ten members of the Permanent Council have
demanded revisions to the Statutes.

At the moment, ambiguity and hidden assumptions appear to
characterise the position regarding action on South Africa by UNESCO and
its affiliated/constituent bodies, where unambiguity and honesty are
obviously absolutely essential. IUPPS itself is also riddled with such
equivocation and obscurity – in August 1985 Secretary-General Jacques
Nenquin wrote to the Secretary-General of the ICPHS about the IUPPS
Statutes that:

> It is so obvious that IUPPS accepts all bona fide scholars irrespective of race,
> religion or politics that it was never thought necessary to formalise this in the
> Statutes[!].

If the September Mainz congress is indeed the IUPPS XIth Congress, then
it will be up to the members present at the Permanent Council meeting and
the 'General Assembly' [Plenary Session] to make their views clearly
known. It can only be hoped that the no doubt predominantly Western
European and American participants at Mainz will bear their Third World
and other colleagues very strongly in mind. If they do not do so, the WAC
Steering Committee has been charged by the Plenary Session to set up an
organisation outside of the IUPPS.

The entry of academia into the public arena with regard to apartheid has
brought to light a series of ambiguous policies, in an area where clarity of
view and policy are vital. Academics have a right to know what action they
can take if they wish to join the fight against apartheid, and must therefore
be able to refer to clear policies of their various relevant organisations.

The call by the ANC and others is for the cultural isolation of South
Africa. The most public archaeological example of the flouting of this policy
is, of course, the forthcoming September 1987 meeting in Mainz to which
some British archaeologists, such as Professor John Coles, will make public
attendance a well-publicised virtue (letter in *British Archaeological News*,
7.11.86). There is growing evidence of at least disquiet, if not distaste,

among German students, academics, and politicians at the idea of their country being seen to host an international congress which appears to the world to be unashamedly opposed to making a stand on the South African apartheid issue. I have just been informed (30.5.87) that there will be no USSR participation at the Mainz Congress.

At a much less publicised meeting in Cambridge in March 1987 on Human Origins, a very clear and detailed message (see Appendix X) was circulated by Anti-Apartheid to all those participating in this meeting which Paul Mellars and Christopher Stringer described as, 'a totally separate, independent meeting [from the WAC] – and emphatically without any exclusion along National or political lines'. The message explained the nature and aims of the boycott, and concluded by urging the participants at the Cambridge meeting to 'ideally, drop out of the conference [or] otherwise, write letters to the organisers protesting about the participation of South Africans here. You can also write to the South African embassy, protesting at the state of emergency and the mass detentions ...'

It is difficult to imagine that UNESCO can continue to operate without clear guidelines for much longer. September 1987 could provide an ideal opportunity for the new Director-General to take a significant and far-reaching decision.

The WAC has raised these questions in a public form, and unambiguous policy statements are badly needed from the relevant organisations and groups. An interesting example concerns the precise definition of those to whom any ban should apply. In the WAC's case, John Evans and I agreed to apply the ban only to those who lived in South Africa/Namibia or those who gained direct financial support from South African sources for employment/ research in those countries. Other organisations have taken the ban to apply to South African/Namibian nationals, wherever they are domiciled. UNESCO's position, and especially the position of its associated non-governmental organisations, remains ambiguous in the extreme about all such matters of concern to academics.

Many colleagues say that they would have been prepared to risk the potential 'divisiveness' of the issue, and would have supported the ban on South Africa/Namibia at the WAC if they had believed that the ban would have produced results. This is a very important point. Several, such as the then South African Ambassador to Britain, maintained that the academic boycott would have no effect on the South African government. John Evans, in the same broadcast – *Heart of the Matter* – gave this as one of his reasons for not supporting the WAC:

> ... I don't think that by doing something of this kind you can really be doing any good, in the first place, to the situation in South Africa, but I think you can be doing a great deal of bad to academic freedom generally ...

The similarities with arguments put forward for academics doing nothing regarding Nazism in Germany – the only real parallel with the South African case of legalised racism – are obvious.

There is a range of views on the importance of academic freedom, from those held by, for example, John Evans (as expressed in *Heart of the Matter*) and Barry Cunliffe (page 140) who believe that there are *no* occasions when academics should take action via their congresses, to those of, for example, by John Evans (when he was a member of the WAC Executive Committee) which seek to distance themselves from apartheid by imposing a ban, to others, such as Trevor Huddleston (in *Heart of the Matter*), who consider that if academics had banned Germans from their deliberations at the right time, it might well have had an impact on the subsequent course of events.

Ralegh Radford, a former Director of the British School of Archaeology at Rome (who was one of the Secretaries of the Organising Committee for the 1932 London Congress), made several important interventions at the National Committee meetings of the WAC. His statements, as well as a letter to me from Professor Christopher Hawkes, and Sigfried De Laet's published review of the history of the IUPPS (and its predecessor the International Congress of Prehistoric and Protohistoric Sciences), suggest that the archaeological world at that time, and earlier, may not have been as academically 'pure' as some are now claiming academia should be.

The claim by the IUPPS to such 'purity' was, of course, hardly likely given the clause in its Statutes (see page 72) which allows nominations to its Permanent Council to derive from Governments. According to Ralegh Radford, political manoeuvering became explicit at the 1931 meeting of IUPPS's predecessor, in Bern. There, two Italian archaeologists were nominated by those present at the Congress for the Permanent Council but one was found to be unacceptable to the Italian Government, and could not represent Italy on it. (Subsequently he was appointed to the 'Comité d'Honneur' of the international archaeological organisation concerned – a compromise which the Italian Government apparently accepted unhappily.)

Also contrary to claims about the inviolate nature of scholarship and international academic organisations was the ban on Italian archaeologists while Italy was involved in Ethiopia. It was the predecessor to the United Nations, the League of Nations, which imposed a ban on all Italian scholars from attending international conferences – including the archaeological Congress in Oslo in 1936.

With specific reference to the Nazis, however, and how archaeologists should, and did, behave, De Laet says, '... during the second conference, in Oslo in 1936, grave difficulties had arisen within the [organisation]. These were caused by the German Nazi government, which had demanded the resignation of a few German colleagues, who did not share the racist theories of the Kossinna school'. The Nazi Government did not consider Dr G. Bersu to be an appropriate representative of their country. They moved him from his Directorship in Frankfurt and placed him in another job in Berlin where he could not be influential, and would not be in contact with foreigners. Dr Bersu could only visit and excavate outside Germany if the other countries concerned paid all the costs; in return for being allowed to do such work, he had to agree to resign as representative of Germany on the Permanent Council. Professor Hawkes informs me that he did so 'under duress; but the Council as sovereign body, had to decide whether to accept it'. After 'anxious debate' the Permanent Council did accept it, apparently without official protest. Such was the influence of a political pressure, and the international archaeological organisation's response to it, although Bersu's only 'crime' had been to disagree with the theories espoused by the German Government.

For academics to claim immunity from the real world gives them a marvellous excuse for never doing anything about anything. All the evidence revealed by the WAC, however, is against such a defeatist view, for the reaction to the ban, and therefore the reasons for the imposition of the ban itself, have made the news nationally and internationally. Directly and indirectly the ban has influenced South African academics to speak out in numerous contexts, and the South African government cannot now safely ignore the academic part of its own constituency. This has been clearly shown very recently with the report (the *Observer*, 8.3.87) of the revolt of '27 top academics at Stellenbosch University, the cradle of Afrikaner Nationalism' who are demanding the 'abolition of the legal definition of race groups' in South Africa. Rightly or wrongly, many Africans see this new development as directly (or, at least, indirectly) related to the WAC's imposition of the ban. Contrary to the views of people like John Evans and the South African Ambassador quoted above, the United Nations Special Committee Against Apartheid, as reported in the British press (*Southern Evening Echo*, 9.3.87), sees the WAC as having established 'an important precedent for the academic community worldwide'.

The WAC decision by academics themselves to ban South Africa/ Namibia from one of its own meetings has stirred the conscience of at least the reader of almost any British newspaper, as well as people in many other countries who read archaeological journals. There is no doubt that the message will spread further, and continue to be debated. Professor Desmond Clark and Professor F Wendorf are behind moves to stage the next Pan African Association's Congress on Prehistory and Related Studies in Cairo in March 1988, with unrestricted participation. The President and the Secretary of the Association have dissociated themselves from this proposal unless South Africans/Namibians are banned from participation, as well as those who choose to attend the September 1987 congress in Mainz.

The WAC is directly responsible for the airing of views and opinions on South Africa in the media and has thereby – whatever the opinions expressed – struck a major blow against apartheid. Each mention of that inhuman regime, must, in the long run, work towards its demise. Shortly after the Congress, Neal Ascherson returned to the subject in the *Observer*, making much use of the views expressed in the *Heart of the Matter* programme:

I am embroiled with Dr Conor Cruise O'Brien, the founder of this column. He hates a recent article of mine about the academic boycott of South Africa – the case of the WAC at Southampton, which 'disinvited' South African scholars – and wrote in *The Times* on 6 September that I had been affected 'by a certain kind of rot in British intellectual life.' Dr O'Brien, as he declared, is himself off to teach at the University of Cape Town for five weeks. His argument is roughly this. By supporting Professor Ucko's decision to 'disinvite' South African archaeologists, I am supporting an odious and pointless form of apartheid by address, rather than by colour. 'A kind of intellectual mob' in Britain is trying to enforce the 'unjust and vindictive punishment of private individuals who neither serve the apartheid regime nor have any power to change it' ... I disagree with most of his article.

The 'intellectual mob' can be found, but it is not important. There will always be sheep, which tells us nothing about the wisdom or integrity of shepherds ...

... In practical terms, I am more certain than ever that Professor Ucko did the right thing. The Southampton Congress not only brought Third World archaeologists and their work into the centre of discussion; it has broken through into defining the social responsibility of the profession – debating, for example, the implications of excavating the graves and removing the funeral deposits of living cultures. If the South Africans had come, black Africa, Asia and Australasia would not have come, and the entire purpose of this pioneering occasion would have disappeared.

What about the South African archaeologists themselves? Last Sunday on television, Professor David Williams, of the University of the Witwatersrand, said with deep emotion that 'we live and work in South African because we want open education, to provide a platform for opposition'. He described as a 'mistake' the idea that 'if you live in South Africa, you must be an active or passive supporter of the regime'.

The personal unfairness to people like that is obvious. But there is a wider issue. Those who want a boycott are saying that they will not accept at international gatherings delegations, official or semi-official, representing areas of South African life which are connected with government or in some sense form part of the apartheid system. South African official research and education, denying knowledge and enlightenment to the majority of the population, are plainly such an area. That is not altered by the fact that within the system there are large numbers of academics and students fighting to change and extend it.

This does not mean that individuals – especially individuals like Professor Williams – should be prevented from meeting their colleagues in Europe or elsewhere. That would be idiotic, as well as impossible. Neither does it mean that British scientists and intellectuals should never visit South Africa – although such visits lay a special duty on them.

... With scientists and academics...if they choose to stay and fight, in their own jobs and in their own country, there is a price to pay. This is not only the risk of dismissal or arrest. It is also that those abroad who want their struggle to succeed are laying on them an extra burden: that they cannot be invited to international meetings of their profession.

This hurts, but it seems to me to be a hurt that goes with the job – like the hurt of ostracism for those who worked for a German occupation regime by day to conceal their work for the Resistance by night. It should not be understood as a real rejection. A South African exile I know commented: 'The onus should be on them. They should say to themselves: I won't go to this or that meeting, for it would mean representing South Africa.'

... Academic or economic boycotts will not achieve dramatic change by themselves. They are all substitutes for the sort of direct action which – apart from the front-line States – is taken only by Cuba, whose troops are on active service in Angola against the South African army. No Western government will go that far.

Or rather – not yet. I believe, as I suspect Dr O'Brien believes, that the West will eventually be drawn into military intervention as South Africa's death struggles tear the continent apart. Sanctions, seen in that light, are an exercise. They are training the world to act towards South Africa in a co-ordinated way, getting the international community used to joint decisions and action. The crisis is coming, and if we have not learnt our drills for it in advance, God help us all.

Dr O'Brien's much-flaunted contribution to the issue turned out to be a fiasco. As *The Times* reported (10.10.86) under the headline 'O'Brien cancels Cape lectures after threat of violence on campus':

> ... Dr O'Brien was visibly upset by his experience, said he had been the target of an 'academic necklace' ... at the University of Witwatersrand in Johannesburg ... Militant students, predominantly black, made it clear that he would be shouted down if he tried to speak ... Before he left for South Africa ... he wrote that he would be glad to have his vist to Cape Town seen as 'a gesture of defiance against an intellectually-disreputable attempt [by the WAC] to isolate what I know to be an honest, open and creative intellectual community'. Students ... offered instead to engage in an 'open debate' with Dr O'Brien on the issue of the academic boycott but he declined what he called 'another punishment session'.

The article went on to say that at both the universities concerned only about 15 per cent of students are black. As the *Guardian* put it (9.10.86):

> The university boycott committee [of the University of Capetown] object[ed] to Dr O'Brien's reported description of the academic boycott of South African universities as 'Mickey Mouse stuff'.

Dr O'Brien's visit to South Africa far from detracting from the importance of the WAC ban, has in fact served to bring added support to it, and has given added strength and resolve to the South African students in their fight against apartheid. A University Inquiry into the disruption laid all blame firmly on Dr O'Brien for having been provocative.

The *Guardian* also used this opportunity in the same issue to publish a long review by David Beresford 'on the way the anti-apartheid boycott is affecting South Africa's academic community', in which it was made clear that the academic boycott was beginning to bite. By May 1987 *Nature* reported that such boycotts were not only biting but 'biting hard', and that 'since [the WAC], South Africans had found that it has become even more difficult to attend conferences overseas'.

There is much to suggest that a full academic boycott of South Africa could have as much effect as the more widely-known sporting ban on South Africa. Certainly, the UN "attaches great importance [to an] academic and cultural boycott of South Africa". John Evans said in *Heart of the Matter*, 'Sport is a difficult problem in many ways. While I don't really like the idea of the interference in sport, it is a different category...[there is a] nationalistic element, [people] represent their country, [and there is a] feeling [that] victory in sport is one up to [the] country concerned – almost chauvanistic feeling about it from time-to-time'. Bishop Huddleston, on the other hand, welcomed the fact that Southampton had brought the whole argument about sanctions into the academic sphere and hoped that it would equal the ban on sport. 'Sport has been the most effective ban so far which has hurt South Africa more than anything else. South Africa feels isolated in sport and look how they try to get them back, even via bribery'. In the same television programme, Bassey Andah stressed that both the sporting and the academic boycotts shared the same feature, the need for 'the individual's interests to be subsumed within the group'.

Although this ban was imposed by a particular group of archaeologists, its message is spreading to other archaeological organisations. In March 1987, for example, the Meeting of Norwegian Archaeologists condemned the IUPPS's removal of its support for the WAC and instructed it instead to remove its support from the congress in Mainz. It also advised the IUPPS 'to revise its statutes so that its organisation is in accord with the needs of present-day world archaeology'. The message is also spreading rapidly to other academic disciplines. Since the Congress there have been major discussions, and in some instances action, on the need for the imposition of such a ban on South Africa/Namibia, amongst the General Medical Council, a conference on Physiotherapy, the International Federation of Information Processing, the World Congress on Diseases in Cattle, the British Psychological Society, and recently, the Society for French Studies, which announced publicly that it does not 'question in any way the cultural boycott of South Africa'. Academic boycotts, and especially the WAC's, feature in a major way in a recent handbook on sanctions (page 292).

Never the less there remain respected academic colleagues who are indeed fundamentally opposed to the South African apartheid regime, but who are not convinced that a boycott of South African/Namibian academics is a suitable, or correct, response to the situation in South Africa. Despite the evidence reviewed in this book they have, until now, been worried and/or suspicious that such a boycott is simply a political act inspired by a particular organisation, the ANC. In that sense, these colleagues have not wanted to take 'political' action. Until now they have had no firm lead to follow. As has been seen, UNESCO itself is ambiguous in its position, and other political organisations which have called for the cultural isolation of South Africa have not made special reference to academics or academia.

This is no longer the case. The Chairman of the UN Special Committee Against Apartheid, General Joseph N Garba, wrote to me (16.3.87):

> On behalf of the Special Committee and on my own behalf I commend the decision of the WAC at its meeting in Southampton in September 1986 for banning South African and Namibian participation in its meetings.
>
> The ban on individual South African and Namibian academics, irrespective of their personal records with regard to *apartheid*, is an important component of the international campaign to assist the struggle against *apartheid*.
>
> The Special Committee takes this opportunity to salute many individuals and organisations who continue to contribute to the international campaign to totally isolate *apartheid* South Africa as called by the resolutions of the United Nations.

From now on the question is clearly posed for those who intend to organise or participate in an academic conference which accepts South African participation. Why are such people defying the United Nations?

An equally important question remains for those South African/Namibian academics who profess to be against apartheid. Why do they continue to flout the wishes of the ANC and of the UN, by insisting on their right to participate in such meetings?

If South African/Namibian academics continue to insist on this right it will, on each occasion, be up to the academics in the host country to decide on their own response. The WAC Executive Committee, faced with this decision in the summer of 1985, banned the South Africans and Namibians from their Congress. The decision was not taken lightly, and, as this book has shown, created almost intolerable dilemmas for the individuals, organisations, academic departments and even for countries considering participation in the Congress. Academics who value the principle of academic free speech, as I and my colleagues involved in the WAC unquestionably do, will have to face the inevitable dilemma again and again until apartheid in South Africa no longer exists.

It is my hope that the story of the World Archaeological Congress may help them to resolve this dilemma, to come out from behind the shaky edifice of their own academic freedom, and turn their attention to the issue of freedom itself.

APPENDIX I
Abbreviations

ANC	African National Congress
AUT	Association of University Teachers
BBC	British Broadcasting Corporation
BP	Before the Present (viz. before 1950)
CBA	Council for British Archaeology
EEC	European Economic Community
FCO	Foreign and Commonwealth Office
GCE	General Certificate of Education
GLC	Greater London Council
HBMC	Historic Buildings and Monuments Commission
IBM	International Business Machines (UK)
ICPHS	International Council for Philosophy and Humanistic Studies
IFA	Institute of Field Archaeologists
IPPA	Indo-Pacific Prehistory Association
IUAES	International Union of Anthropological and Ethnological Sciences
IUPPS	International Union of Prehistoric and Protohistoric Sciences
MSC	Manpower Services Commission
NUS	National Union of Students
RAI	Royal Anthropological Institute
SAA	Society for American Archaeology
UK	United Kingdom
UN	United Nations
UNESCO	United Nations Educational, Scientific and Cultural Organisation
USA	United States of America
USSR	Union of Soviet Socialist Republics
WAC	World Archaeological Congress

APPENDIX II

Glossary

ABORIGINES Derived from the Latin 'ab origine'. When used with a capital 'A', usually refers to the indigenous (qv) peoples of Australia. Without a capital it is often used to refer to any indigenous group.

AFRICAN NATIONAL CONGRESS Founded in Bloemfontein in 1912, with the intention of working for a racially integrated and democratic South Africa. Banned in 1961 after the Sharpeville massacre, and with many of its leaders (including Nelson Mandela), imprisoned, it continued in exile, with its headquarters in Lusaka, Zambia, and representatives throughout the world. The movement has constantly called for the total isolation of South Africa, including academic isolation.

ANTHROPOLOGY The study or science of man, which began to develop as a separate discipline in the 19th century. In its widest sense anthropology embraces human physiology and psychology as well as the study of human societies and all other aspects of human culture including archaeology (qv). This is still the sense in which it is usually used in North America. In Britain the non-physical side of anthropology is traditionally divided into 'social' and 'cultural' anthropology. Cultural Anthropology, a term often also used in North America, covers the whole range of human activities which are learned and transmitted. Social Anthropology is more concerned with social institutions, social values and social organisation and structure.

APARTHEID Literally means 'apart-ness', a system introduced in South Africa in 1948. Apartheid policy recently described by the State President of South Africa as 'co-operative co-existence', and by opponents to it as 'institutionalised racism'. Under South African legislation all South Africans are classified by race and from this classification, so are their lives regulated (eg where to live and work, where and how to be educated, and where and how they are governed). Described most recently by the *Commonwealth Group of Eminent Persons* (qv) as 'awesome in its cruelty. It is achieved and sustained only through force, creating human misery and deprivation and blighting the lives of millions'.

ARCHAEOLOGY The study of the past mainly using non-documentary sources, mainly material culture (qv).

244

ASSOCIATION OF UNIVERSITY TEACHERS Professional and Trade Union organisation with 30,000 members representing academic staff in UK universities. Affiliated to the National Trades Union Congress.

AVEBURY A ritual monument of Neolithic (qv) date in Wiltshire, consisting of a large circle of massive stones surrounded by a ditch and an outer bank. The four original entrances now admit roads leading to the village established in the centre of the site.

BBC (British Broadcasting Corporation) A publicly financed corporation ultimately responsible to Parliament but in practical terms largely independent. Founded 1927. Maintained a broadcasting monopoly until 1957.

BEACON HILL A hill in Hampshire topped by a largely unexcavated defended Iron Age settlement, or 'hillfort'.

BENIN A kingdom in southern Nigeria famous for bronze casting. Using the *cire perdue* technique, metalworkers cast human heads and relief plaques in a long series which stylistic analyses suggest lasted perhaps from the 15th to the 19th century AD.

BP Means Before Present, and is a term used in the radiocarbon dating technique (qv). Dates are measured and expressed with reference to a fixed 'present' which is set at 1950 when the technique was first developed and used.

BRITISH ACADEMY Founded in 1901 and comprising 17 Sections, including archaeology.

BRITISH ANTI-APARTHEID MOVEMENT A national movement with the aim of bringing the system of apartheid (qv) to an end and of informing the British public about apartheid and what it means to the people of Southern Africa. The Movement supports Southern African organisations, such as the African National Congress (qv), campaigning for the elimination of apartheid. It has numerous local groups, such as the Southampton Anti-Apartheid Group, affiliated to it.

BRITISH COUNCIL Founded by Government in 1934 for the promotion of a wider knowledge of Britain and the English language abroad and the development of closer cultural relations with other countries.

BRONZE AGE Defines the period when metalworkers used the alloy of copper and tin to hammer and cast weapons, tools, ornaments and vessels, before the discovery of the way to work iron. A term used in the archaeology of many parts of the world, to describe a technological stage.

CENTRE-PERIPHERY RELATIONS The economic and political relationship existing between one more highly developed country or region (the 'centre') and the less developed countries or regions in contact with it (the 'periphery').

COMMONWEALTH Comprises 49 sovereign nations who acknowledge the Queen as their Head. It holds self-determination as a central principle and has been concerned to help extend political freedoms to all the people of South Africa. South Africa was forced to leave the

Commonwealth in 1961 because of its racist policies.

COMMONWEALTH GROUP OF EMINENT PERSONS Appointed at Nassau (qv) and comprising: Malcolm Fraser (Co-Chairman) (Australia), General O Obasanjo (Co-Chairman) (Nigeria), Lord Barber (Britain), Dame Nita Barrow (Barbados), John Malecela (Tanzania), Sardar S Singh (India), Reverend E W Scott (Canada). Report submitted June 1986 which concluded that there was no prospect in view of the establishment of a non-racial and representative government in South Africa.

COPPER AGE Also called the Chalcolithic. A period when copper metallurgy had been developed but before bronze technology was introduced.

COUNCIL FOR BRITISH ARCHAEOLOGY Founded 1944 to represent archaeological opinion in Britain, both professional and amateur. It has a full-time Director and is based in London.

CULTURAL RESOURCE MANAGEMENT Refers to the protection and development of archaeological sites.

DANEBURY A defended Iron Age site, or hillfort, in Hampshire, the subject of several years of intensive excavation by Professor B.W. Cunliffe.

DIFFUSION The spread of ideas, items of material culture, and peoples from one area to another. It does not imply necessarily a movement of people, for ideas can move through trade and other contact. Nevertheless, diffusion as the only explanation of similarities in material culture (qv) has long been undermined by the certain evidence for independent invention and parallel, unconnected, development associated with the refining of radiocarbon dating.

DOMESTICATION The control of fauna and flora by early agriculturalists through selective breeding so that desirable traits might be encouraged and the dependence on hunting and gathering reduced.

DRUIDS The priests of the Celtic Iron Age (qv) in Europe, named and described by classical writers. Links with Stonehenge (qv) and other Neolithic (qv) ritual monuments, archaeologically untenable now, were suggested in the 17th century, and have been kept alive by the revived Druid movement which has no direct connection with the pre-Roman Druids.

ECOLOGY The study of all aspects of the natural living environment.

EGYPTOLOGY The study of Egypt's ancient past.

ENGLISH HERITAGE See Historic Buildings and Monuments Commission.

ETHNICITY The ascription, or claim to belong, to a particular cultural group on the basis of genetics or language or other cultural manifestation. Definitions of what constitutes an ethnic group have varied over time and place.

ETHNOLOGY A term often used in Britain to describe those working particularly on material culture (qv). In its wider sense it is also concerned with the classification of peoples in terms of their racial and cultural characteristics, and the explanation of these by reference to their history or prehistory. In Western Europe the term is used in a way that is much closer to the use in Britain of the term Anthropology (qv).

EUROPEAN ECONOMIC COMMUNITY (EEC) Also known as the 'Common Market'. Established in Rome, 1957, with the principal aim of promoting economic relations in Europe, but also formulating joint European policies.

FOREIGN AND COMMONWEALTH OFFICE Government department headed by the Secretary of State for Foreign and Commonwealth Affairs, dealing with British foreign policy.

FOURTH WORLD Members of the indigenous (qv) peoples (eg Aborigines (qv)) in countries, such as Australia, and in the New World (qv), where an alien majority has now become established in government.

GEOGRAPHY The study of the earth's surface, its form, physical attributes and uses, its natural and political divisions, climates and produce. Human geography describes the study of population distribution, density and spatially focused activities.

GLENEAGLES AGREEMENT Decision by Commonwealth leaders in 1977 to force South Africa into sporting isolation.

GREAT ZIMBABWE A group of finely-built, massive stone structures of considerable complexity constructed in the 14th – 15th centuries in Zimbabwe.

GREATER LONDON COUNCIL A local authority deriving its finances from local government rates. It took the place of the London County Council and it was abolished by Government in 1986.

HAUT MOYEN-AGE/HIGH MIDDLE AGES A European continental term for the early Medieval period up to about 1100 AD.

HISTORIC BUILDINGS AND MONUMENTS COMMISSION A government organ which became established and separate from the Department of the Environment in 1984. Its brief is to protect and preserve monuments, buildings and towns and to promote public interest in visiting them. It advises the Secretary of State for the Environment.

HISTORY The study of the past using mainly documentary sources, and thus concentrated on societies where writing has been adopted.

HOLOCENE The most recent part of the Quaternary period, from about 10,000 BP (qv) to the present day.

HOMINID A family of mammals represented by the single genus Homo. Used to describe the family of Man and its evolutionary predecessors.

HUANACO PAMPA An Inca (qv) city, a provincial capital, in the Andes, and the subject of a major project linking excavated archaeological evidence with historical data.

INCA A people and kingdom in South America which incorporated the Andes mountains and the Pacific coast, with a capital at Cuzco. The Inca state flourished between 1200 AD and the first part of the 16th century.

INDIGENOUS Native to the land, the original inhabitants.

INDO-PACIFIC PREHISTORY ASSOCIATION (IPPA) An Association with individual and institutional members, to promote cooperation in the study of the prehistory of related subjects of eastern Asia and the Pacific and prehistorically related areas.

INSTITUTE OF FIELD ARCHAEOLOGISTS Founded 1982 to represent professional archaeologists.

INUIT The indigenous (qv) word meaning 'the people', which is the term much-preferred by the people themselves over 'Eskimos' or 'Esquimaux'.

IRON AGE The period during which the technology of iron was perfected and gradually took over from bronze as the metal for arms, tools and some prestigious and display items.

LAURA ROCK ART A complex of Aboriginal (qv) rock paintings and pecking in Cape York, northern Queensland, Australia. Excavations have dated the peckings to *c* 12,000 BC while the most recent art works probably continued to be painted until at least the 1930s.

LEPENSKI VIR A small Neolithic (qv) settlement in Yugoslavia discovered in 1976 and dating from before *c* 5,300 BC. The site includes seven successive settlements of hunters and fishers who constructed houses and carved stone sculptures.

LEY LINERS People who believe that archaeological and historical sites of various dates are linked by mystical lines running invisibly across the countryside.

MANPOWER SERVICES COMMISSION Since 1982 responsible for a Community Enterprise Programme on behalf of the Secretary of State for Employment to help long-term unemployed adults obtain work experience on projects of benefit to the community.

MATERIAL CULTURE A term used to describe the objects produced by human beings. As such, material culture is the main source of information about the past from which archaeologists can make inferences. This material culture evidence is often analysed typologically (qv) in an attempt to trace patterns of diffusion (qv). The study of material culture (and see Ethnology) and primitive technology often also examine man's adaptation to the environment.

MEDIEVAL PERIOD Also known as the Middle Ages. When used in Britain, the term defines the whole period between 1066 and 1485 AD, though in practise it is often divided into early Medieval and late Medieval.

MOUVEMENT CONTRE LE RACISME ET POUR L'AMITIE ENTRE LES PEUPLES A French anti-racist movement with its headquarters in Paris.

MYCENAEAN Pertaining to the site or culture associated with Mycenae, a Bronze Age palace in Greece.

NAMIBIA Country in Southwest Africa bordered by Angola, Zambia and

South Africa. A German colony before World War I, it was administered by South Africa until 1966 when the United Nations (qv) revoked the mandate. South Africa has never acted on the UN decision and has maintained effective jurisdiction over the area.

NASSAU ACCORD Decision by Commonwealth (qv) leaders in October 1985 to promote political dialogue in South Africa aimed at replacing apartheid (qv) by popular government through pressure from the Commonwealth Group of Eminent Persons (qv).

NEOLITHIC (lit: New Stone Age) A period of prehistory originally defined by the occurrence of polished stone tools and pottery. Now used most frequently in connection with the beginnings of farming.

NECROPOLIS Cemetery or burial place.

NEW WORLD Another name for the Americas.

OLD SARUM The embanked site of the town which was a precursor to Salisbury, Wiltshire, now containing the foundations of the cathedral. Possibly originally an Iron Age (qv) defended site.

OLD WORLD Often used to refer to Europe when opposing Europe to the New World (qv).

PARIETAL Pertaining to a wall, as in rock art.

PHOENICIAN A people from the eastern Mediterranean renowned as traders in later prehistory who have erroneously been credited with the construction of Great Zimbabwe (qv) among other worldwide activities.

PIDGIN ENGLISH A product of initial contacts between English and West European explorers and non-English speaking peoples. Pidgin English, sometimes referred to as Creole, has now become a recognised language in several parts of the world, eg Melanesia, and has developed its own literature and grammar.

PLEISTOCENE The earliest part of the Quaternary period, from about 2 million years BP (qv) to 10,000 BP.

PREHISTORIC SOCIETY Founded in 1908 to further prehistoric archaeology.

PROTOHISTORY A period when one area may be still theoretically 'prehistoric' but be in contact with another area where writing and thus 'historical' documents exist. Another use of the term refers to the beginnings of the use of writing by a society.

PUBLIC ARCHAEOLOGY See Cultural Resource Management. It is also used to refer to the management of, and legislation concerning, sites.

RADIOCARBON DATING TECHNIQUE All living matter contains a small but constant proportion of the radioactive isotope of carbon, C14. When the living matter dies the isotope is no longer replenished from the atmosphere and it decays at a constant rate. By measuring the radioactivity of the carbon remaining in a specimen its age can be calculated.

RESCUE ARCHAEOLOGY Term coined in the 1960s in Britain for field archaeology carried out on sites under threat of destruction, time and money being the main parameters of any research element.

ROYAL ANTHROPOLOGICAL INSTITUTE OF GREAT BRITAIN AND IRELAND Established in 1843 to promote the study of the science of man, it is one of the few institutions in Britain which still attempts to cater for all the different interests of anthropology (qv).

ROYAL SOCIETY One of the oldest scientific societies in Europe, founded in 1660 to promote 'natural knowledge'.

SAMI (or Saami) Formerly often known as the Lapps and traditionally practising reindeer pastoralism, they inhabit areas of northern Scandinavia, the USSR, and Greenland.

SAQQARA Major necropolis (qv) in southern Egypt associated with 2nd and 3rd Dynasty pharaohs (rulers).

SCIENCE-BASED ARCHAEOLOGY (or Archaeological Science) The use of methods of the physical and biological sciences to answer archaeological questions.

SCIENTIFIC ARCHAEOLOGY See Science-Based Archaeology.

SMITH REGIME A term used to describe the period following Rohodesia's unilateral declaration of independence and the setting up of a new constitution on 11 November 1965 with Ian Smith as Prime Minister. In retaliation, Britain imposed economic sanctions with UN (qv) approval. Great Britain recognised the independence of the country under the name Zimbabwe in 1971.

SOCIETY OF ANTIQUARIES OF LONDON Founded 1752 for the 'Encouragement, Advancement and furtherance of the Study and knowledge of Antiquities and History of this and other countries'.

STONEHENGE A Neolithic (qv) and Bronze Age (qv) ritual site on Salisbury Plain, Wiltshire, consisting of a bank and ditch enclosing a complex of structures such as pits and stone circles, which were rebuilt to different patterns several times. Served as a focus for other ritual monuments between 2500 and 1200 BC and has attracted a variety of 'alternative' religions including the Druids (qv) and, more recently, the 'Peace Convoy'.

SUTTON HOO A site in Suffolk where a very rich 7th Century AD boat burial was excavated in the 1930s and where new excavations are taking place.

THIRD WORLD Nations which are not part of the Capitalist industrialised West nor of the Communist Eastern bloc; they are poorer, less economically developed, and are frequently exploited by the other two 'worlds'. See also **FOURTH WORLD**.

TYPOLOGY The classification of traits in objects, remains and specimens according to classes and types which they are supposed to exhibit, in order to trace their evolution and development.

UNITED NATIONS (UN) Founded in 1945 as the successor to the League of Nations, its member countries have all signed an international charter to promote world peace and to further economic, social and cultural cooperation. Switzerland is one of the few countries still voting against joining the 159 members of the organisation, whose central organisation is situated in New York.

UNITED NATIONS EDUCATIONAL, SCIENTIFIC AND CULTURAL ORGANIZATION (UNESCO) Established 1946 for the purpose of advancing, through the educational, scientific, and cultural relations of the peoples of the world, the objectives of international peace and the common welfare of mankind. In August 1986, it had 158 member countries, with the USA and Britain having recently withdrawn from it.

WORLD COUNCIL OF INDIGENOUS PEOPLES Founded in 1975 to represent the Fourth World (qv) (with membership from more than 19 peoples). The Council has Observer Status with the UN (qv) and a secretariat based in Canada.

Chronology of main events

1976 September 13 – 18

IXth Congress of the IUPPS in Nice, France. IUPPS Commissions created, following a suggestion by the then Secretary-General, Professor Henry de Lumley.

1981 October 19 – 24

Xth Congress of the IUPPS in Mexico City. Britain was mentioned as a possible host of the XIth Congress.

1981 October – November

Professor Peter Ucko first approached by the four British members of the IUPPS to become its National Secretary.

1982 April 23

First meeting of the National Committee. The location of the 1986 Congress was tentatively agreed as Southampton and London.

1982 May 3-5

Meeting of the International Executive Committee of the IUPPS in Florence. XIth Congress of the IUPPS formally offered to Britain, under the Presidency of Professor John Evans and Professor Peter Ucko as National Secretary.

1983 January

Circulation of the Congress's First Announcement.

1983 March 23

Executive Committee meeting. Congress formed as a registered Company with six Directors.

1983 May 10

Executive Committee meeting. Martlet Conference Services appointed.

1983 May 16 – 18

Meeting of the International Executive Committee of the IUPPS in Lund.

1983 June 20

Executive and National Committee meetings. Principles and basic outline of the academic programme approved.

1983 October 19

Executive Committee meeting. Implications for the Congress of the IUAES Congress in Canada explored.

1984 January 4

> *Executive Committee meeting.* Pan African Congress's ban on South Africa reported. Detailed budgets for 2000 and 3000 potential participants examined and accepted.

1984 July 6

> *Executive Committee meeting.* Plans for the British Museum fund-raising evening finalised. Student Liaison Officer appointed.

1984 September 3,5

> *Meeting of the International Executive Committee of the IUPPS* in Bucharest.

1984 September 27

> *Executive and National Committee meetings.* Official launch of XIth Congress of IUPPS, henceforth named the World Archaeological Congress (the WAC). Announcements in the Congress's Second Announcement of sponsorship from the City of Southampton and English Heritage, and that George Allen & Unwin were to be the Congress's principal publishers.

1984 October 2

> *Executive Committee meeting.* Finances of the Congress reviewed, including arrangements for the BM fund-raising evening.

1984 December 17

> *Executive Committee meeting.* Several further sponsors announced, including major sponsorship from Cultural Resource Management Ltd. (York).

1985 March

> Reprint of the Congress's Second Announcement. First written indications of trouble about South African participation from local Southampton organisations.

1985 April 24,26

> *Meeting of the International Executive Committee of the IUPPS* in Madrid.

1985 May 10

> *Executive Committee meeting.* Draft of Final Announcement approved.

1985 June

> Meetings with local Southampton anti-apartheid groups.

1985 July 20

> Proclamation of State of Emergency in South Africa.

1985 August 3

> Private meeting between John Evans and Peter Ucko, to discuss the possibility of a ban on South African participation, and the growing evidence of non-participation by the Third World if South Africans were to attend.

1985 September 7

> *Executive Committee telephone conference.* South African

participation in the Congress banned.

1985 September 19

WAC Press Release regarding the ban, including the statement that 'South Africa and its apartheid regime placed it outside all normal principles and regulations'.

1985 October 15

Executive Committee meeting. Namibian participation also banned from the WAC.

1985 October

Circulation of Congress's Final Announcement with names of South African and Namibian participants removed, and including a statement from the President, John Evans, giving only pragmatic reasons for the ban.

1985 November 20

Executive and National Committee meetings. Reaffirmation of the bans, despite the threatened withdrawal of £150,000 sponsorship from Heritage Projects Ltd. (York) (Formerly Cultural Resource Management Ltd. (York)).

1985 November

Circulation of President's letter to all registered participants, including the statement that 'the ban has been accepted by us only on the basis that it is a protest against the explicitly racialist political system in South Africa and the inequitable society it has created, not against individuals'.

1985 December 13

Executive Committee meeting. Strategy finalised for the International Executive Committee meeting in Paris.

1986 January 4

Unforseen cancellation of IUAES Inter-Congress in Alexandria.

1986 January 17

Meeting of the International Executive Committee of the IUPPS in Paris. Decisions taken (1) to expel the WAC from IUPPS, (2) to move the XIth IUPPS Congress to Mainz, Germany on the same September dates in 1986, and (3) to appoint Professor K. Weidemann as IUPPS National Secretary, and Dr K. Böhner as IUPPS President – unless South African and Namibian participation in the WAC is reinstated before 15 February.

1986 January 23-25

Contact with ANC and others about the possibility of re-admission of South African and Namibian participants if the WAC were to be regarded as an exception to normal policies.

1986 January 24

Resignation of Professor John Evans from the International Executive Committee.

1986 January 25

Executive Committee meeting. Decision to explore the

possibility of readmission of South African and Namibian participants, if the ANC and others agreed.

1986 January 27

Resignation of Professor John Evans from the WAC.

1986 February 6

ANC and Anti-Apartheid refuse to recognise the WAC as an exception.

1986 February 8

Executive and National Committee meetings. Resignation of three members of the Executive Committee/Board of Directors, thereby allowing the remaining two members to continue to organise the WAC.

1986 February 13

Executive Committee meeting. Appointment of eight new Directors of the Company. First meeting of the newly-constituted Executive Committee. Decision taken to circulate all 3000 potential participants with the news that the WAC would continue as planned, and that the Mainz Congress would not take place until September 1987.

1986 March 14

Executive Committee meeting. Two more Directors of the Company appointed. Decision to keep the Academic Programme as intact as possible, and in fact to expand it.

1986 May 15

Executive Committee meeting. Budgets adjusted to envisaged participation of between 1000 and 2000. Reiteration of decision not to return registration fees that were being requested, at least until after the Congress. Adjustments to both Academic and Non-Academic Programmes, and timing of distribution of pre-circulated papers approved.

1986 June 19

Circulation of all participants with contents pages of pre-circulated paper volumes, and a letter from the Secretary on the occasion of the 1000th registration.

1986 June 24

Executive Committee meeting. Adoption of budget based on 1,750 participants.

1986 July 24

Executive Committee meeting. Preparation of budget based on 1,500 participants.

1986 August 24

All grant expenditure stopped by the Secretary.

1986 August 28

Executive Committee meeting. Recognition that there would be losses of *c* £100,000 unless there was a significant number of late registrations.

1986 August 31

Registration of participants, and Vice Chancellor's Reception at the University of Southampton.

1986 September 1 – 6

World Archaeological Congress.

1986 September 6

Plenary Session in the Guildhall. One-year Steering Committee established.Mayor's Reception, City of Southampton.

1986 September 7

Participants travel to London and visit British Museum exhibition.

1986 September 9

First meeting of the WAC Steering Committee. Professor Michael Day elected as Chairman and Professor Peter Ucko elected Secretary of the Steering Committee. Preliminary discussion of reforms that should be put to the IUPPS. Agreement that the Steering Committee supports 'the UN and UNESCO position on South Africa/Namibia and cultural contact'.

1986 October 20

Executive Committee meeting. Committee informed that the Congress had made a loss of c. £90,000, which was well within the insured amount of £150,000 for overall loss if less than 3000 participants registered. Insurance companies refusing to accept liability, and some potential participants who had withdrawn claiming return of registration fees. Decision taken not to liquidate the Company, but to pursue the insurance claim, after taking Counsel's opinion.

1987 January 21-23

Second meeting of the WAC Steering Committee. Agreed that 'There should be no South Africans/Namibians on the Ruling Council of an international archaeological body'. Also agreed that a full public discussion of the issues concerning South African/Namibian participation in IUPPS's affairs and congresses should be discussed once revisions to the IUPPS Statutes had been implemented. Decided that, if possible, a WAC Bulletin should be produced. Details of the maximum and minimum changes to the IUPPS Statutes were decided upon. Strategies for approaching IUPPS, ICPHS, and UNESCO were devised. Further agreed that 'questions of principle surrounding the study and conservation of skeletal remains are of central concern to the archaeological profession, and that human skeletal material should always be treated with dignity and respect'.

1987 February

Publication of the *World Archaeological Bulletin* No. 1, and of the edited Proceedings of the WAC Plenary Session.

Revised World Archaeological Congress Second Announcement

ان هذا الاجتماع لعلماء الآثار وغيرهم من المهتمين بالماضي سيكون حقا اجتماعا عالميا .

وستكون معظم المواضيع الرئيسية قيد المناقشة بذات اهمية للشعوب في جميع انحاء العالم .

ستعقد الجلسات العملية في جامعة ساوثمبتون ، كما ان الحدث الهام الذي سيقع خلال المؤتمر سوف يكون افتتاح معرض كبير جديد في المتحف البريطاني بلندن .

Questo Congresso di Dimensioni Internazionali vedrà la partecipazione di Archeologi di tutto il mondo e di tutti coloro che si interessano ai problemi del passato.
I principali argomenti di discussione sono stati scelti in base alla loro Universalità.
I lavori si svolgeranno presso l'Università di Southampton e comprenoeranno un'importantissima iniziativa: l'inaugurazione di una esposizione presso il British Museum a Londra.

考古学者ならびに人類の過去の遺産に関心を抱いている人々が集うこの会議は、真の意味で国際的な性格をもつものとなりましょう。
討論の主な議題のほとんどが、世界中の人々にとって興味あるものとなっています。
会議はサウサンプトン大学で行われます。会議開催期間中、ロンドンの大英博物館において重要な大展示会の幕が切っておとされることになっています。

这次考古学家与其他对历史有兴趣人士的聚会，将是个国际性的会议。
全世界大多数将会讨论的主要论题都将令人感兴趣。
这次大会工作会将在南安或南普敦大学举行，这次大会议主要项目是在英国博物馆开幕的一个主要新展览会。

Dispela kibung em i bilong ol lain saveman ol digim i graun long painim ol samting bilong ol tumbuna na tu bilong olgeta lain man meri ol i laik kisin ...
Ol dispela toktok yet bai i kamap long Universiti bilong ples Southampton long Sauten England. Tasol long namel taim tu wanpela bikpela samting bai i kamap insait long British Museum long London, long wonem bai ol i opim dua long Museum na insait bai ol soim sampela kain kain nupela samting ol i stretim gut na putim. Huset i stap long kibung yet i ken go long London tu na lukim ol dispela nupela samting.

This meeting of archaeologists and others who are interested in the past is to be a truly international one.
Most of the main subjects to be discussed should be of interest to people all over the world.
The working sessions will take place at the University of Southampton and a significant event during the Congress will be the opening of a major new exhibition at the British Museum in London.

Данная встреча археологов и других специалистов, проявляющих интерес к прошлому, станет поистине международной. Большинство основных вопросов, по которым будут проводиться дискуссии, должны представлять интерес для людей во всем мире.
Рабочие заседания будут проводиться в университете города Саутхамптона. Во время проведения Конгресса будет открыта новая большая выставка в Британском музее в Лондоне, что явится важным событием.

Ce congrès de dimension vraiment internationale rassemblera les archéologues du monde entier ainsi que tous ceux qui s'intéressent au passé.
Les principaux sujets de discussion ont été définis en fonction de leur intérêt et de leur accessibilité.
Les séances de travail auront lieu à l'Université de Southampton. Un grand événement qui fera partie du Congrès sera l'ouverture au Musée britannique, à Londres, d'une importante exposition de préhistoire.

Dieses Treffen von Archäologen und anderen Personen, die an der Vorzeit interessiert sind, wird einen wirklich internationalen Charakter haben.
Die meisten Hauptthemen der Tagung dürften für Menschen in aller Welt von Interesse sein.
Die Arbeitssitzungen werden in der Universität Southampton stattfinden. Ein wichtiges Ereignis während des Kongresses wird die Eröffnung einer großen neuen Ausstellung im Britischen Museum in London sein.

Esta reunión de arqueólogos y otras personas interesadas en el pasado será realmente internacional.
La mayoría de los principales temas que se discutirán serán de interés para personas en todo el mundo.
Las sesiones de trabajo tendrán lugar en la Universidad de Southampton, y un importante acontecimiento durante el Congreso será la apertura de una importante nueva exposición en el Museo Británico en Londres.

पुरानी वस्तुओं और दूसरे प्रकार के आदमियों की जो भूत युग में दिलचस्पी रखते हैं मीटिंग वास्तव में एक अन्तर्राष्ट्रीय है ।
बड़े विषयों में से अधिकतर जिन पर बहस हो वह सारे संसार की दिलचस्पी के लिये होने चाहियें ।
काम वाले इजलास साउथेम्पटन के विश्वविद्यालय में होंगे और सभा में एक महत्वपूर्ण कार्य ब्रिटिश म्यूजियम, लन्दन में एक बड़ी नई प्रदर्शनी का उद्घाटन करना होगा ।

Mkutano huu wa wataalamu wa historia-chimbo pamoja na watu wengine wanaoshughulika na mambo ya kale, utakuwa ni mkutano wa kimataifa.
Sehemu kubwa ya maswala makuu yatakayojadiliwa yawe yatawapendeza na kuwafaidi watu wengine ulimwenguni kote.
Mkutano huo utafanyika katika Chuo Kikuu cha Southampton; na tukio kubwa la mkutano huo litakuwa ni kufunguliwa kwa maonyesho makubwa katika Jumba la Makumbusho mjini London.

The World Archaeological Congress
Royal Patron H.R.H., The Prince of Wales
The 11th Congress of the
International Union of Prehistoric and Protohistoric Sciences
1-7 September 1986
Southampton and London

The following Theme meetings will be based on precirculated papers and will be devoted to discussion. They will not include verbal presentation of papers.

Cultural Attitudes to Animals, including Birds, Fish and Invertebrates

Overall organisers:

T. Ingold, Lecturer, Department of Social Anthropology, University of Manchester.
M. Maltby, Research Fellow, Faunal Remains Unit, Department of Archaeology, University of Southampton.

Symposium based on precirculated papers   *4½ days*

All human societies, past and present, have coexisted with populations of animals of one or many species. This symposium explores the multiple dimensions of man's relation to animals as these are reflected by the historical diversity of cultural traditions. Whilst prehistory has much to contribute on the role of animals in the human past, the theme also touches on the central concerns of disciplines such as social and cultural anthropology, ethology and sociobiology, psychology, history and philosophy. The range of expected contributions reflects this variety of disciplinary perspectives. There will be four major themes.

What is an animal?   *½ day*

The first, *What is an animal?* which is organised by **T. Ingold,** sets out to show how the differing answers to this question reveal the ways we see ourselves, highlighting general issues about humanity and animality that will inform discussion of more specific problems in the subsequent three themes. Definitions of animality, whether 'folk' or 'scientific', and whether inclusive or exclusive of humanity, can reveal much about the way the definers see themselves. Contributors to this session, representing a range of academic disciplines, will consider how the man-animal distinction appears to them from their personal or disciplinary points of view. By isolating what is peculiarly 'western' in the scientific conception of the animal, we can better comprehend the attitudes towards animals of people of other cultures, present and past, and thereby reach a broader understanding of what it means to be human.

The appropriation, domination and exploitation of animals   *1½ days*

The second theme, *The appropriation, domination and exploitation of animals,* (in association with Commission 13(2), The Beginnings of Animal Domestication) is organised by **J. Clutton-Brock,** Principal Scientific Officer, Department of Zoology, British Museum (Natural History) and **P. A. Jewell,** Professor, Physiological Laboratory, University of Cambridge. This theme will focus on cultural attitudes towards, rather than biological aspects of, animals in archaeology and anthropology. It will consider how animals have been made to provision and to work for man, how they have been brought under human control, and how they have become the objects of social relations. In what respects do the forms of exploitation and control depend upon the properties of the animals concerned (comparing, for example, mammals, birds, fish, and shell-fish)? Should exploitative activities be characterised on the basis of the types of food or raw materials obtained, or the behaviours involved in obtaining them? What are the different uses, including non-food uses, to which animal products can be put? How are wild and domestic animals to be distinguished and what are the behavioural correlates of domestication? What factors underlie the transition from hunting to pastoralism, and the development of animal husbandry?

A number of contributions have already been offered from Europe, America, China and Australia and it is hoped that further precirculated papers will cover the following topics: the role of livestock in changing the face of the earth; the lack of diversity of species among mammals that have been domesticated; the selected forces that have affected animal and human behaviour; and the role of animals in ancient warfare and conquest of new lands.

Semantics of animal symbolism   *1 day*

The third theme, *Semantics of animal symbolism*, is organised by **R. Willis,** Honorary Research Fellow, Department of Social Anthropology, University of Edinburgh. It is concerned with how people in different cultures incorporate animals into their systems of meaning, and involve them in religious practice. In recent years symbolic anthropology has moved beyond an opposition between 'structuralist' and 'interactionalist' perspectives, towards a unified framework including both views. A major focus for these theoretical issues is the symbolic representation of animals and of animality, in both 'western' and other cultures. In this context anthropologists have become increasingly aware of ethnocentric bias in their own preconceptions of humanity and animality, and cognate dualities such as mind and body, and gender distinctions. Ideas and relevant material in the area of animal symbolism will be discussed, covering such topics as the ritual use of animals, totemism and principles of classification, the definition of boundaries (species, group, gender), animals as mythic characters, representations of animal society as reflections of human society, and the animal as metaphor and metonym. The aim is to assess the current anthropological and archaeological understanding of animal symbolism, and to review a wide range of ethnographically and prehistorically documented cases, to discover possible semantic universals.

A number of contributions have already been offered from Europe, North and South America, Africa, Australia and India. Papers for precirculation are equally welcome from anthropologists and archaeologists working in this field.

Cultural attitudes towards animals in art   *1½ days*

The final theme, *Cultural attitudes towards animals in art* is organised by **M.W. Conkey,** Associate Professor, Department of Anthropology, State University of New York at Binghamton, and **J.D. Lewis-Williams,** Senior Lecturer, Department of Archaeology, University of Witwatersrand, Johannesburg. This theme will concentrate on two broad issues: first, the bases for the interpretation of depictions in prehistoric art, particularly zoomorphic depictions; and second, the inferences that can be made from visual images about the ways the people who created and used the art thought about the relations between humans and animals. Some papers will deal with interpretative methods, while others will take a contextual approach to art forms, regarding them as manifestations of a system of visual communications whose elements combine to constitute a set of meanings regarding humans and animals.

Contributions already offered deal with both prehistoric and contemporary artistic production in Europe, North and South America, Southern Africa, Australia and India.

Comparative Studies in the Development of Complex Societies

Overall organisers:

T.C.Champion, Senior Lecturer, Department of Archaeology, University of Southampton.
J.F. Cherry, Assistant Lecturer, Department of Classical Archaeology, University of Cambridge.
M.J. Rowlands, Reader, Department of Anthropology, University College London.

Symposium based on precirculated papers $4^{1}/_{2}$ days

This symposium will review recent work in the study of complex societies and look ahead to new directions. A wide range of topics in the development, functioning and decline of complex societies will be approached through comparative studies. There will be six major themes within the symposium.

Conceptualising complex societies $^{1}/_{2}$ day

The first, *Conceptualising complex societies,* organised by **M.J. Rowlands,** will question some of the assumptions made concerning 'complex societies'. Archaeology has the problem of explaining both the form and the content of asymmetries in social relations. Thinking on this subject has been shaped by the experience of European expansion and a negative reflection on what was perceived to be 'other cultures'. The utility of such Eurocentric concepts as status, rank, class, power, state and non-state, even complexity itself, for cross-cultural understanding must be assessed.

Political centralisation: social inequality and modes of dominance $^{1}/_{2}$ day

The second theme, *Political centralisation: social inequality and modes of dominance,* also organised by **M.J. Rowlands,** assumes that while asymmetries in social relations are universal features of human societies, their form and content are not. Questions proposed to orientate the discussion include: How are power and authority conceived and represented in different societies? How is access to the resources and knowledge necessary for the reproduction of society restricted? How should we best conceptualise the apparently cyclical tendency to political centralisation and decentralisation?

Ritual, legitimation and authority

½ day

The third theme, *Ritual, legitimation and authority* organised by **J.F. Cherry**, is concerned with the various cultural resources and idioms employed in the definition of authority, including the ways in which power and authority are symbolised and legitimised in complex societies. It will include topics such as ritual practice, religious cults, iconography, the cosmological ordering of space and time, and antagonistic/syncretistic systems of ideas and moral codes

Centre-periphery relations

1½ days

The fourth theme, *Centre-periphery relations*, organised by **T.C. Champion,** picks up a major theme of the archaeological study of complex societies and will deal with regional analysis of centre-periphery relations at various scales. As well as the wide variety of interactions between central places and their hinterlands, and the cultural differences between them, other scales of centre-periphery relationship will be discussed: 'civilised'/'barbarian', urban/non-urban, sedentary/nomadic, and agriculturalist/pastoralist.

Imperialism, colonialism and acculturation

1 day

The fifth theme, *Imperialism, colonialism and acculturation*, also organised by **T.C. Champion,** will include discussion of the mechanisms of imperial expansion, internal and external conflict, cultural diversity within large-scale complex societies, modes of incorporation, maintenance of centrality, and fission at the periphery. Also included will be the ideology of 'empire', cross-border relationships, the impact of empires on their neighbours, and colonialism in modern historical archaeology.

Literacy, tradition and communication

½ day

The final theme, *Literacy, tradition and communication*, organised by **J.F. Cherry,** will focus mainly on the varying roles of literacy in emergent and established complex societies. Topics will include the ways in which literacy, by reason of its frequent restriction to esoteric ritual contexts or to learned elites, may objectify modes of consciousness; this includes the invention and preservation of knowledge and cultural traditions, the shaping of forms of social domination, and the denial or impeding of change.

Archaeological 'Objectivity' in Interpretation

Overall organiser:
P.J. Ucko, Professor, Department of Archaeology, University of Southampton.

Symposium based on precirculated papers

4½ days

This symposium is concerned with the way that the evidence of the past, including archaeological evidence itself, has been used and viewed by particular groups at different times. The reasons for particular choices of interpretation are explored within four major themes.

Multi-culturalism and ethnicity in archaeological interpretations   *1 day*

The first, *Multi-culturalism and ethnicity in archaeological interpretations*, is organised by **C. Haselgrove,** Lecturer, Department of Archaeology, University of Durham, and **S.J. Shennan,** Lecturer, Department of Archaeology, University of Southampton. Within archaeology, concepts of multi-culturalism and ethnicity have traditionally been used to explain cultural variation in space and time; in the modern world these concepts affect the way the past is reconstructed and presented. They are equally relevant to the very possibility of extracting information about the past from the prehistoric archaeological record, if this is seen as the ultimate result of culturally-specific, rule-bound behaviour to which we do not have access. Questions therefore arise in two main areas: the recognition and meaning of spatial variations at the regional scale in the archaeological record; and the genesis and maintenance of ethnic and cultural diversity, and its significance in different social contexts.

Material culture and symbolic expression   *1 day*

The second theme, *Material culture and symbolic expression*, is organised by **I. Hodder,** Lecturer, Department of Archaeology, University of Cambridge. The discussions will focus on how artifacts and their spatial arrangements come to have symbolic meanings, and how these meanings become involved in social strategies, leading to considerations of style, ideology, ritual and art. Social dimensions of age, sex and hierarchical domination will be examined, as well as the relationship between an individual and society. Papers will cover both contemporary and past societies in different parts of the world, in social systems both simple and complex, and in material traditions of varying character.

Offers of precirculated papers already include several on style, the interpretation of Iron Age art, pottery symbolism, the symbolic organisation of settlement space, and symbolic expression in complex societies. There will also be discussion of precirculated papers on body painting, tattooing, burial practices, bone and stone tool production.

The politics of the past: museums, media and education   *1½ days*

The third theme, *The politics of the past: museums, media and education*, is organised by **P. Gathercole,** Dean of Darwin College, University of Cambridge, **M. Leone,** Associate Professor, Division of Behavioural and Social Sciences, The Department of Anthropology, University of Maryland, and **C. Schrire,** Professor, Department of Human Ecology, Rutgers State University of New Jersey. Archaeology has always played a part in national politics, but only recently has the impact of politics on archaeology become apparent. This theme will explore the political component in museums, travelling displays, documentaries, "blockbuster movies", slide shows, text books, tour guides, and national monuments. The mediating role played by inherently political institutions in interpreting the archaeological record for current purposes will be discussed.

Topics to be explored will include such things as: Who owns the past?; Reconstruction as interpretation; Museums and national identity; and The presentation of the past to the public.

The fourth theme, *Indigenous perceptions of the past*, is organised by **D. Bellos,** Professor, Department of French, University of Southampton and **R. Layton,** Reader, Department of Anthropology, University of Durham. All human cultures have traditions concerning their own past, expressed in written records, legends or myths orally transmitted or dramatised in ritual, and often seen to be embodied in the past's material remains. Concepts of time vary radically: cyclic concepts view the present as a re-embodiment of the past, linear concepts view time as progress, or as decline from a "golden age". The value attached to the past and its remains will depend on its significance for the present. A comparison of alternative indigenous views may promote understanding of the general characteristics of peoples' perceptions of their past.

In this context the term 'indigenous' encompasses cultural views worldwide and without restriction by chronology or by degree of literacy, thus there will be a sub-section devoted to *Mediations of the past in modern Europe*. This will bring together work from a variety of humanistic disciplines (literary, historical, sociological, philosophical, etc.) which illuminates the processes by which erudite and popular perceptions of the past and related concepts (such as the "primitive", the "remote", the "exotic", etc.) have been formed and mediated in western European cultures from the 18th Century on.

The Social and Economic Contexts of Technological Change

Overall organisers:

R.J. Bradley, Reader, Department of Archaeology, University of Reading.
R.W. Chapman, Lecturer, Department of Archaeology, University of Reading.
S. Van der Leeuw, Lecturer, Institute for Pre- and Proto-History, Amsterdam.

Symposium based on precirculated papers
4 days

Since the 19th Century, archaeologists and anthropologists have studied changes in technology as major thresholds in cultural evolution. While much of this analysis has been essentially descriptive, equating technological innovations with socio-economic stages, some scholars have attempted to explain the adoption and spread of new technologies as well as their effects on culture evolution (eg, Wittfogel's hydraulic theory and the origins of State society). One of the major deficiencies of exact approaches to these problems has been the lack of analysis devoted to the social and economic contexts of the processes of technological innovation and change. This symposium will attempt to remedy this deficiency and will be contextual and explanatory, rather than simply descriptive. Case studies from all parts of the world, from the earliest industries to contemporary societies and especially including ethno-archaeological perspectives, will be discussed. The symposium will be divided into four major themes.

The first theme, *Contexts and innovation and adoption of new technologies*, is organised by **R.J. Bradley** and **R.W. Chapman.** Offers of precirculated papers on archaeological, ethno-archaeological, and anthropological subjects have already been received, the latter concerned with processes of modernisation and change in non-industrial societies. Among the questions to be discussed are: the nature of archaeology's contribution to the modelling and diffusion processes; the relationship between the length of time of the innovation process and the costs and benefits of the innovation; the determinants of the length of time over which a new technology achieves wide-spread adoption; the identification of those social and economic processes which may accelerate or retard the length of time taken for innovations to change from being socially advantageous to being economically and technologically necessary for subsistence production; feedback processes between technological and social change and the variation of the innovation process between hierarchical and non-hierarchical societies. All of these topics require consideration of both general and middle-range theories.

Strategies of raw material procurement and Social and economic contexts of production *2 days*

The second and third themes, *Strategies of raw material procurement,* and *Social and economic contexts of production,* are organised by **R. Torrence,** Lecturer, Department of Prehistory and Archaeology, University of Sheffield, and **S. Van der Leeuw,** respectively. The organisation of technologies will be examined in terms of the related processes of procurement and production. How far do these processes explain variations within an between technologies, whether these be lithic, ceramic or other technologies? In which contexts do the procurement of raw materials become specialised and separate from other social and economic activities? For example, when do lithic procurement strategies cease to be "embedded" in subsistence strategies? Which factors determine the presence of curative rather than expedient technologies? Production for consumption and exchange will be discussed, as will the contexts in which time-budgeting and craft-specialisation are selected in production strategies. In which contexts will the rearrangement of the time allocated to production be preferred to the adoption of a new technology when a major increase in production is contemplated?

Technology and the intensification of subsistence production *1 day*

In the final theme, *Technology and the intensification of subsistence production,* organised by **R.J. Bradley** and **R.W. Chapman,** discussion will be devoted not only to the effect of technological innovation on intensification and cultural evolution, but also to the determinants of technological innovation. What are the relationships between capital and labour intensification and stratification? How do competitive social and political strategies determine intensification? While anthropological research has generated much of the theory of technological change and intensification processes, it is the archaeological record of irrigation systems, field systems, and other evidence for the exploitation and organisation of land, which has the potential to consider these important questions within a temporal context.

MAN AND CULTURE IN THE PLEISTOCENE

Several thematic and specialist sessions of the Congress will be devoted to this particular period of prehistory. Because of the extensive interest in this area of Congress activity, the Pleistocene affords a convenient way of illustrating the complexity of the overall organisation of the Congress, as well as the sorts of choices which will confront each participant in September 1986.

Those with especial interests in the Pleistocene may choose between various meetings (I-IX).

I. Four sequential days of discussion based on precirculated papers on

The Pleistocene Perspective: Critical Periods of Cultural Change   *4 days*

Overall organisers:

C.S. Gamble, Lecturer, Department of Archaeology, University of Southampton.
P.A. Mellars, Lecturer, Department of Archaeology, University of Cambridge.

This symposium will have four major themes based on precirculated papers:

The Origins of Culture   *½ day*

(organised on behalf of Commission 5, The Earliest Industries: Africa; and Commission 6, The Earliest Hominids).

Organisers:

J. Desmond Clark, Professor, Department of Anthropology, University of California, Berkeley.
G. Isaac, Professor, Peabody Museum, University of Harvard.

The aim of this theme is to examine a broad range of questions bearing on the origins and early development of cultural behaviour prior to the emergence of *Homo sapiens* populations. Precirculated papers will focus mainly on the African evidence, but will also make relevant comparisons with parallel developments in Asia and Europe. The archaeological evidence will be combined with relevant studies of palaeoecological data, taphonomic studies, dating methods, and the relationships between behavioural patterns and the early evolution of the *Homo* lineage.

The afternoon will be devoted to a discussion based on precirculated papers (and oral presentation of recent results) on:

Scientific Dating Techniques in the Pleistocene   *½ day*

Organisers:

M.J. Aitken, Deputy Director, Research Laboratory for Archaeology and the History of Art, Oxford University.
S.G.E. Bowman, Senior Scientific Officer, Research Laboratory, British Museum.

A firm chronological framework is critical to the understanding of the pattern and tempo of cultural change in the Pleistocene. This sub-theme will deal with techniques such as radiocarbon, thermoluminescence, electron spin resonance, uranium series, potassium-argon, amino acid, magnetic reversal stratigraphy, fission tracks, in so far as they are relevant to the overall theme. It will be non-specialist from the technical point-of-view and aims to present to archaeologists (a) the basic principles, (b) guidelines for sample collection, (c) limitations and potentialities, and (d) important recent results.

Archaeology and the Origins and Dispersal of Modern Man   *1 day*

Organiser:
P.A. Mellars.

This theme will review recent developments bearing on both the evolutionary origins of *Homo sapiens sapiens* populations, and the wide range of associated changes in cultural patterns in different areas of the world. The precirculated papers will focus on such questions as the evolutionary relationship between early *sapiens* populations and more archaic forms (e.g. Neanderthals); the origins of various cultural innovations (technological, economic, social, demographic, symbolic etc.) which are conventionally taken to define the transition from 'Middle' to 'Upper' Palaeolithic cultures: and the earliest expansion of *sapiens* populations into south-east Asia, Australasia and other areas of the world.

World Population at 18,000 BP   *1 day*

Organisers:
C.S. Gamble, jointly with **J.K. Kozlowski** (on behalf of Commission 8, Problems of the Upper Palaeolithic), Institute of Archaeology, Jagiellonian University, Cracow.

The purpose of this theme will be to compare the archaeological records from many parts of the world at the moment of the last glacial maximum which has been established from the oceanic record at 18,000 BP. The particular millenium cannot always be accurately pinpointed with archaeological materials; thus the time 'spike' to be used in such comparisons runs from 22,000 to 14,000 BP.

This symposium will provide Palaeolithic specialists from around the world with an opportunity to assemble information on this particular time 'spike'. The climatic data gives us a fixed point of reference to compare archaeological sequences from different regions and environments both within and between continents in order to establish the impact of environment on world population. It is the first step to more detailed comparisons of population density, changes in adaptive strategies to cope with environmental problems, and the intensity of regional exploitation. The aim of this theme is, therefore, to draw together information on the distribution of world population 18,000 years ago, and to examine the various associated environmental and archaeological records. Discussion will focus on explanations for the differences between the archaeological records of 18,000 BP. from the four continents then inhabited, as well as considering variation among regional archaeological signatures of settlement systems and histories.

Organisers:

P.A. Mellars, jointly with **S.K. Kozlowski** (on behalf of Commission 12, Cultures, Economies and Ecologies of post-Palaeolithic Hunters), Department of Archaeology, University of Warsaw.

The rapid and dramatic changes in environmental conditions which marked the transition from the Pleistocene to the Holocene periods presented a major challenge for human communities in all parts of the world. The aim of this meeting is to examine the varying patterns of human response to these environmental changes over the widest possible geographical range. The fine chronological control that exists for this time-range can be used to compare patterns of change in many different aspects of human behaviour and organisation (economic, technological, demographic, social, symbolic etc.) and to synchronise these developments closely with associated changes in climate, vegetation patterns, animal populations, sea levels, and other aspects of the environment. Other discussions will focus on the patterns of colonisation of habitats previously abandoned under late glacial climates, and the expansion of population into previously unoccupied territories. The relevant time-range may be defined broadly as 14,000 to 7,000 BP., though individual contributions may well focus on narrower chronological ranges in order to illustrate more specific aspects of the adaptive processes.

II. A half day based on oral presentations on:

The Palaeoecology of Prehistoric Man (Commission 3) *½ day*

Organiser:

H. de Lumley, Professor, Laboratoire de Préhistoire, Musée National d'Histoire Naturelle, Paris.

This meeting will focus mainly on the methodology and theoretical approaches to palaeoecological studies with particular attention to the application of recently developed techniques. Topics covered will include: problems of climatic and vegetational reconstruction, faunal studies, dietary analysis, and the reconstruction of overall subsistence and settlement strategies within a palaeoecological framework.

III. A day based on oral presentations on:

The Earliest Industries: Europe and the Near East (Commission 5) *1 day*

Organisers:

J. Combier, Director of Research, Centre Nationale de la Recherche, France.
H. de Lumley.

This session will provide an up-to-date review of the most recent work bearing on the Lower and Middle Palaeolithic occupation of Europe and the Near East. Special attention will be paid to the earliest stages of occupation, with particular reference to the problems of relative and absolute chronology, technological variation, economic and settlement patterns, and associations with fossil Hominids.

IV. A half day based on oral presentations on:

Biology, Culture and Environment of Earliest Hominids in Asia
(on behalf of Commission 5, The Earliest Industries: Asia) *½ day*

Organiser:
A.K. Ghosh, Senior Reader, Department of Anthropology, University of Calcutta.

This meeting will deal with a broad range of topics concerned with the distribution, dating and cultural behaviour of early Hominids in Asia. Special attention will be paid to the evolutionary biology of early populations and their relationships to environmental and ecological conditions. Major topics will include: early Hominid finds and implications for biological evolution; the development of technology and other aspects of culture; and the palaeoecological framework of early Hominid occupation.

V. A half day based on oral presentations on:

The Earliest Industries: Africa (Commission 5) *½ day*

Organiser:
J. Desmond Clark.

This symposium will present a review of recent work on the earlier Stone Age occupation of Africa, with particular reference to the results of new fieldwork and new developments in the fields of dating, economic and social interpretation, and palaeoecological analysis.

VI. Up to two days based on oral presentations on:

The Earliest Hominids (Commission 6) *1½-2 days*

Organisers:
Y. Coppens, Professor, Collège de France, Laboratoire d'Anthropologie, Musée de l'Homme, Paris.
M.H. Day, Professor, Department of Anatomy, St. Thomas's Hospital Medical School, London.

This meeting will focus on Hominoid and Hominid evolution from the viewpoints of cranial, postcranial and dental anatomy, taxonomy, physical evolution, functional morphology and the environmental context of fossil finds, including palaeoecology and palaeoethology.

VII. Two and a half sequential days of discussion based on precirculated papers and oral presentations.

The Peopling of the Americas: Problems and results of recent research on Pleistocene Man in America (Commission 10) *2½ days*

Organiser:
A.L. Bryan, Professor, Department of Anthropology, University of Alberta, Edmonton.

This meeting will deal with the essential, and complex, problems of cultural and biological origins of American Indians; subdivisions will be geographical, North America and South America. It is anticipated that the results of new research will be presented from the following areas and sites: Old Crow, Yukon; California; Monte Verde, Chile; Sao Raimundo Nonato, Piaui, Brazil; and the States of Bahia and Minas Gerais.

VIII. Some Pleistocene experts may also be particularly interested in a two day meeting based primarily on oral presentations on:

Communal Land Mammal Hunting and Butchering	2 *days*

Organisers:

L.B. Davis, Professor, Department of Sociology and Anthropology, Montana State University.
N. Noe-Nygaard, Lecturer, Institute of Historical Geology and Palaeontology, University of Copenhagen.
B.O.K. Reeves, Professor, Department of Archaeology, University of Calgary.

The focus of this meeting will be on large mammal hunting and butchering from archaeological, ethnohistorical and ethnological perspectives. Species to be included are: reindeer, caribou, musk-ox, bighorn sheep, antelope, bison, North American elk/European red deer, wapita/European elk, North and South American deer, camelids, camels, horse, mastodon and mammoth.

Emphasis will be placed on synthesis of information and interpretation for the various species, relative to provisional procurement and butchering techniques from various perspectives. Discussion will focus on the fact that organised communal hunting and butchering of large land mammals was a characteristic adaptive pattern of both recent prehistoric and much more ancient butchering and occasionally agricultural societies. The following countries are amongst those about which participants have already agreed to speak: America, Canada, Argentina, Norway, Denmark and France.

IX. Some of those interested in World Population at 18,000 BP may well be particularly interested in art. They will have to choose between the sessions described above and a three day meeting based on oral presentations on:

Cultural Contexts of Rock Art (on behalf of Commission 9, Prehistoric Art)	3 *days*

Organiser:

H.-G. Bandi, Professor, Seminar Für Urgeschichte, Universität Bern.

In this meeting rock art experts from all over the world will come together not primarily to discuss their particular new discoveries, but for the first time to consider a much more fundamental question – the relationship between rock art of a particular culture and other known activities. The contributions presented will, therefore, concentrate on the similarities and differences of style and content between rock art and other artistic works (such as ostrich shell, pottery, wood, bone, etc.) of the same culture. Discussion will focus on such questions as how the chronology of rock-art works in a particular culture correspond, or do not correspond, to other evidence of dating the material culture of the societies concerned. Contributors will be asked to try to explain the way that their rock art studies have been used by them, and others, to characterise the nature of the prehistoric culture whose remains they are studying.

Those participants who are interested in the analysis of art-works in general may have to make difficult decisions regarding their participation in the above meeting and theme meetings on *Cultural attitudes towards animals in art, Material culture and symbolic expression,* and the specialist meeting on *Celtic art: images of interaction and identity,* which may in fact clash.

Those participants who are particularly interested in *Communal land mammal hunting and butchering* may well wish to attend the discussions on *The appropriation, domination and exploitation of animals* within the overall symposium on *Cultural attitudes to animals, including birds, fish and invertebrates.* The provisional timetabling of the Congress endeavours to avoid a major clash of these particular interests.

The History of Early and More Recent Developments in Social and Economic Archaeology
(on behalf of Commission 1, History of Prehistoric and Protohistoric Archaeology.)

Organiser:
A.C. Renfrew, Professor, Department of Archaeology, University of Cambridge.

Symposium based on oral presentations	*Up to 1 day*

The explanation in social and economic terms of culture change in the past, as evident earlier in this century, may be contrasted with the long-dominant taxonomic approach. More recent developments towards processual archaeology or "new archaeology" which came to prominence in the 1960s, owed much to Marxist writers such as Gordon Childe and Leslie White and to the lively intellectual climate in Europe in the 1920s. It is time to set the origins of social and economic archaeology in a broader geographical and chronological context.

Physical and Chemical Dating Techniques in Prehistory (Commission 2)

Organisers:
M.J. Aitken, Research Laboratory for Archaeology, Oxford University.
S.G.E. Bowman, Senior Scientific Officer, Research Laboratory, British Museum.

Symposium based on oral presentations	*Up to 2 days*

This meeting will bring together those who are actively involved in scientific dating techniques. The papers will be of a specialist and technical nature with emphasis on recent research advances and problems.

Data management and mathematical methods in archaeology
(Commission 4)

Organisers:
B.S. Ottaway, Honorary Fellow, Department of Archaeology, University of Edinburgh.
A. Voorrips, Professor, Department of Archaeology, University of Amsterdam.
R. Whallon, Professor, Museum of Anthropology, University of Michigan.

Symposium based on oral presentations	*3 days*

This symposium will present an overview of the interaction between quantitative methods and archaeological theory and methodology.

There will be three major themes. The first, on Methodology, will include papers on simulation, seriation and ordering, classification and typology, image enhancing techniques, locational analysis, intra-site spatial analysis and sampling and data management. The second, on Regional overviews, will include papers on the USSR, Middle and South America, and Australia. The final theme, devoted to Theory, will include papers on statistical and mathematical modelling in archaeological theories and models.

Participants will include not only archaeologists but also mathematicians, and the symposium will make use of poster sessions as far as possible, and particularly for microcomputer/data-management systems.

Recent Advances in the Understanding of Plant Domestication and Early Agriculture
(on behalf of Commission 13(1), The Beginnings of Agriculture).

Organisers:

D.R. Harris, Professor, and **G.C. Hillman,** Lecturer, Department of Human Environment, Institute of Archaeology, London.

Symposium based on precirculated papers   *2 days*

In recent years studies of the evolution under cultivation of individual crops have extended the biological framework of our understanding of domestication. At the same time, the application of new techniques to the recovery and analysis of archaeo-botanical data has greatly increased the evidence available for interpreting the early history of agriculture. The symposium will adopt a comparative, worldwide perspective and will include contributions on individual taxa as well as regional case studies. It will also include papers on plant use and management by non- (or pre-) agricultural peoples. The precirculated papers will include reviews of some of the major cereals, pulses and tuberous crops; presentations of new evidence for early agriculture in tropical and temperate areas of Eurasia, Africa, Australasia and the Americas; and discussions of new techniques of bioarchaeological analysis.

Participants will include botanists and archaeologists, and papers already offered include contributions from North and South America, Western and Eastern Europe, Africa, Israel, India, China, Indonesia, Australia and New Zealand.

The Neolithic of Europe
(on behalf of Commission 14, The Neolithic of the Old World).

Organiser:

A. Fleming, Reader, Department of Prehistory, University of Sheffield .

Symposium based on precirculated papers   *3 days*

There will be three regionally-based sessions dealing with the European Neolithic: Northern and Western Europe, Central and Eastern Europe, and Southern Europe. Prominent themes will include chamber tombs and neolithic ritual practices; the character and spread of the earliest neolithic in several contrasting regions; fortification and neolithic trade.

The Neolithic of Africa
(on behalf of Commission 14, The Neolithic of the Old World).

Organisers:
B. Andah, Professor, Department of Archaeology, University of Ibadan.
T. Shaw, Professor Emeritus, Department of Archaeology, University of Ibadan.

Symposium based on oral presentations	*1-2 days*

The 'Neolithic' is not as easy to define in Africa as in some other parts of the Old World, where the definition has become primarily an economic one. Consideration will be given both to courses towards pastoralism and crop agriculture and to technical innovations in material equipment. It is hoped that contributors will attempt spatial, social and linguistic reconstructions.

Iron-Using Peoples in Sub-Saharan Africa
(on behalf of Commission 17, Iron Age Cultures).

Organiser:
D.W. Phillipson, Curator, University Museum of Archaeology and Anthropology, University of Cambridge.

Symposium based on oral presentations	*1 day*

The symposium will provide both overview papers and up-to-date regional studies on the archaeology of the past 2,500 years in Africa south of the Sahara. Emphasis will be on evaluation of the evidence for indigenous innovation in the development of iron-using societies.

The Copper and Bronze Ages of The Old World
(on behalf of Commission 15, The Origins of Metallurgy, and Commission 16, Copper and Bronze Age Cultures).

Organisers:
A.F. Harding, Lecturer, Department of Archaeology, University of Durham.
I.H. Longworth, Keeper, Department of Prehistoric and Romano-British Antiquities, British Museum.

Symposium based on oral presentations	*3-4 days*

This symposium will be concerned with aspects of Old World archaeology from the origins of metallurgy through to the regular use of iron. The meeting will, as far as possible, be thematic and will include settlement and population studies; metallurgy and metalwork; inter-cultural contacts; and economic and social implications. There will also be a section devoted to regional and site studies.

Archaeology and Ethnology in Iron Age Europe
(on behalf of Commission 17, Iron Age Cultures).

Organisers:
B. Cunliffe, Professor, Institute of Archaeology, University of Oxford.
V. Kruta, Professor, Ecole Pratique des Hautes Etudes, Paris.

To cover as much as possible of work in progress this symposium will focus on the cultural characterisation and development of the different communities comprising non-classical Europe during the Iron Age. Major themes within the symposium include: Stress, isolation and the need for defence; Production and distribution as mechanisms for cultural integration; and Celtic art: images of interaction and identity.

In the light of these themes it is hoped to explore the antithesis between isolation and integration in Iron Age Europe.

Iron-Age Societies in South Asia
(on behalf of Commission 17, Iron Age Cultures).

Organiser:

R. Knox, Assistant Keeper, Department of Oriental Antiquities, British Museum.

Symposium based on oral presentations *1 day*

The general theme of the symposium will focus on the Iron Age of the sub-continent, particularly the origins of iron metallurgy, the character of early iron technology in South Asia, and on associated phenomena such as the growth of urbanisation.

Settlement, Cultural and Religious Relationships between People and States in the Early Middle Ages
(on behalf of Commission 19, The Archaeology of the Early Middle Ages).

Organisers:

K. Böhner, Professor, Römisch-Germanisches Zentralmuseum, Mainz.
B. Stjernquist, Professor, Department of Archaeology, University of Lund.
D. Wilson, Director, British Museum.

Symposium based on oral presentations *2 days*

Public Archaeology and Cultural Resource Management

Organiser:
Council for British Archaeology, London.

Symposium based on oral presentations *2 days*

There will be three major themes in the symposium. The first, *History and Development of Systems of Cultural Resource Management,* will examine the evolution of governmental structures designed to protect and administer material evidence of the past in different regions of the world. Half a day will be devoted to a discussion of Stonehenge, the most famous of all British monuments, particularly in the context of plans for its management by the newly-formed Historic Buildings and Monuments Commission.

The second theme, *Archaeology in legislation, administration, and planning,* will compare and contrast contemporary cultural resource management systems in operation around the world. The final theme will be *Training and qualification of archaeologists for cultural resource management,* and will concentrate on the special requirements of archaeologists working in this relatively new field of activity.

APPENDIX V

Organisational Structure
of International Academic Bodies

(mentioned in text)

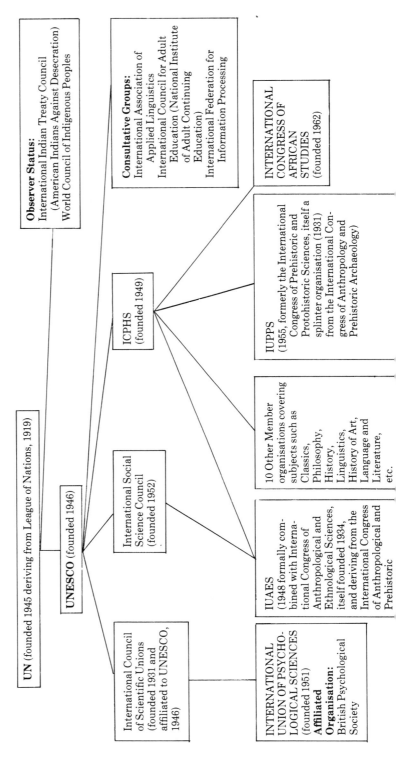

UN (founded 1945 deriving from League of Nations, 1919)

Observer Status:
International Indian Treaty Council
(American Indians Against Desecration)
World Council of Indigenous Peoples

UNESCO (founded 1946)

Consultative Groups:
International Association of Applied Linguistics
International Council for Adult Education (National Institute of Adult Continuing Education)
International Federation for Information Processing

INTERNATIONAL CONGRESS OF AFRICAN STUDIES (founded 1962)

ICPHS (founded 1949)

IUPPS (1955, formerly the International Congress of Prehistoric and Protohistoric Sciences, itself a splinter organisation (1931) from the International Congress of Anthropology and Prehistoric Archaeology)

International Social Science Council (founded 1952)

10 Other Member organisations covering subjects such as Classics, Philosophy, History, Linguistics, History of Art, Language and Literature, etc.

International Council of Scientific Unions (founded 1931 and affiliated to UNESCO, 1946)

IUAES (1948 formally combined with International Congress of Anthropological and Ethnological Sciences, itself founded 1934, and deriving from the International Congress of Anthropological and Prehistoric

INTERNATIONAL UNION OF PSYCHO-LOGICAL SCIENCES (founded 1951)
Affiliated Organisation:
British Psychological Society

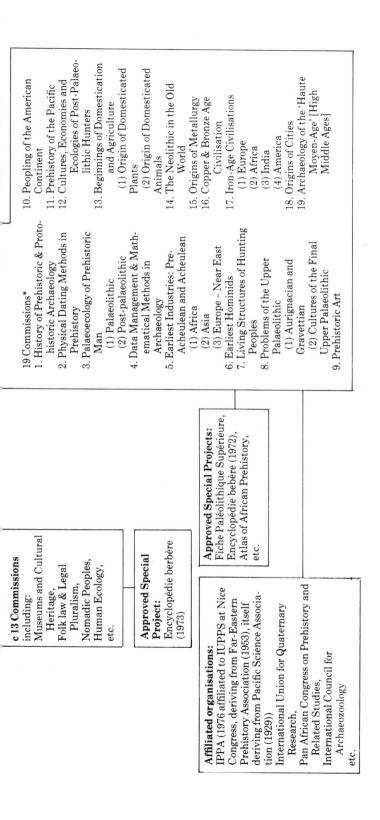

c 13 Commissions
including:
Museums and Cultural Heritage,
Folk law & Legal Pluralism,
Nomadic Peoples,
Human Ecology,
etc.

Approved Special Project:
Encyclopédie berbère (1973)

Approved Special Projects:
Fiche Paléolithique Supérieure,
Encyclopédie bebère (1972),
Atlas of African Prehistory,
etc.

Affiliated organisations:
IPPA (1976 affiliated to IUPPS at Nice Congress, deriving from Far-Eastern Prehistory Association (1953), itself deriving from Pacific Science Association (1929))
International Union for Quaternary Research,
Pan African Congress on Prehistory and Related Studies,
International Council for Archaeozoology
etc.

19 Commissions*
1. History of Prehistoric & Proto-historic Archaeology
2. Physical Dating Methods in Prehistory
3. Palaeoecology of Prehistoric Man
   (1) Palaeolithic
   (2) Post-palaeolithic
4. Data Management & Mathematical Methods in Archaeology
5. Earliest Industries: Pre-Acheulean and Acheulean
   (1) Africa
   (2) Asia
   (3) Europe – Near East
6. Earliest Hominids
7. Living Structures of Hunting Peoples
8. Problems of the Upper Palaeolithic
   (1) Aurignacian and Gravettian
   (2) Cultures of the Final Upper Palaeolithic
9. Prehistoric Art
10. Peopling of the American Continent
11. Prehistory of the Pacific
12. Cultures, Economies and Ecologies of Post-Palaeolithic Hunters
13. Beginnings of Domestication and Agriculture
    (1) Origin of Domesticated Plants
    (2) Origin of Domesticated Animals
14. The Neolithic in the Old World
15. Origins of Metallurgy
16. Copper & Bronze Age Civilisation
17. Iron-Age Civilisations
    (1) Europe
    (2) Africa
    (3) India
    (4) America
18. Origins of Cities
19. Archaeology of the 'Haute Moyen-Age' [High Middle Ages]

* These Commissions were those supposedly in operation when Britain became the host for the XIth IUPPS Congress (having been reduced from 21 to 19 at the Florence meeting of 1982). Several changes were made to the list of Commissions at subsequent meetings.

International Executive Committee of IUPPS[1]

VOTING MEMBERS
(*absent from Paris meeting, 17.1.86)
H.-G. Bandi (Switzerland)
K. Böhner (West Germany)
* A.J. Dani (Pakistan)
* C.A. Diop (Senegal)
J. Evans – President of the XIth Congress (– 24.1.86) [Statutes silent about vote but legal opinion that probably so entitled]
* M. Garasanin (Yugoslavia)
* A. Ghosh (India)

* P. Graziosi (Italy)
* J. Lorenzo (Mexico)
* R. Nunoo (Ghana)
E. Ripoll-Perello (Spain)
* B. Rybakov (USSR)
J. Sackett (USA)
B. Stjernquist (Sweden)
P. Ucko – National Secretary of the XIth Congress [Statutes self-contradictory about vote but legal opinion that clearly so entitled]

NON-VOTING MEMBERS
L. Balout (France)(President of the IXth Congress – 1976)
* A. Beltran Martinez (Spain)(National Secretary of the IVth Congress – 1954)
* A. Benac (Yugoslavia)(National Secretary of the VIIIth Congress – 1971)
* W. Dehn (West Germany)(National Secretary of the Vth Congress – 1958)
* J. Garcia Barcena (Mexico)(President of the Xth Congress – 1981)
* W.U. Guyan (Switzerland)(National Secretary of the IIIrd Congress – 1950)
* S.J. De Laet (Belgium)(former Secretary-General of the IUPPS)
H de Lumley (France)(National Secretary of the IXth Congress – 1976)
J. Nenquin – Secretary-General of the IUPPS
* M. Pallottino (Italy)(President of the VIth Congress – 1962)
* J. Poulik (Czechoslovakia) (National Secretary of the VIIth Congress – 1966)

ALSO PRESENT DURING PART OR ALL OF PARIS MEETING OF 17.1.86
D. Bellos – interpreter
J.D. Clark (USA) [apparently as Coordinator of the Special Project, *Atlas of African Prehistory*[2].]
G. Camps (France) [apparently as General secretary of the Special Project, *Encyclopédie berbère*]
H. Faure – President, International Union for Quaternary Research
J. d'Ormesson – Secretary-General, IPCHS
M. Otte (Belgium) [apparently as representative of the Special Project, *Fiche Paléolithique Supérieure*[3]]

[1] The IUPPS Statutes state that the International Executive Committee includes 15 members (including the President and the Secretary-General). In addition, previous Presidents, Secretary-Generals, National Secretaries, and Presidents of Committees responsible for the organisation of Special Projects, may attend International Executive Committee meetings.

[2] However, the Minutes of the International Executive Committee meeting in Bucharest in 1984 state that this 'Entreprise patronnée' would be taken over by the Malawi Antiquities Service.

[3] Approved at the meetings in Bucharest in 1984.

Members of the WAC Executive Committee/Board of Directors

(See Name Index for further details)

Professor Leslie Alcock (by 16.11.81 – 8.2.86; 14.3.86 -)

Dr Timothy Champion (13.2.86 -)

Dr Juliet Clutton-Brock (14.3.86 -)

Professor Michael Day (13.2.86 -) Chairman

Professor John Evans (by 16.11.81 – 27.1.86) Chairman

Mr Andrew Fleming (13.2.86 -)

Professor David Harris (13.2.86 -)

Mr Derek Hayes (23.3.83 -) Treasurer

Dr Ian Hodder (13.2.86 -)

Professor Colin Renfrew (by 16.11.81 – 8.2.86)

Dr Michael Rowlands (13.2.86 -)

Professor Thurstan Shaw (13.2.86 -)

Dr Stephen Shennan (13.2.86 -)

Professor Peter Ucko (by 23.3.82 -) Secretary

Dr (later Sir) David Wilson (by 16.11.81 – 8.2.86)

Countries Represented
at the World Archaeological Congress

Argentina	Madagascar
Australia	Malawi
Austria	Mexico
Bangladesh	Mozambique
Belgium	The Netherlands
Bolivia	New Zealand
Botswana	Nigeria
Brazil	Norway
Burkina Faso	Pakistan
Cameroon	Papua New Guinea
Canada	Peru
Chile	Philippines
China	Poland
Colombia	Portugal
Cyprus	Puerto Rico
Czechoslovakia	Rumania
Denmark	Rwanda
East Germany	Senegal
Easter Island	Solomon Islands
Ecuador	South Korea
Egypt	Spain
Finland	Sri Lanka
France	Sweden
French Guiana	Switzerland
Ghana	Syria
Greece	Tanzania
Hungary	Thailand
Iceland	UK
India	USA
Indonesia	USSR
Ireland	Venezuela
Israel	West Germany
Italy	Yugoslavia
Japan	Zambia
Kenya	Zimbabwe
Lebanon	

Letter to UNESCO Non-Governmental Organisations Unit

9 February 1987

Dear Mr Malempré

Thank you for your most helpful discussion with me on the telephone on 13 January. As I told you, our Steering Committee met from 21-23 January and I am writing to you on its behalf.

I believe that I need not set out all the details leading up to the ban on South African/Namibian participants in the WAC (which was held from 1-7 September 1986) as you have the details in your file. However, if you so wish, I can easily send you various announcements issued by the then National and Executive Committees which were organising the Congress. Please let me know.

As you are also aware the International Executive Committee of the IUPPS met on 17 January 1986 in Paris and decided not to recognise the WAC as the 11th Congress of the IUPPS, because of its ban on South African/Namibian participation which was taken to contravene the remark in Statute 3 referring to the 'collaboration with scholars in all countries' (the sole mention of this point in the IUPPS Statutes). Professor Nenquin, Secretary-General of the IUPPS, subsequently wrote to members of the Permanent Council, with a deadline of 15 February for a reply, informing them of the Executive's decision and seeking their ratification of the decision. All those who did not respond were counted as 'votes' in the affirmative.

Since then the Chairman of our Steering Committee, Professor Michael Day, wrote to Professor Nenquin on 5 December 1986 as attached, but has received no reply. I wrote to Mr d'Ormesson of ICPHS on 6 November, 26 November and 12 December 1986, and I also telephoned him on numerous occasions in Paris and also once in Cairo during the recent ICPHS General Assembly, at a time pre-arranged with one of the Vice-Presidents of ICPHS, but he chose not to take any of the telephone calls. He then wrote as attached.

The Steering Committee has three major points to put to UNESCO:

1. *South African/Namibian participation*

Mr Kaboré set out UNESCO's position for me in a letter of 29 November 1985, and he included various attachments, most particularly the 'directives concerning UNESCO's relations with international non-governmental organisations' as well as UNESCO resolutions regarding South Africa.

As I understand it, the UNESCO resolutions of 1974 and 1976 (iii. 8, 9, 16, 17, 19) still stand. They make it clear that UNESCO will not assist the 'racialist government of the Republic of South Africa' and it invites UNESCO members 'to have the Republic of South Africa ... excluded from any meeting or activities concerning the organisation in which (this) country might presume to participate'. Elsewhere UNESCO urges intensification of a cultural boycott and it urges all possible measures to prevent 'non-governmental organisations participating in any way in the policy of the Government of South Africa ...'. UNESCO has, as I understand it from you and Mr Kaboré, chosen to interpret these overall resolutions as meaning that individual South African/Namibian participants in congresses and in organisations are acceptable if they are clearly not supporters of the apartheid regime.

As I understand it, ICPHS interprets the same UNESCO resolutions by saying that it 'does not wish to have any South African on any of the ruling bodies of member organisations of ICPHS' (letter from the Secretary-General of ICPHS to the Secretary General of IUPPS of 7 January 1986), and it anyway protects itself by stating that it does not have to conform to any of UNESCO's policies.

IUPPS, affiliated through ICPHS to UNESCO, chooses to allow all South African/Namibian participants irrespective of their views on apartheid, and allows up to four South African members on its ruling Council and these members may be suggested to the Permanent Council by Government. At the same time, and contradictorily, affiliated to the IUPPS is the Pan African Congress on Prehistory and Related Studies which banned all contact with South African individuals and institutions at its meeting in Jos, Nigeria, in December 1983.

Mr Kaboré, and you subsequently by telephone, referred to a response from ICPHS in 1971 which satisfied UNESCO regarding its members from the Republic of South Africa. I am not at all clear whether or not the members concerned were those in IUPPS. It is in any case, as you must be well aware, argued by many that the acceptance of South Africans in any international group is actually to give support to the Government of South Africa.

Our Steering Committee formally requests UNESCO's response to the following two questions: (1) whether the banning of South African/Namibian participation from business meetings is or is not in line with UNESCO resolutions; and (2) whether the banning of South African/Namibian participation from congresses is or is not in line with UNESCO resolutions. Furthermore, it urges UNESCO to consider whether or not such a ban is more in line with its resolutions than are either the practices of ICPHS or of the IUPPS. (It is not suggested that either ICPHS or IUPPS are in any way constitutionally 'out of order' because both of these organisations have written into their Statutes that they may be politically independent of either UNESCO or ICPHS respectively).

It is known to us that clarification of UNESCO's position on these matters is also of concern to several African academic organisations and I am sure that you will be receiving requests for such clarification direct from them also.

2. *IUPPS's decision not to recognise [the] WAC*

It has been brought to the Steering Committee's notice, subsequently confirmed by legal opinions from Britain, Denmark and France, that the actions taken to disenfranchise the WAC as the 11th Congress of the IUPPS infringed the existing IUPPS Statutes.

The list of such infringements is long but the main ones of relevance here, are:

(a) IUPPS Statute 35 makes it clear that the question of where and when Congresses be held is a matter for the Permanent Council, and not for the Executive Committee. Statute 13 makes it clear that such a decision can only be taken at an actual meeting of the Permanent Council. The last meeting of the IUPPS Permanent Council took place on 3 and 5 September 1984 when it was decided that its next meeting would be in Southampton, in 1986, on the occasion of the 11th Congress of the Union;

(b) even if the postal procedure had been in order the Executive Committee's decision of 17 January 1986, as minuted, was to hold the 11th Congress of the IUPPS in September 1986, and this is what the Permanent Council members were asked to agree to. The so-called 11th Congress of the IUPPS is now scheduled for 31 August – 5 September 1987;

(c) the term of the Secretary Generalship runs for five years; it would therefore appear that currently there is no IUPPS Secretary-General;

(d) several members of the IUPPS Permanent Council and Executive Committee had retired from their academic positions prior to the Permanent Council meeting on 3 and 5 September 1984. According to the Secretary-General's usual interpretation of the Statutes they should then have become members of the Comité d'Honneur and were therefore not eligible to take part in the special Executive meeting in Paris. This is all the more significant as the Secretary-General at that Paris meeting refused all consideration of the known views of some of the absent voting members of the Executive Committee.

The Steering Committee formally requests UNESCO to examine the unconstitutional actions of the IUPPS regarding the WAC, here alleged to have infringed its Statutes, and to give the Steering Committee its view as to the constitutional status of (a) the WAC of September 1986; (b) the proposed meeting in Mainz in August/September 1987; and (c) the validity of the decisions taken at the extraordinary meeting of the IUPPS Executive Committee on 17 January 1986 in Paris.

3. *The future*

(a) As already mentioned, we have been put into a situation where we so far have been unable to 'negotiate' with either the IUPPS or with ICPHS. If the meeting scheduled for August/September 1987 in Mainz is not the 11th Congress of the IUPPS, then it is obscure as to how matters can progress. A Permanent Council meeting seems to be the only way that revisions to the Statutes, the location of the next congress of the IUPPS, and many other matters, can be resolved. At this stage it is not clear even who constitutes the IUPPS Bureau (the Secretary-General and President, both of whose incumbency must be in question). To make matters worse, whereas the IUPPS Statutes lay down the criteria for calling special meetings of the Executive Committee, they do not make any mention of special meetings of the Permanent Council. (It is legally possible that a special meeting of the Permanent Council could be called by the Bureau or even by the President alone, but the situation is certainly not clear).

The Steering Committee, therefore, suggests to UNESCO that the most constructive way forward is for there to be a special meeting of at least the Permanent Council called specifically to discuss significant changes to the organisation including revisions to its Statutes. Otherwise the Statutes appear to make it almost inevitable that there must be a two to three year delay for any revisions to be made to the Statutes and, in the current situation, such a delay would be bad for everyone concerned. It urges UNESCO to finance such a meeting in a way that would allow true world-wide participation in such a special meeting. As I have explained to you, IUPPS historically has not provided financial support for those attending either Executive Committee or Permanent Council meetings. It is only at such a special meeting, with adequate financial support for travel costs, that the Third World and certain Eastern European countries could attend. Furthermore it is only at such a special meeting when the agenda is known to include a discussion of the revision of Statutes with possible implications for South African/Namibian future participation in its affairs, that the Third World and certain Eastern European countries might agree to participate (even with South Africans present).

(b) If UNESCO finds itself unable to assist in the regularisation of the IUPPS position so that there may be co-operation between WAC and IUPPS, then the Steering Committee may wish to apply to UNESCO for formal relations within UNESCO category A or B under the terms of clause (ii)6 where 'as an exception the Executive may ... admit an international non-governmental organisation directly to Category A or B'. I believe that it is not necessary at this point to spell out why the Steering Committee wishes to adopt the procedure of (ii)6. I enclose a copy of the edited version of the Plenary Session of the WAC 1986 for you to be able to judge the breadth and depth of views expressed by the 502 participants at the Plenary Session of the WAC, well over half of those who attended the Congress.

The Steering Committee would be most grateful for as early a reply as possible. It does, of course, realise that you will wish to consult with several organisations but points out that the next crucial date appears to be the proposed IUPPS Executive Committee meeting (if that is still what it is) apparently scheduled to meet in Czechoslovakia on 4-6 May 1987.

Finally, and in any case, may I suggest that Professor Essomba (a member of our Steering Committee) and I come to talk to you about UNESCO's policy on South African participation in associated non-governmental organisations, before he returns to Cameroon (in the middle of March). I myself return from the United States at the end of February so it sounds as if sometime during the first two weeks of March would be best from our side. Could you please let us both know when you suggest ...

Yours sincerely,
P.J. Ucko
Secretary of Steering Committee
World Archaeological Congress.

Message from Anti-Apartheid

TO ALL THOSE ATTENDING THE CONFERENCE ON 'THE ORIGIN AND DISPERSAL OF MODERN HUMANS'

As you may know, the WAC was held in Southampton last year. As a result of much effort, debate and lobbying by principled opponents of Pretoria's apartheid regime in the AUT and elsewhere; the conference organisers agreed to support the United Nations call for an academic boycott of South Africa. In view of this, we feel that the participation of South Africans in this conference is doubly sad.

THE ANTI-APARTHEID MOVEMENT URGES ALL ACADEMICS, INSIDE AND OUTSIDE SOUTH AFRICA, TO SUPPORT THE BOYCOTT.

What is the boycott? The academic boycott of South Africa is part of a world-wide campaign to get nations and individuals to sever all their links – economic, cultural, sporting and academic – with the apartheid state. The boycott was originally a tactic used by black people inside South Africa as a form of protest – for example when bus fares rose unacceptably.

Who called it? The boycott was first called for by Albert Luthuli, the then President of the African National Congress (ANC), in 1959. Since then, the call has been repeated time and time again by all the legitimate representatives of black people in South Africa and illegally occupied Namibia.

Who supports it? Inside South Africa, the call is supported by the ANC, the South West Africa People's Organisation (SWAPO), the United Democratic Front (UDF), Bishop Desmond Tutu, Revd. Alan Boesak, and all black people struggling against apartheid. The largest black students' union – the Azanian Students' Organisation (AZASO) – has added its voice to the chorus for an academic boycott. Outside South Africa the call is supported by the UN, UNESCO, and the Revd. Jesse Jackson among others. In this country, the Anti-Apartheid movement, the Labour Party, the World University Service, and all the major educational trade unions – NUT, NUS, AUT etc. – support the boycott.

What's it for? The boycott aims at nothing less than the total isolation of South Africa from the International community. Its purpose is to make

South Africa a pariah, to cut it off completely from the rest of the world, and
to emphasise the moral and political unacceptability of apartheid.

Can it work? Yes – with your help. Public pressure recently forced
Barclays bank, General Motors, and many other large firms to pull out of
South Africa. The US and EEC have applied sanctions, South African
sports teams have been banned from International events, and principled
entertainers, such as Stevie Wonder, have refused to tour there.

But what about South African academics who oppose apartheid? The
purpose of the boycott is certainly not to punish individual South Africans,
least of all those who oppose apartheid. If such individuals are
inconvenienced by it, this is unfortunate, but the boycott is aimed at
apartheid, which permeates every aspect of South African society, and the
lives of everyone who lives there, to talk about its effects on individual
academics is to miss the point.

Why should we support the boycott? Because it is what black people in
South Africa want. Because it is up to us to take a stand against apartheid
here and now, in what ever way we can. Because the presence of South
African representatives at this conference – no matter what their personal
views are – lends credence and respectability to one of the most brutal
states in the world. Because it is immoral to have any dealings with a
regime which treats a majority of its citizens as sub-human, and has
imprisoned tens of thousands of children aged between 10 and 16 years.

But would you boycott every regime with a bad human rights record?
No. South Africa is special. The UN has recognised this; it has said that
apartheid is 'a crime against humanity'. We too must realise that South
Africa is almost unique in human history, and act accordingly.

What's so special about South Africa? It is the only country in the
world where systematic discrimination against people on the basis of their
race is a part of the constitutional and legal framework. The only parallel
we can draw is with Nazi Germany.

So should this conference have gone ahead? Not with South African
participants. The decision of the organisers of the WAC was the right one.
Those who are organising and participating in this conference are out of
step, not just with world opinion, but with the opinions of the academic
community.

But why mix politics and education? Because they are already mixed.
In South Africa, education is one of the major ways in which apartheid
operates and is reinforced. Black people are systematically discriminated
against in this as in all other spheres. They are not taught their own history.
They are not taught the truth about their country. They are not taught to
think for themselves. They are taught about the innate inferiority of their
people and their culture. The boycott of apartheid schools by children and
their parents in the townships, and the actions of students on university
campuses shows that black and white people are aware of this, and struggle
against it.

But what good will the boycott do? At best it will hasten the downfall of apartheid. Obviously the severing of economic ties is most important in this respect. At worst it will emphasise and make real our determination, as an academic community, to isolate apartheid, but the boycott is also a moral and political step which we must take if we are not to be implicated in the evil which is South Africa today.

So what should we do now? Ideally, drop out of the conference. Otherwise, write letters to the organisers protesting about the participation of South Africans here. You can also write to the South African embassy, protesting at the state of emergency and the mass detentions. Above all, find out more about apartheid and how to fight it by ringing the Anti-Apartheid Movement on 01-387-7966.

P&P Cambridge Anti-Apartheid.

Suggested Revisions by the WAC Steering Committee of IUPPS Statutes

PROPOSITION DE REVISION DES STATUTS

3. '... par la collaboration de savants de tous les pays *respectant les principes de l'UNESCO dans le cadre des droits de l'homme.*'

6. Il-y-aura avantage a déterminer le droit national duquel les Statuts relèveront à tout jamais.

7. '... correspondance officielle, *sont toutes les langues officielles de l'UNESCO*'.

9. Les Statuts doivent clarifier les pouvoirs statutaires eventuels de l'Assemblée générale.

10. 'Il est composé *d'au moins quatre membres* par pays, *chaque pays disposant d'une voix, en plus au moins quatre membres qui représentent le Conseil Mondial de Peuples Indigènes* [ou une organisation semblable] *disposant ensemble d'une seule voix*.

    A partir de 1987/1988 des nouveaux membres désignés par chaque pays remplaceront les membres courants qui ont été choisis par la Conférence de Berne en 1931. *Par la suite la moitié du Conseil sera renouvelée tous les cinq ans, le mandat des membres particuliers étant renouvelable. Les pays/CMPI désignants sont tenus de soumettre leur propositions pour remplir les sièges vacantes assorties pour chaque nom d'un Curriculum Vitae complet. Dans le cas où le délégué désigné n'est pas acceptée, le CE signalera la raison au pays/CMPI designant.*

    Les membres du Cp de chaque pays comporteront au possible à la fois des hommes et des femmes aussi bien que des étudiants et des jeunes archéologues.

    Effacez 'Ils cessent ... CP.'

12. Les Statuts doivent stipuler que l'ordre du jour des réunions du CP soit distribué bien avant la réunion pour donner assez de temps pour la consultation à l'intérieur de chaque pays. Les Statuts doivent aussi stipuler que si aucun des délégués officiels d'un pays est empeché d'assister à la réunion du CP, et que si le Président reçoit cette notification antérieurement, le pays dont il s'agit peut autoriser la delégation officielle d'un autre pays de voter à sa place.

13. Les Statuts doivent stipuler les modalités par lesquelles les sessions extraordinaires peuvent être réunies.

13. A la discrétion du CP des conférences peuvent être organisé entre les réunions des Congrès proprement dits dans des pays qui n'ont pas les moyens ni les ressources de monter un Congrès mondial.

    L'organisation de telles conférences sera pareille à celle des Congrès, sujet à des modifications approuvées éventuellement par le CP dans le but de faciliter la tâche du pays invitant. Notamment le comité de gestion invitant peut limiter les nombres de participants aux conférences et peut, par une invitation sélective ou bien par un autre dispositif de sélection approuvé par le Comité de gestion et le CP ou le CE, recevoir une proposition ou la totalité des participants.

18. Les Statuts doivent permettre la possibilité qu'on tienne compte de toutes les opinions au sein du CE, soit en admettent l'envoi par la poste des opinions/voix délibératives, soit par d'autres moyens comme une autorisation officielle ou bien l'envoi d'un délégué alternatif.

20. *Remplacez* 'Le CE ... le CP' *par: Le CE prend des décisions de principe au nom de, et sujet à, l'autorité du CP, établit des comités auxquels il délègue les pouvoirs appropriés, autorise le budget, établit les inscriptions d'affiliation, et autorise des programmes d'activité de nature internationale, scientifique et professionnelle, et fait toute autre demarche nécéssaire au nom de l'Union, et reste responsable devant le CP.*

    Périodiquement le CE établit le barême des inscriptions pour chaque catégorie d'affiliation, et a le droit d'annuller le paiement des inscriptions ou bien de les réduire dans le cas où il estime que des raisons financières ou autres renderont la charge onéreuse ou le paiement non-faisable.

    A moins que le CE ait dûment renoncé au paiement des inscriptions, les membres qui manquent de payer leur inscriptions seront privés du droit de vote.

22. *Effacez.*

26. 'Le Bureau ... *du trésorier* et du Sècrétaire général'. *Le Secrétaire général nomme et dirige les employés de l'Union.*

29. 'Le mandat du Secrétaire général dur 5 ans *ou* jusqu'au prochain Congrès, ...'

30. 'Durant la durée de son mandat, le Secrétaire général cesse de représenter son propre pays *ou circonscription* au CP'.

33. *Le trésorier* 'est également chargé de la gestion financière de l'UISPP. Il reçoit du Comité national ... que le Secrétaire devra entreprendre pour l'UISPP, etc).' 'Dans cette somme ... du prochain congrès'. *Le trésorier est responsable au CE pour l'établissement du budget.* 'A chaque réunion du CE, *le trésorier* présente *les comptes vérifiés* ... absolue des votants. Ces *comptes sont* ensuite soumis à l'approbation du CP lors de chaque réunion de celui-ci'.

34. 'Le CISPP se réunit *normalement* tous les cinq ans'.

35. 'La date ... du CP' *ou bien si cela s'avère impossible, par une réunion extraordinaire du CE convoqué par le Bureau.*

38. *Effacez complètement.*

39. Deuxième paragraphe – *effacez complètement.*

40. *Les langues des Congrès et leurs publications sont toutes les langues officielles de l'UNESCO.*

43/ Ces Statuts doivent être réformulés à la lumière des nouvelles
44. responsabilités du CE indiquées dans le Statut 20, amendé.

45. 'Des modifications ... (b) soit par 10 *membres votant* du CP ... être adressées par écrit au *Secrétaire général* de l'UISPP.'

Ces modifications doivent parvenir au Secrétaire général neuf mois avant la réunion du CP à laquelle ils figureront à l'ordre du jour. Puis le Secrétaire général les distribue aux membres du CP au moins six mois avant la réunion dont il s'agit. Les modifications aux Statuts sont adoptées si elles sont approuvées par les deux tiers des voix déposées à une séance du CP formellement convoqué.

Further Reading

Pratap, Ajay and Nandini Rao (eds) 1986 Archaeology and Politics. *Archaeological Review from Cambridge*. Vol. 5(1).

The Commonwealth Group of Eminent Persons 1986 *Mission to South Africa: The Commonwealth Report*. Penguin Special.

Hanlon, Joseph and Roger Omond 1987 *The Sanctions Handbook*. Penguin Special.

Hodder, Ian 1986 *Reading the Past*. Cambridge University Press.

Omond, Roger 1985 *The Apartheid Handbook, a guide to South Africa's everyday racial policies*. Penguin Special.

Whitehouse, Ruth (ed) 1983 *The Macmillan Dictionary of Archaeology*.

Name Index

General Index

Primary Mathematics: Audit and Test
Assessing your knowledge and understanding

Claire Mooney
Mike Fletcher

Learning Matters

First published in 2001 by Learning Matters Ltd.

© Claire Mooney and Mike Fletcher

British Library Cataloguing in Publication Data
A CIP record for this book is available from the British Library.

ISBN 1 903300 21 5

Cover design by Topics – The Creative Partnership
Text design by Code 5 Design Associates Ltd
Project Management by Deer Park Productions
Typeset by PDQ Typesetting
Printed and bound in Great Britain by The Baskerville Press Ltd, Salisbury, Wiltshire.

Learning Matters Ltd
58 Wonford Road
Exeter EX2 4LQ
Tel: 01392 215560
Email: info@learningmatters.co.uk
www.learningmatters.co.uk

About this book

This book has been written to help support the needs of all primary trainees on all courses of Initial Teacher Training (ITT) in England and other parts of the UK where a secure subject knowledge and understanding of mathematics is required for the award of Qualified Teacher Status (QTS). A secure subject knowledge and understanding of mathematics is now widely acknowledged as a critical factor at every point in the complex process of planning, teaching and assessing mathematics itself. The audit and test materials presented here in seven parts are intended to help you to identify your own strengths and weaknesses in mathematics and to help you to set clear, appropriate and achievable targets for your own mathematical development:

→ *Part 1: Mathematics background;*

→ *Part 2: Interest in mathematics;*

→ *Part 3: Perceived competence and confidence in mathematics;*

→ *Part 4: Mathematics test;*

→ *Part 5: Answers;*

→ *Part 6: Targets for further development;*

→ *Part 7: Suggestions for revision and further reading.*

It is quite likely that you will be required to undertake further auditing and testing of your subject knowledge and understanding of mathematics at the start of your own course of ITT. You may wish to retain the audit and test results here for your own records and use them as working documents to return to as and when necessary. Your ITT provider may also wish to use them for their records too.

You may indeed find the auditing and testing of your mathematics subject knowledge a daunting prospect, especially if you have not studied mathematics for several years. However, most people simply take it all in their stride and you should aim to do the same. Undertaking a self-audit and testing you own mathematical knowledge is just one part of the assessment process you will experience both during training and throughout your career in teaching. There is certainly nothing to worry about when auditing and testing yourself in the comfort of your own home, and your ITT provider will take every step they can to help you towards your goal of becoming an effective and successful primary school teacher.

For trainees wishing to undertake some revision or who feel the need for a mathematics study aid there are several excellent books written specifically for primary trainees with diverse backgrounds in mathematics, all available from good booksellers. The *Learning Matters QTS Series* includes *Primary Mathematics: Knowledge and Understanding* by Mooney et al. (full details in References). Additional ideas for revision and further study are included in Part 7.

The ITT National Curriculum for Primary Mathematics

As mentioned earlier, it is now a statutory requirement that all trainees on all courses of Initial Teacher Training must, when assessed, demonstrate that they have a secure knowledge and understanding of the subject content of mathematics as specified in the Initial Teacher Training National Curriculum (ITTNC) for Primary Mathematics in order to support mathematics teaching at primary level. Details of the ITTNC for Primary Mathematics can be found in Annex D of DfEE Circular 4/98 *Teaching: High Status, High Standards — Requirements for Courses of Initial Teacher Training*. Where gaps in subject knowledge and understanding are identified, ITT providers are required to ensure that those areas needing attention are addressed and that, by the end of their course, trainees are both competent and confident in using their knowledge and understanding of mathematics in their teaching. The specified subject content of mathematics includes:

→ *the real number system;*

→ *indices;*

→ *number operations and algebra;*

→ *equations, functions and graphs;*

→ *mathematical reasoning and proof;*

→ *measures;*

→ *shape and space;*

→ *probability and statistics.*

The self-audit and test materials presented here will introduce you to the content items listed above in detail.

Mathematics: the National Curriculum for England

So just what is it that all of this subject knowledge and understanding supports? In 1989, all maintained schools throughout England and Wales experienced the introduction of a National Curriculum for Mathematics. Mathematics in the National Curriculum is organised on the basis of four Key Stages of which Key Stage 1 for 5- to 7-year-olds (Years 1 and 2) and Key Stage 2 for 7- to 11-year-olds (Years 3 to 6) are for primary. The components of each Key Stage include Programmes of Study, which set out the mathematics that children should be taught; Attainment Targets, which set out the mathematical knowledge, skills and understanding that children should attain; and Level Descriptions, which describe the types and range of performance that children working at a particular level should be able to demonstrate within each Attainment Target. A brief summary of Programmes of Study is presented as follows:

→ *Ma 1: Using and applying mathematics;*

→ *Ma 2: Number and algebra;*

→ *Ma 3: Shape, space and measures;*

→ *Ma 4: Handling data (Key Stage 2).*

The statutory Mathematics National Curriculum is now supported by the National Numeracy Strategy's *Framework for Teaching Mathematics* (non-statutory).

References

DfEE (1998) *Teaching: High Status, High Standards (Requirements for Courses of Initial Teacher Training)*. Circular Number 4/98. London: DfEE. (Also available online at *http://www.open.gov.uk/dfee/dfeehome.htm* and *http://www.teach-tta.gov.uk*.)

DfEE/QCA (1999) *Mathematics: the National Curriculum for England*. London: HMSO. (Also available online at *http://www.nc.uk.net*.)

DfEE (1999) *The National Numeracy Strategy: Framework for Teaching Mathematics*. London: DfEE. (Also available online at *http://www.standards.dfee.gov.uk/numeracy/NNSframework/*.)

Mooney, C. et al. (2000) *Primary Mathematics: Knowledge and Understanding*. Exeter: Learning Matters .

Provide as many background details as you can. Don't worry if it looks a bit 'blank' in places, you won't be alone.

→ personal details

Name

Date of birth

Year(s) of course

Subject specialism

Elected Key Stage

→ mathematics qualifications

GCSE/O level (equivalent)

Date taken

Grade(s)

GCE A level (equivalent)

Date taken

Grade(s)

→ mathematics degree

Year of graduation

Class of degree

Other mathematics courses

→ other (e.g. work related)

A positive attitude towards mathematics will help you to learn and teach it well, whether it is your favourite subject or not. Be honest with yourself and think carefully about your responses below. It is possible that you might have a healthy interest in mathematics even if you currently think you don't know much about it, and unfortunately the converse might be true!

Circle as appropriate using the key provided.

1 = *I am very interested in mathematics.*
2 = *I am interested in mathematics.*
3 = *I am uncertain about my interest in mathematics.*
4 = *I am not interested in mathematics.*

→ *Interest*   **1   2   3   4**

A **1** or a **2** is fantastic, a **3** encouraging, a **4** – well, you have yet to be inspired! Reflect critically on your attitude towards mathematics, positive or negative, and use the space below to comment further. Can you identify the experiences that gave rise to your interest or lack of interest in mathematics?

→   *experiences statement*

As you undertake the following self-audit you might notice that you feel quite competent in an area of mathematics but lack the confidence to teach it. Competence and confidence are clearly quite different things. By the end of your training you will have greater competence within mathematics and greater confidence to teach the subject.

Competence

The areas within the self-audit are drawn directly from Section C of the ITTNC for Primary Mathematics (Annex D of DfEE Circular 4/98). There are rather a lot of them and you will need some time to read through and complete this part thoroughly. You do not need to know about or feel competent with everything listed here right now. This will develop throughout your training.

Please respond to the following statements using the key provided.

1 = *Very good. Existing competence perceived as* exceeding *the stated requirements.*

2 = *Good. Existing competence perceived as* meeting *the stated requirements comfortably.*

3 = *Adequate. Existing competence perceived as* meeting *the stated requirements but* some *uncertainties still exist.*

4 = *Not good. Existing competence perceived as* not meeting *the stated requirements.*

As part of all courses trainees must demonstrate that they know and understand:

C13a Number and algebra

	1	2	3	4
i the real number system				
• **the arithmetic of integers, fractions and decimals**	○	○	○	○
• **forming equalities and inequalities and recognising when equality is preserved**	○	○	○	○
• **the distinction between a rational number and an irrational number making sense of simple recurring decimals**	○	○	○	○
ii indices				
• **representing numbers in index form including positive and negative integer exponents**	○	○	○	○
• **standard form**	○	○	○	○
iii number operations and algebra				
• **using the associative, commutative and distributive laws**	○	○	○	○
• **use of cancellation to simplify calculations**	○	○	○	○
• **using the multiplicative structure of ratio and proportion to solve problems**	○	○	○	○

- finding factors and multiples of numbers and of simple algebraic expressions
- constructing general statements
- manipulating simple algebraic expressions and using formulae
- knowing when numerical expressions and algebraic expressions are equivalent
- number sequences, their *nth* terms and their sums

iv equations, functions and graphs

- forming equations and solving linear and simultaneous linear equations, finding exact solutions
- interpreting functions and finding inverses of simple functions
- representing functions graphically and algebraically
- understanding the significance of gradients and intercepts
- interpreting graphs, and using them to solve equations

C13b Mathematical reasoning and proof

1 2 3 4

- the correct use of $=$, $\equiv$, $\Rightarrow$, $\therefore$
- the difference between mathematical reasoning and explanation, as well as the proper use of evidence
- following rigorous mathematical argument
- familiarity with methods of proof, including simple deductive proof, proof by exhaustion and disproof by counter-example

C13c Measures

1 2 3 4

- understanding that the basis of measures is exact and that practical measurement is approximate
- standard measures and compound measures, including rates of change
- the relationship between measures, including length, area, volume and capacity
- understanding the importance of choice of unit and use of proportion

C13d Shape and space

1 2 3 4

- Cartesian coordinates in 2-D
- 2-D transformations
- angles, congruence and similarity in triangles and other shapes
- geometrical constructions
- identifying and measuring properties and characteristics of 2-D shapes
- using Pythagoras' theorem

- **recognising the relationships between and using the formulae for the area of 2-D shapes; including rectangle and triangle, trapezium, and parallelogram**
- **the calculation of the area of circles and sectors, the length of circumferences and arcs**
- **recognise, understand and use formulae for the surface area and volume of prisms**
- **identifying 3-D solids and shapes and recognising their properties and characteristics**

C13e probability and statistics

	1	2	3	4
using discrete and continuous data and understanding the difference between them	○	○	○	○
tabulating and representing data diagrammatically and graphically	○	○	○	○
interpreting data and predicting from data	○	○	○	○
finding and using the mean and other central measures	○	○	○	○
finding and using measures of spread to compare distributions	○	○	○	○
using systematic methods for identifying, counting and organising events and outcomes	○	○	○	○
understanding the difference between probability and observed relative frequencies	○	○	○	○
recognise independent and mutually exclusive events	○	○	○	○

Making sense of your perceived competence

Look back over the **perceived competency** grades within your self-audit. Summarise each area in the following table by looking at the distribution of responses. For example, if you ticked *1*s, *2*s and *3*s in *The real number system* but no *4*s, you should fill in your Range as *1*s to *3*s. If you ticked more *3*s than anything else, you should fill in your Mode, the most frequently occurring response, as *3*.

	range	mode
The real number system		
Indices		
Number operations and algebra		
Equations, functions and graphs		
Mathematical reasoning and proof		
Measures		
Shape and space		
Probability and statistics		

Mostly 1s Areas summarised as mostly **1**s suggest that most competency requirements are exceeded. Your perceived competence would place you at a level beyond that indicated for a non-mathematics specialist. Well done.

Mostly 2s Areas summarised as mostly **2**s suggest that most competency requirements are met comfortably. Some attention is necessary locally, certainly in weaker elements. Your perceived competence places you at a level about that of a non-mathematics specialist. With this sort of profile you probably have little to worry about.

Mostly 3s Areas summarised as mostly **3**s suggest that most competency requirements are met adequately. However, attention is necessary throughout. Your perceived competence places you at a level best described as approaching that specified for a non-mathematics specialist. You are probably in good company and with a little effort you will be up there with the best of them.

Mostly 4s Areas summarised as mostly **4**s suggest that most competency requirements are hardly being met at all, but remember, you only have to get there by the end of your training – not before! Given the nature of the requirements, a profile like this is not surprising. Consistent effort throughout your training will certainly result in a much improved competency profile, so don't worry.

Confidence

Carefully examine the Programmes of Study for Key Stages 1 and 2 in the Mathematics National Curriculum given below. Overall, how would you describe your confidence in terms of **teaching** them? Respond using the key provided.

1 = Very good. Might even feel happy to support colleagues!

2 = Good. Further professional development required in some aspects.

3 = Adequate. Further professional development required in most aspects.

4 = Poor. Help! Further professional development essential in all aspects.

Ma2: Number

	1	2	3	4
• using and applying number	○	○	○	○
• numbers and the number system	○	○	○	○
• calculations	○	○	○	○
• solving numerical problems	○	○	○	○

Ma3: Shape, space and measures

	1	2	3	4
• using and applying shape, space and measures	○	○	○	○
• understanding patterns and properties of shape	○	○	○	○
• understanding properties of position and movement	○	○	○	○
• understanding measures	○	○	○	○

Ma4: Handling data (Key Stage 2)

1 2 3 4

- using and applying handling data
- processing, representing and interpreting data

Making sense of your perceived confidence

1s and **2**s are fantastic – what's kept you away from the profession for so long?! **3**s are encouraging and we would imagine many people would have this sort of profile. If you ticked any **4**s, don't worry, you are being honest with yourself and that is good. If you felt so confident about teaching mathematics at this stage, it would be difficult to convince you that there was any point in training you to do it! Reflect critically on your perceived confidence about teaching mathematics and use the space below to comment further. Can you identify the 'source' of your confidence or the 'source' of your lack of it?

confidence statement

Perceived competence and confidence is one thing. How would you do if actually put to the test! It really doesn't matter how well or how badly you do in the test now, you have lots of time to make up for the mathematics you have forgotten or never knew in the first place. The following pages explore your knowledge and understanding in the areas of mathematics identified in Section C of the ITTNC for Primary Mathematics (Annex D of DfEE Circular 4/98). Take as long as you need and try not to cheat too much by looking at the answers! The marking system is quite straightforward and easy to use.

Number

1 Using a method for long multiplication work out the following:

   (i) 45×24 (ii) 146×234 (iii) 312×235

(3 marks)

2 Use a long division algorithm to solve:

   (i) $1768 \div 34$ (ii) $1638 \div 63$ (iii) $3335 \div 23$

(3 marks)

Key vocabulary: *algorithm, place value, operation, dividend, divisor, quotient*

3 Using $p = \frac{2}{3}$, $q = \frac{1}{2}$, $r = 2\frac{4}{7}$ and $s = 1\frac{1}{5}$ find:

(i) $p + q$	(ii) $p + r$	(iii) $q + s$
(iv) $p - q$	(v) $r - q$	(vi) $r - s$
(vii) $p \times q$	(viii) $q \times s$	(ix) $r \times s$
(x) $p \div q$	(xi) $q \div p$	(xii) $q \div r$

(12 marks)

Key vocabulary: *fraction, numerator, denominator, proper fraction, improper fraction*

4 Convert the following into decimal fractions:

   (i) $\frac{5}{8}$ (ii) $\frac{7}{20}$ (iii) 65%   (iv) 0.1%

(4 marks)

5 Convert the following to vulgar fractions:

   (i)   0.375   (ii) 0.28   (iii) 76%

(3 marks)

6 Express the following fractions in their simplest forms:

   (i) $\frac{84}{96}$ (ii) $\frac{84}{91}$

(2 marks)

7 Convert the following into percentages:

   (i) $\frac{5}{8}$ (ii) 0.375   (iii) $\frac{7}{20}$ (iv) 0.28

(4 marks)

⑧ Prior to Christmas the cost of the latest computer game was increased by 20%. In the sales after Christmas it was reduced by 20%. How do the two prices compare?

(1 mark)

⑨ As it was so desirable, the cost of the latest mobile phone was increased by 25%. A month later it was no longer fashionable and was reduced by 20%. How did the reduced price compare with the original price before the increase?

(1 mark)

⑩ A school basketball team scored 24 points in one game and 30 points in the next. What was their percentage increase in the points scored?

(1 mark)

⑪ Two children undertake a sponsored swim. In total they raise £160. The ratio of the contributions of Edward to Katherine was 2:3. How much did each child raise?

(2 marks)

⑫ A junior school shares out library books to year groups based on the ratio of the number of children in the year groups. 1000 books are to be distributed to Years 3, 4, 5 and 6. There are 52 children in Year 3, 68 in Year 4, 44 in Year 5 and 36 in Year 6. How many books does each year group get?

(4 marks)

⑬ Place a tick in the box next to the numbers that are rational and a cross next to the numbers that are irrational.

(i) 0.3636363…   □   (ii) $\sqrt{2}$ □   (iii) $\sqrt{4}$ □

(iv) 0.101001000100001… □   (v) $\frac{1}{9}$ □   (vi) $\sqrt{\frac{4}{9}}$ □

(vii) π □   (viii) 2^3 □   (ix) 2^{-3} □

(9 marks)

⑭ Place the numbers from question 13 in numerical order. Also include the following numbers:

$\frac{1}{7}$ $-\sqrt{5}$ $-(2^2)$ $-(2^{-2})$ $0.\dot{3}$

(7 marks)

⑮ 0.33333… can be written as $0.\dot{3}$. Write the following recurring decimals using the same notation:

(i) 0.27272727…   (ii) 0.277777777…
(iii) 0.904904904904…   (iv) 18.18181818…

(4 marks)

⑯ Write these numbers in index form:

(i) 100 000 (ii) 0.1 (iii) 100

(3 marks)

⑰ Convert these numbers from standard form into ordinary form

(i) 6.6×10^3 (ii) 7.07×10^{-2}

(2 marks)

⑱ Write these numbers in standard form

(i) 523000 (ii) 0.0606

(2 marks)

Key vocabulary: *index form, exponent, standard form*

⑲ Put a tick in the box if the statement is **true** and a cross if the statement is **false**.

(i) $(24 + 8) \div 4 = (24 \div 4) + (8 \div 4)$ ☐

(ii) $(96 \div 12) \, 4 = 96 \div (12 \div 4)$ ☐

(iii)   17% of £50 = 50% of £17   ☐

(iv) $(20 + 8) \times (30 + 9) = (20 \times 30) + (8 \times 9)$ ☐

(4 marks)

Key vocabulary: *commutative, associative, distributive, order of precedence, (BODMAS)*

⑳ Find all the factors of each of the following numbers:

(i)   18 (ii)   60

(2 marks)

㉑ Find all the prime factors of each of the following numbers:

(i)   48 (ii)   105

(2 marks)

㉒ Find the highest common factor of each of the following:

(i)   6 and 15 (ii)   18 and 54
(iii) $12a^2$ and $4ab$ (iv) a^2b and a^3b^2

(4 marks)

Key vocabulary: *factor, common factor, prime factor, multiple*

Algebra – patterns and relationships

❶ If $a = 5$, $b = 15$, $c = 2$, $d = 3$, $de = 15$ and $df = 18$ find:

(i) ab

(ii) ac

(iii) e

(iv) f

(v) $a(b + c)$

(vi) $d(e + f)$

(vii) $a(b - c)$

(viii) $d(e - f)$

(ix) $2a^2b$

(x) $2d^2e$

(xi) $\frac{1}{a}$

(xii) $\frac{1}{d}$

(12 marks)

❷ Lydia is doing a mathematics investigation and obtains the results 1, 4, 9, 16, 25.

(i) What would be the next term in this sequence?

(1 mark)

(ii) The 10th term?

(1 mark)

(iii) The nth term?

(2 marks)

❸ Tom is investigating the number of slabs that would be required to pave around a square garden pond as follows:

pond 1   *pond 2*   *pond 3*   *pond 4*   *pond 5*

(i) Write down the number pattern that he found.

(1 mark)

(ii) How many slabs would be needed to pave around the 10th pond?

(1 mark)

(iii) What would be the nth term of this sequence?

(2 marks)

❹ Jess is doing a mathematics investigation and obtained the results 1, 2, 4, 8, 16, 32.

(i) What would be the next term in this sequence?

(1 mark)

(ii) The 10th term?

(1 mark)

(iii) The nth term?

(2 marks)

5 Henry is investigating multilink staircases as follows:

staircase 1

staircase 2

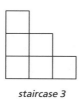
staircase 3

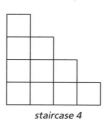
staircase 4

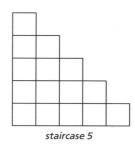
staircase 5

(i)   Write down the number pattern that he found.

(1 mark)

(ii) How many cubes would be needed for the 10th staircase?

(1 mark)

(iii) What would be the nth term of this sequence?

(2 marks)

Key vocabulary: *generalise, nth term, number sequence, equation, expression*

6 Solve the following equations:

(i) $\dfrac{1}{x+2} = 3$ (ii) $\dfrac{1}{5x-4} = \dfrac{1}{x}$

(iii) $\dfrac{3}{1+b} = \dfrac{5}{b+3}$

(3 marks)

Key vocabulary: *term, expression, equation*

7 Solve the following pairs of simultaneous equations:

(i) $\begin{cases} y - 2x = 4 \\ y + x = 7 \end{cases}$

(ii) $\begin{cases} 2a - 3b = 2 \\ 4a + 6b = 4 \end{cases}$

(iii) $\begin{cases} 2x - y = 5 \\ 3x + 2y = 11 \end{cases}$

(3 marks)

Key vocabulary: *simultaneous linear equation*

Shape and space

❶ If angle *a* is 100°, work out angles *b*, *c*, *d*, *e* and *f*.

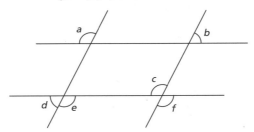

(1 mark)

❷ If angle *a* = 95°, angle *b* = 110° and angle *c* = 105°, what does angle *d* equal?

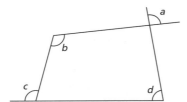

(1 mark)

Key vocabulary: *opposite angles, complementary angles, supplementary angles, interior angles*

❸

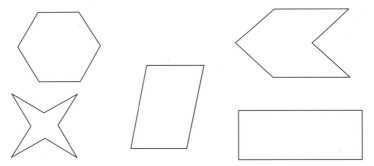

    (i)   Identify the lines of symmetry of the shapes above.

(5 marks)

    (ii)   Identify the orders of rotational symmetry of the shapes above.

(5 marks)

Key vocabulary: *reflective symmetry, order of rotational symmetry*

❹ Identify which of the angles in the following shape are acute, obtuse, right or reflex.

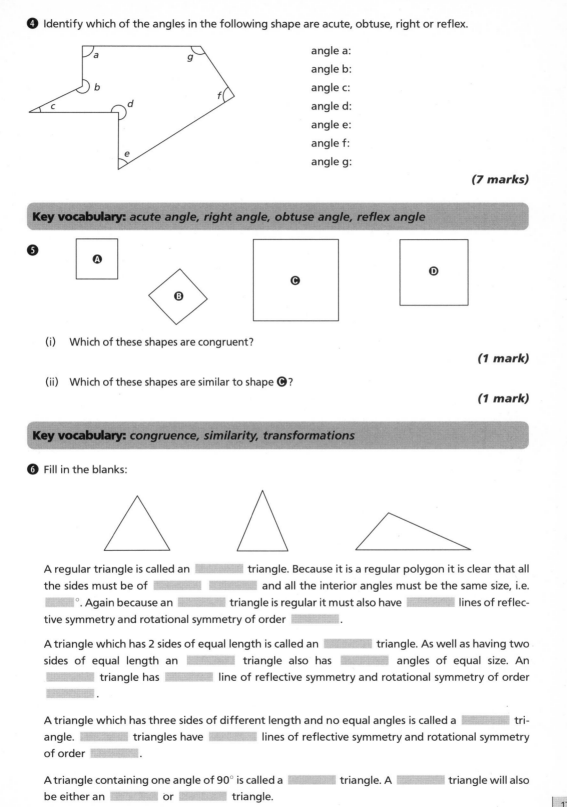

angle a:

angle b:

angle c:

angle d:

angle e:

angle f:

angle g:

(7 marks)

Key vocabulary: *acute angle, right angle, obtuse angle, reflex angle*

❺

(i)   Which of these shapes are congruent?

(1 mark)

(ii)   Which of these shapes are similar to shape ⓒ?

(1 mark)

Key vocabulary: *congruence, similarity, transformations*

❻ Fill in the blanks:

A regular triangle is called an ▓▓▓▓ triangle. Because it is a regular polygon it is clear that all the sides must be of ▓▓▓▓ ▓▓▓▓ and all the interior angles must be the same size, i.e. ▓▓▓°. Again because an ▓▓▓▓ triangle is regular it must also have ▓▓▓▓ lines of reflective symmetry and rotational symmetry of order ▓▓▓▓.

A triangle which has 2 sides of equal length is called an ▓▓▓▓ triangle. As well as having two sides of equal length an ▓▓▓▓ triangle also has ▓▓▓▓ angles of equal size. An ▓▓▓▓ triangle has ▓▓▓▓ line of reflective symmetry and rotational symmetry of order ▓▓▓▓.

A triangle which has three sides of different length and no equal angles is called a ▓▓▓▓ triangle. ▓▓▓▓ triangles have ▓▓▓▓ lines of reflective symmetry and rotational symmetry of order ▓▓▓▓.

A triangle containing one angle of 90° is called a ▓▓▓▓ triangle. A ▓▓▓▓ triangle will also be either an ▓▓▓▓ or ▓▓▓▓ triangle.

The number of lines of reflective symmetry and the order of rotational symmetry of a ▨▨▨▨▨▨ triangle depends on whether it is an ▨▨▨▨▨▨ or ▨▨▨▨▨▨ triangle.

(24 marks)

Key vocabulary: *triangle, equilateral, isosceles, scalene, right-angled*

❼ Put a tick in the box if the following triangles have right angles:

(i)   AB = 3   BC = 4   AC = 5   ☐

(ii) XY = 4   YZ = 5   XZ = 6   ☐

(2 marks)

Key vocabulary: *Pythagoras' theorem, Pythagorean triples*

❽ What is the area of this triangle?

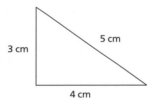

(1 mark)

❾ What is the area of this parallelogram?

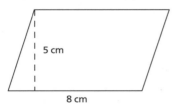

(1 mark)

❿ What is the area of this trapezium?

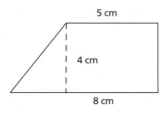

(1 mark)

18

⓫ Work out the perimeter and area of the following shape:

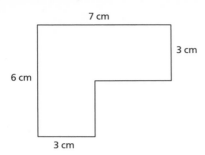

7 cm

3 cm

6 cm

3 cm

Perimeter =

Area =

(2 marks)

⓬ Work out the perimeter and area of the following shape (you will need to calculate a sensible value for *L*).

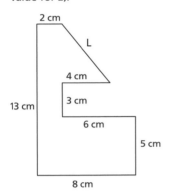

2 cm

L

4 cm

3 cm

13 cm

6 cm

5 cm

8 cm

L =

Perimeter =

Area =

(3 marks)

Key vocabulary: *perimeter, area*

⓭ Find the circumference and area of a circle with a diameter of 10 cm.

(2 marks)

⓮

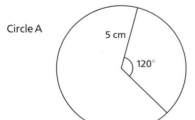

Circle A

5 cm

120°

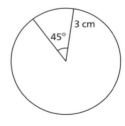

Circle B

3 cm

45°

(i)   Calculate the area of the sector marked in each circle.

(2 marks)

(ii) Calculate the length of the arcs marked on each circle above.

(2 marks)

Key vocabulary: *radius, diameter, circumference, area, sector, arc*

⑮ This rectangle has the following coordinates:

a (1, 1)

b (1, 3)

c (5, 3)

d (5, 1)

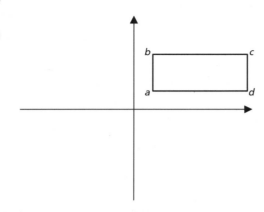

Work out the new coordinates when the rectangle is reflected in:

(i)   the *y*-axis

(ii)   the line *x* = *y*

(2 marks)

Key vocabulary: *Cartesian coordinates, quadrant, abscissa, ordinate*

⑯ Name the *five* Platonic solids. What links the solids in this group?

(6 marks)

⑰ Draw *two* different nets for a tetrahedron.

(2 marks)

18 Draw three different nets for a cube.

(3 marks)

19 Identify the number of faces, vertices and edges on the following solids:

Solid	Faces	Edges	Vertices
Cube			
Tetrahedron			
Triangular prism			

(9 marks)

Key vocabulary: *face, edge, vertex, net*

20 A cuboid has edges of lengths 3 cm, 4 cm and 6 cm.

   (i)   What is the area of each face?   *(3 marks)*
   (ii)   What is the total surface area of the cuboid?   *(1 mark)*
   (iii) What is the volume of the cuboid?   *(1 mark)*

21 Find the surface area and volume of the following cylinder, with radius 5 cm and length 10 cm.

Surface area =

Volume =

(2 marks)

22 Find the surface area and volume of the following triangular prism:

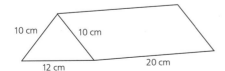

10 cm   10 cm

12 cm   20 cm

Surface area =

Volume =

(2 marks)

Key vocabulary: *surface area, volume*

21

Statistics

❶ The following tables show the results of a test taken by two classes. Inspect each of the sets of data and complete the table underneath.

Class A results

12	13	15	15	16	16	16	17	17	17
17	17	18	18	18	19	19	20	20	20

Class B results

10	11	8	11	14	17	15	12	19	11
18	20	17	19	16	11	20	17	15	19

	Class A data	Class B data
Mean		
Mode		
Median		
Range		

(8 marks)

❷ The wages of 10 workers in a factory are £30k, £22k, £6k, £6k, £6k, £6k, £6k, £6k, £6k, £6k. Find:

(i)   the mode

(ii)   the mean

(iii)   the median

If you were the union representative, which average would you use to justify a wage rise for the workers? Explain your reasoning.

(4 marks)

Key vocabulary: *mode, median, mean, range, discrete data, continuous data*

(Statistics ____ out of 12

Probability

❶ Dice are numbered 1–6. Two fair dice are thrown and the numbers added. Find the probability that the total is:

(i) 2   (ii) 7   (iii) 6   (iv) 14

(4 marks)

❷ (i)   A fair die is rolled. What is the probability that a 5 will be rolled?

(ii)   A coin is flipped. What is the probability of achieving tails?

(iii)   A fair die is rolled and a coin is flipped. What is the probability of achieving a 5 and tails?

(3 marks)

❸ A card is drawn from a pack of 52. What is the probability:

(i) it is a heart?

(ii) it is a black card?

(iii) it is a card less than a 10? (Ace is high)

(iv) is it likely or unlikely that the card is higher than a Jack? (Ace is high)

(4 marks)

❹ Delyth has the following cards:

21	30	15	39	18	34	42	27
☹	☺	☹	☺	☺	☹	☺	☺

(i) Gareth takes a card without looking. He says, 'I'm more likely to have an even number than an odd number.' Is he correct? Explain.

(1 mark)

(ii) Choose one of the following words to complete the sentences below.

likely   impossible   certain   unlikely

(a) It is ▭ that Gareth's card will contain ☹

(b) It is ▭ that Gareth's number will be greater than 10.

(2 marks)

Key vocabulary: *mutually exclusive, independent, tree diagram, outcome, relative frequency*

Measures

❶ What imperial and metric units could be used to measure the following:

	Imperial	Metric
Distance		
Speed		
Volume		
Capacity		
Mass		
Area		

(12 marks)

❷ James is following a recipe which is written using metric units of measurement.

  (i)   The recipe suggests using a mixing bowl with a diameter of 30 cm. How many inches should the diameter of the bowl be?

  (ii) The recipe requires 1 litre of milk. How many pints must James use?

  (iii) It also requires 500 g of flour. How many pounds and/or ounces are required?

  (3 marks)

❸ Put the following in size order, starting with the lightest:

  1 lb   250 g   ½ oz   1 kg   ½ lb   500 g   10 oz   25 g

  (1 mark)

❹ Put the following in size order, starting with the shortest:

  5.4 m   349 cm   16 m   2.4 km   1780 m   2567 m   1780 cm   5650 mm

  (1 mark)

Key vocabulary: *Imperial, metric, conversion*

Equations and graphs

❶ Amelia is setting out from home for a bike ride. The simplified graph shows the journey.

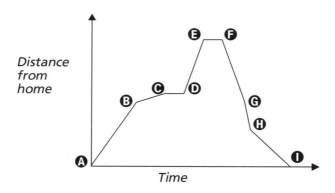

  (i)   Which part of the graph shows Amelia cycling up a steep hill?

  (1 mark)

  (ii) Which parts of the graph show her having a rest?

  (2 marks)

  (iii) Which point on the graph shows her arriving home?

  (1 mark)

❷ This is the graph of $y = 10x + 8$

What is:

(i)   the gradient of the line?

(ii) the y-intercept?

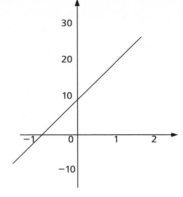

(2 marks)

❸ Write down the equation of the following graph:

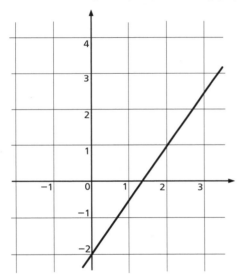

(1 mark)

❹ Write down the gradient and y-intercept of each of the following linear equations:

(i) $y = \frac{2}{3}x + 6$ Gradient =
                              y-intercept =

(ii) $2y = 3x - 6$ Gradient =
                              y-intercept =

(4 marks)

Key vocabulary: *gradient, y-intercept, linear*

Reasoning and proof

1 Say whether the following statements are **true** or **false**. Explain your reasoning.
    (i)   The product of two consecutive numbers is always divisible by 2. (The product of 3 and 4 is 12.)
    (ii) The sum of three consecutive numbers is always even
    (iii) The product of three consecutive numbers is always divisible by 6

                                                                        (3 marks)

2 Which of the following are **true** and which are **false**? (*x* is a real number.)
    (i) $2(x + 4) \equiv 2x + 8$
    (ii) $3(x - 3) \equiv 3x - 6$
    (iii) $x^2 = -4$

                                                                        (3 marks)

3 Prove that there are exactly four prime numbers between 10 and 20

                                                                       (1 mark)

4 Prove that the sum of any two odd numbers is even.

                                                                       (1 mark)

5 Show that when two six-faced dice are thrown a total of 6 is more likely than a total of 4.

                                                                       (1 mark)

> **Key vocabulary:** *prove, show, deductive proof, proof by exhaustion, disproof by counter example, $\equiv$, $\therefore$, $\Rightarrow$)*

Making sense of your test results

How well did you do? Determine a separate % score for each area, and then determine an overall score for the test. Remember that your percentage score is relative to the nature of the material tested and the time at which the test took place.

	Score		Percentage
Number	**Marks**	(max. 79)	%
Algebra	**Marks**	(max. 34)	%
Shape and space	**Marks**	(max. 92)	%
Statistics	**Marks**	(max. 12)	%
Probability	**Marks**	(max. 14)	%
Measures	**Marks**	(max. 17)	%
Equations and graphs	**Marks**	(max. 11)	%
Reasoning and proof	**Marks**	(max. 9)	%
Overall	**Marks**	(max. 268)	%

Consider the following divisions against which your separate and overall test scores can be measured. The scale is based upon our experiences of testing trainees in this way. It should be used for guidance and to aid target setting and not taken as some sort of absolute test measure.

80–100%   In the areas tested, your score is very good and indicates that you probably exceed the level expected of a non-mathematics specialist. Well done.

60–80%   In the areas tested, your score is good and indicates that you probably meet the level expected of a non-mathematics specialist. Some attention is necessary in weaker questions. However, with these marks you probably have little to worry about.

50–60%   In the areas tested, your score is adequate and probably indicates that you are moving towards the level expected of a non-mathematics specialist. However, attention is necessary throughout. Just like the self-audit, you are probably in good company and with a little effort you'll be up there with the best of them.

0–50%   In the areas tested, your score is probably a bit on the low side. Use the test positively to target the areas you need to work on. Remember, you only have to get there by the end of your training. Your score wouldn't concern us at this stage, so don't let it concern you unduly.

A useful tip would be to take a break from testing for now. Use the test questions as a guide for some revision (see Part 7 for further recommendations). Come back to the different sections of the test later and see how much progress you have made.

Number

❶ (i) $45 \times 24 = 1080$

x	40	5	
20	800	100	900
4	160	20	180
			1080

(ii) $146 \times 234 = 34\,164$

(iii) $312 \times 235 = 73\,320$

```
      312
  ×   235
     1560
     9360
    62400
    73320
    1 1 1
```

❷ (i) $1768 \div 34 = 52$

```
          52
    34)1768
        1700    (50 × 34)
          68
          68    (2 × 34)
           0
```

(ii) $1638 \div 63 = 26$

```
         26
    63)1638
       126
        378
        378
          0
```

(iii) $3335 \div 23 = 145$

```
        1 4 5
    23)3 3 3 5
         10  11
```

❸ (i) $p + q = \frac{2}{3} + \frac{1}{2} = \frac{4}{6} + \frac{3}{6} = \frac{7}{6} = 1\frac{1}{6}$

(ii) $p + r = \frac{2}{3} + 2\frac{4}{7} = \frac{2}{3} + \frac{18}{7} = \frac{14}{21} + \frac{54}{21} = \frac{68}{21} = 3\frac{5}{21}$

(iii) $q + s = \frac{1}{2} + 1\frac{1}{5} = \frac{1}{2} + \frac{6}{5} = \frac{5}{10} + \frac{12}{10} = \frac{17}{10} = 1\frac{7}{10}$

(iv) $p - q = \frac{2}{3} - \frac{1}{2} = \frac{4}{6} - \frac{3}{6} = \frac{1}{6}$

(v) $r - q = 2\frac{4}{7} - \frac{1}{2} = \frac{18}{7} - \frac{1}{2} = \frac{36}{14} - \frac{7}{14} = \frac{29}{14} = 2\frac{1}{14}$

(vi) $r - s = 2\frac{4}{7} - 1\frac{1}{5} = \frac{18}{7} - \frac{6}{5} = \frac{90}{35} - \frac{42}{35} = \frac{48}{35} = 1\frac{13}{35}$

(vii) $p \times q = \frac{2}{3} \times \frac{1}{2} = \frac{2}{6} = \frac{1}{3}$

(viii) $q \times s = \frac{1}{2} \times 1\frac{1}{5} = \frac{1}{2} \times \frac{6}{5} = \frac{6}{10} = \frac{3}{5}$

(ix) $r \times s = 2\frac{4}{7} \times 1\frac{1}{5} = \frac{18}{7} \times \frac{6}{5} = \frac{108}{35} = 3\frac{3}{35}$

(x) $p \div q = \frac{2}{3} \div \frac{1}{2} = \frac{2}{3} \times \frac{2}{1} = \frac{4}{3} = 1\frac{1}{3}$

(xi) $q \div p = \frac{1}{2} \div \frac{2}{3} = \frac{1}{2} \times \frac{3}{2} = \frac{3}{4}$

(xii) $q \div r = \frac{1}{2} \div 2\frac{4}{7} = \frac{1}{2} \times \frac{7}{18} = \frac{7}{36}$

❹ (i) $\frac{5}{8} = 0.625$

$$8\overline{)5.^50^20^40}\quad 0.625$$

(ii) $\frac{7}{20} = 0.35$

$$20\overline{)7.^70^{10}0}\quad 0.35$$

(iii) $65\% = 0.65$

(iv) $0.1\% = 0.001$

❺ (i) $0.375 = \frac{375}{1000} = \frac{3}{8}$

(ii) $0.28 = \frac{28}{100} = \frac{14}{50} = \frac{7}{25}$

(iii) $76\% = \frac{76}{100} = \frac{38}{50} = \frac{19}{25}$

❻ (i) $\frac{84}{96} = \frac{42}{48} = \frac{21}{24} = \frac{7}{8}$

(ii) $\frac{84}{91} = \frac{12}{13}$

❼ (i) $\frac{5}{8} = 0.625 = 62.5\%$

(ii) $0.375 = 37.5\%$

(iii) $\frac{7}{20} = 0.35 = 35\%$

(iv) $0.28 = 28\%$

❽ 4% cheaper:

Let the original price be n

A 20% increase is equal to $0.2n$

So the pre-Christmas price is $n + 0.2n = 1.2n$

A post-Christmas 20% decrease is equal to $0.24n$

So the post-Christmas price is $1.2n - 0.24n = 0.96n$

The percentage decrease from n to $0.96n$ is 4%

Hence the game is only 4% cheaper.

9 The two prices are the same:

> Let the original price be n
> A 25% increase is equal to $0.25n$
> So the increased price is $n + 0.25n = 1.25n$
> The 20% reduction is equal to $0.25n$
> So the reduced price is $1.25n - 0.25n = n$
> Hence the reduced price is equal to the original price.

10 In the first game the team scored 24 points; in the second game they scored 30 points. There was an increase of 6 points from the first game to the second game. As a percentage this increase can be represented as $\frac{6}{24} \times 100\% = 25\%$.

11 For every £5 raised Edward contributed £2 (i.e. $\frac{2}{5}$) and Katherine contributed £3 (i.e. $\frac{3}{5}$). Applying this to the £160 total raised gives:

> Edward: $\frac{2}{5} \times £160 = £64$
>
> Katherine: $\frac{3}{5} \times £160 = £96$

12 This is the same type of problem as question 11, only slightly larger.

The books are shared in the ratio 52 (i.e. $\frac{52}{200}$) to 68 (i.e. $\frac{68}{200}$) to 44 (i.e. $\frac{44}{200}$) to 36 (i.e. $\frac{36}{200}$). Applying this to the 1000 books to be distributed gives:

> Year 3: $\frac{52}{200} \times 1000$ books $= 260$ books
>
> Year 4: $\frac{68}{200} \times 1000$ books $= 340$ books
>
> Year 5: $\frac{44}{200} \times 1000$ books $= 220$ books
>
> Year 6: $\frac{36}{200} \times 1000$ books $= 180$ books

13 (i) ☑   (ii) ☒   (iii) ☑

(iv) ☒   (v) ☑   (vi) ☑

(vii) ☒   (viii) ☑   (ix) ☑

14 $-(2^2)$ $-\sqrt{5}$ $-(2^{-2})$ $0.1010010001...$ $\frac{1}{9}$ 2^{-3} $\frac{1}{7}$

$0.\dot{3}$ 0.363636 $\sqrt{\frac{4}{9}}$ $\sqrt{2}$ $\sqrt{4}$ π 2^3

15 (i) $0.\dot{2}\dot{7}$ (ii) $0.2\dot{7}$ (iii) $0.9\dot{0}\dot{4}$ (iv) $18.\dot{1}\dot{8}$

16 (i) $100\,000 = 10^5$ (ii) $0.1 = 10^{-1}$ (iii) $100 = 10^2$

17 (i) $6.6 \times 10^3 = 6600$ (ii) $7.07 \times 10^{-2} = 0.0707$

18 (i) $523\,000 = 5.23 \times 10^5$ (ii) $0.0606 = 6.06 \times 10^{-2}$

19 (i) ☑   (ii) ☒   (iii) ☑   (iv) ☒

20 (i) Factors of 18: 1, 2, 3, 6, 9, 18
(ii) Factors of 60: 1, 2, 3, 4, 5, 6, 10, 12, 15, 20, 30, 60

㉑ (i) Factors of 48: 1, 2, 3, 4, 6, 8, 12, 16, 24, 48
Of these only 2 and 3 are prime, hence these are the prime factors.

(ii) Factors of 105: 1, 3, 5, 7, 15, 21, 35, 105
Of these only 3, 5 and 7 are prime, hence these are the prime factors.

㉒ (i) Factors of 6: 1, 2, 3, 6
Factors of 15: 1, 3, 5, 15
1 and 3 are factors common to both 6 and 15.
3 is the highest common factor.

(ii) Factors of 18: 1, 2, 3, 6, 9, 18
Factors of 54: 1, 2, 3, 6, 9, 18, 27, 54
1, 2, 3, 6, 9 and 18 are factors common to both 18 and 54.
18 is the highest common factor.

(iii) Factors of $12a^2$: 1, 2, 3, 4, 6, 12, a, $2a$, $3a$, $4a$, $6a$, $12a$, a^2, $2a^2$, $3a^2$, $4a^2$, $6a^2$, $12a^2$
Factors of $4ab$: 1, 2, 4, a, $2a$, $4a$, b, $2b$, $4b$, ab, $2ab$, $4ab$
1, 2, 4, a, $2a$ and $4a$ are factors common to both $12a^2$ and $4ab$.
$4a$ is the highest common factor.

(iv) Factors of a^2b: 1, a, a^2, b, ab, a^2b
Factors of a^3b^2: 1, a, a^2, a^3, b, b^2, ab, a^2b, a^3b, ab^2, a^2b^2, a^3b^2
1, a, a^2, b, ab, a^2b are factors common to both a^2b and a^3b^2.
a^2b is the highest common factor.

Algebra – Patterns and relationships

❶ (i) $ab = 5 \times 15 = 75$

(ii) $ac = 5 \times 2 = 10$

(iii) $de = 15$ and $d = 3$, hence $e = 15 \div 3 = 5$

(iv) $df = 18$ and $d = 3$, hence $f = 18 \div 3 = 6$

(v) $a(b + c) = 5(15 + 2) = 85$

(vi) $d(e + f) = 3(5 + 6) = 33$

(vii) $a(b - c) = 5(15 - 2) = 65$

(viii) $d(e - f) = 3(5 - 6) = -3$

(ix) $2a^2b = 2 \times 5^2 \times 15 = 750$

(x) $2d^2e = 2 \times 3^2 \times 5 = 90$

(xi) $\frac{1}{a} = \frac{1}{5}$ or 0.2

(xii) $\frac{1}{a} = \frac{1}{3}$ or 0.333

❷ (i) 36

(ii) 100

(iii) n^2

❸ (i) 8, 12, 16, 20, 24

(ii) 44 slabs

(iii) $4n + 4 = 4(n + 1)$

❹ (i) 64

(ii) 512

(iii) $2^{(n-1)}$

❺ (i) 1, 3, 6, 10, 15

(ii) 55 cubes

(iii) $\dfrac{n(n + 1)}{2}$

6 (i)

$$\frac{1}{x + 2} = 3$$

$$
\begin{aligned}
1 &= 3(x + 2) \\
1 &= 3x + 6 \\
-5 &= 3x \\
x &= \tfrac{-5}{3}
\end{aligned}
$$

(ii)

$$\frac{1}{5x - 4x} = \frac{1}{x}$$

$$
\begin{aligned}
x &= 5x - 4 \\
4 &= 4x \\
x &= 1
\end{aligned}
$$

(iii)

$$\frac{3}{1 + b} = \frac{5}{b + 3}$$

$$
\begin{aligned}
3(b + 3) &= 5(1 + b) \\
3b + 9 &= 5 + 5b \\
4 &= 2b \\
2 &= b
\end{aligned}
$$

7 (i)
$$
\begin{cases}
y - 2x = 4 \ (1) \\
y + x = 7 \ (2)
\end{cases}
$$

$(2) - (1)$:

$$
\begin{array}{r}
y + x = 7 \\
- \quad y - 2x = 4 \\
\hline
3x = 3 \\
x = 1
\end{array}
$$

Substitute in (2):

$$
\begin{aligned}
y + x &= 7 \\
y + 1 &= 7 \\
y &= 6
\end{aligned}
$$

(ii)
$$
\begin{cases}
2a - 3b = 2 \ (1) \\
4a + 6b = 4 \ (2)
\end{cases}
$$

rearranging (1) gives:

$$a = \frac{2 + 3b}{2}$$

Substituting for a in (2) gives:

$$4a + 6b = 4$$

$$4\left(\frac{2 + 3b}{2}\right) + 6b = 4$$

$$
\begin{aligned}
4 + 6b + 6b &= 4 \\
12b &= 0 \\
b &= 0
\end{aligned}
$$

Substituting for b in (1) gives:

$$
\begin{aligned}
2a - 3b &= 2 \\
2a - 0 &= 2 \\
a &= 1
\end{aligned}
$$

(iii) $\begin{cases} 2x - y = 5 \\ 3x + 2y = 11 \end{cases}$

By drawing the graphs represented by the two equations it is possible to find the common solution. The common solution is found where the two lines cross. At this point the values for x and y in both of the equations are the same.

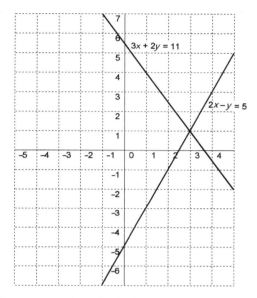

In this case the lines cross at the point (3,1), giving the common solution:

$x = 3$ and
$y = 1$

Shape and space

1 $b = 80°$ $c = 100°$ $d = 80°$ $e = 100°$ $f = 100°$

2 angle $d = 80°$

3

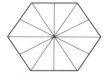

6 lines of reflective symmetry
rotational symmetry of order 6

no lines of reflective symmetry
rotational symmetry of order 2

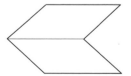

1 line of reflective symmetry
rotational symmetry of order 1

4 lines of reflective symmetry
rotational symmetry of order 4

2 lines of reflective symmetry
rotational symmetry of order 2

④   angle a: right   angle b: reflex   angle c: acute   angle d: reflex

        angle e: acute   angle f: right   angle g: obtuse

⑤ (i)   shapes **Ⓐ** and **Ⓑ** are congruent
     (ii)   all of the other shapes, **Ⓐ**, **Ⓑ** and **Ⓓ** are similar to shape **Ⓒ**

⑥   A regular triangle is called an **equilateral** triangle. Because it is a regular polygon it is clear that all the sides must be of **equal length** and all the interior angles must be the same size, i.e. **60°**. Again because an **equilateral** triangle is regular it must also have **three** lines of reflective symmetry and rotational symmetry of order **3**.

    A triangle which has two sides of equal length is called an **isosceles** triangle. As well as having two sides of equal length an **isosceles** triangle also has **two** angles of equal size. An **isosceles** triangle has **one** line of reflective symmetry and rotational symmetry of order **1**.

    A triangle which has three sides of different length and no equal angles is called a **scalene** triangle. **Scalene** triangles have **no** lines of reflective symmetry and rotational symmetry of order **1**.

    A triangle containing one angle of 90° is called a **right-angled** triangle. A **right-angled** triangle will also be either an **isosceles** or **scalene** triangle.

    The number of lines of reflective symmetry and the order of rotational symmetry of a **right-angled** triangle depends on whether it is an **isosceles** or **scalene** triangle.

⑦   Right-angled triangles satisfy Pythagoras' theorem, i.e. $a^2 + b^2 = c^2$

    (i) $3^2 + 4^2 = 5^2$, hence the triangle has a right angle

    (ii) $4^2 + 5^2 = 41$ not 6^2, hence the triangle does not have a right angle

⑧   Area of the triangle is equal to half × base × height = 2 cm × 3 cm = 6cm^2

⑨   Area of the parallelogram is equal to base × height = 8 cm × 5 cm = 40 cm^2

⑩   Area of the trapezium is found by dissecting it into a parallelogram and a triangle, then adding the area of the parallelogram and the area of the triangle:

$$\begin{aligned} \text{Area of parallelogram + Area of triangle} \ &= (5 \text{ cm} \times 4 \text{ cm}) + (1.5 \text{ cm} \times 4 \text{ cm}) \\ &= 20 \text{ cm}^2 + 6 \text{ cm}^2 \\ &= 26 \text{ cm}^2 \end{aligned}$$

⑪ $$\begin{aligned} \text{Perimeter} \ &= 7 \text{ cm} + 3 \text{ cm} + 3 \text{ cm} + 6 \text{ cm} + (7-3) \text{ cm} + (6-3) \text{ cm} \\ &= 7 \text{ cm} + 3 \text{ cm} + 3 \text{ cm} + 6 \text{ cm} + 4 \text{ cm} + 3 \text{ cm} \\ &= 26 \text{ cm} \end{aligned}$$

$$\begin{aligned} \text{Area} \ &= (7 \times 6) \text{ cm}^2 - (4 \times 3) \text{ cm}^2 \\ &= 42 \text{ cm}^2 - 12 \text{ cm}^2 \\ &= 30 \text{ cm}^2 \end{aligned}$$

⑫ Using Pythagoras' theorem to calculate L:

$$4^2 + 5^2 = L^2$$
$$16 + 25 = L^2$$
$$41 = L^2$$
$$\sqrt{41} = L$$
$$L \approx 6.4 \text{ cm}$$

Perimeter $\approx$ 2 cm + 13 cm + 8 cm + 5 cm + 6 cm + 3 cm + 4 cm + 6.4 cm
$\approx$ 47.4 cm

Area $= (2 \times 13) \text{ cm}^2 + (6 \times 5) \text{ cm}^2 + (\frac{1}{2} \times 4 \times 5) \text{ cm}^2$

$= 26 \text{ cm}^2 + 30 \text{ cm}^2 + 10 \text{ cm}^2$
$= 66 \text{ cm}^2$

⑬ Circumference $= \pi d$
$= 10\pi$ cm
$\approx$ 31.4 cm   (taking π to be 3.14)
Area $= \pi r^2$
$= 25\pi \text{ cm}^2$
$\approx$ 78.5 cm² (taking π to be 3.14)

⑭ (i)   Area of circle **Ⓐ** $= \pi r^2$
$= 25\pi \text{ cm}^2$
$\approx$ 78.5 cm²

The sector marked in circle **Ⓐ** represents $\frac{1}{3}$ of the circle because 120° is $\frac{1}{3}$ of 360°. Hence the area of the sector in circle **Ⓐ** is $\frac{1}{3} \times$ 78.5 cm² = 26.17 cm²

Area of circle **Ⓑ** $= \pi r^2$
$= 9\pi \text{ cm}^2$
$\approx$ 28.26 cm²

The sector marked in circle **Ⓑ** represents $\frac{1}{8}$ of the circle because 45° is $\frac{1}{8}$ of 360°. Hence the area of the sector in circle **Ⓑ** is $\frac{1}{8} \times$ 28.26 cm² = 3.53 cm²

(ii) The circumference of circle **Ⓐ** $= 2\pi r$
$= 10\pi$ cm
$\approx$ 31.4 cm

The length of the arc marked in circle **Ⓐ** represents $\frac{1}{3}$ the length of the circumference because 120° is $\frac{1}{3}$ of 360°.

Hence the length of the arc in circle **Ⓐ** is $\frac{1}{3} \times$ 31.4 cm = 10.47 cm

The circumference of circle **Ⓑ** $= 2\pi r$
$= 6\pi$ cm
$\approx$ 18.84 cm

The length of the arc marked in circle **Ⓑ** represents $\frac{1}{8}$ the length of the circumference because 45° is $\frac{1}{8}$ of 360°.

Hence the length of the arc in circle **Ⓑ** is $\frac{1}{8} \times$ 18.84 cm = 2.36 cm

⑮ (i) Reflection in the *y*-axis has the effect of multiplying the *x*-coordinate (or abscissa) by −1, giving:

a′ = (−1, 1)
b′ = (−1, 3)
c′ = (−5, 3)
d′ = (−5, 1)

(ii) Reflection in the line *x* = *y* has the effect of exchanging the *x* and *y* coordinates (abscissa and ordinate), giving:

a″ = (1, 1)
b″ = (3, 1)
c″ = (3, 5)
d″ = (1, 5)

⑯ The five Platonic solids are:

- **regular tetrahedron**
- **cube**
- **regular octahedron**
- **regular dodecahedron**
- **regular icosahedron**

The Platonic solids are the only regular solids. A polyhedron is defined as regular if all faces are congruent and all the angles between the faces (i.e. the dihedral angles) are the same size.

⑰
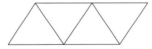

⑱
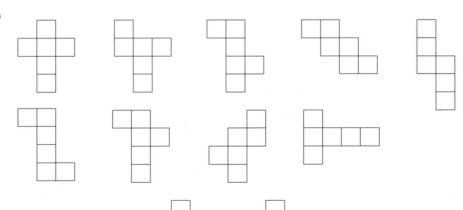

⑲

Solid	Faces	Edges	Vertices
Cube	6	12	8
Tetrahedron	4	6	4
Triangular prism	5	9	6

⑳ (i) The cuboid has:

2 faces with an area of 3 cm × 4 cm = 12 cm^2
2 faces with an area of 4 cm × 6 cm = 24 cm^2
2 faces with an area of 3 cm × 6 cm = 18 cm^2

(ii) The total surface area = (2 × 12 cm^2) + (2 × 24 cm^2) + (2 × 18 cm^2)
$$= 24 \text{ cm}^2 + 48 \text{ cm}^2 + 36 \text{ cm}^2$$
$$= 108 \text{ cm}^2$$

(iii) The volume of the cuboid = 3 cm × 4 cm × 6 cm
$$= 72 \text{ cm}^3$$

㉑ Surface area:

Area of each circular face = πr^2
$$= 25\pi \text{ cm}^2$$
$$\approx 78.5 \text{ cm}^2$$

Area of curved surface = 10 × 2πr cm^2
$$= 10 \times 10\pi \text{ cm}^2$$
$$\approx 314 \text{ cm}^2$$

Total surface area = (2 × 78.5 cm^2) + 314 cm^2
$$= 157 \text{ cm}^2 + 314 \text{ cm}^2$$
$$= 471 \text{ cm}^2$$

Volume:

Area of circular face × length = 78.5 cm^2 × 10 cm
$$= 785 \text{ cm}^3$$

㉒ Surface area:

Area of each triangular face = 6 cm × 8 cm
$$= 48 \text{ cm}^2$$

Area of 2 rectangular faces = 10 cm × 20 cm
$$= 200 \text{ cm}^2$$

Area of remaining rectangular face = 12 cm × 20 cm
$$= 240 \text{ cm}^2$$

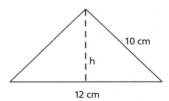

Total surface area = (2 × 48 cm^2) + (2 × 200 cm^2) + 240 cm^2
$$= 96 \text{ cm}^2 + 400 \text{ cm}^2 + 240 \text{ cm}^2$$
$$= 736 \text{ cm}^2$$

Using Pythagoras $10^2 = 6^2 + h^2$
$$10^2 - 6^2 = h^2$$
$$100 - 36 = h^2$$
$$64 = h^2$$
$$h = 8 \text{ cm}$$

Volume:

Area of triangular face × length = 48 cm^2 × 20 cm
$$= 960 \text{ cm}^3$$

Statistics

❶

	Class A data	Class B data	
Mean	17	15	
Mode	17	11	
Median	17	15.5	
Range	8	12	

❷ (i)   mode = £6k

(ii)   mean = £10k

(iii)   median = £6k

Either the mode or the median would be an appropriate average to justify a wage increase.

Probability

❶ (i) $\frac{1}{36}$ (ii) $\frac{6}{36} = \frac{1}{6}$ (iii) $\frac{5}{36}$ (iv) 0

❷ (i) $\frac{1}{6}$ (ii) $\frac{1}{2}$ (iii) $\frac{1}{6} \times \frac{1}{2} = \frac{1}{12}$

❸ (i) $\frac{13}{52} = \frac{1}{4}$ (ii) $\frac{26}{52} = \frac{1}{2}$ (iii) $\frac{32}{52} = \frac{16}{26} = \frac{8}{13}$ (iv) $\frac{12}{52} = \frac{6}{26} = \frac{3}{13}$

❹ (i) He is not correct. There is an equal number of even and odd cards, therefore it is equally likely that he will have an even number or an odd number.

(ii) (a) unlikely

(b) certain

Measures

❶

	Imperial	Metric
Distance	mile	km
Speed	mph	kmh^{-1}
Volume	cubic foot	m^3
Capacity	pint	litre
Mass	lb	kg
Area	square foot	m^2

❷ (i)   taking approx. 2.5 cm to the inch gives 12 inches

(ii)   appox. 1.75 pints

(iii)   approx 2.2 pounds to the kilogram, hence 1.1 pounds in 500 g. 1.1 pounds is about 1 lb $1\frac{1}{2}$ oz.

❸ $\frac{1}{2}$ oz   25 g $\frac{1}{2}$ lb   250 g   10 oz   1 lb   500 g   1 kg

❹ 349 cm   5.4 m   5650 mm   16 m   1780 cm   1780 m   2.4 km   2567 m

Equations and graphs

❶ (i) B − C   (ii) C − D and E − F   (iii) I

❷ Using $y = mx + c$ as the general equation of a straight line, where m is the gradient and c is the y-intercept gives:

   (i)   gradient $= 10$

   (ii) y-intercept $= 8$

❸ Using $y = mx + c$

   m = gradient $c = y$-intercept

     $= \frac{3}{2}$ $= -2$

   Substituting into the general equation gives:

   $y = \frac{3}{2}x - 2$

❹ (i)   gradient $= \frac{2}{3}$ y-intercept $= 6$

   (ii) gradient $= \frac{3}{2}$ y-intercept $= -3$

Reasoning and proof

❶ (i) **True** – The product of an odd number multiplied by an even number always gives an even number. As one of the two numbers is even, it has a factor of 2; hence the product will have a factor of 2.

   (ii) **False** – This can be shown using disproof by counter example:

            Let the three consecutive numbers be 2, 3, 4

            Summing gives $2 + 3 + 4 = 9$

            This is not even, hence the statement is false.

   (iii) **True** – The product of three consecutive numbers is always divisible by 6. Within any three consecutive numbers one must be even and therefore have a factor of 2, and one must have a factor of 3. Hence the product will have a factor of 2×3, i.e. 6.

❷ (i) **True**   (ii) **False**   (iii) **False**

❸ Consider the factors of all the numbers from 10 to 20:

        10 has factors: 1, 2, 5, 10   11 has factors: 1, 11

        12 has factors: 1, 2, 3, 4, 6, 12   13 has factors: 1, 13

        14 has factors: 1, 2, 7, 14   15 has factors: 1, 3, 5, 15

        16 has factors: 1, 2, 4, 8, 16   17 has factors: 1, 17

        18 has factors: 1, 2, 3, 6, 9, 18   19 has factors: 1, 19

        20 has factors: 1, 2, 4, 5, 10, 20

   This method of proof by exhaustion shows that there are exactly four prime numbers between 10 and 20: 11, 13, 17, 19.

4 Let the two odd numbers be $2a + 1$ and $2b + 1$ (where a and b are both integers)

Adding gives $(2a + 1) + (2b + 1) = 2a + 2b + 2$
$$= 2(a + b + 1)$$

$a + b + 1$ is an integer, which implies that $2(a + b + 1)$ is even

5 A table can be used to show all the possible outcomes:

Die 1	Die 2	Total	Die 1	Die 2	Total	Die 1	Die 2	Total	Die 1	Die 2	Total	Die 1	Die 2	Total	Die 1	Die 2	Total
1	1	2	2	1	3	3	1	4	4	1	5	5	1	6	6	1	7
1	2	3	2	2	4	3	2	5	4	2	6	5	2	7	6	2	8
1	3	4	2	3	5	3	3	6	4	3	7	5	3	8	6	3	9
1	4	5	2	4	6	3	4	7	4	4	8	5	4	9	6	4	10
1	5	6	2	5	7	3	5	8	4	5	9	5	5	10	6	5	11
1	6	7	2	6	8	3	6	9	4	6	10	5	6	11	6	6	12

From the table it can be seen that when throwing two dice the probability of obtaining a 6 is $\frac{5}{36}$ and the probability of obtaining a 4 is $\frac{3}{36}$, which shows that 6 is a more likely outcome than 4.

Teachers are constantly engaged in target setting, for example when assessing and marking children's work, when keeping records and when evaluating their own performance. Target setting is seen as a positive step towards ensuring progress and raising attainment. As your own training gets under way, you might well be asked to set targets for yourself. Targets will almost certainly be set for you!

Formally record your targets for further development below. Make **clear** and **specific** reference to areas within your self-audit and mathematics test that require attention. Don't forget to indicate where, when and how the targets will be achieved.

targets
(areas identified from the audit and test results requiring attention)

Number	Algebra – patterns and relationships	Shape and space

Statistics	Probability	Measures

Equations and graphs	Reasoning and proof	

Well done indeed for getting this far! By working through this book you are well on your way towards developing your mathematical knowledge and understanding. Having set targets it is useful to know where to go for further subject knowledge support. This section outlines some of the possible choices.

There are many books to support the development of mathematical knowledge currently available. As a trainee teacher it is probably more appropriate to look at books written specifically to address the requirements of 4/98, Annex D. Since publication of this document various books have been written to support students as they work to develop the subject knowledge requirements outlined in Section C. Some books look solely at the subject knowledge identified, others attempt to place it more firmly within a classroom context. It depends on your own needs when developing your subject knowledge, which of these is most appropriate for you. Two books which address the learning within a classroom context are detailed below.

- Mooney, C. et al. (2000) *Primary Mathematics: Knowledge and Understanding.* Exeter: Learning Matters.

  This book addresses all of the subject knowledge requirements of 4/98, Annex D, Section C. The approach adopted endeavours to tackle the subject knowledge through a series of misconceptions that children may demonstrate in the classroom. The subject knowledge required by the teacher to effectively support and extend the child is then detailed. It also includes a review of research in each of the areas, as well as self-assessment questions to check understanding.

- Haylock, D. (2001) *Mathematics Explained for Primary Teachers*, 2nd edn. London: Paul Chapman.

  This book has been thoroughly revised and updated for the second edition and addresses the subject knowledge requirements of 4/98, Annex D. It is firmly rooted within the classroom context of learning mathematics and again includes self-assessment questions to check understanding.

It is also possible to buy plenty of GCSE revision texts which help develop knowledge at a similar level to that required by 4/98, Annex D, Section C. However, if you are just seeking to improve your knowledge in the areas outlined within 4/98, then a potential problem using these books could be that the knowledge covered is not necessarily the knowledge required by 4/98. In some areas it may be wider, in others more limited. If you are a little uncertain about mathematics, the format and the level might be a little intimidating. If you are more confident and just a little 'rusty' in a few areas they might be a suitable option.

A further option is to use the Internet to support your learning. Including specific website addresses in a book is rather risky as they tend to change quite regularly. Included here are a couple which are well established and were current at the time of writing.

- For help with revision at GCSE level, the BBC's Bitesize site is quite useful:

  http://www.bbc.co.uk/education/gcsebitesize/maths/index.shtml

- Considering mathematics more broadly, the Math Forum home page is a useful starting point. From here it is possible to search their Internet mathematics library for useful pages related to an incredibly diverse number of mathematical topics. It is also possible to e-mail Dr. Math with their Ask Dr. Math facility. Using this, any mathematical questions you have can be e-mailed to the Forum, who will endeavour to answer your question and publish the answer on the site.

http://mathforum.com/

Also, remember that study groups with other trainees can be invaluable. Choosing the most appropriate resource for your needs, setting clear, achievable targets and identifying specific time to develop your mathematical knowledge, skills and understanding will all support you as you work towards achieving all the requirements for gaining QTS and becoming a confident and successful teacher.

Achieving QTS

Our Achieving QTS series now includes over 15 titles, encompassing *Audit and Test*, *Knowledge and Understanding*, *Teaching Theory and Practice*, and *Skills Tests* titles for each of the core subject areas in the primary curriculum. The Teacher Training Agency have identified books in this series as high quality resources for trainee teachers. You can find general information on each on these ranges on our website: *www.learningmatters.co.uk*

Primary English
Audit and Test
Doreen Challen
£6.99   64 pages   ISBN: 1 903300 20 7

Primary Mathematics
Audit and Test
Claire Mooney and Mike Fletcher
£6.99   48 pages   ISBN: 1 903300 21 5

Primary Science
Audit and Test
John Sharp and Jenny Byrne
£6.99   80 pages   ISBN: 1 903300 22 3

Primary English
Knowledge and Understanding
Jane Medwell, George Moore, David Wray, Vivienne Griffiths
£14.99   224 pages   ISBN: 1 903300 01 0

Primary English
Teaching Theory and Practice
Jane Medwell, Hilary Minns, David Wray, Vivienne Griffiths
£14.99   208 pages   ISBN: 1 903300 02 9

Primary Mathematics
Knowledge and Understanding
Claire Mooney, Lindsey Ferrie, Sue Fox, Alice Hansen, Reg Wrathmell
£14.99   176 pages   ISBN: 1 903300 03 7

Primary Mathematics
Teaching Theory and Practice
Claire Mooney, Mary Briggs, Mike Fletcher, Judith McCullouch
£14.99   176 pages   ISBN: 1 903300 04 5

Primary Science
Knowledge and Understanding
Rob Johnsey, Graham Peacock, John Sharp, Debbie Wright
£14.99   224 pages   ISBN: 1 903300 05 3

Primary Science
Teaching Theory and Practice
John Sharp, Graham Peacock, Rob Johnsey, Shirley Simon, Robin Smith
£12.99   144 pages   ISBN: 1 903300 06 1

Primary ICT
Knowledge, Understanding and Practice
Jane Sharp, John Potter, Jonathan Allen, Avril Loveless
£14.99   256 pages   ISBN: 1 903300 07 X

Professional Studies
Primary Phase
Edited by Kate Jacques and Rob Hyland
£14.99   224 pages   ISBN: 1 903300 09 6

Passing the Numeracy Skills Test (second edition)
Mark Patmore
£6.99   64 pages   ISBN: 1 903300 11 8

Passing the Literacy Skills Test
Jim Johnson
£6.99   80 pages   ISBN: 1 903300 12 6

Passing the ICT Skills Test
Clive Ferrigan
£6.99   64 pages   ISBN: 1 903300 13 4

Succeeding in the Induction Year
Neil Simco
£12.99   144 pages   ISBN: 1 903300 10 X

To order, please contact our distributors:
Plymbridge Distributors, Estover Road, Plymouth, PL6 7PY
Tel: 01752 202301 Fax: 01752 202333 Email: orders@plymbridge.com